西北政法大学国际法研究中心
西北政法大学郑斌航空与空间法研究所 主办

本书获陕西省哲学社会科学重点研究基地——
西北政法大学国际法研究中心专项基金、陕西省国际法学科
"三秦学者"科研创新团队专项资金资助

CHINA AVIATION LAW REVIEW

中国航空法评论

（第四卷）

王瀚／主编

《中国航空法评论》
编委会

目　录

特　稿

航空环境治理

临空经济法治

第 五 航 权

航空法基础理论

航空法热点前沿

资　　讯

特　　稿

制裁不循规旅客的国际立法与消费者保护的“拉锯战”

柯莉娟*

一、前　　言

民航发展的根基在“飞安”，随着制造航空器技术的进步，确保“飞安”的机制着重于建立不得干扰飞航安全的“航空安保措施”，但不断增加的这类安保措施却在某种程度上造成旅客抱怨，民航业者为考虑消费者感受，在执行安保程序时亦多有疑惑，化解制裁不循规旅客的国际立法与消费者保护的“拉锯战”，是本文探讨重点。

在航空安保措施方面，美国“9·11”事件可谓是促使“新”国际航空安保立法急速发展的转折点，在此之前，国际民航组织（International Civil Aviation Organization，ICAO）以芝加哥公约第17号附约及第8973号文件建置航空安保的法制基础。“9·11”事

* 加拿大麦吉尔大学法学博士，资深职业律师，加拿大麦吉尔大学航空与空间法研究所客座教授，东吴大学兼职教授。

件之后,ICAO 修订第 17 号附约加强航空安保的措施,中国代表团还建议制定《制止危害民用航空安全的非法行为的公约》(以下简称《北京公约》)以取代 1971 年《关于制止危害民用航空安全的非法行为的公约》(以下简称《蒙特利尔公约》)及其 1988 年议定书;[①]另外,随着国际民用航空运输业的飞速发展,在航空器上不循规旅客案件数量呈现激增趋势,1963 年《关于在航空器内的犯罪和其他某些行为的公约》(以下简称《东京公约》)已远远不能实现对该类案件的有效规制,加上其在管辖权方面的规定过窄,导致很多案件出现"管辖空白"的情况,ICAO 于 2014 年通过《关于修订〈关于在航空器内的犯罪和其他某些行为的公约〉的议定书》(以下简称 2014 年《蒙特利尔议定书》),作为《东京公约》现代化的最终成果。[②] 至此,《北京公约》《北京议定书》与 2014 年《蒙特利尔议定书》,分别成为规范与航空器有关之非法行为、[③]劫机及制裁航空器上干扰飞航秩序的新国际航空安保立法。

综上,本文主要以实务案例观点说明制裁不循规旅客的国际立法与消费者保护在实践上的疑惑,并以管辖权、对不循规旅客的认定及管束与裁处问题等为例说明《北京公约》与 2014 年《蒙特利尔议定书》立法重点的适用疑惑;且简要说明 2014 年《蒙特利尔议定书》国际立法上未决问题以彰显不循规旅客规范不足之处;并在结论中提出审视国际航空安保立法效益时,应考虑平衡制裁不循规旅客与保护消费者的必要性,以确保航空运输发展的实质意义。

---

① 参见 ICAO 国际航空法会议,中国代表团对《蒙特利尔公约议定书(草案)》和《海牙公约议定书(草案)》的意见,DCAS Doc No. 15,27/8/10。中国代表团建议用《北京公约》取代 1971 年《蒙特利尔公约》及其 1988 年议定书;同时赞同用议定书的形式,即《北京议定书》来修订 1970 年《海牙公约》。

② 参见杨彩霞:《国际民航不循规旅客管辖权问题研究》,载《北京航空航天大学学报》(社会科学版)2015 年第 6 期。

③ 《北京议定书》已于 2018 年 1 月 1 日生效,《北京公约》亦于 2018 年 7 月 1 日生效;由国际航空运输协会(IATA)力推的 2014 年《蒙特利尔议定书》迄今为止尚未生效。

二、立法重点的适用疑惑

因航空产业自第一次世界大战爆发后才正式进入商业运转，航空法规范在国际法中相较于海商法等显得“新”，故除以传统国际法原则为依循外，也逐渐就航空产业特性调整国际法适用原则，以弥补某些“真空”。在处理与航空器有关的不循规旅客非法干扰行为议题上，新国际航空安保立法重点中的管辖权、对不循规旅客的认定及管束与裁处问题三个重点，在加入消费者保护的因素后，实务运用上确实存在一些疑惑，故简要比较说明如下。

（一）管辖权问题

自 1963 年《东京公约》起的几个规范航空器上非法干扰行为之航空保安事项的公约，如 1970 年《海牙公约》与 1971 年《蒙特利尔公约》及其议定书，除了从基于航空器为领土之延伸法理而赋予航空器登记国管辖权之外，增加航空器营运人永久居所及主要营业地国亦取得管辖权。早期与航空器有关的非法干扰行为，如劫机，多发生于航空器内，故上述公约规定的管辖权在适用上似乎无大问题。唯自 1980 年起，科技进步使航空器犯罪已不限于在航空器内，尤其是 2001 年的“9・11”事件后，为弥补利用民用航空器对地面目标进行攻击的行为，或对重大恐怖袭击事件的幕后策划者和组织者无法进行刑事追究的真空，ICAO 提出 2010 年《北京公约》及《北京议定书》寻求 ICAO 会员国支持，补上“航空犯罪发生地”的属地管辖权。同样，面对日益增加的航空器内“不循规”及/或“滋扰”行为，2014 年《蒙特利尔议定书》亦增加刑事管辖权选项，简单比较一下上述公约的管辖权如表 1 所示。

表1 管辖权比较

1963年《东京公约》第3条、第4条	1970年《海牙公约》第4条	1971年《蒙特利尔公约》第5条	2014年《蒙特利尔议定书》第3条	2010年《北京公约》第8条《北京议定书》第7条
• 航空器登记国 • 非航空器登记国之缔约国行使对飞航中航空器上所犯罪行之刑事管辖权之五种情形	• 航空器登记国 • 航空器降落地国 • 承租人主要营业地(如无则以其永久居所) • 罪犯在缔约国领土内,且该国没有引渡罪犯的	• 航空器登记国 • 航空器降落地国 • 承租人主要营业地(如无则以其永久居所) • 犯罪行为发生地国	• 航空器登记国 • 航空器降落地国 • 承租人主要营业地(如无则以其永久居所) • 当降落地国行使其管辖权时,国家应考虑相关的犯罪或行为是否构成经营人所在国的犯罪	• 航空器登记国 • 航空器降落地国 • 承租人主要营业地(如无则以其永久居所) • 犯罪行为发生地国 • 犯罪人发现国(辅助性管辖) • 犯罪人国籍国 • 被害人国籍国 • 无国籍犯罪行为人居所地国 • 罪犯在缔约国领土内,且该国没有引渡罪犯的

虽然在制裁航空器上干扰飞航秩序及犯罪的行为增列管辖权可助于世界各国加强防范或吓阻在航空器内之犯罪或不法行为,在实务运作上,出现受害的旅客、空勤组员等欲对该违反公约规定之行为人主张民事求偿时,因民事、刑事或行政违规行为之管辖法院不同,以及跨境证据取得不易的问题,增加了航空公司处理组员与消费者申诉争议上的复杂度及成本。

实务真实案例有:某外籍航空公司地勤因错误,将某商务舱机位重复划给一名中国台湾地区旅客与一名美籍旅客,导致该中国台湾地区旅客于机舱内口出恶言污辱请他下机的空勤组员,当欧洲籍机长下令拒载该旅客要求其下机后,该旅客又在空桥至候机处不停咆哮,并导致航班严重迟延,致使某些转机旅客错过航班。该外籍航空公司对旅客的干扰行为根据其航空安保计划向机场航警处陈报违规事件,并将该名旅客列为"拒载旅客"(俗称"黑名单"),该名中国台湾地区旅客回到中国台湾地区后竟于子夜打电话到空勤组员下榻饭店要求澄清，吓得空勤组员在两名警员戒护下才敢搭车前往机场服勤。该外籍航空公司事后派处理客诉案件之经理与该名旅客联络欲了解情况，但旅客情绪仍相当激动，于电话访谈中再次出言：“若认识恐怖分子本·拉登将会拿两颗炸弹来炸该航空公司或到空勤组员住宿酒店对其不利”，甚至在中国台湾地区桃园市地方法院以总经理及客诉经理为被告提出“诬告”的刑事告诉。因中国台湾地区不受任何公约拘束，在中国台湾地区桃园地方法院地检署检察官对与确保航空保安的规范所知有限的情况下，分析该旅客是“境外”干扰飞航行为、骚扰空勤组员与电话中出言威胁航班与组员安全仅是争取消费者权益的“意气用事”，无具体危险，对诬告的刑事告诉为不起诉处分而结案，对于该名旅客涉嫌构成刑事犯罪或不当行为却也未主动侦查，更不认为有刑事管辖权，究其缘故，因中国台湾地区保护消费者权益的意识高涨，在航空公司自费处理迟延旅客要求，又未主动提刑事诉讼的情况下，主管机关虽知悉此案也皆采息事宁人态度。

简言之，纵使新国际航空保安立法增列管辖权选项，许多航空公司斟酌适用法律时还考虑《北京公约》仅适用于“可信威胁”①，且在“舱门未关”条件下，也无法适用《东京公约》或《蒙特利尔议定书》，加上不同国内法对消费者保障意识强弱等因素，所以，新国际安保立法中对管辖权的修订虽有所进步，但还不能解决实务上的诸多问题。

（二）对不循规旅客的认定及管束问题——以谎报炸弹、机舱内滋扰为例

ICAO 第 8973 号文件的 9 版附录 24——“航空运营人安保计划”（Appendix 24—“Aircraft Operator Security Programme”）第 26 点写明：“Basic responsibility for the security of aircraft rests with the operator.”（航空器使用人承担航空器保安之基本责任），②故发生不循规旅客事件时，航空

① ICAO，工作文件 HLCAS-WP/15，2012 年 7 月 12 日。

② 资料来源：http://img2.caa.gov.vn/2017/10/02/16/04/Appendix-24.pdf，最后访问日期：2018 年 12 月 5 日。

公司必须先根据其安保计划判定是否为“不循规旅客违规行为”。又“不循规旅客违规行为”可根据 ICAO 第 17 号附约及第 288 号通告(Circular 288 – 2002:Guidance Material on the Legal Aspects of Unruly/Disruptive Passengers)概括分为“非法干扰行为”(Acts of Unlawful Interference)①及“滋扰性行为”(Unruly and Disruptive Behaviour)两大类;第 288 号通告对“滋扰性行为”的定义为:“A passenger who fails to respect the rules of conduct at an airport or on board an aircraft or to follow the instructions of the airport staff or crew members and thereby disturbs the good order and discipline at an airport or on board the aircraft.”(旅客不遵守机场或飞机上的行为守则,或不遵守机场工作人员或机组人员的指示,从而扰乱机场或飞机上的良好秩序和纪律)唯“非法干扰行为”或“滋扰性行为”是否属于“犯罪行为”而具有“可责性”②,则应依据管辖法院适用准据法之“罪行法定”原则认定。所以产生适用不同国内法后亦会出现对不循规旅客有不一致的管束措施。

另根据国际航空运输协会(International Air Transport Association,IATA)于 2018 年 5 月提出“不循规旅客”事实报告,③不循规旅客事件包括对机组

---

① ICAO 第 17 号附约第一章定义“非法干扰行为”:These are acts or attempted acts such as to jeopardize the safety of civil aviation, including but not limited to:

- unlawful seizure of aircraft,
- destruction of an aircraft in service,
- hostage-taking on board aircraft or on aerodromes,
- forcible intrusion on board an aircraft, at an airport or on the premises of an aeronautical facility,
- introduction on board an aircraft or at an airport of a weapon or hazardous device or material intended for criminal purposes,
- use of an aircraft in service for the purpose of causing death, serious bodily injury, or serious damage to property or the environment,
- communication of false information such as to jeopardize the safety of an aircraft in flight or on the ground, of passengers, crew, ground personnel or the general public, at an airport or on the premises of a civil aviation facility。

② See Barbara E. Young, “Responsibility and Liability for Unlawful Interference in International Civil Aviation”, supplement AASL, Vol. 28/1 – 1, Feb. 2003, at 4.

③ See Fact Sheet Unruly Passengers, IATA, Accessed May 2018. https://www.iata.org/pressroom/facts_figures/fact_sheets/Documents/fact-sheet-unruly-passengers.pdf.

人员和其他旅客的暴力、骚扰、辱骂、吸烟、不遵守安全指示和其他形式的闹事行为。虽然这种行为是极少数旅客所为，但却产生了不同程度的影响。它们造成不便，威胁其他旅客和机组人员的安全和安保，并导致运营严重中断和增加航空公司营运成本；且

(1)于2016年，平均每1424航班出现一例“不循规旅客”(2015年平均每1205航班出现一例)；

(2)大多数“不循规旅客”事件报告都是属一级事件，是指属口头违规性质，通常可以由经过训练的组员处理后结案；

(3)事件报告中的12%属于二级事件，涉及对他人的人身攻击或对飞机的损害；

(4)在报告的事例中，33%的事例是由饮用酒精或食用毒品引起的；

(5)国际航空运输协会的统计资料并没有覆盖全球所有航空公司，因此很可能大大低估了问题的真实程度。

从上述“不循规旅客”增加的事实来看，新国际航空保安立法的吓阻效果尚不明显。实务上的适用疑惑还包括：根据2014年《蒙特利尔议定书》第13条新增《东京公约》第18条之2规定，缔约国可制定国家法律，由航空公司取得向在机上违规的不循规旅客“要求补偿所产生任何损失”的请求权；又ICAO于2018年9月第37届会议的工作文件中亦重申此一重点，强调“议定书还载有关于处理包括各国间的协调、正当程序和公平待遇以及根据国家法律要求补偿的权利等问题的各项规定”。[①] 比较《北京公约》及2014年《蒙特利尔议定书》在处理“不循规旅客”事件时可发现：该议定书提供航空公司因处理“不循规旅客”事件而产生之费用或损失明确请求权，某程度上可支持航空公司执行安保计划，但是，除非不循规旅客的行为已构成《北京公约》明列的“犯罪行为”，否则对航空公司还需自行认定违法行为是否为犯罪行为；更何况，《北京公约》第4条规定了法人犯罪，并进一步明确了法人和负责

① ICAO LC/37 - WP/2 - 3,17/5/18.

管理或控制该法人的个人实施犯罪时应承担的刑事、民事以及行政责任。①万一因航空公司地勤人员未查核旅客托运行李有危险品而造成"飞安"问题,航空公司甚为担心援引《北京公约》裁罚不循规旅客的管束措施时亦须承担刑事与民事责任。

实务上出现的"不循规旅客"实例有:某欧籍航空公司在准备飞曼谷之航班上收到来自美国的网络电话告知机上有炸弹,为确保航空安全,该航空公司命令准备起飞的飞机停飞,飞机紧急自跑道撤回停机坪,将旅客和行李全部卸除后重新进行保安检查,无异样后才起飞,导致全机旅客行程严重延误。事实上,经事后查明,是因为机上某名中国籍旅客配偶怀疑其出轨而谎报机上有炸弹,但这一行为已经给航空公司和广大旅客带来巨大的经济损失和心理伤害。该航空公司虽然根据航空器注册国应遵循的欧盟法规,如2008年EC 300/2008法规,所制订的运送人保安计划可对谎报炸弹的中国籍行为人在欧洲主要营业地行使刑事追诉权,但采取诉讼程序太旷日废时,成本太高,且若适用国际公约而选择其他管辖法院,则应择哪一个国际公约较为适合?例如,《北京公约》第1条(e)规定"传送该人明知是虚假的情报,从而危及飞航中的航空器的安全"是适用该公约的"犯罪"的行为;然而,2014年《蒙特利尔议定书》第1条规定公约适用范围中亦包括:"危及或能危及航空器或其所载人员或财产的安全,或危及航空器上的良好秩序和纪律的行为,无论其是否构成犯罪行为。"当发生谎报炸弹的案例时,已然发生同一行为可同时适用《北京公约》而成立"犯罪行为",以及适用《蒙特利尔议定书》可能尚未构成犯罪但属于危害航空安保行为的事例。简言之,《北京公约》与2014年《蒙特利尔议定书》的规范范围有相似(如犯罪行为)及差异(如议定书新增安保员的权利可立即处理危及航空器上的良好秩序和纪律的行为)之处。从而,在新国际安保立法下,就本事例而言,反而让航空公司在谎报炸弹之违规行为是否构成刑事犯罪的认定上出现困惑,而该航空公司最期待的是行为人

① 参见张莉琼:《国际航空犯罪法人行事责任及国内立法转化研究》,载中国法学网:www.iolaw.org.cn/showNews.aspx?id=58241,最后访问日期:2018年12月5日。

的所在国法律可容许航空公司经由陈报航空保安事件后，让当地航空警察经由侦办程序找到行为人进行诉追或行政裁罚，遏制此类事件发生，再借由刑事侦办得到的证据向保险机构申请理赔处理旅客航班迟延的损失，或可向违规的行为人求偿。

此外，机舱内滋扰事件更是层出不穷，据报载：美国空服员工会首次发布性骚调查报告，受访者包括 29 家美国航空公司的 3500 名空服人员，其中 80% 为女性、20% 为男性，统计出有高达 68% 的空服人员曾遭遇性骚扰。① 且于 2017 年 1 月 4 日民航资源网亦报道女旅客申诉一名男旅客趁其熟睡时性侵新闻，②可见航空器上性骚扰问题严重。值得注意的是，在备受争议的“凯莉·莫里斯诉荷兰皇家航空公司”(*Kelly Morris v. KLM Royal Dutch Airlines*)③案件中，欧洲法院几经审酌，最终支持女旅客因男旅客趁其熟睡性侵导致身体损伤而援引规范航空器运送人私法责任的华沙公约向航空公司请求赔偿。当时，尚无如 2014 年《蒙特利尔议定书》具体确认航空公司可向加害人求偿的国际法位阶的立法，航空公司必须研议向加害人求偿的较有利的国内法。

又航空公司也饱受因航班延误而出现“空闹”事件，有些旅客从地面闹到空中，直接威胁航空安全，澳门国际机场网站上迄今还载明：“2013 年 5 月国际民航组织法律委员会第 35 届会议资料披露，在近 5 年内，平均每 1200 次飞行中即发生 1 起此类事件。国际航空运输协会对 2008 年至 2011 年各会员公司呈报情况的统计表明，4 年间全球共报告 1.5 万起此类案件，而实际发生的案件数量可能远不止于此。”④航空公司在处理旅客拒下飞机求偿之

---

① 参见《空服员遭狼爪比例高！美国调查：68% 曾被性骚》，载自由时报网：http://news.ltn.com.tw/news/world/breakingnews/2422479，最后访问日期：2019 年 1 月 10 日。

② 参见《网曝高管飞机上性骚扰女旅客　公安机关介入调查》，载民航资源网：http://news.carnoc.com/list/386/386009.html，最后访问日期：2019 年 1 月 10 日。

③ *Kelly Morris v. KLM Royal Dutch Airlines*，[2001] EWCA Civ. 790.

④ 《航空“不循规”行为是国际社会共同对治的顽症》，载澳门国际机场网：http://www.macau-airport.com/cn/media-centre/news/news/12862，最后访问日期：2014 年 12 月 23 日。

“空闹”事件,或如白人男性旅客要求某航空女性空服人员协助上厕所①等涉嫌构成机舱内滋扰事件时,常因考虑不循规旅客主张消费者权益保护而出现执行制裁不循规旅客与消费者保护的“拉锯战”,最终未向不循规旅客的行为求偿,难起吓阻之效。

(三)裁处问题——以机舱内吸烟为例

实务上在滋扰性行为的裁处结果上亦经常出现歧义,甚至对相同违规行为而有不同裁处结果,民航主管机关及航空公司亦深感困惑。举例而言:2018 年 7 月中国国际航空(以下简称国航)CA106 航班从中国香港特别行政区飞往大连市的飞行途中,有机组员在机舱吸烟,误触系统设备,导致飞机飞行高度瞬降、失压,连紧急氧气罩都落下,吓坏不少旅客。而在中国交通部 2017 年颁布的《大型飞机公共航空运输承运人运行合格审定规则》规定中,全机舱(包含驾驶舱)都是禁烟状态。② 换言之,任何人皆不能于驾驶舱及客舱内吸烟,对于航空公司的违规行为,民航局可根据《大型飞机公共航空运输承运人运行合格审定规则》第 121. 597 条认定是违规行为,而可根据第 121. 763 条规定责令其停止违法行为,并处以警告或者人民币 10,000 元以上 30,000 元以下罚款;对于在客舱内吸烟的旅客,可根据《公共航空旅客运输飞行中安全保卫工作规则》第 47 条规定而适用《中华人民共和国治安管理处罚法》第 23 条第 3 款规定,认定是“扰乱航空器秩序”之违规行为,得处以警告,或者 200 元以下罚款,情节严重者处 5 日以上 10 日以下拘留,可以并处 500 元以下罚款。

事实上,客舱内吸烟的“滋扰性行为”在实务上适用法规的裁处结果可能更加复杂,假设:中国籍旅客购买加拿大航空(以下简称加航)机票自蒙特

① 李宜秦:《洋男逼擦屁股 长荣空服员崩溃》,载中国时报网:http://www. chinatimes. com/newpapers/20190121000489—260114? chdtv,最后访问日期:2019 年 1 月 21 日。

② 参见李靖棠:《真是驾驶抽烟惹祸! 陆国航班机空中瞬降惊魂》,载中国电子报网:https://www. chinatimes. com/realtimenews/20180713002187 - 260409,最后访问日期:2018 年 7 月 13 日。

利尔经温哥华、中国台湾地区台北市(停留数日后)前往四川省成都市的往返机票,于从温哥华到中国台湾地区台北市约13小时航班上,烟瘾难耐,躲到厕所抽烟,被后进厕所中国台湾地区旅客发现告知空服员,加航机长应如何处置?应注意:加拿大已批准《东京公约》,[①]但迄今尚未批准《北京公约》及2014年《蒙特利尔议定书》,所以根据《东京公约》,航空器登记国——加拿大法律取得管辖权,加航在网站上写明:“成为世界上首家提供北美和欧洲之间完全无烟航班的定期航班。在此之前,1988年9月,加航成为加拿大首家禁止在北美和加勒比境内的所有包机和定期航班吸烟的航空公司。”[②]再查加拿大《非吸烟者健康保护法》(Non-smokers' Healthy Act)第3(2)条及第5(1)条规定,似乎可容许加航对飞行时间超过2小时航班上划定“吸烟区”。然而,加拿大仍应遵守ICAO第29届大会A29－15号决议(Smoking Restrictions on International Passenger Flights)禁止国际旅客在机舱内吸烟,所以,驾驶员与旅客在客舱内吸烟是否同属“滋扰性行为”?是否应视为“航空保安事件”?在本事件中,加航考虑用降落地法(中国台湾地区“民用航空法”)处罚该名中国籍旅客又担心“敏感问题”,若不处理,又无法给检举的中国台湾地区旅客交代,可能面对民事求偿风险,因为,中国台湾地区“最高法院”曾判定美国西北航空应对于坐在非吸烟区的中国台湾地区旅客以受到二手烟危害身体为由,构成“债务不履行”而支付赔偿。[③] 加航机长如何妥善处理显非易事,益证制裁不循规旅客的国际立法与消费者保护的“拉锯战”不断上演的复杂原因,亟须各国政府共同协助及统一化法规适用,才能获得实质预防及抑制“滋扰性行为”的效果。

---

① See ICAO Current lists of parties to multilateral air law treaties, Accessed December 5, 2018. https://www.icao.int/secretariat/legal/List%20of%20Parties/Tokyo_EN.pdf.

② “Non-smoking airlines(October 1990) Air Canada became the first scheduled airline in the world to offer exclusively smoke-free flights between North America and Europe. Prior to this date, in September 1988, Air Canada became the first Canadian airline to ban smoking on all of its charter and scheduled flights within North America and the Caribbean.” Accessed December 5, 2018. https://www.aircanada.com/ca/en/aco/home/about/media/facts-about-air-canada.html.

③ 参见中国台湾地区“最高法院”九十一年度台上字第一四九五号判决。

三、制裁不循规旅客规范不足

(一)2014年《蒙特利尔议定书》缺失

就公约拘束力而言,已批准《北京议定书》及《北京公约》的国家,若亦是1971年《蒙特利尔公约》、1988年《蒙特利尔补充议定书》之缔约国而产生竞合时,《北京公约》将优先适用(《北京公约》第19条及第24条)。况且,2014年《蒙特利尔议定书》主要目的在作为《东京公约》现代化结果,所以,纵使2014年《蒙特利尔议定书》生效,仅生《北京公约》与2014年《蒙特利尔议定书》同时存在、并立的结果。实务现况是,在2019年2月前,《北京公约》仅获得50国批准,[①]距离ICAO的192个会员国批准《北京公约》与2014年《蒙特利尔议定书》,以及在两者生效后建构国际合作的确保航空安保机制尚有一段距离,从而,许多航空公司尚在观望其所属国或营业所在地国对实践新国际航空安保的政策。

有中国学者主张,虽然2014年《蒙特利尔议定书》是为修补《东京公约》的缺陷。例如,对"飞行中"定义过窄、欠缺对刑事犯罪行为与其他危害行为明确界定、管辖权有空缺而无法对航空器降落地国的离机加害人主张追诉、欠缺统一执行程序规则及对机长职权规定过宽等,但却仍有疏失。[②] 也有外国学者持相似见解,批判2014年《蒙特利尔议定书》仍无法对《东京公约》主要缺陷提供有效的解决。[③] 例如,就管辖权而言,2014年《蒙特利尔议定书》第3条明文规定降落地国取得管辖权之条件:(1)缔约国须采取必要措施;(2)某项犯罪是在其前一起飞地点或下一个预备降落地点在其领土内的航

---

① 资料来源:https://www.icao.int/secretariat/legal/List%20of%20Parties/Beijing_Conv_EN.pdf,最后访问日期:2018年12月5日。

② 参见郑派:《论2014年〈蒙特利尔议定书〉对1963年〈东京公约〉的修订》,载《北京理工大学学报》(社会科学版)2015年第2期。

③ See Jennifer A. Urban, "The Protocol to amend the Convention on offences and certain acts committed on board aircraft: A missed opportunity or a sufficient modernization?", *Indiana Law Review* 49, pp. 738 – 743.

空器所犯;(3)随后航空器在其领土内降落;(4)且嫌犯仍在机上。2014年《蒙特利尔议定书》未清楚罗列违规态样,在适用上不免又需参考《东京公约》第1条第1项第2款规定之定义:“危害或能危害航空器或其所载人员或财产的安全,或危害航空器上的良好秩序和纪律的行为,无论是否构成犯罪行为。”最终还是回到ICAO第17号附约与第288号通告对“不循规旅客”的定义来认定违规行为可责性,甚至是以管辖法院当地法令来认定,如此一来,自然无法为实务上亟待取得能在制裁不循规旅客与保护消费者间“拉锯战”问题上提供有效解决的策略。

(二)平衡制裁不循规旅客与保护消费者的必要性

相较于2014年《蒙特利尔议定书》,《北京公约》第1条明列对“飞行中”与“使用中”航空器构成“犯罪”的行为,与《蒙特利尔公约》及其1988年议定书在违规行为范围上相比,明显差异处还包括增加了使用生物、化学和核物质对民用航空进行攻击和使用民用航空器非法传播生物、化学和核物质的条款,较能符合违规行为“现代化”的要求。但是,正因《北京公约》规范之行为侧重于“犯罪”行为,而2014年《蒙特利尔议定书》系以解决航空公司于实务上处理不断上升的不循规旅客事例为重点,ICAO于2018年9月第37届会议的工作文件引言中仍肯认《蒙特利尔议定书》的规范意义为:“……议定书的执行条款部分承认了在特定条件下,降落地国和经营人所在国对机上和其他行为行使管辖权。如果议定书中规定的标准得到满足,则确立对犯罪行为的此类管辖权即为强制性的。议定书从法律上认可了机上保安员的地位,并为其提供特别的保护措施。议定书还载有关于处理包括各国间的协调、正当程序和公平待遇以及根据国家法律要求补偿的权利等问题的各项规定。”ICAO为研议制裁不循规旅客的机制还成立“不循规旅客法律问题的工作队”,借由审查第288号通告,更新指导材料、审视2014年《蒙特利尔议定书》的管辖权问题、推出刑事处分与行政制裁或任何其他形式的法律程序以期有效威吓“不循规旅客”、考虑是否对“不循规”和“滋扰性”提出定义等,可见

ICAO 还试图解决 2014 年《蒙特利尔议定书》尚未解决的问题,若要让 ICAO 会员国及其航空公司有效遏制"不循规"和"滋扰性"旅客以确保航空保安,建议"不循规旅客法律问题的工作队"应正视相关的消费者保障问题,考虑以实务运作观点讨论如何寻得平衡制裁不循规旅客与保护消费者的法制。

四、结　论

纵使新国际航空安保立法将航空安保措施带入新纪元,就航空公司处理安保的实务案例而言,影响航空业者的威胁来源除少数有意危害飞航安全的分子,多数的威胁来自不守法的内部员工,常见的行为包括偷窃、破坏、运送毒品等,但更多的威胁是来自旅客,原因有很多种,最常发生的干扰行为如饮酒后的不理性举动或骚扰空勤组员等。各国航空公司也开始思考如何处理此类不循规旅客的事件,例如,将某些旅客列入"黑名单"而拒载。当航机迟延时,也经常发生旅客咆哮航空公司人员,拒绝下机等干扰航空器继续飞行的作为,航空公司不得不求助航空警察遏止旅客滋扰行为,但是,这些安保举措也同时遭受到消费者保护团体指谪航空公司侵害消费者权益,因此,纵使有《北京公约》及 2014 年《蒙特利尔议定书》等制裁不循规旅客的新国际立法作为国家或航空公司制订其航空安保计划之参考,仍经常让航空公司在实际采取航空安保措施时又得考虑与消费者保护,两者间形成"拉锯战",此一议题持续困扰着民航主管机关、业者与旅客。

无疑,《芝加哥公约》第 17 号附约、其他附件(如第 1 号、第 6 号、第 8 号、第 11 号、第 13 号、第 14 号、第 19 号附约)及第 8973 号文件建构国际航空保安法制的标准及建议措施是 ICAO 会员国应遵守的最低标准,[①]也是维护全球航空安保的基石。当《北京公约》生效后,因该公约除包含数个航空保安

---

① See ICAO PowerPoint Presentation Template, Accessed December 5, 2018. http://www.icao.int/safety/SafetyManagement/Documents/Annex%2019%20-%20ICAO%20presentation%20-%20self%20instruction%2024September2013.pdf.

公约的违规行为类型外，还明确包含未规定的适用范围，例如，对“飞行中”“使用中”“不适用国家航空器”“国际因素”等；对管辖权则加入有关“人的因素”赋予犯罪人国籍国、被害人国籍国及无国籍犯罪行为人居所地国等管辖权（《北京公约》第8条）；除维持“或起诉或引渡原则”外还规范“排除政治罪不引渡原则”及“得拒绝引渡或司法互助之情形”（《北京公约》第12条至第14条）；及赋予法律实体民事、刑事或行政上之责任（《北京公约》第4条）；强调国际法规定之国家和个人的其他权利、义务和责任等（《北京公约》第6条），对于不循规旅客构成犯罪的行为提供较明确的处置机制。唯不可否认的是，《北京公约》及2014年《蒙特利尔议定书》规范重点确有不同，从本文列举的实务案例中适用管辖权、对不循规旅客的认定及管束与裁处等三个重点的说明，更可发现相同但又有差异处，在加入消费者保护的因素后，实务运用上确实存在一些疑惑，经常让航空公司在实际采取航空安保措施时又得考虑消费者保护的平衡，使两者间形成“拉锯战”，两者失衡的结果将不利航空产业的健全发展。

然而，在确保“万无一失”及“零风险”的飞安前提下，鼓励ICAO会员国批准《北京公约》遏制与航空器有关的犯罪，其最终结果是由国家的意志支持航空公司及消费者共同协力保证航空运输上的飞航安全，更是具体保障消费者权益的实践；相同道理，若ICAO“不循规旅客法律问题的工作队”修改2014年《蒙特利尔议定书》或其他确保航空安保措施时，能正视相关的消费者保障问题，或许可减少制裁不循规旅客的国际立法与消费者保护间在个案权衡上的两难，亦能促使会员国考虑批准修改后的2014年《蒙特利尔议定书》，或借此取得更完善的国际航空保卫立法，以建置吓阻及制裁不循规旅客的航空安保机制，在发展健全航空运输的最终目标上应该更有实质意义。

Legal and Aeropolitical Implications of Brexit on European and International Air Transport

Andrea Trimarchi *

The decision of exiting the EU, stemming from the pre-legislative referendum held on 23 June 2016, whereby the majority of UK citizens expressed their desire for the UK to leave the EU, marked a momentous socio-political event not only in European, but also in international history, triggering a transitional phase, due to expire on 29 March 2019 (now 31 October 2019). It is believed that the exit of the UK from the EU, commonly known as 'Brexit', will have a remarkable impact on a number of fields, including inter alia trade, finance, telecommunications and, not of lesser importance, air transport. The UK represents the world's third most developed aviation network

---

* Research Assistant in Air Law at the Institute of Air, Space and Cyber Law at Universität zu Köln, Germany.

behind the US and China and the largest aviation market worldwide with its airport carrying 200 million passengers annually, 49% of which travelling from or to the EU. As a member of the EU, the UK has tremendously benefitted from the creation and consolidation of an EU single air transport market and from air traffic rights being negotiated at the EU supranational level vis-à-vis third countries. The current legal scenario allows for an unconditional provision of air services to, from and within the Union and the UK. In aviation, the essential corollary of the UK's membership in the EU is that UK airlines enjoy a plethora of traffic rights, including the right to provide air services between two points located within the EU, as well as within an individual EU member State (i. e. cabotage). However, there is no doubt this may drastically change once the UK will leave the EU, with significant repercussions on the whole international air transport sector.

1. Introduction

Since 2016, the portmanteau "Brexit" has become part of the common English vocabulary, attracting increasing attention globally. As a matter of fact, in 2017 and 2018, "*what is Brexit*" and "*when is Brexit*" have been among the most googled questions worldwide. ①

The decision of exiting the European Union (hereinafter also referred to as the "EU") stems from the pre-legislative *referendum* held on 23 June 2016 whereby on a turnout of 72.2% of the eligible electorate, some 17,410,742 voters (or 51.9% of those voting) voted to leave the EU, while 16,141,241 (48.1% of those voting) voted to remain. This democratic response marked a

---

① See Accessed March 10, 2019. https://www.express.co.uk/news/uk/1018417/brexit-news-what-is-brexit-google-searches.

momentous socio-political event not only in European, but also in international history, triggering a transitional phase, which was originally due to expire on 29 March 2019(now extended until 31 October 2019).

The exit of the UK from the EU will cause numerous repercussions on the EU and global economy. Such impact is expected to increase even more should a "hard-Brexit" or "no-deal Brexit" occur, that is, should the UK leave the EU without an agreement allowing for access to the EU single market or entitling the UK to benefit from current EU's trade agreements.

Today, the UK represents the world's third most developed aviation network behind the US and China and the third largest aviation market worldwide with its airports carrying 200 million passengers annually, 49% of which travelling from or to the EU. As a member of the EU, the UK currently enjoys the EU single air transport market and all agreements that the EU has concluded with third countries.

This paper intends to discuss and analyse possible post-Brexit scenarios concerning air transport. While potential implications of Brexit in aviation may be indefinite, the research will be delimited to three macro thematic areas. Firstly, from an intra-EU perspective, speculations will be moved with regard to potential *UK-EU aviation relations* and as to whether UK airlines will still be allowed to take advantage of the unique commercial features and spirit of the EU aviation single market. Secondly, emphasis will be placed on the legal and regulatory issues concerning the *relations between the UK and third countries*. This, particularly in a Hard-Brexit scenario, will be likely to result in a political debate as to whether concluding new air services agreements (hereinafter also referred to as "ASAs") or determining the automatic revival of old agreements, which were in force prior to the conferral of an horizontal mandate to the EU Commission in the field of external aviation relations. Furthermore, the study will briefly consider the repercussion that Brexit will have in another relevant commercial sphere of air transport, namely, *EU consumer protection law*, which, as will be shown, does not only constitute a regional concern.

2. Legal Basis for Brexit

Following the outcome of the *referendum*, the UK invoked the machinery *ex* Art. 50 of the Treaty on the Functioning of the European Union (hereinafter also referred to as "TFEU"), ① which entitles any EU member State to "*withdraw from the [European] Union in accordance with its own constitutional requirements*". ②

Interestingly, an express "withdrawal clause" was only introduced in 2007 in Lisbon with the drafting of Art. 50. However, as literature has observed, this does not necessarily imply that, even before 2007, States could not withdraw their participation in the EU. The Vienna Convention on the Law of Treaties (hereinafter also referred to as "VCLT"), indeed, includes the well-recognised customary principle of public international law according to which States can withdraw from a treaty either with the consent of all the parties③ or if the nature of a treaty even implicitly admits withdrawal. ④

While much has been debated with respect to the constitutional aspects of a potential withdrawal from the EU, it is fundamental to draw the attention to paragraph 2 of the same Art. 50, which explicitly requires the "withdrawing State" to negotiate future relations with the EU:

---

① Consolidated version of the Treaty on the Functioning of the European Union [2008], O. J. C 115/47.

② Art. 50 (1) TFEU.

③ Art. 54 (b) VCLT.

④ Art. 56 (1) (b) VCLT.

"[...] In the light of the guidelines provided by the European Council, the Union shall negotiate and conclude an agreement with that State, setting out the arrangements for its withdrawal, taking account of the framework for its future relationship with the Union". ①

Negotiations, which were originally due to result in a deal by 29 March 2019, have been, however, further extended upon decision of the European Council and the EU member States (not including the UK). A new "Exit-date" is now set for 31 October 2019.

3. Brexit in the Air

The UK aviation market is the third largest worldwide. It is estimated that, only in 2016, more than 258 million passengers have travelled or transited through airports located in the UK, with over 370 direct connections currently linking the UK to the rest of the world. ②

Yet, while more than 8 million business trips between the UK and the EU take place each year, making the EU one of the most important trade partners of the UK, more than 70% of persons travelling to the UK does so by air. ③

While holding a central position as a current EU member in the horizontal negotiations conducted by the EU Commission with key third countries, the UK represents and will continue to represent an attractive and stand-alone major partner for transatlantic and middle-east/east-Asian countries.

---

① Art. 50(2) TFEU.

② International Air Transport Association (IATA), "A Study of the Effects of the United Kingdom leaving the European Union on Airlines Flying to and from the UK", 2018, p. 4.

③ Association of UK Airlines, "Brexit and Aviation: Market Access", 2017, p. 3.

4. Repercussions on the EU Single Aviation Market: Post-Brexit Scenarios

Following a gradual process of liberalisation which took place between 1987 and 1993, ① the EU has progressively built a unique liberalised aviation market within its boundaries. This liberalisation wave eventually culminated with the adoption of the Regulation (EC) No. 1008/2008, ② which now provides the basic EU legislation for the provision of air services within the Union.

The so-called EU single aviation market now allows air carriers established in any of the EU Member States to provide air services indistinctively and indiscriminately through the whole territory of the Union, thereby including the territory of the UK. From a policy standpoint, the most significant corollaries of the EU aviation sector can be identified in the freedom of establishment for airlines-directly stemming from the introduction of the "Community (now

---

① Starting from December 1987, the Council of the European Union (then European Communities) adopted several legal instruments intended to achieve liberalisation of air transport between the Member States. Such legislative instruments were gathered in so-called "legislative packages". The first legislative package (1987) did not remove all restrictions on competition, but introduced a scheme of fare zones, within which the airlines were to be allowed to act freely. The second legislative package (1990) dealt with liberalising access to the market and to "deregulate" capacity and frequency of air services within the Union. It also introduced the concept of multiple designation, allowing an indefinite number of airlines to be designated in ASAs. The third legislative package (1992), which introduced new requirements concerning air carrier licensing and established the "community air carrier" notion, allowing free market access to all airlines capable of meeting the requirements set forth in EU law. See for a more detailed analysis Elmar M. Giemulla and Ludwig Weber (eds), *International and EU Aviation Law: Selected Issues*, Kluwer Law International, 2011, pp. 142 - 150. See also Pablo Mendes De Leon, *Introduction to Air Law*, Tenth Edition, Kluwer Law International, 2017, pp. 91 - 96.

② Regulation (EC) No. 1008/2008 of the European Parliament and of the Council on common rules for the operation of air services in the Community, 2008 O. J. L 293 3.

Union) Air Carrier"[①] notion and the abolition of the cabotage reserve within the EU's territory.[②]

This has resulted in a radical transformation of the EU aviation market, which is now strongly characterised by the presence and success of low cost airlines, which established in an EU Member State (e.g. UK for EasyJet and Norwegian; Ireland for Ryanair), provide any sort of intra-EU air services, including cabotage services (e.g. Porto-Lisbon; Berlin-Cologne; London-Manchester).

It naturally follows that the exit of the UK from the EU will have a tremendous impact on the EU single aviation market at large. It may be interesting, therefore, to address the main issues and potential scenarios, which may outline with respect to the post-Brexit relations between the EU and the UK. The following regulatory options specifically refer to a hard-Brexit hypothetical scenario, as previously described.

4.1 Towards an EU-UK Open Skies Agreement

In the event the EU and the UK failed to negotiate a withdrawal agreement capable of maintaining unchanged aviation relations, the two parties may anew

---

① Art. 2(11) of Regulation (EC) No. 1008/2008 defines a "Community air carrier" as "an air carrier with a valide operating licence granted by a competent licensing authority in accordance with Chapter II", that is, granted by a competent licensing authority of any of the EU Member States.

② The term cabotage in aviation is characterised by a strong economic connotation. However, as the etymology of the word demonstrates, this concept finds its roots in maritime law and does not relate to economic activities or phenomena. In aviation law, cabotage refers to the carriage of traffic between two points, which are both located within the territory of one state. *See inter alia* Paul S. Dempsey, *Public International Air Law*, McGill University Institute and Centre for Research in Air and Space Law, 2008, pp. 517 – 522; Pablo Mendes De Leon, *Cabotage in Air Transport Regulation* Martinus Nijhoff Publishers, 1992, p. xi. Practical examples of cabotage air services include flights between New York (US) and Los Angeles (UK); Shanghai (China) and Shenzhen (China); New Delhi (India) and Mumbai (India); St. Petersburg (Russia) and Moscow (Russia).

negotiate a specific bilateral ASA, possibly in the liberal form of an Open Skies agreement.[①] The new ASA may be shaped on the basis of the EU/Switzerland Agreement on Air Transport concluded in 2014,[②] which grants Swiss airlines traffic rights both between any point in Switzerland and the EU, and between points in different EU Member States.[③]

Such a possibility would still guarantee a rather high degree of competitiveness and flexibility in the provision of air services between the Union and the UK. However, notably, it would be very unlikely that the EU and the UK would grant reciprocal fifth and seventh freedom[④] and cabotage rights. In such a case, hence, market access would be significantly limited.

---

① Open Skies ASAs are generally liberal ASAs, which are characterised by a number of elements, including but not limited to: no limitations with regard to capacity; opening of all routes; unlimited exchange of third and fourth freedom rights, with, occasionally, also inclusion of fifth freedom rights, subject to approval from the third country involved; multiple, i. e. unlimited designation; strong competitive connotation.

② Agreement between the European Community and the Swiss Confederation on Air Transport [2002] OJ L114/73. It shall be observed that the EU/Switzerland Agreement on Air Transport was included in broader umbrella negotiations for a comprehensive EU/Swiss Agreement, which composed of several sector-specific agreements, allows Switzerland to maintain its competitiveness in the EU market and secure its quality as a business location.

③ See Roberto Cassar, "Survival of the Freest: The Impact of Brexit on EasyJet p. l. c.", 66 *ZLW* 3, 2017, pp. 428 – 429.

④ Rights granted in ASAs are usually denominated as "freedoms of the air", although some authors have notably observed that it would be more appropriate to refer to such rights as pure "*privileges*", see for instance Brian F. Havel and Gabriel S. Sanchez, *The Principles and Practice of International Aviation Law*, Cambridge University Press, 2014, p. 78. The fifth freedom of the air entails the right of an airline of a state A to carry passengers and/or cargo between two foreign states B and C, provided such service is the continuation of a service originating in the territory of state A. It is often referred to as "beyond freedom" or "beyond traffic right". Practical examples include the right of Singapore Airlines to fly from Singapore to Dubai (AUE), picking up new passengers from Dubai (AUE) to London (UK). The seventh freedom of the air, which is notably rather frequent in the cargo sector, grants the right of the airline of a state A to carry passengers and/or cargo between two foreign states B and C, without any link with the territory of its home state A. This would be the case of an air services operated by the US carrier Delta Air Lines between Frankfurt (Germany) and Astana (Kazakhstan).

As a result, for example, UK carriers, e.g. EasyJet or British Airways, would no longer be granted the right to operate air services between Paris and Frankfurt or between Barcelona and Madrid. Similarly, EU airlines would find a diriment legal obstacle in operating intra-UK routes (e.g. London-Edinburgh; Bristol-Manchester).

In practice, a good share of UK/EU traffic would be safeguarded and the UK would, aviation wise, *de facto* become one of the major key partners of the EU, pretty much like the US, Canada and Brazil.

4.2 Revival or Renegotiation of Individual Bilateral Air Services Agreements

One must also take into account a potential scenario in which the EU fails to horizontally conclude an aviation agreement with the UK. This would, by far, be the most detrimental solution for the Union itself.

Should an EU/UK deal not be reached, the UK may opt for negotiating individual bilateral ASAs with each EU member State. This could potentially jeopardise the operation of the EU single aviation market. From a policy perspective, indeed, the UK may arbitrarily choose the partner countries with which negotiating an ASA. Therefore, while negotiating ASAs with Germany, France and Italy, the UK may decide not to start negotiations with countries, such as Croatia and Estonia.

What is more, the UK may opt to seek Open Skies relations with key EU partners, while simply invoking the revival of older bilateral ASAs, of the Bermuda Ⅱ style, ① with some other countries. Thus, this scenario would call for a fragmented patchwork, which would considerably undermine the unique

① Agreement Concerning Air Services, United States-United Kingdom, 1977, 28 UNTS 5367 (Bermuda Ⅱ Agreement).

level of harmonisation and liberalisation that the EU has attained so far.

4.3 The Norway-Iceland Option: Joining the European Common Aviation Area

At present, the benefits of the EU single aviation market are not exclusive to the EU Member States. The Agreement on the European Common Aviation Area (ECAA), ① concluded in 2006, has indeed extended the single market to a number of neighbouring countries. These, in addition to the EU member States, include Serbia, Iceland, Norway, Montenegro, Albania, Bosnia and Herzegovina, Kosovo, Georgia, Armenia, Moldova and Azerbaijan. ② The ECAA liberalises air transport relations between State parties by allowing any airline established in any ECAA State to fly between any airports located within the ECAA area, including cabotage services.

By ratifying the ECAA Agreement, the UK could maintain its position in the single aviation market. Under this scenario, there would be no change to the regulations, ownership conditions or traffic rights facing UK carriers or facing EU carriers operating routes to and within the UK. Notably, the economic impact to aviation would be "*equivalent to not leaving the European Union at all*". ③ Although very beneficial for the industry, such a solution seems to currently undergo some political resistance, also in light of the fact that the UK would not *de facto* occupy a prominent position in the ECAA and would, therefore,

---

① Multilateral Agreement between the European Community and Its Member States, the Republic of Albania, Bosnia and Herzegovina, the Republic of Bulgaria, the Republic of Croatia, the Former Yugoslav Republic of Macedonia, the Republic of Iceland, the Republic of Montenegro, the Kingdom of Norway, Romania, the Republic of Serbia and the United Nations Interim Administration Mission in Kosovo on the Establishment of a European Common Aviation Area, [2006] OJ L285.

② As of May 2019.

③ International Air Transport Association (IATA), "A Study of the Effects of the United Kingdom leaving the European Union on Airlines Flying to and from the UK", 2018, p. 15.

passively accept the decisions of the EU.

5. The UK's External Aviation Relations

Upon "Exit-day", the UK will immediately cease to be part of all Open Skies ASAs, which cover EU's external aviation relations with third countries, including, for instance, the US and Canada. This means that, on one hand, UK airlines will no longer be granted the necessary rights to carry traffic between any point in the EU to any point in the US or Canada. On the other hand, US or Canadian airlines will no longer have unlimited access and extensive freedom to operate air services from/to the UK.

This section will address the potential scenarios arising from a hard-Brexit. In particular, the focus will be laid on the case of the UK/US relations and which regulatory options could be available.

5.1 A New UK/US Open Skies Air Services Agreement

As of today, the most plausible scenario would entail that the UK will no longer be bound by the EU/US Open Skies agreement and may decide to individually negotiate a bilateral ASA with the US.

From a political perspective, the new UK/US agreement would be likely to take the form of a liberal Open Skies ASA. The UK is one of the strongest aviation partner of the US, with London Heathrow being a crucial gateway for transatlantic leisure passengers and business traffic. Therefore, both parties are in need of strategically maintain good relations and offer the largest possible number of connections.

Already in early 2018, talks have been made public as to the possibility of shaping the UK/US ASA on the current EU/US Open Skies agreement, by simply replacing the parties concerned.① However, remarkably, ownership and control requirements would need to be renegotiated and kept in line with the Chicago tradition.② In fact, at present, by virtue of the EU/US Open Skies agreements, air carriers willing to operate an international service from London to Los Angeles must only demonstrate to meet the "Community air carrier" requirements (majority owned and effectively controlled by nationals of any EU Member State).

The nationality clause shall be therefore amended in order to foresee a UK ownership and control. Notably, however, there is today some uncertainty as to whether some of the major UK-based transatlantic carriers, namely Virgin Atlantic and Norwegian UK, will meet the ownership criteria, since ownership is distributed across Europe.

5.2 A New Era for Bermuda Ⅱ Agreement?

History of international aviation relations has been strongly characterised by the bilateral ASAs concluded between the UK and the US. The iconic Bermuda Ⅰ (1946)③ and Bermuda Ⅱ (1947)④ agreements-between the UK and the US, but adopted as a model by almost all countries worldwide-have significantly marked the arena of bilateral aviation relations for almost half a century before leaving the scene to agreements of the Open Skies type.

Accordingly, from a legal perspective, should the EU/US Open Skies agreement not be applicable to the relations between the UK and the US, the two

---

① Bloomberg, "US Offers UK Worse 'Open Skies' Deal After Brexit", 5 March 2018.

② Bilteralism stems from the failure of the Convention on International Civil Aviation (Chicago Convention) of 1944 to provide a systematic regulation of commercial air transport.

③ Air Services Agreement between the United States and the United Kingdom, Feb. 11, 1946, 60 Stat. 1499, T. I. A. S. No. 1507 (Bermuda I Agreement).

④ Agreement Concerning Air Services, United States – United Kingdom, 1977, 28 UNTS 5367 (Bermuda II Agreement).

States may opt to invoke the automatic revival of the old bilateral Bermuda Ⅱ Agreement, which was in force until 2007.

This would have a tremendous impact on transatlantic UK/US air transport as Bermuda Ⅱ framework remarkably places restrictions on designation (single or dual) and routes. Additionally, the whole Bermuda Ⅱ system is still characterised by rigid predetermination (capacity, frequency, pricing), and, therefore, leaves little room to free competition. ①

5.3 Multilateralism through the European Common Aviation Area

As above discussed, the UK may opt for a membership in the ECAA, which would allow it to continue enjoying the benefits of the comprehensive horizontal Open Skies agreements concluded by the EU, including, for instance, the EU/US Open Skies ASA. For instance, Norway, despite not being a member of the EU, is a party to the EU/US Open Skies ASA as a third-party by virtue of the ECAA.

However, at present, this solution is not likely to receive widespread approval. Principal reasons include: (i) the UK would passively benefit from the EU's external aviation strategy, but would no longer have a determinant weight in the decision-making/negotiation phase; and (ii) the tripartite scheme EU/US/UK would imply the consent of the US to allow the UK to benefit from the agreement as a "third party". However, the US may privilege the idea of individually negotiating its traffic relations with the UK.

---

① Predetermination and restrictions permeated the spirit of the Bermuda Ⅱ agreement as the UK intended to prevent a univocal domination of the transatlantic air transport market by US carriers. As to the historical background of the Bermuda Ⅱ agreement, see inter alia Andreas F. Lowenfeld, "The Future Determines the Past: Bermuda I in Light of Bermuda Ⅱ", 3 *Air & Space Law* 1, 1978, pp. 2 – 10; Robert R. Gray, "The Impact of Bermuda Ⅱ on Future Bilateral Agreements", 3 *Air & Space Law* 1, 1978, pp. 17 – 22.

6. The Impact on the Airline Sector: The Cases of British Airways and EasyJet Europe

As observed, following "Exit-Day", airlines established or having their principal place of business in the territory of the UK will immediately cease to be considered EU air carriers, in line with the requirements set out in Art. 4 of Regulation (EC) No. 1008/2008. ①

British Airways, Easyjet, Jet2 and Norwegian UK are currently the major UK airlines. Upon the exit of the UK from the EU, these airlines will no longer be granted the right to operate intra-EU services (e.g. Paris-Barcelona; Rome-Frankfurt) and intra-EU Member State services (e.g. Porto-Lisbon; Cologne-Berlin; Paris-Toulouse). Furthermore, as specified above, UK airlines will not be able to be "designated" under the Open Skies agreements which the EU is currently a party to.

At the same time, EU carriers having operational bases located in the UK (e.g. Ryanair, which operates more than 200 destinations from London

---

① Pursuant to Art. 4 of Regulation (EC) No. 1008/2008 "An undertaking shall be granted an operating licence by the competent licensing authority of a Member State provided that: (a) its principal place of business is located in that Member State; (b) it holds a valid AOC issued by a national authority of the same Member State whose competent licensing authority is responsible for granting, refusing, revoking or suspending the operating licence of the Community air carrier; (c) it has one or more aircraft at its disposal through ownership or a dry lease agreement; (d) its main occupation is to operate air services in isolation or combined with any other commercial operation of aircraft or the repair and maintenance of aircraft; (e) its company structure allows the competent licensing authority to implement the provisions of this Chapter; (f) Member States and/or nationals of Member States own more than 50% of the undertaking and effectively control it, whether directly or indirectly through one or more intermediate undertakings, except as provided for in an agreement with a third country to which the Community is a party; (g) it meets the financial conditions specified in Article 5; (h) it complies with the insurance requirements specified in Article 11 and in Regulation (EC) No. 785/2004; and (i) it complies with the provisions on good repute as specified in Article 7."

Stansted) will significantly be affected. In order to continue operations, these carriers shall demonstrate that majority ownership of the company(50% plus 1 of equity shares and voting rights) and effective control (e.g. the identity of the board of directors, the structure and nationality of those entrusted with decisional powers) lie with UK nationals. ①

There is uncertainty, for instance, as to whether British Airways will satisfy this nationality criteria. As known, after the merger with Iberia in 2011, British Airways is now majority owned by International Airlines Group (IAG), an Anglo-Spanish holding company registered in Madrid and, operationally, headquartered in London. ② It is, therefore, not clear if British Airways would qualify as UK majority owned and effectively controlled air carrier. As a result, in the context of a new EU/UK ASA, the EU could legitimately refuse to grant traffic rights to the UK designated airline British Airways, as the company does not substantially meet the ownership and control requirements.

UK airlines have immediately reacted tothe Brexit referendum. This is the case, for instance, of EasyJet, which, in 2017, applied and was subsequently granted an Air Operator Certificate (AOC) from the Austrian Ministry of Transport, thereby establishing a business base in Austria with a European operating permit, EasyJet Europe. ③ By way of holding an Austrian, that is, an EU AOC, EasyJet is considered an EU air carrier and can be granted the right to

---

① See, for instance, Pablo Mendes De Leon and Esther Maarsen-Neumann, "Foreign Air Carriers with Their Principal Place of Business in the EU/EEA", *in* Stephan Hobe, Nicolai von Ruckteschell and David Heffernan eds., *Cologne Compendium on Air Law in Europe*, Carl Heymanns Verlag, 2013, p. 509.

② IAG, which also comprises of EU air carriers, such as Level, Aer Lingus and Vueling, is the world's third-largest airline group in terms of annual revenue and the second-largest in Europe.

③ See *inter alia* https://www.theguardian.com/business/2017/jul/14/easyjet-austria-eu-flights-brexit. See also Roberto Cassar, "Survival of the Freest: The Impact of Brexit on EasyJet p. l. c", pp. 431 - 432.

operate intra-EU cabotage services. However, despite operating now more than 100 aircraft from Vienna Airport, it is still doubtful if the majority ownership and effective control of the new "EU" established subsidiary rests with EU nationals. Failing to comply with such requirement would determine the suspension of the AOC.

7. Post-Brexit EU Air Passenger Rights in a Nutshell

Consumer protection in air transport concerning the rights of air passengers constitutes a stand-alone subfield of aviation law, having captured significant attention over the last years, not only in Europe. The basic EU legislation in this context is the Regulation (EC) No. 261/2004, ① which sets out a standardised scheme under which airlines are liable to compensate passenger in cases of denied boarding, delay and flight cancellation. ②

Pursuant to its Art. 3, this Regulation is applicable only to passengers flying:

- From an EU airport on any air carrier (regardless of the air carrier's nationality);
- To an EU airport from a non-EU airport provided the flight being operated by an EU air carrier. ③

---

① Regulation (EC) No. 261/2004 of the European Parliament and of the Council establishing common rules on compensation and assistance to passengers in the event of denied boarding and of cancellation or long delay of flights, and repealing Regulation (EEC) No. 295/91, [2004] OJ L 46.

② Art. 7 of Regulation (EC) No. 261/2004 provides a systematic and standardised compensation scheme, which differentiates the exact amount of compensation on the basis of the distance flown: (a) EUR 250 for all flights of 1500 kilometres or less; (b) EUR 400 for all intra-Community flights of more than 1500 kilometres, and for all other flights between 1500 and 3500 kilometres; and (c) EUR 600 for all flights not falling under (a) or (b).

③ Art. 3 of Regulation (EC) No. 261/2004 further specifies that the Regulation does not apply if passengers "received benefits or compensation and were given assistance in that third country".

It naturally follows that Brexit will have considerable impact on the applicability of Regulation (EC) No. 261/2004, as its geographical scope of application will be significantly reduced with UK airports no longer being considered EU airports for the purpose of passenger compensation. This would probably result in uncertainty as to whether Regulation(EC) No. 261/2004 would still apply to flights between the EU and the UK or, if no EU legislation is to apply, what legal regime would then be in place.

In February 2018, in a notice to stakeholder concerning consumer protection and passenger rights the EU Commission stated that, following the UK's exit from the EU, Regulation (EC) No. 261/2004 will no longer apply to flights departing—as of "Exit-Day" —from the UK to an airport located in the EU with a non-EU air carrier. ① However, compensation and assistance rights will still be granted to passengers travelling from the UK to the EU on an EU air carrier.

It is still unclear whether the UK will continue applying the Regulation or if it will decide to revert to the standards-which however do not cover all situations foreseen by EU law! —prescribed in the Montreal Convention 1999. ② While the latter seems impracticable as Montreal Convention 1999 is only concerned with the category of flight delay and does not take into account denied boarding and flight cancellation, the former represents a rather utopian possibility as, in fact, applying the Regulation(EC) No. 261/2004 would implicitly mean that the UK accepts the jurisdiction of the Court of Justice of the European Union(CJEU), which was repeatedly pointed as one of the most critical element of the "Brexit

① See EU Commission, Notice to Stakeholders, "Withdrawal of the United Kingdom and EU Rules on Consumer Protection and Passenger Rights", 2018, pp. 4 – 5.

② Convention for the Unification of Certain Rules for International Carriage by Air, opened for signature at Montreal on 28 May 1999(ICAO Doc. No. 4698).

wave".[①] Realistically, the UK may implement an independent regulatory act, by which foreseeing adequate and equivalent legal protection to travellers and consumers.

Below it is a summary of the post-Brexit scenario in relation to the applicability of Regulation (EC) No. 261/2004 to flights within the UK and between the UK and the EU.

FROM	TO	TO DATE	POSSIBLE CHANGES
UK airport	UK airport	Valid under Regulation(EC) No. 261/2004	No longer eligible for compensation
UK airport	EU airport with an EU carrier(e.g. Air France)	Valid under Regulation(EC) No. 261/2004	No Change
UK airport	EU airport with a non-EU carrier(e.g. Thomas Cook)	Valid under Regulation(EC) No. 261/2004	No longer eligible for compensation
UK airport	Non-EU airport	Valid under Regulation(EC) No. 261/2004	No longer eligible for compensation
Non-EU airport	UK airport	Valid under Regulation(EC) No. 261/2004	No longer eligible for compensation

Furthermore, the exit of the UK from the EU is believed to cause repercussions in relation to passengers with reduced mobility. Reduced mobility is the focus of several regulations, internationally and domestically, as well as on an

① HM Government, Department of Transport, "Beyond Horizon-The Future of UK Aviation", 2018.

EU level. In fact, the International Civil Aviation Organization (ICAO) has set guidelines for the non-discrimination of passengers with reduced mobility in aviation, in line with the Convention on the Right of Persons with Disabilities adopted by the United Nations (UN) General Assembly in 2006. ①

Accessibility of passengers with reduced mobility in the UK is currently also governed by the Regulation (EC) No. 1107/2006, ② which provides that air carriers shall not refuse access to passengers on the basis of disability or reduced mobility, provided that the person concerned holds a valid ticket and reservation.

However, to date, it seems reasonable to expect that standards relating to passengers with reduced mobility will not be lowered. The UK Government has already pointed out that it has not only no intention of diminishing the rights of disabled people, but also to make flying for disabled persons as seamless as possible. ③

8. Concluding Remarks and Future Perspectives

The legal environment concerning air transport in the post-Brexit era appears highly fragmented and clearly uncertain. In particular, the current political uncertainty, which permeates the future relations between the UK and the EU, evidently affects speculations and potential future scenarios.

This paper has tried to lay emphasis on the repercussions of the exit of the UK from the EU in air transport. The post-Brexit position of the UK will be a

---

① United Nations, Convention on Rights of Persons with Disabilities, General Assembly, A/RES/61/106, (24 January 2007).

② Regulation (EC) No. 1107/2006 of the European Parliament and of the Council concerning the rights of disabled persons and persons with reduced mobility when travelling by air, [2006] OJ L204/1.

③ See House of Commons Library, Briefing Paper, *Brexit and Transport*, No. CBP 7633, (April, 2018). See also HM Government, "Beyond the Horizon-The Future of UK Aviation", 2018.

peculiar one, both in "internal" relations with the EU and "externally" with third countries. Negotiations concerning an EU/UK Open Skies ASA, which would guarantee a relatively significant freedom of air transport between the EU and the UK, are still taking place.

From a global standpoint, it may be rather interesting how the UK will negotiate its aviation relations following its exit from the EU (and the EU horizontal agreements). In particular, the analysis has contemplated potential scenarios concerning new UK/US aviation relations. Again, political uncertainty still raise doubts as to whether the UK will decide to conclude a new ASA with the US, to invoke revival of the old Bermuda II agreement, or, instead, to join the ECAA and continue benefitting from the EU/US Open Skies ASA as a third party.

The last part of the study has focused on the specific category of air passenger rights and has discussed legal future developments post-Brexit. Unlike for air transport relations, it seems reasonable to affirm that, despite the UK leaving the EU and no longer being bound by EU legislation, the UK is committed to, at least, maintain an adequate level of protection to passengers and passengers with reduced mobility, thereby implementing domestic legislation in line with current international and European standards.

从美国航空产品责任司法实践优先权原则的适用管窥埃航空难的几个法律问题

吴建端*

一、前　　言

本文所称的优先权,英文表述为"preemption",与民法一般意义上的优先权(priority or preemptive right)是不同的。民法意义上的优先权(priority),是指在某个特殊债权关系中债权人依照法律的规定而对债务人的财产所享有的优先于一般债权人受偿的权利。民法上"优先权"这一名词译自外文,罗马法中就已经设立了优先权,①拉丁文为"*priviledia*",法文为"priviledes",日本译为"先取特权","priority"中文表述的含义更趋向于优先受偿权。在民商法中虽然也有"preemptive right"的表述,主要是指股东的优

---

* 荷兰莱顿大学航空法学博士,西北政法大学郑斌航空与空间法研究所特约研究员,上海璞燕信息科技有限公司总经理。

① 如有妻之嫁资返还优先权、受监护人优先权、丧葬费用优先权等。

先投票权、房产承租人的优先权等。哈佛大学的学者将优先投票权表述为"preemptive voting right",简称"preemptive right";①而房产承租人的优先权(tenant's preemptive right)只在房产所有人准备将房产出售时才产生。

本文探讨的优先权,在"穆泽维茨诉科达拉"一案中,宾夕法尼亚州联邦法院的弗拉赫蒂(Flaherty)法官作出了解释:"preemption"可以理解为取代的同义词。优先适用上级(本案中为国家)对某一地区进行全面、广泛的监管,以防止下级监管共存的情况。②

美国哈佛大学的研究表明,本文所指的优先权(preemption)是美国法律体系中重要组成部分,有关联邦法律优先于州法律的案例美国最高法院作出了不少裁决,不仅是因为裁决对人民生活有重大影响,也决定某些州法律的命运,这些裁决实质上也影响了国家和州之间的权力平衡。

优先权是一种源自《美国宪法》第6条的精神。《美国宪法》第6条第2款规定:"本宪法及依本宪法所制定之合众国法律;以及根据合众国的授权已经缔结及将要缔结的一切条约,应成为全国的最高法律;每个州的法官都应受其约束,不管任何一州宪法或法律中有任何相反的规定。"③该条款列举了三项高于州法的"国土最高法律"(supreme law of the land),即《美国宪法》、依据《美国宪法》制定的美国联邦法律和美国缔结的国际条约。这个条款通常被称为"至上条款"(Supremacy Clause),也有人称为"宪法至上条款"。

人们普遍认为,依据至上条款,美国联邦法律将优先于或取代与联邦法律相冲突的州法律。但是,也有人认为,历史上受州监管的领域一般不会被

---

① 资料来源:http://blogs.harvard.edu/bankruptcyroundtable/tag/preemption-rights/,最后访问日期:2019年6月18日。

② "[P]reempts may be understood as a synonym for supersedes. Preemption... applies to situations where a higher authority (in this case, the State) regulates an area so comprehensively and pervasively as to preclude the coexistence of regulation by a lower authority (in this case, the County)."

③ "This Constitution, and the laws of the United States which shall be made in pursuance thereof; and all treaties made, or which shall be made, under the authority of the United States, shall be the supreme law of the land; and the judges in every state shall be bound thereby, anything in the Constitution or laws of any State to the contrary notwithstanding."

随后的联邦法律取代,除非国会立法有清晰和明确的意图来优先于州法律。①

内华达州最高法院法官南希(Nancy Saita)根据《美国宪法》第6条关于至上原则的规定,较为全面地解释了优先权含义并且认为,当联邦法和州法存在冲突时,有效的联邦法优先于其他有效的州法。联邦立法是否从根本上先于州法律是国会意图的问题。国会是否明示或隐含地打算先于州法律?即使是隐含的,国会也会有优先于州法律的意图。

在确定国会是否明晰表达优先于州法律的意图时,法院必须审查法定语言。任何明示的优先权语言通常都支配优先权的范围。② 当国会不包括明示优先于州法律的法定语言时,国会的优先于州法律的意图可能在两种情况下被隐含:领域优先或者冲突优先。在领域优先情况下,联邦法律彻底地占据了该立法领域,从而合理地推断国会没有为各州留出补充空间。③

在领域优先下,当国会的立法完全占据立法领域,或涉及联邦利益主导地位的领域时,即意味国会实际上没有为各州在该领域监管行为留下空间。为了确定国会是否已经在某一法律领域实施优先权,必须审查整个监管方案,以确定国会是否打算根据其综合性水平或所监管领域的性质,阻止各州也对该领域实施监管。如果根据这一审查,可以推断国会打算占领这一立法领域,那么无论具体的法律冲突如何,州的要求都会被优先掉。

如果国会的立法没有对一个涉及联邦利益的领域进行规范,国会想要优先于州法的意图在一定程度上是隐含的。冲突优先权分析从整体上审查联

---

① "Clear and manifest purpose of Congress."

② Express preemption: "Congress expressly preempts state law when it explicitly states that intent in a statute's language. Thus, when determining whether Congress has expressly preempted state law, a court must examine statutory language—any explicit preemption language generally governs the extent of preemption."

③ Under field preemption, "federal law so thoroughly occupies a legislative field 'as to make reasonable the inference that Congress left no room for the States to supplement it.'" 资料来源:http://www.duhaime.org/LegalDictionary/P/PreemptionDoctrine.aspx,最后访问日期:2019年3月12日。

邦法规,以确定一方是否不可能同时遵守联邦和州的要求,或者根据联邦法规的目的和预期效果,州法律是否对实现国会意图构成障碍。

综上所述,我们可以发现,美国联邦法律的优先权适用包括两类三种情形:明示优先(express preemption)与隐含优先(implied preemption),其中隐含优先又包括冲突优先(conflict preemption)和领域优先(field preemption)。

因为涉及美国联邦法律与地方法律的冲突问题,优先权在美国的司法案例的出现次数比较多。例如,在美国"摩西伯格"(Morseburg)一案中,杰伊·拜比(Jay S. Bybee)法官认为,在1976年《版权法案》生效之后,《加州转售版税法案》规定的追续权被1976年《版权法案》优先,原告无权主张追续权;在《加州转售版税法案》生效而1976年《版权法案》未生效的期间,《加州转售版税法案》规定的追续权属于1909年《版权法案》未涉及的额外权利,符合州与联邦保护之间的平衡,原告有权主张追续权。①

在航空领域,美国各级法院对优先权裁定会出现不一致的情况。② 但在多数航空产品责任案件审理中,优先权(preemption)是制造商的有效抗辩手段。由于美国州一级的法律规定赔偿额往往要高出联邦法院和国际公约的赔偿额,自美国联邦第三巡回上诉法院1999年对"阿卜杜拉诉美国航空公司案"作出裁决以来,③优先权一直是最受争议的航空法问题。本文将结合案例,重点阐述优先权在航空产品责任争议中的应用,结合当前普遍关注的波音737MAX空难法律问题,通过案例分析优先权在航空产品责任中的适用问题。

① 资料来源:http://www. ncac. gov. cn/chinacopyright/contents/519/387450. html,最后访问日期:2019年3月18日。

② 资料来源:https://harvardlawreview. org/wp-content/uploads/pdfs/new_evidence_on_the_presumption. pdf,最后访问日期:2019年6月1日。

③ 181 F. 3d 363,3d Cir. 1999.

二、航空领域的优先权

(一)概述

美国联邦航空法律针对优先权的问题,明确规定了由联邦政府独家行使航空管理的一些重要权限,而实践中,优先权的范围还会更大些。1958 年《美国联邦航空法》规定:“州或其政治分支机构,两个或两个以上州的州际机构或其他政治机构不得颁布或执行任何涉及任何航空承运人的费率、航线或服务的法律、规则、法规、标准或其他具有法律效力的规定。”①在美国的法院审理航空案件的过程中,法官常常会决定是否适用优先权。在“阿卜杜拉诉美国航空公司”(Abdullah v. Am. Airlines, Inc)一案中,法院就指出“相应的,国会的意图是优先权分析的最终试金石”。在涉及优先权的案件中,法官会设法确定立法意图。②

美国联邦最高法院 1998 年在“以色列 EL. AL 航空公司诉陈某(女)”一案中,认定在国际航空运输中《华沙公约》为索赔创立了特别诉因,认为“当她的诉求无法满足《华沙公约》规定的责任条件时,《华沙公约》就排除了该旅客根据当地法来进行人身伤害的诉讼”。③ 也就是说,人身伤害的诉讼请求不可以超越《华沙公约》设定的赔偿条件和限额。《华沙公约》被美国政府批准加入,也就成为美国联邦法律,相对于州等地方法律具有优先权。

该判决为后来美国法院对类似案件的审判,产生了深远的影响,也从心理上阻断了一些律师绕过适用的国际公约,而利用当地法来帮助当事人获得更高赔偿的念头。美国国内绝大部分的航空法律和法规都是由国会及联邦政府包括美国联邦航空局制定的,州政府可自己制定并修改其航空法,但州

---

① 49 U. S. C. 41713(b)(1).

② Abdullah v. Am. Airlines, Inc. ,181 F. 3d 363,366(3d Cir. 1999)("Accordingly, '[t]he purpose of Congress is the ultimate touchstone' of pre-emption analysis.").

③ Diane Westwood Wilson and Joanne L Geraghty, "The Progeny of Tseng", *Air & Space Law* XXV, 2000, p. 64.

航空法不可与联邦航空法有冲突。

以美国无人机的立法为例,美国的绝大多数州都对无人机进行了立法管理,甚至有些市政府都参与了有关无人机管理的法案制定。但州政府以及地方政府有些立法行为已逾越了现行联邦法律框架,虽说州政府与地方政府在制定无人机相关法规时,都曾向美国联邦航空局咨询,然而很显然美国运输部及其联邦航空局更情愿自己对无人机法规进行全盘监管。

美国联邦航空局称,当州政府以及地方政府尝试着通过制定法规来管理无人机时,真正的安全问题才刚刚浮现。州与州的法规不同,甚至镇与镇的法规也不同,这严重制约了美国联邦航空局对空域的统一管理,这事实上无法保障空中飞行的安全,反而还影响了空中交通的效率。

2015 年 12 月 17 日美国联邦航空局发表《情况说明书》,①引用联邦法律、美国最高法院判决和上诉法院判决,给无人机系统不断变化的监管环境划定了界限,书面通知州和地方政府不得颁布同联邦航空局已经颁布或计划颁布的,有关无人机在国家空域(National Air Space,NAS)飞行和安全的法律法规相冲突的法律或者法规。②

美国联邦法律虽然没有规定涉及无人机的联邦航空法规优先适用于(preemptive)州和当地有关无人机法律的范围。③ 美国《联邦航空局现代化和改革法案》(FAA Modernization and Reform Act of 2012,FMRA)、《联邦航空局延期,安全和保安法案》(Federal Aviation Administration Extension, Safety,and Security Act,FESSA)或者第 107 部也都没有包含明确的优先规定,尽管如此,在美国判例法中依然可以找寻到联邦法律优先的依据。而当

① 资料来源:https://www.faa.gov/uas/resources/uas_regulations_policy/media/uas_fact_sheet_final.pdf,最后访问日期:2017 年 12 月 8 日。

② 资料来源:https://www.faa.gov/uas/regulations_policies/media/UAS_Fact_Sheet_Final.pdf,最后访问日期:2017 年 12 月 18 日。

③ "Preemption"源自美国《联邦宪法》第三章(The Supremacy Clause of Article Ⅲ),大概意思是联邦宪法以及依照《联邦宪法》授权制定的法律属于上位法,优先适用[the Constitution, and laws and treaties made pursuant to it, are the supreme law of the land(the USA)]。也就是说,联邦法若与州法有冲突,除非法院判定该联邦法违宪,否则优先适用联邦法。

联邦法和州法之间存在直接冲突时,就存在优先权适用的问题。①

优先权在航空案件中起着重要作用。事实上,历史上美国联邦政府航空业对航空业的管制很广,对航空业的管制的主要法律法规几乎完全是联邦的。②在美国的运输行业中,航空运输与联邦政府关联性是独一无二的,也曾是唯一一个几乎完全在联邦管辖范围内开展业务的行业。在美国,无论是联邦政府,还是各州政府都出台了航空法规,并建立专门的管理机构来对空中交通进行管制。根据《美国宪法》的规定,国会有权出台与空中导航相关的各项法案对美国空域的州际及外国航空活动进行监管。③ 目前联邦政府已颁布的航空法有:

1926 年出台的《商业航空法》,该法对州际及国外飞行器的核实与记录作了法律规定。

1938 年出台《民用航空法》,对 1926 年的《商业航空法》进行了修订,并成立民用航空专家小组——一个由 5 人组成的专门小组,负责管理美国联邦司法权限内的一切航空事务。后来,该专家小组改名为民用航空委员会,并将大部分权力转交给了商务部。

1958 年美国通过了《联邦航空法》,由此成立了联邦航空局。之后,联邦政府又相继出台了 1970 年《机场与航线发展法》及 1978 年《航空公司放松管制法》等。

2001 年"9·11"恐怖袭击事件发生后,2011 年美国国会又出台了《航空与运输安全法》,据此在美国交通部下成立美国交通安全管理局(Transportation Security Administration,TSA),后 TSA 隶属美国国土安全部。

美国绝大部分的航空法都是由联邦政府制定的,州政府可自己制定并修改其航空法,但州航空法不可与联邦航空法有冲突,更不可超越联邦法

① Sikkelee v. Precision Airmove Corp. ,822 F. 3D 680688(3d Cir).

② Abdullah v. Am. Airlines,Inc. ,181 F. 3d 363,368(3d Cir. 1999)citing S. Rep. No. 1811, 85th Cong. ,2d Sess. 5(1958).

③ 根据《美国宪法》,美国国会有权宪法授予合众国政府或政府中任何机关或官员的其他一切权力所必要的和恰当的法律。

律法规。

(二)行业导向

发生航空事故后,航空产品制造商通常会面临索赔与诉讼。这些索赔与诉讼往往会声称飞机上使用的一种或多种产品"有缺陷",并导致事故发生。原告需要收集大量的证据,开展广泛的调查,并聘请专家来证明所谓缺陷的主张,诉讼成本通常很高。对被告来说,聘用律师进行抗辩成本很高,需要在法庭上进行技术性解释来支持本方主张的费用也不少。这对于美国民航业的发展十分不利。为此美国通过以下几种途径来解决航空产品责任诉讼偏多的问题。

一是通过立法。美国为振兴通用航空产业,1994 年制定了《通用航空振兴法》,确立了除斥期间制度,对通用航空事故受害人向航空器制造商提起产品责任诉讼设置了时间限制。在以往的通用航空的产品责任诉讼中,航空器制造商面临的最大问题是责任期限问题。通用航空的机龄通常很长,美国现阶段的通用航空器的平均机龄通常在 30 年左右,一旦发生事故,制造商仍需对此承担严格产品责任。随着产品责任诉讼成本和赔偿金额的增加,责任保险的费用也在不断增长,制造商不得不将这些成本加入产品售价。其结果是,通用航空器的售价不断攀升,而销售数量锐减,由此产生恶性循环。

出于振兴美国通用航空产业和增加就业、刺激经济的需要,美国制定了《通用航空振兴法》,①限制对通用航空器制造商提起产品责任诉讼,其核心内容就是规定 18 年的除斥期间。② 通过限定时间,既免除制造商过重的潜在产品责任,也可以减轻甚至免除诉讼压力,将其从诉讼"泥潭"中拯救出来。另外,即使产品质量没有问题,许多原告在提起诉讼时并无充分依据,但被告

① The General Aviation Revitalization Act of 1994, also known by its initials GARA, is Public Law 103 – 298, an Act of Congress on Senate Bill S. 1458 (103rd Congress), Amending the Federal Aviation Act of 1958.

② The GeneralAviation Revitalization Act immunizes aircraft manufacturers from liability for defects in their Products once those products turn 18 years old.

仍将被迫应诉和抗辩,需要为此支付大量的诉讼费用,许多被告为避免被拖入漫长的诉讼中,往往不得已选择与原告和解并向原告支付和解金。实践表明,保障产品安全性的途径有许多种,而产品责任仅是其中之一,对于通用航空器的安全性关注,重点不应放在事后的产品责任诉讼上,而应强调事先的监管;在监管体系健全的前提下,可以考虑对航空器制造商的产品责任适当放松,以求得各方之间的利益平衡。

二是依循先例。由于在普通法系中,上级法院的判决特别是最高法院的判决不仅最终解决了当前的法律争议,而且案件的判决也被视为对未来有法律影响的先例(precedent)。依据普通法法系的"依循先例原则"(stare decisis),美国最高法院的判决影响了下级法院对新的案件的审理。例如,美国联邦第三巡回上诉法院引用了最高法院的优先权裁决来指导其分析。第三巡回上诉法院在阿卜杜拉诉美国航空公司(Abdullah v. American Airlines, Inc.)一案中指出,在确定是否存在优先权上,"国会的意图是最终的试金石"。[①]法官引用了最高法院在伯班克市等诉洛克希德航站楼案[②]中对美国1958年《联邦航空法》立法历史的广泛审查结果。[③] 美国最高法院认为,1958年的《联邦航空法》要求在安全和效率之间保持微妙的平衡。如果要实现联邦航空法所依据国会的意图,要求联邦法规的统一和优先权相互依赖。

当允许无限多的陪审团对联邦航空局的安全和型号认证决定进行二次猜测时,如何实现国会意图的两个要求是无法实现的。这种类型的法律结构不仅会破坏国会在通过1958年《联邦航空法》时希望保持的"安全与效率之间的微妙平衡",而且会明显破坏国会创建联邦航空局以实现的"统一与排他性"的联邦法规体系努力。法官认为,联邦航空局的型号认证过程非常复杂,陪审员缺乏联邦航空局的技术专长和经验来理解这些标准,更不用说应

---

① 资料来源:https://caselaw. findlaw. com/us - 3rd-circuit/1461468. html,最后访问日期:2018年12月11日。

② City of Burbank et al. , Appellants, v. Lockheed Air Terminal Inc. et al.

③ 资料来源:https://www. law. cornell. edu/supremecourt/text/411/624,最后访问日期:2018年12月11日。

用它们了。法官甚至表示,原告经验丰富的律师"完全无法协助法院"。产品的认证过程是漫长的、非常复杂和详细的。这不是律师、法官或陪审团能够或打算完成的事情。这点国会和最高法院很久以前就已经意识到,这就是为什么联邦航空局成立并被授予了维护"安全和效率之间微妙平衡"所需的独家权力。

最终法院认为,整个航空安全领域都是联邦政府的优先。① 但法院也作出一点让步的解释,阿卜杜拉案件的诉求只适用于操作飞机,而不适用于飞机的设计或制造。②

(三)新近案例

美国关于航空产品责任的诉讼,被告大多数成功通过利用优先权的规定来免除、限制或减轻自身的赔偿责任。而斯科利(Sikkelee)一案则有所不同。该案涉及一名已故飞行员的妻子对与其丈夫大卫·斯科利(David Sikkelee)有关的多家制造商提起诉讼,后者在2005年塞斯纳172N飞机起飞后不久坠毁身亡。化油器是争议的焦点。原告认为,事故发生的原因是化油器,它有两个半部分,浮筒和节气门体,用螺栓固定在一起。这些螺栓松动,导致发动机在起飞后不久失去动力。这起事故发生在彻底检修之后仅400小时。

因此,其遗孀于2007年在宾夕法尼亚州地区法院对17名被告提起诉讼,声称州法律要求严格责任、违反保证、疏忽、虚假陈述和一致行动。而被告提出了一项简易判决动议,主张发动机及其部件(包括化油器)在颁发型式认证时已获得联邦航空局的批准,从而符合联邦航空局的相关规定。地方法院同意并批准了简易判决推理,即当联邦航空局为发动机颁发型式认证时,它确定联邦注意标准(standard of care)已作为法律问题得到满足。2010

---

① The entire field of aviation safety is federally preempted, See Abdullah v. American Airlines, Inc., 181 F. 3d 363(3rd Cir. 1999).

② 资料来源:http://www. mondaq. com/unitedstates/x/486980/Aviation/Third + Circuit + Limits + Federal + Aviation + Act + Preemption + For + Product + Liability + Claims,最后访问日期:2019年3月5日。

年地方法院批准了被告的简易判决动议,裁定原告根据州法律的注意标准(standards of care)提出的州法律索赔被联邦注意标准所优先。原告随后提出了一项修改后的诉求,继续主张按州法索赔,但也指控被告多次违反联邦航空局条例的行为。①

美国联邦第三巡回上诉法院以往在一系列案件中,大多支持联邦航空法对州法航空产品责任索赔的领域优先权。但在此案中,②上诉法院采取了与过往有所不同的立场。2016 年 4 月 19 日第三巡回上诉法院就斯科利一案,发表了长达 61 页的意见,缩小了联邦法律优先权的范围。意见认为,航空产品责任索赔应按照州侵权法的注意标准而不是联邦注意标准。这一观点可能会使航空产品制造商面临潜在的责任,以及各州不统一标准的不可预测性。

2018 年第三巡回上诉法院在新的判决中认为,原告对事故飞机上发动机的型号合格证持有人莱康明(被告)提出的设计缺陷索赔,并未被冲突优先,因为莱康明有能力对其型号合格证进行更改,并且无法证明联邦航空局不会批准该发动机的替代设计。法院强调,允许州法律对型号证书持有人提起诉讼是对联邦计划的补充,并进一步促进了其确保飞机安全的目的。因此,如果该裁定成立,航空产品制造商将承担相应的责任。

第三巡回上诉法院与以往不同的判决引起了很大的关注,该案的被告于 2019 年 2 月 24 日向美国最高法院提起上诉,虽然美国最高法院已经受理此案,但由于美国最高法院收到大量的上诉案件,但只能够开庭审理上诉案件总数的 3%,何时开庭审理并形成最终判决尚须等待。密切关注此案件的美国航空航天协会(Aerospace Industries Association of America)、产品责任建议

---

① 资料来源:http://plpdblog. com/2016/05/02/federal-preemption-narrowed-for-aviation-suppliers-in-sikkelee-v-precision-airmotive-corp/,最后访问日期:2019 年 2 月 12 日。

② Sikkelee v. Precision Airmotive, et. al.

理事会(Product Liability Advisory Council, Inc.)、美国实验飞机协会[①]、空客美国公司、通用航空制造商协会等,纷纷于2019年4月下旬提交了非当事人意见陈述(又称法庭之友陈述,英文正式表述为"brief of amicus curiae")并刊登在美国最高法院网站上,表现出对此案的高度关注。

美国法庭之友陈述是指非案件当事人,可能或可能没有被当事人请求,通过提供与案件有关的信息、专门知识或见解来协助法庭。这项做法,对于法官作出客观公正的裁决有益,特别是涉及一些专业领域。在两家美国企业诉中国维生素C企业的案件中,我国商务部第一次以法庭之友的身份参与美国法院的诉讼进程,委派律师作为支持中国企业的法庭之友向美国最高法院提供口头陈述。[②] 美国哈佛大学法学院于2012年也曾向法庭提交过法庭之友陈述,对案件审理影响很大。[③] 美国法院的这种实践值得我们借鉴。

三、波音737 MAX空难产品责任

(一)波音公司产品责任

埃航空难发生之后,波音公司可能面临各种类型的法律索赔,其中包括对飞机或其飞行控制系统缺陷的产品责任,未对飞行员进行系统变更方面的培训责任,以及在首次坠毁后未采取措施解决任何问题的疏忽甚至刑事责任,但波音也可能有下列几种救济的手段。

一是向问题零部件的制造商追索。飞机是由许多零部件组成的复杂机器,通常由几十家或数百家制造商生产。也有人推测,美国罗克韦尔柯

---

① 美国实验飞机协会(Experimental Aircraft Association, EAA)是美国航空爱好者自发的群众性的飞行大会。EAA的全称是:全美实验飞机协会,每年的夏季都隆重的举行一次,每次都有上万架大小各异的飞机和近百万狂热的美国航空爱好者参加这个飞行盛会。

② 参见李友根:《法学研究的反思:美国最高法院维C企业垄断案的启示》,载《经贸法律评论》2019年第1期。

③ 资料来源:https://harvardmagazine.com/2012/08/harvard-files-amicus-brief,最后访问日期:2016年12月21日。

林斯公司①提供了相关软件产品,也可能成为被追索的对象。②

二是由保险支付赔偿。由于在不到半年的时间里发生两起同一类型的飞机波音737 Max 8坠毁事故,这引起了人们对其安全性的质疑,将会对其追究产品责任。印尼狮航空难遇难者家属已经从2018年11月起陆续起诉波音公司。波音公司将面临印尼狮航和埃塞俄比亚航空公司飞机失事受害者家属的巨额索赔,以及飞机停飞所造成的损失最终由波音公司的承保人,也就是保险公司承担。保险公司通常组成一个联合体来分担巨额索赔的风险,由主要保险公司承担更大比例的风险。

三是利用美国法律体系中的优先权来限制自身的责任。波音可能会主张,公司是依据联邦法律,通过法定手续获得产品的适航许可,产品是合格的。

四是利用购机合同的免责条款。早先通过订立免责条款来转移损失或责任风险。该条款表面上平等,实质上由比较强势的一方主导,作出对其比较有利的规定。

诉讼是一个耗时耗力的漫长过程,在美国,90%以上的案件都是通过庭外和解予以解决。未来涉及波音公司的诉讼有可能出现经典的判例,也可能庭外解决,无法预测,但更多解决方案应当是以诉讼双方签订和解赔偿协议(包含保密条款)而告终。

(二)联邦航空局的责任问题

此次埃航飞机坠毁之后,人们也关注美国联邦航空局的安全认证过程是否完善,是否履行了自身的安全管理职责,是否应当承担产品责任等问题。

---

① 罗克韦尔柯林斯公司(Rockwell Collins Inc.)是美国跨国性的航空电子设备供应商,总部位于爱荷华州的锡达拉皮兹(Cedar Rapids),致力于为各政府部门和商业客户提供广泛应用的航空电子和通信产品,如现正为波音787提供显示设备、通讯和监视系统、飞行员操控系统和网络核心构架。

② 资料来源:https://www.latimes.com/business/la-fi-boeing-737-max-crash-faa-alert-20190505-story.html,最后访问日期:2019年5月16日。

航空产品的认证需要相当长的时间,需要联邦航空局与航空公司合作,试图找出最佳的安全管理和运行方法。但是现在有人质疑这个过程是否被依法真正遵循。① 在美国联邦航空局与波音公司等制造商的互动问题方面,美国联邦航空局曾让 79 家航空产品制造商的工程师或其他被视为合格的工作人员负责安全检查工作,向联邦航空局报告被认为不是最关键的系统的安全,而不是由联邦航空局负责完成所有的检查工作。② 什么系统是真正安全系统,系统是否有完善的备份手段。传统上,飞机都有很好的安全举措,例如,单个发动机可以飞行。而目前这个系统说是安全,却导致新的飞机坠毁。

美国联邦航空局负责飞行员行为、飞行操作和飞机制造商的安全标准制定和审查。在美国诉瓦里格航空公司(United States v. Varig Airlines)一案中,美国最高法院讨论了"自由裁量职能抗辩"(discretionary function defense)的问题。该案源于一起机上失火,造成 124 人死亡。火灾是由于厕所不符合适用的安全规定造成的。受害者亲属控告联邦航空局,声称联邦航空局在审查飞机安全时疏忽大意。

原告认为,美国联邦航空局只是简单地"抽查"波音公司的设计工作,但美国最高法院裁定,联邦航空局的抽查工作是在行使其自由裁量权,因此不能被起诉,政府有权决定如何履行其维护安全的责任。③ 有人认为,在埃航一案中,联邦航空局允许波音公司自我认证其设计的做法似乎完全放弃了其责任,应当承担疏忽的责任。④

需要指出的是,针对政府机构的索赔受《联邦侵权索赔法》(Federal Tort

---

① 资料来源:https://www.npr.org/2019/03/21/705418083/plane-safety-is-a-shared-responsibility-former-faa-administrator-says,最后访问日期:2019 年 5 月 16 日。

② 资料来源:https://www.usatoday.com/story/news/nation/2019/04/20/did-faa-outsource-air-safety-boeing-and-other-companies/3497255002/,最后访问日期:2019 年 5 月 16 日。

③ 资料来源:https://supreme.justia.com/cases/federal/us/467/797/,最后访问日期:2019 年 5 月 16 日。

④ 资料来源:https://www.aviationlawmonitor.com/2019/03/airlines/ethiopian-airlines-flight-302-can-families-hold-the-faa-liable-for-certifying-the-boeing-737-max-800-as-safe-when-it-wasnt/,最后访问日期:2019 年 5 月 16 日。

Claims Act,FTCA)管辖。[①]《联邦侵权索赔法》对美国政府普遍享有的主权豁免规定了例外情况,即规定了联邦政府雇员因在其职责范围内的疏忽造成人身伤害、死亡或财产损失的赔偿。[②]

在美国,因联邦雇员在其公务范围内的不当或疏忽行为而受伤或财产受损的个人,可向政府提出索赔,要求赔偿其受到的伤害。为了陈述一项有效的索赔,索赔人必须证明:(1)受到联邦政府雇员的伤害或财产受到损害;(2)雇员在其职责范围内行事;(3)雇员的行为疏忽或错误;(4)造成伤害或损害的疏忽或错误行为。[③]

依据美国相关规定,联邦政府雇员对被视为单纯的"自由裁量"的行为不承担责任。此外,美国政府对判决前的利息或惩罚性赔偿不承担责任,其责任由法官而非陪审团评估。[④]

四、结　　论

综上所述,我们可以发现,优先权在美国航空产品责任中的应用是随着美国的现代工业包括航空制造的发展而逐步完善的一项制度,在给予航空事故受害人充分的索赔权的同时,通过规则与判例来给予美国高新产业予以一定程度的保护。美国的发达与领先一是在于创新发展所带来的优势,二是在于法律体系的建立,三是在于规则制定权的掌控与权威性的维护。虽然近期的波音空难事件对美国民用航空产品安全管理体系和声誉造成了很大的损害,也将给美国现有的产品责任制度重塑带来冲击,这个过程需要时间和实践来完善,其做法可以探究,其经验可以借鉴,其教训值得思考。

---

① 参见《美国法典》28 篇第 2671 节及以下(28 USC section 2671 et seq.)。

② 参见《美国法典》28 篇第 1346(b)条。

③ 资料来源:https://www.house.gov/doing-business-with-the-house/leases/federal-tort-claims-act,最后访问日期:2019 年 5 月 16 日。

④ 《联邦侵权索赔法》(FTCA)。

航空环境治理

国际航空减排机制研究

王思炜 *

随着人们环保意识的不断提升与国际航空业的发展,国际航空减排的概念也越发深入人心。全球温室气体排放单位中交通工具的排放量占13%,在这13%的温室气体排放总量中航空运输的排放量又占其中的13%。而单从二氧化碳排放来讲,来自航空(国际和国内)的二氧化碳排放总量就占到全球二氧化碳排放总量的2%[联合国政府间气候变化专门委员会(IPCC)第五次评估报告],国际航空大约占全球二氧化碳排放总量的1.3%,①占到航空运输总排放量的65%。且随着航空经济的不断发展,国际航空的温室气体排放量势必还会大幅增长。仅2017年一年民用航空大约排放了8.59亿吨二氧化碳,约占人为制造二氧化碳排放总量的2%。② 通过这些数据

* 西北政法大学国际法学院2016级硕士研究生。

① ICAO, On board a sustainable future, p. 2.

② See Fact sheet: climate change & CORSIA, Accessed December 28, 2018. https://www.iata.org/pressroom/facts_figures/fact_sheets/Documents/fact-sheet-climate-change.pdf.

不难看出,航空运输尤其是国际航空运输减排工作的开展迫在眉睫。但同时,国际航空运输领域关乎一国的经济发展,涉及一国的国民经济利益。建立何种形式的减排规则,如何构建能够平衡不同国家间的利益的减排体系,是今后开展整个国际航空减排活动的基础和关键。从1992年的《联合国气候变化框架公约》到1997年的《京都议定书》,再到2007年的《巴厘路线图》、2009年的《哥本哈根议定书》、2015年的《巴黎协定》,以及2018年12月刚刚结束的波兰卡托维兹气候变化大会;从欧盟的EU ETS体系再到现阶段国际民用航空组织(International Civel Aviation Organization,ICAO)的国际航空碳抵消和减排计划(Carbon Offsetting and Reduction Scheme for International Aviation,CORSIA),从欧盟委员会、联合国再到国际民用航空组织、国际航空运输协会,它们都见证并推动了国际航空减排的发展。可见国际民用航空减排并非一朝一夕就能完成,不仅需要一个统一的规制平台、一整套减排运行规则,还需要各个国家之间乃至不同的国际组织之间相互配合,共同努力。本文将沿着国际公约的发展与国际组织减排机制的运行脉络进行介绍,并以ICAO项下的减排措施作为切入点着重进行分析,此外还将通过对比发达国家与发展中国家的国家行动计划对ICAO碳减排机制对两者国内经济发展的影响进行分析。

一、国际航空减排机制的源起和演进

(一)国际公约的发展

1.《联合国气候变化框架公约》

《联合国气候变化框架公约》(United Nations Framework Convention on Climate Change,UNFCCC)是1992年5月9日通过的一项国际环境公约,于1992年6月3日至14日在里约热内卢进行开放签字,1994年3月21日生效。① 1992

① 资料来源:https://en.wikipedia.org/wiki/United_Nations_Framework_Convention_on_Climate_Change,最后访问日期:2018年12月29日。

年的 UNFCCC 为全球首个以控制 CO_2 等温室气体排放为目标，也是首个应对由于气候变化对全球经济和生存环境带来的不利影响的国际层面的立法。[①] 且自 1995 年以来，每年都会举行 UNFCCC 的缔约方会议，对气候变化的进展进行评估和考量。但是综观 UNFCCC 全文，其主要通过附件一与附件二两份文件将发达国家与发展中国家的责任进行了区分和界定，例如，在第 4 条中就分别规定了附件一所列国家的带头义务和附件二所列国家的资金、技术的援助义务，来具体实施“共同但有区别的责任”原则。除此之外，在 UNFCCC 中并未规定义务的履行强制性标准及不履行或不完全履行情形下的惩罚机制，而是用“促进”和“便利”等词汇来进行表述。这种规则模式必然在日后会引起附件一、附件二所列发达国家的不满，实际上也是一部没有任何强制性约束的国际条约。

2.《京都议定书》

《京都议定书》(以下简称《议定书》)作为《联合国气候变化框架公约》下的补充，旨在减少温室气体的排放。《议定书》于 1997 年 12 月 11 日在日本京都第三届缔约方会议中通过，并于 2005 年 2 月 16 日生效。[②]《京都议定书》的先进性首先在于为了缩减全球的温室减排成本而创造性地建立了三个以市场为基础的灵活机制，即针对附件 B 所列国家减排的排放权交易机制和共同执行机制，以及帮助发展中国家减排的清洁发展机制。[③] 分别规定在《议定书》第 17 条、第 6 条和第 12 条。但是该议定书也以“共同但有区别的责任”原则为基础，并进一步的强调了附件 B 中发达国家的特定减排义务。《议定书》规定发达国家以 1990 年确立的排放量削减水准为基线，将在 2008

---

① 参见孙玉娇：《全球航空碳排放交易机制法律研究》，中国民航大学 2018 年硕士学位论文，第 14 页。

② 资料来源：https://en.wikipedia.org/wiki/Kyoto_Protocol，最后访问日期：2019 年 1 月 3 日。

③ 参见何晶晶：《从“京都议定书”到“巴黎协定”：开启新的气候变化治理时代》，载《国际法研究》2016 年第 3 期。

年至2012年把六种温室气体的排放总量减少5.2%。[①] 但是由于在《议定书》中也欠缺对缔约国履行承诺的一个制约机制和未履行承诺的惩罚机制,所以如果附件B的国家不对《京都议定书》第二轮承诺目标进行谈判(如加拿大),[②]那委员会可能对此无法采取任何有效的制约措施,因为委员会的唯一惩罚机制就是按照惩罚率扣减第二个承诺期的分配数额。[③] 除此之外,白俄罗斯、哈萨克斯坦和乌克兰已经明确表示,他们可能会退出《京都议定书》或者不将第二轮减排目标付诸本国的法律,日本、俄罗斯和新西兰在第二轮中没有提出新的目标,此外加拿大于2012年退出《议定书》,美国甚至仅签署但并未批准该《议定书》。[④] 从批准国家的实践情况来讲,第二轮减排目标实际上只覆盖了极少数的国家,涉及的排放总量也只占据了排放整体中很小的一部分,这样来讲《议定书》实际上并不能发挥出其原先所设想出的作用,故从其所产生的推动效果上来讲并不成功。

3.《巴黎协定》

《巴黎协定》也是《联合国气候变化框架公约》下的一项协议,是对2020年后应对世界气候变化所作出的安排。经历了哥本哈根气候大会的破裂后,《巴黎协定》确立了以自下而上(bottom-up)的治理机制为主,兼有自上而下(up-bottom)治理成分的混合型治理模式(hybrid climate governance structure),

---

① 参见李威:《从"京都议定书"到"巴黎协定":气候国际法的改革与发展》,载《上海对外经贸大学学报》2016年第5期。

② Canada sued for abandoning Kyoto Climate Commitment' Environmental News Service, http://www.ens-newswire.com/ens/may2007/2007-05-29-02.asp (29 May 2007) and Impossible for Canada to meet Kyoto targets' CBC News, http://www.cbc.ca/canada/story/2006/04/07/kyoto060407.html.

③ Procedures and mechanisms relating to compliance under the Kyoto Protocol' in the Report of the Conference of the Parties serving as the meeting of the Parties to the Kyoto Protocol on its first session, held at Montreal from 28 November to 10 December 2005, Addendum, Part Two: Action taken, FCCC/KP/CMP/2005/8/Add.3, 2006.

④ Lavanya Rajamani, "Addressing the 'Post-Kyoto' Stress Disorder, Reflections on the Emerging Legal Architecture of the Climate Regime", *International and Comparative Law Quarterly* 58, 2009, p.7.

无疑开启了新的气候变化治理时代。① 截至 2018 年 11 月,194 个国家和欧盟签署了协议,其中 183 个国家和欧盟代表超过 87% 的全球温室气体排放国已经签署或接受该协议,包括在 UNFCCC 中 4 个最大的温室气体排放国中的 3 个:中国、美国和印度。② 但是 2017 年 8 月 4 日,美国总统特朗普向联合国正式发出通知,要求在符合法律条件的情形下尽快退出《巴黎协定》,尽管根据《巴黎协定》第 28 条第 1 款的规定:"自本协定对一缔约方生效满三年后可以提出退出的通知",《巴黎协定》于 2016 年 11 月 4 日对美国生效,那么至少要到 2019 年 11 月 4 日美国才能退出《巴黎协定》。或者美国也可以通过直接退出《联合国气候变化框架公约》的方式于保存人收到退出通知一年期满后生效。但美国此举将会大大动摇国际社会的减排决心,甚至会造成国际航空减排工作的经济与技术缺失问题。

《巴黎协定》为所有国家设定了同样的核心义务,抛弃了《联合国气候变化框架公约》中以附件形式对不同国家区别对待的方式,这样就能考虑到不同国家间的环境状况和发展能力,并针对不同的因素采取不同的方式。③ 在《巴黎协定》中不仅考虑到了发达国家缔约方的继续带头作用还认识到了发展中国家缔约方的减排目标。但是,《巴黎协定》实际上也存在一系列的实施困境。首先,《巴黎协定》的目标为:把全球平均气温升幅控制在工业化前水平以上低于 2℃之内,并努力将气温升幅限制在工业化前水平以上 1.5℃之内。④ 这条大幅缩减剩余碳空间的道路,将会给印度等发展中国家带来不安,⑤因为

---

① Daniel Bodansky, Seth Hoedl, "Gilbert Metcalf and Robert Stavins: Facilitating linkage of climate policies through the Paris outcome", *climate policy*, 2015, p. 2.

② 资料来源:https://en. wikipedia. org/wiki/Paris_Agreement,最后访问日期:2019 年 1 月 5 日。

③ Daniel Bodansky, "Notes And Comment: The Paris Climate Change Agreement: Anewhope", 110 *A. J. I. L.* 288, 2016, p. 5.

④ 《巴黎协定》第 2 条。

⑤ Jason Maclean, "Will We Ever Have Paris? Canada's Cliamte Change Policy and Federalism 3.0", 55 *Alberta L. Rev.* 889, 2018, p. 6.

这些国家尚需通过发展航空经济改善国民生活水平。① 其次,综观《巴黎协定》全文不难看出通篇均将国家的减排责任认定为国家的自主贡献,这其实是国家间利益对抗的妥协产物,在会议召开之前以欧盟和小岛屿国家为首的部分缔约方都认为应将国家的贡献成果法律化,来确保国家对义务的履行,但是却遭到了美国、中国和印度等排放大国的强烈反对。换言之,《巴黎协定》在国家自主贡献等核心内容上的法律约束力更多的是程序上的而非实质性的,即缔约国并没有实现国家资助贡献承诺目标的强制结果义务。②

4. 波兰卡托维兹气候变化会议

2018 年 12 月 2 日联合国新一轮的气候变化大会在波兰卡托维兹举行。共有 197 个国家参加会议,其中包括 196 个缔约国和 1 个观察国。③ 目的在于对《巴黎协定》的实施细则进行商定,确保行动透明的实际实施细则。缔约方会议第 24 届会议主要解决三个问题:各国履行承诺所适用的规则和程序,如何为气候行动提供资金,以及"宏伟目标"——各国可能愿意做出什么努力。④ 会议主要包括《联合国气候变化框架公约》第 24 届缔约方大会(COP24)、第 14 届《东京议定书》缔约方会议(CMP14)、第 1 届《巴黎协定》缔约方会议第 3 部分(CMA1 -3),以及《巴黎协定》特设工作组第 1 届第 7 次会议(APA1 -7)、公约附属科学技术咨询机构第 49 次会议(SBSTA49)、公约附属履行机构第 49 次会议(SBI49)等几个部分。在 COP 24 国家适应计划的决定中,其第 3 条就首先明确:"现阶段还没有足够的信息对国家适应

---

① Lavanya Rajamani, "Ambition and Differnetiation in the 2015 Paris Agreement: Interpretative Possibilites and Underlying Politics", *International and Comparative Law Quarterly* 65, 2016, p. 493.

② 参见何晶晶:《从"京都议定书"到"巴黎协定":开启新的气候变化治理时代》,载《国际法研究》2016 年第 3 期。

③ 资料来源:https://unfccc. int/sites/default/files/resource/i03. pdf,最后访问日期:2019 年 1 月 6 日。

④ 资料来源:http://www. un. org/zh/climatechange/cop24. shtml,最后访问日期:2019 年 1 月 6 日。

计划的实施成效进行评估。"[①]对此,应从加强实施过程的重要性、[②]在国家、次国家和地方层面上加强监督和评估、[③]对发展中国家的技术和资金援助[④]等几个方面的信息获取与收集。除此之外,为了确保行动的透明性和有效性,该决定第 19 条还明确了附属履行机构的行动细化义务并以此来确保在 2021 年 11 月第 55 届会议上能够取得发展,且不迟于 2025 年启动评估和盘点工作。在专门针对最不发达国家制定的工作方案第 6 条,还设置了最不发达国家专家工作组来促进南南合作,以使《京都议定书》和《巴黎协定》能够在最不发达缔约国有效适用。[⑤] 通过上述文件不难看出在 COP 24 会议上的确取得了明显的进步,但是就如何确保缔约国履行气候承诺的问题仍然未得到实质性解决。

(二)欧盟区域性碳排放交易规则

1. 欧盟碳交易体系的缺陷

1997 年,当时的欧洲共同体及其成员国根据《京都议定书》承诺,在 2008 年至 2012 年,使温室气体排放总量在 1990 年的基础上减少 8%,虽然那时英国和德国在减排方面取得了重大的进展,但是其他许多会员国却仍在苦苦挣扎。[⑥] 1998 年欧盟委员会发布了一份名为《气候变化—指向欧盟的后京都议定书战略》的文件,强调应迅速制定政策以确保欧盟能够履行《京都议定书》的承诺。2001 年,欧盟委员会通过了一项对欧盟范围内的排放交易指令,紧接着 2003 年 10 月欧盟碳排放交易体系(European Union Emissions Trading System,EU ETS)正式上升为法律,并于 2005 年在欧盟当时的 25 个成员国内

---

① 资料来源:https://unfccc.int/sites/default/files/resource/cop24_auv_nap.pdf,最后访问日期:2019 年 1 月 6 日。

② Decision-/CP.24:National adaptation plans,Article 5.

③ Decision-/CP.24:National adaptation plans,Article 8.

④ Decision-/CP.24:National adaptation plans,Article 15.

⑤ Decision-/CP.24:Least developed countries work programme.

⑥ Wil Burns,"The European Union's Emissions Trading System: Climate Policymaking Model,or Muddle? (Part 1)",30 *Tul. Envtl. L. J.* 189,2017,p.6.

适用。在 EU ETS 框架下受监管的实体有三种减排途径可以选择:进行投资以实现减排;减少生产并销售排放额度以及扩大或维持生产并购买排放额度。[①] 欧盟的碳排放交易体系已发展为阶段性模式,共分为四个交易阶段:其中 2005～2007 年的第一个交易阶段为"在实践中学习",在这个阶段只涵盖发电厂和能源密集型产业的二氧化碳排放。[②] 第二个阶段为 2008～2012 年,这个阶段恰逢《京都议定书》的第一承诺期,所以在该排放交易体系下的国家需要有具体的减排目标,且航空部门也于 2012 年 1 月 1 日在该阶段下被纳入 EU ETS(但是来自或飞往非欧盟国家的航班申请暂停),超额的惩罚也从第一阶段的每吨 40 欧元增加为每吨 100 欧元。[③] 第三个阶段则为"后京都"阶段(2013 年以后)。[④]

2008 年 11 月 19 日欧盟通过再次修订 2003 年 10 月 13 日的 2003/87/EC 指令所形成的 2008/101/EC 指令,将航空业纳入排放交易机制。欧盟境内的航空业将于 2011 年纳入,境外的航空业(以下简称国际航空)2012 年纳入。[⑤] 在 2008/101/EC 指令中规定:"'航空排放'指附件一所列航空活动的飞行排放,其中航线包括由成员国境内机场离港和由第三国到达成员国境内机场。[⑥] 2012 年总限额为历史排放量的 97%,其中 82% 用于免费分配,3% 用于特别保留,另外 15% 通过拍卖方式使用"。该指令一经公布很多航空公司甚至包括印度、中国、俄罗斯和美国等国家都对欧盟有关航空业碳交易体系

---

① Mirzha de Manuel Aramendia, Bruges European Econ. Research Papers, Market Efficiency in the EU Emissions Trading Schewe 5 (2011), hetps://www. coleurope. eu/Content/studyprogrammes/eco/publications/BEER/BEER 20. pdf.

② 资料来源:https://ec. europa. eu/clima/policies/ets/pre2013_en,最后访问日期:2019 年 1 月 7 日。

③ 资料来源:https://ec. europa. eu/clima/policies/ets/pre2013_en,最后访问日期:2019 年 1 月 7 日。

④ See Josephine Van Zeben, "Subsidiarity in European Environmental Law: A Competence Allocation Appeoach", *Harv Envtl. L. Rev.* 415, p. 6.

⑤ 参见刘衡、黄志雄:《论欧盟航空碳税"停摆"的原因与启示》,载《法治研究》2013 年第 10 期。

⑥ 2003/101/EC, Article 3(r).

的规定表示了反对。[①] 美国等一些国家认为欧盟没有权利管辖非欧盟国家的国际航班,[②]其中中国和美国明确禁止其本国的航空公司遵守 EU ETS 的规定。2012 年 11 月 27 日美国出台了《欧盟排放交易计划禁止法案》,中国则声称要扣留空客 600 亿元的订单,甚至法国也施压要求冻结该计划。[③] 随后,欧盟气候行动司司长德贝克表示若未来国际上能够建立一套优于 EU ETS 的体系则可以暂停适用。基于此,2012 年 11 月鉴于国际民航组织理事会会议通过了相关决定,欧盟即决定暂停向非欧盟国际航班征收航空碳税。[④] 欧盟的碳交易体系虽然未能顺利在国际航空领域进行适用,但是却不能否认欧盟在减排领域的优势和其 ETS 体系的贡献作用。在第二阶段末,EU ETS 在全球碳排放交易市场中的交易占比高达 80% 以上,甚至引领了全球碳排放市场的走向。[⑤]

2. 欧盟碳排放交易体系的发展

EU ETS 的第三个交易阶段为 2013 ~ 2020 年。这与 2012 年 12 月在多哈达成的《京都议定书》的第二个承诺期相一致。[⑥] 其中最大的变化是在欧盟范围内引入了排放上限(每年减少 1.74%),此外还逐步向拍卖配额转变,

---

① 资料来源:https://en. wikipedia. org/wiki/European_Union_Emission_Trading_Scheme,最后访问日期:2019 年 1 月 8 日。

② See David P. Stewart, "Air Transport Association of America v. Secretary of State for Energy and Climate Change. Case No. C – 366/10", *American Journal of International Law*, 2013, p. 4.

③ See Katelyn E. Ciolino, "Up in the Air: The Conflict Surrounding the European Union's Aviation Directive and the Implications of a Judicial Resolution", 38 *Brooklyn J. Int' l L.* 1151, 2013, p. 3.

④ 参见刘衡、黄志雄:《论欧盟航空碳税"停摆"的原因与启示》,载《法治研究》2013 年第 10 期。

⑤ 参见孙悦:《欧盟碳排放交易体系及其价格机制研究》,吉林大学 2018 年博士学位论文,第 38 页。

⑥ 资料来源:https://ec. europa. eu/clima/sites/clima/files/docs/ets_handbook_en. pdf,最后访问日期:2019 年 1 月 11 日。

以取代免费配额。① 并为新加入者拨入3亿元的储备津贴。② 除了整个欧洲经济区(European Economic Area,EEA)以及冰岛、挪威和列支敦士登以外,2013年1月1日克罗地亚也加入了EU ETS体系中,2014年克罗地亚的航空业也将被纳入该体系中。欧盟的碳排放交易体系在总结、吸取经验的基础上也取得了新的发展。

(1)碳排放交易的范围变大

欧盟排放权交易体系所涵盖的温室气体范围越来越大,从第三个阶段开始,欧盟的排放交易体系大约能够占到欧盟温室气体排放总量的一半,涵盖的部门范围逐步扩大:包括铝、碳捕获以及储存、石化产品等多个化学产品在内;温室气体的覆盖范围在EU ETS的第三阶段也从二氧化碳扩展至包括所有由硝酸、己二酸和乙醛酸所产生的二氧化氮(N_2O)排放。欧盟成员国经欧盟委员会的批准后,也可以向EU ETS中增加更多的部门和温室气体的排放种类。③ 但与此同时,随着欧盟排放交易阶段的不断变化,排放上限也变得越来越严格,单就航空部门在第三阶段的排放上限来讲,也仅达到历史排放总量的95%。④

(2)排放配额的分配数额不断减少

欧盟后一个阶段的排放交易政策总是通过总结先前的经验与教训并加以改进和完善。⑤ 故第三个阶段,在总结第一个阶段和第二个阶段中因配额发放的过多所导致的欧盟排放配额(European Union Allowance,EUA)价格过低的问题的基础上,改变原有将配额分配给成员国再由成员国内部分配的模

---

① The EU Emissions Trading System (EU ETS), Accessed January 8, 2019. https://ec.europa.eu/clima/sites/clima/files/factsheet_ets_en.pdf.

② 资料来源:https://ec.europa.eu/clima/policies/ets_en,最后访问日期:2019年1月8日。

③ 资料来源:https://ec.europa.eu/clima/sites/clima/files/docs/ets_handbook_en.pdf,最后访问日期:2019年1月11日。

④ Main EU ETS features over the years, Accessed April 10, 2019. https://ec.europa.eu/clima/sites/clima/files/docs/ets_handbook_en.pdf.

⑤ Josephine van Zeben, "Subsidiarity in European Environmental Law: A Competence Allocation Approach", 38 *Harv. Envtl. L. Rev.* 415, 2014, p. 25.

式,变更为直接由欧盟分配到企业。① 此外,在第三阶段总体减排 20% 的目标下按照线性递减系数每年下降 1.74% 的比例,②这意味着欧盟的排放配额每年将减少 38,264,264 项津贴。与第一、第二阶段免费发放津贴不同,在第三阶段中将以拍卖分配为主,免费分配将限制在分配上限的 43% 左右,且主要集中在工业部门。③ 而在航空部门,82% 的航空津贴将免费分配给报告了 2010 年经核实的吨公里数据的运营商,15% 的航空津贴将被拍卖,剩余 3% 的航空津贴将作为特别储备用于日后新进入市场的公司和快速增长的运营商,根据这一标准,航空公司在第三阶段每 1000 吨公里航程仅可获得 0.6422 个津贴。④ 但鉴于 2016 年国际民航组织大会通过了一项关于全球减排措施的决议,即通过市场措施来解决国际航空的二氧化碳排放问题。欧盟即决定从 2017 年起将 EU ETS 体系的地理范围限制在欧洲经济区内。EU ETS 中的航空部分将会根据 CORSIA 体系作出新的审议,通过审议将会认定如何在欧盟的 EU ETS 法律中适用全球措施,如果没有新的修正案,欧盟将从 2024 年起恢复原来的实施范围。⑤

EU ETS 的第四个阶段为 2021 ~ 2030 年,欧盟委员会提议于 2015 年 7 月修订阶段四旨在实现 2030 年气候和能源政策框架,EU ETS 相较于 2005 年将削减 43% 的排放,从 2021 年起补贴总额也将于每年 2.2% 的速度下降。该框架包括一个具有约束力的目标,即到 2030 年,欧盟领土的碳排放量至少比 1990 年的水平减少 40% 。⑥

综上所述,尽管欧盟的 ETS 规则整体优势性较强且后期也取得了较大

---

① 温琪:《碳排放权交易制度研究》,江西财经大学 2018 年硕士学位论文,第 24 页。

② Wil Burns, "The European Union's Emissions Trading System, Climate Policymaking Model, or Muddle? (Part II)", 31 *Tul. Envtl. L. J.* 51, 2017, p. 7.

③ EU ETS Handbook,资料来源:https://ec.europa.eu/clima/sites/clima/files/docs/ets_handbook_en.pdf,最后访问日期:2019 年 1 月 11 日。

④ EU ETS Handbook, Allocation of aviation allowances, p. 91.

⑤ 资料来源:https://ec.europa.eu/clima/policies/transport/aviation_en,最后访问日期:2019 年 1 月 11 日。

⑥ 资料来源:https://ec.europa.eu/clima/policies/strategies/2030_en,最后访问日期:2019 年 1 月 12 日。

程度的发展,但是其2008/101/EC指令将EU ETS规则强制适用于进入或离开欧盟领域的非欧盟国家的国际航班的行为,则受到了从违反“共同但有区别的责任”原则、国家主权与公平性及其贸易的平等与非歧视性原则等几个方面的谴责。[①] 且根据国际航空运输协会(International Air Transport Association,IATA)估计,若EU ETS未限制其适用范围则可能会给整个国际社会的航空运输产业增加数十亿美元的成本;此外,中国民航总局分析,欧盟的航空碳税将于2012年给中国航空运输额外增加800万人民币的支出(相当于120万美元),到2020年将达到每年30亿人民币,到2020年将累计支出176亿人民币。[②] 2008年欧盟最初将航空业纳入ETS体系中时便在国际社会中引发了强烈的反弹,这不仅被认为是对第三世界国家主权的侵犯,而且这些税将在很大程度上转嫁到乘客身上。[③] 总体来说,欧盟ETS体系的单边性和其明显的“一刀切”特点,很难得到国际社会的认可和遵守。国际组织统一平台的建立和以“共同但有区别的责任”原则为基础的减排规则才是目前解决国际航空减排问题最可行的方法。

(三)国际民用航空组织的减排规则

根据上文对欧盟ETS体系的介绍,欧盟于2013年至2016年将ETS指令涵盖的航空活动限制在欧洲经济区机场之间的航班的“停摆”决定,就是由于2013年10月国际民航组织大会上就制定全球市场减排机制达成决议,以在2016年前限制航空排放,该机制将在2020年前实施。欧盟将在国际民航组织2016年大会取得成果后进行审议,以便对2017年以后的EU ETS的适用范围提出建议。随后国际民航组织在2016年第39届大会上针对国际航空的减排问题取得了一系列丰硕的成果:通过了《国际民航组织关于环境保

---

① 参见党玺:《欧盟强征航空碳税及其应对措施》,载《浙江理工大学学报》2013年第5期。

② Wenqiong Liang and Liying Zhang, “Legal Issues Concerning the EU Unilateral Aviation Ets: A Chinese Perspective”, 11 *S. C. J. Int’l L. & Bus.* 1, 2014, p. 3.

③ Kaylin Gaal, “‘Soaring’ Gas Prices: Policy Considerations for The European Union Emissions Trading System and Aviation”, *Wm. & Mary Envtl. L. & Pol’y Rev.* 38, 2013, p. 5.

护的持续政策和做法的综合声明——气候变化》和《国际民航组织关于环境保护的持续政策和做法的综合声明——全球市场措施机制》两份重要的文件。[①] 且将在2021年之前通过采取全球市场措施来解决国际航空二氧化碳的减排问题。据此,欧盟决定2017年将排放权交易体系的适用范围限制在欧洲经济区内。

国际民用航空组织在国际航空环保方面的组织与指导作用早在《京都议定书》中就进行了肯定:"附件一所列缔约方谋求或限制温室气体的排放应通过国际民用航空组织作出努力。"[②]且在1944年《国际民用航空公约》(《芝加哥公约》)中就明确国际民用航空组织的宗旨和目的就是促进国际民用航空在各方面的发展,[③]其中当然包括减排和能源的发展,同时也肯定了其在缔约国领土内为履行职责所享有的法律上的能力。[④] 单就其建立的减排规则的国际影响力来讲,也是现阶段期望最高、希望最大、可行性最强的措施。

1. ICAO减排规则的设立背景

根据联合国政府间气候变化专门委员会(Intergovernmental Panel on Climate Change,IPCC)2018年报告的介绍:据估计,人类活动将导致全球变暖高于工业化前水平大约1.0℃。如果按照现在这样的速度发展下去的话到2030年至2052年将会达到1.5℃。[⑤] 且在IPCC目前进行的第六次评估工作周期中第三个工作组所通过的关于气候变化减缓的文件中也再次强调了航空业方面减排工作的重要性。[⑥] 早在2005年12月的一份报告中就预计,到2050年航空业将会产生大约4300Gt(Gigatonne = 10^9 Tonnes)的碳污染,接近全球气候剩余预算的5%,如果没有监督,到21世纪中叶全球航空排

① 参见李炎瑾:《国际民用航空器市场减排规则研究》,华南理工大学2018年硕士学位论文,第24页。

② 《京都议定书》第2条。

③ 《芝加哥公约》第44条。

④ 《芝加哥公约》第47条。

⑤ 资料来源:https://www.ipcc.ch/sr15/chapter/summary-for-policy-makers,最后访问日期:2019年1月13日;IPCC,Global Warming of 1.5℃,p.447。

⑥ IPCC,The IPCC and the Sixth Assessment cycle,p.2.

放将会增加2倍,每年将会排放超过300Gt的碳。① 在过去的40年里,全世界民用航空的乘客公里数以每年5%的速度增长,与此同时二氧化碳的排放量也以每年2%的速度增长。② 国际社会在很早就认识到了航空运输减排的重要性,1972年联合国人类环境大会的一项决议中就认为国际航空运输将会给环境造成危害。对此,1983年ICAO就设立了航空环保委员会(Committee on Aviation Environmental Protection,CAEP),就民用航空环保问题向大会和理事会提供建议。而在国际条约的制定方面,1992年《联合国气候变化框架公约》首先达成了温室气体减排的约束机制;在此后的《京都议定书》中就紧接着对国际航空运输的减排工作进行了规定并同时明确了ICAO对国际航空减排问题的法律指导地位;另外,欧盟通过2008/101/EC指令企图主导国际航空减排行为的失利,也进一步地肯定了ICAO在制定国际统一减排体系、平衡不同国家之间经济利益方面的独特优势。

2. ICAO在国际民航减排领域地位的确立与发展

(1)《芝加哥公约》

第二次世界大战期间,庞大的客运和货运需求无法得到满足,推动了飞机技术的发展,继而加速了国际民用航空会议的举行。1944年54个国家起草了《国际民用航空公约》(《芝加哥公约》),这一公约为国际航空运输奠定了标准和程序基础,其目的和宗旨就是:以安全、有序的方式发展国际民用航空运输。③ 根据《芝加哥公约》的规定,将设定一个临时的国际民用航空组织(Provisonal ICAO PICAO),当第26个国家批准该公约时该临时性组织将由一个常设性的国际民航组织(ICAO)所取代。1947年3月5日第26个国家批准了公约,故1947年4月4日PICAO正式被ICAO所取代。紧接着,1947

① 资料来源:https://en.wikipedia.org/wiki/Environmental_impact_of_aviation,最后访问日期:2019年1月13日。

② Giel Op't Veld,Aleksandra Mandic,Laszlo Daniel Toth,Joachim Ciers,"Carbon Footprint of Academic Air Travel:A Case Study in Switzerland",Dec 2018,p.5.

③ 资料来源:https://www.icao.int/about-icao/History/Pages/default.aspx,最后访问日期:2019年1月15日。

年10月ICAO成为联合国经社理事会(Economic And Social Council, ECOSOC)的专门机构。[①] 现阶段,国际民航组织共有192个成员国,包括193个联合国成员国(除多米尼加、列支敦士登外)[②]中的191个,以及库克群岛。在1944年《芝加哥公约》第47条中就已经明确了国际民航组织具有的法律能力,且凡与国家的宪法与法律不抵触时,ICAO都具有完全的法人资格。制定和维护国家标准和建议措施及空中航行服务程序,既是《芝加哥公约》的根本原则,也是国际民航组织的核心使命。[③] 其后,《芝加哥公约》虽然于1959年、1963年、1969年、1975年、1980年、1997年、2000年和2006年多次进行修订,并分别针对第45条、第48条、第49条、第50条、第51条、第56条、第61条、第90条等进行修改,但始终对国际民用航空组织的法律能力及其完全的法人资格充分的认可和肯定。

(2)《京都议定书》

1997年《京都议定书》在航空减排的发展中起到了关键的作用,在《议定书》第2条中就明确了附件一所列缔约国应通过国际民用航空组织来谋求限制或减少由航空燃料所产生的温室气体排放。ICAO也在具备法律资格的前提下积极履行其国际航空环保义务,2001年10月5日至11月25日举行的国际民用航空第33届大会上就认识到了航空活动可能对环境带来的损害及对应责任,[④]明确自己将在最大限度内促使各成员国在环境保护领域内和谐共处。迄今为止,在推动国际航空绿色发展及碳减排方面,ICAO发挥着无可替代的作用。

(3)第24届波兰气候变化缔约方会议

2018年12月2日至14日于波兰卡托维兹举行的第24届联合国气候变

---

① 资料来源:https://en.wikipedia.org/wiki/International_Civil_Aviation_Organization,最后访问日期:2019年1月15日。

② 列支敦士登已经委托瑞士执行该条约,使其适用于列支敦士登领土范围内。

③ 资料来源:https://www.icao.int/about-icao/AirNavigationCommission/Pages/CH/how-icao-develops-standards_CH.aspx,最后访问日期:2019年1月15日。

④ 参见覃华平:《欧盟航空减排交易机制(EU ETS)探析——兼论国际航空减排路径》,载《比较法研究》2011年第6期。

化缔约方会议(COP 24)中又强调了全球航空碳减排问题:即在没有额外的政策措施的情形下,预计到2035年,全球航空运输的碳排放量大约能够达到10.9亿吨,与2015年相比排放量将增长23%,且在2050年以前每年约以3%的速度增长。可见,在全球贸易流量持续增长的情形下,让更多的利益相关方加入减排进程中来是十分重要的。[①] 2018年12月4日举行的全球气候行动高级别会议的活动目标是为政党、国际组织与国际合作提供机会和平台,而ICAO的工作正是构建统一的国际减排体系与交流合作平台。不仅如此,国际民航组织也在本届缔约方会议的边会中专题介绍了CORSIA抵消计划、强调了ICAO所具备的法律优势地位。[②] 综上所述,COP 24不仅肯定了ICAO的减排工作,也为国际民用航空组织进一步的发展提供了宝贵的经验教训。

3. ICAO航空减排的发展进程

正如ICAO于COP 24边会上的介绍一样,为什么国际民用航空组织在管理和限制国际航空排放问题上具有优势呢?一方面,是国际民用航空组织自1944年《芝加哥公约》建立之日起就是旨在服务和促进国际航空运输发展的专门性国际组织,也是迄今为止在国际航空发展方面影响力最大的国际组织;[③]另一方面,就是ICAO框架下的国际航空减排规则之间环环相扣,具有统一的标准和程序基础,各部门之间能够相互联系合力促进国际航空减排工作的运行。[④]

(1)ICAO第33届大会

国际民航组织2001年第33届大会首次对国际民用航空与环境保护作

---

① 资料来源:https://unfccc.int/sites/default/files/resource/1012MPGCA_Cross-cutting_RT_conceptnote_Oceans_Transport_FINAL.pdf,最后访问日期:2019年1月16日。

② 资料来源:https://attend-emea.broadcast.skype.com/zh-CN/2a6c12ad-406a-4f33-b686-f78ff5822208/42a9995e-7673-456e-933c-cad119d587a5/player?cid=zjlqx6vhfbvwy7dq2inl2suob3r7thwpf3b3w5svu4tswdioxhuq&rid=EMEA,最后访问日期:2019年1月16日。

③ See Daniel B. Reagan, "Putting International Aviation into the European Union Emissions Trading Scheme: Can Europe Do It Flying Solo", 35 *B. C. Envtl. Aff. L. Rev.* 349, 2008, p. 5.

④ 参见刘萍:《国际航空碳排放全球机制的构建》,载《法律科学》(西北政法大学学报)2013年第4期。

出了综合性的声明(A33 -7)。[①] 在决议中提出将通过技术的提升、适当的运营机制、空中交通管理和土地、机场的规划等综合措施来缓解航空运输对环境造成的不利影响。在该项决议中对国际航空的环保问题给予了足够的重视,在 A33 -7 决议中通过 A 到 I 九个附件,从标准和程序的制定、噪声的控制、土地的规划和发动机减排等几个方面进行了综合规定。

该决议进一步指出对于航空器排放进行收税与收费的区分,大会强烈建议应通过收费的形式代替收税,并将所收取的费用首先应用于航空运输的减排方面。此外,大会敦促理事会制定行动指南与方针,鼓励各缔约国在国内与国际层面积极采取措施。从 ICAO 第 33 届大会起,理事会就被要求在每届常会上提交一份国际民航组织关于环境保护政策和措施的综合说明以供审查,至此国际航空环保问题就成为历届常会的普遍性议题。

(2)ICAO 第 35 届大会

因美国发生“9·11”恐怖袭击事件,国际民航组织临时决定召开第 34 届大会。[②] 故主要议程仅限于选取另外三个缔约国为理事国与大会 A33 -10 和 A33 -27 有关的航空安保活动及国际航空安全财务机制筹资。[③] 并未涉及国际航空减排领域。故本文将介绍 2004 年举行的 ICAO 第 35 届大会,以及大会有效决议(Doc 9848)中通过的《国际民航组织关于环境保护的持续政策和做法的综合声明》(A35 -5),该声明包含了限制或减少航空器噪声、航空器排放对当地空气质量,以及航空温室气体对全球气候的影响三个方面。本次大会首先明确了各成员国在国际航空减排过程中所发挥的重要作用以及与国际民航组织之间的关系,大会强调:民航组织在与环境有关的一切民航实务工作中发挥着领导作用,但同时也请求各缔约国给予支持并提供必要的科学资料以使民航组织的工作能够有据可循。国际民航组织在明确

---

① ICAO, Doc. 9790, Assembly Resolution, A33 -7.

② 参见杨万柳:《国际航空排放全球治理的多维进路》,吉林大学 2014 年博士学位论文,第 46 页。

③ 资料来源:https://www.icao.int/Meetings/AMC/Pages/Archived-Assembly.aspx?Assembly=a34,最后访问日期:2019 年 1 月 18 日。

其所发挥的协调、指导作用的同时也注意到各缔约国本国已经存在的相关政策和法规,故大会在鼓励各缔约国以成本效益为基础一视同仁的对待国内与国际航班、自愿采取限制或减少航空排放措施的同时也应尽量避免对各国民航产业的发展产生不利影响。

而在排放权交易方面,为了敦促各缔约国采取与国际民航组织保持高度一致的排放权交易政策和措施,进一步构筑统一的国际民航排放权交易制度。大会要求理事会在接下来的工作中主要采取以下两种做法:一种是国际民航组织将支持缔约国与其他国际组织的自由交易制度;另一种则是国际民航组织提供指导原则,各缔约国根据本国的实际发展状况在符合《联合国气候变化框架公约》的要求下具体适用。但无论采取何种方式理事会都应确保交易制度的基本原则和法律基础,例如,监督、报告等关键性问题。① 由此,ICAO 开始真正致力于解决国际航空排放问题。②

(3)ICAO 第 36 届大会

2007 年 9 月国际民用航空组织召开了第 36 届大会,在本次大会中通过了 A36-22 号决议:《国际民航组织关于环境保护的持续政策和做法的综合声明》,该声明由 A 至 L 共 12 个附录构成,其中附录 A、I、J、K、L 5 个附录与航空排放有关。③ ICAO 第 36 届大会中关于航空减排问题的规定,相较于前几届会议更加全面,除了环境质量标准和程序的制定、航空对当地空气质量的影响外,在对全球气候的影响方面还增加了科学理解、与联合国等其他机构的合作、ICAO 对国际航空和气候变化的行动方案以及排放权交易等几个方面。在本次决议中,ICAO 以 UNFCCC 防止危险的人为活动干预气候体系的最终目标、《芝加哥公约》的不歧视和平等、公平的发展机会原则、共同但有区别的责任和各自能力的原则为基础,确保在国际民航领域继续发挥领导作用的同时,加强与《联合国气候变化框架公约》缔约方大会和科学技术咨

① ICAO, Assembly Resolution A35-5.

② 参见杨万柳:《国际航空排放全球治理的多维进路》,吉林大学 2014 年博士学位论文,第 47 页。

③ ICAO, Doc. 9902, Assembly Resolution A36-22.

询附属机构的联系，尽快制定出能够充分考虑到对发展中国家的航空及其成长影响的具体方案。

在航空减排的问题上大会首先肯定了减排工作所取得的重大进展，以及国际航空公司在2020年年前再将燃油效率提高25%的承诺，并进一步强调了尽可能地减少航空器减排工作对经济发展的不利影响。① 为了促进上述目标的实现，在A36－22号决议中，ICAO提出在保持航空环境保护委员会所发挥的评价、预测和指导作用的基础上，组建一个新的航空和气候变化组（Group on International Aviation and Climate Change，GIACC），由发达国家和发展中国家平等的参与，旨在形成一个以所有缔约国自愿为基础的国际航空与气候变化的行动方案，以此来指导理事会接下来措施的制定。除了机构的建立与基本原则的把握，为了达到国际民航组织对于限制或减少航空器排放的目标，大会要求理事会从制定航空器燃油中长期目标、空中交通管理及效率、新程序的开发以及航空器与航线的设计等多个具体的方面入手，来推动缔约国之间的合作、促进成果的监测与报告。此外，在航空排放权交易领域，大会再次建议通过以升级航空器为目的的收费形式来进行款项的征收，各缔约国也应尽可能地避免单方面的费用收取行为。② 可见，相较于前几届会议，ICAO在其第36届大会中关于航空减排问题逐步朝着精细化和统一化的方向发展，且其对于国际民用航空减排工作的发展规划也越来越清晰明确，涵盖的范围也越来越细致具体。

另外，ICAO还于2007年首次发布了环境报告，该报告主要介绍了2007年2月举行的国际民航组织航空环境保护委员会第七次会议（CAEP/7）和2007年5月举行的国际民航组织航空排放讨论会，此外还特别强调了IPCC的报告，以及《联合国气候变化框架公约》等与航空有关的联合国论坛的相

---

① See Miranda M. Jensen, "Ready for Takeoff: Embarking on a Journey to Regulate Aircraft Greenhouse Gas Emissions at Home and Abroad", 42 *Vt. L. Rev.* 833, 2018, p. 4.

② See Jon M. Truby, "Reforming the Air Passenger Duty as an Environmental Tax", *ELR* 12 3 (200), 2010, p. 11.

关内容。[①] 在本次环境报告中 ICAO 将国际航空的排放问题分为几个板块进行了详细的介绍,并从技术、燃料燃烧效率的提升、制定运营措施改善航空交通管理以及以市场为基础的措施这四个方面入手,主张以此推行综合性的减排规则。其中,在以市场为基础的航空减排措施中,环境报告主要考虑了排放交易、自愿措施和与排放相关的收费三个方面,而在碳排放交易计划中又进一步提出了"设定总体限制、允许配额买卖"的具体实施措施,并发布了相关指导文件(Doc 9885);在自愿措施方面 ICAO/CAEP 又配套编写了"航空自愿排放交易报告"。

ICAO 于 2007 年发布的环境报告实际上是对国际航空环境问题的汇总与梳理,在总结航空环保与碳减排规则的同时,还创新地汇集了众多专家学者对国际航空排放问题的研究成果与理论文章,这无疑使 ICAO 关于航空排放体系的介绍更加充实丰满。例如,在其中的一篇文章中就介绍了自愿交易体系在灵活性、竞争力与实践性等几个方面的优势,并结合 CAEP 的报道描述了:日本和英国的排放交易计划、芝加哥气候交易所(Chicago Climate Exchange)、蒙特利尔气候交易所(Montreal Climate Exchange)、欧洲气候交易所(European Climate Exchange)、亚洲碳交易所(Asia Carbon Exchange)以及航空公司的碳抵消计划。[②]

(4)ICAO 第 37 届大会

2010 年 10 月召开的 ICAO 第 37 届大会通过了 A37 - 18:《国际民航组织关于环境保护的持续政策和做法的综合声明——一般规定、噪声和当地空气质量》;A37 - 19:《国际民航组织关于环境保护的持续政策和做法的综合声明——气候变化》两项决议。在 A37 - 18 号决议中仍采用附录的形式具体分为总则、标准建议措施与指导材料的制定、噪声管理、土地使用规划及航空器对当地空气质量的影响等几个方面。大会强调要求理事会进一步加强

① ICAO, Environmental Report 2007.

② Andreas Hardeman and Kalle Keldusild, "Voluntary Emission Trading for Aviation", ICAO Environment Report 2007, p. 150.

与国际组织、缔约国之间的联系与合作，并对2010年5月理事会批准的关于二氧化碳排放标准的计划表示欢迎。

在本次大会中，将国际航空排放对气候变化影响的问题单独列为一个议题进行讨论研究，就足以表明国际民用航空组织已经认识到限制或减少国际航空排放对全球气候变化所产生不利影响的重要性。大会仍然以《联合国气候变化框架公约》的最终目标、《京都议定书》的发展原则及各种灵活工具［比如，清洁发展机制（Clean Development Mechanism，CDM）］、IPCC评估小组的特别报告为理论基础，并在此基础上提出新的发展规划与政策指导。在A37－19号决议中首先肯定了国际航空运输业的集体承诺：2009年至2020年以每年平均1.5%的比率持续提升二氧化碳效率，从2020年起实现碳平衡增长，并在2050年前将碳排放与2005年的水平相比减少50%。[①] 大会决定在2020年以前，实现全球年平均燃油效率提高2%，2021年至2050年全球年平均燃油效率提升2%的目标。坚持《联合国气候变化框架公约》与《京都议定书》“共同但有区别的责任”，区分发达国家与发展中国家的不同发展情况、能力以及排放数量，有差别的自愿实施。为了促进该目标的实现，大会鼓励各成员国向国际民航组织提交其国家行动计划、阐述其政策措施，并每年报告二氧化碳的排放状况。大会认为，限制或减少国际航空排放对全球气候变化的不利影响需要通过国际组织或区域性的多边、双边的形式，为了尽快形成能够在国际层面统一适用的航空减排规则，大会要求理事会制定一个国际航空基于市场措施（MARKET－based Measures，MBMs）的框架，供ICAO第38届会议审议，并以总吨公里收益1%的国际航空活动作为划分是否应用MBMs的门槛值，低于门槛值或是其他非常小的航空器运营人应有资格免除适用。理事会应定期向《气候变化框架公约》报告国际航空二氧化碳的排放情况，评估所取得的成果。但该决议的目标、微量豁免以及市场机制等几个

① ICAO，Assembly Resolution A37－19.

部分,受到包括中国在内的近 60 个国家的保留。①

ICAO 于 2010 年发布的第二次环境报告相比于 2007 年发布的第一次环境报告而言是一次完全致力于气候变化的报告。国际民航《2010 年航空与气候变化环境报告》包括航空燃料的可持续替代、绿色融资以及国际民航组织与联合国及其他国际组织的合作等八个部分组成,②并通过评估航空运输对气候变化的影响,来指导国际航空减排方案的实施;此外,在 2010 年的环境报告中还专门介绍了 CAEP 2010 年 2 月举行的第八次会议的结果,结合了在该领域知名专家的研究和报告,为促进国际社会对航空减排工作知识的获取与交流提供了更加便利的平台和渠道。

在航空对气候变化的影响这一章节中,首先,介绍了全球气候变化是由于底层大气中温室气体(Greenhouse Gas,GHG)的累计造成的,其中最令人担忧的就是二氧化碳,民用航空则是二氧化碳排放主体中一个"小而重要"的贡献者。其次,在《环境报告航空温室气体排放》一文中大卫·S. 李(David S. Lee)提到二氧化碳的量化(过去和未来)是非常有力的航空减排政策之一,但必须以累计的总排放量为基础,而不是以排放率为基础。③ 这个观点实际上就是"共同但有区别的责任"在二氧化碳排放量化领域的实际运用,也是发达国家与发展中国家减排责任的分配在二氧化碳领域的具体解读。最后,在 2010 年环境报告中还着重强调了制定一个统一、透明的碳排放量计算工具的重要性。通过分析 ICAO 2010 的环境报告不难看出,ICAO 对治理国际航空排放对气候变化的不利影响逐步从整体化、框架化向精细化过渡。

(5)ICAO 第 38 届大会

国际民航组织 2013 年 10 月第 38 届大会的有效文件(Doc 10022)中通

---

① 参见李炎瑾:《国际民用航空器市场减排规则研究》,华南理工大学 2018 年硕士学位论文,第 23 页。

② ICAO,Environment Report 2010.

③ See David S. Lee,"Aviation Greenhouse Gas Emissions",ICAO Environmental Report 2010,p. 42.

过了 A38－17:《国际民航组织关于环境保护的持续政策和做法的综合声明——一般规定、噪声和当地空气质量》以及 A38－18:《国际民航组织关于环境保护持续政策和做法的综合声明——气候变化》两项具体决议,延续了 ICAO 第 37 届大会的决议模式。①

在 A38－17 这项决议中仍旧在肯定国际民用航空组织指导作用的基础上从航空器噪声、航空器排放对当地空气质量的影响以及航空器温室气体排放对全球气候的影响三个方面分别进行审议,并强调了不同方面的相互依存性。而在 A38－18 项决议中 ICAO 则进行了更为深入细致的探讨:大会首先肯定了航空技术部门所取得的重大进步:相比于 20 世纪 60 年代,现阶段航空器的燃油效率提高了约 80%。除了航空器的制造,为了更进一步实现国际航空的减排目标,大会又列举了 ICAO 在其他层面制定的减排方案:《全球空中航行计划》规定了空中交通管理(Air Traffic Management,ATM)措施、第 12 次空中航行会议通过了航空系统组块升级战略、航空环境保护委员会商定了航空器的全球二氧化碳排放标准、航空与代用燃料会议制定了航空代用燃料全球框架、开发国际民航组织燃料节省估算工具(ICAO Fuel Savings Estimation Tool,IFSET)、可持续的航空代用燃料等。基于这一系列的综合措施,大会指出航空业反对分散的国家或地区基于市场的措施,支持制定单一的全球碳抵消政策,形成一整套的全面减排措施。实质上,这也是国际社会对于欧盟 ETS 措施的抵制以及对 ICAO 所制定的全球统一减排规则的肯定在第 38 届大会上的反映。大会表示截至 2013 年年底,已有代表国际收费吨公里总量 81.60% 的 71 个成员国编制并自愿向国际民用组织提交了其国家行动计划,其中就包括国际航空产生的二氧化碳排放。② 并进一步的鼓励其他国家向国际民航组织提交行动计划,报告国际民航的二氧化碳排放情况,确保 IPCC 及其他联合国组织能够获取由航空器引起的对大气任何影响的最

① ICAO,Doc 10022,Assembly Resolutions.

② 资料来源:https://www.icao.int/annual-report－2013/Pages/CH/progress-on-icaos-strategic-objectives-strategic-objective-c1－environmental-protection-states-action-plans_CH.aspx,最后访问日期:2019 年 1 月 24 日。

新消息。[①] 除此之外,大会强调所有的措施都将虑及各成员国特别是发展中国家的不同情况和各自能力、航空市场的成熟程度通过微量豁免或分段实施的方式,尽量减少对市场的扭曲。但是,包括中国、印度、巴西、澳大利亚在内的多个国家,对国际民航组织的中期全球理想目标,以及以发达国家为主的一系列国家对国际民航组织的豁免措施提出了保留,而这些方面也正是发达国家与发展中国家间的冲突点。

在 ICAO 2013 年的环境报告中主要介绍了国际民航组织第 38 届大会就制订全球航空《关于全球基于市场的措施(MBM)计划的观点》(以下简称 MBM 计划)所取得的新突破,这也说明了国际民航组织成员国对于国际航空排放基于市场措施解决方案的支持。[②] 预计到 2016 年将提出 2020 年以后实施全球 MBM 计划的建议,推动全球性排放措施的实现。[③] 根据 2013 年环境报告的介绍,ICAO 第 37 届大会发挥着承上启下的作用,不仅承担着促进全球航空减排目标的实现、加强与成员国或其他国际组织的合作、研究国际航空温室气体减排的解决方案;还要对制订全球航空 MBM 计划,以及从 2020 年起的实施机制、中期目标的实现等在 2016 年第 39 届大会中需要审议的事项进行估计、监察与核实。国际民用航空组织的全球航空减排工作正处于一个关键时期:航空运输总量不断增加,碳减排要求的程度不断提升,相应的配套措施也需要尽快制定,所以 2013 年环境报告指出在 A38 - 18 决议中以第 37 届大会以来所取得的一系列的成就为基础纳入了一些关键因素,包括度量、监察国际航空排放的全球温室气体;制定了全球飞机二氧化碳排放标准,争取在 2016 年由国际民航组织理事会通过;此外,还介绍了 CAEP 第九次会议中三次指导小组会议所通过的航空噪声标准、减少航空器燃料的燃烧和排放、航空器交通管理业务的变化以及颗粒物标准的研究等方面所取得的成果。

---

① ICAO, Assembly Resolution A38 - 18.

② ICAO, Environment Report, 2013.

③ Assembly Resolution on International Aviation and Climate Change (A38 - 18), ICAO 2013 Environmental Report, p. 13.

ICAO第38届大会共有184个会员国和54个观察组织参加，成为与此前相比规模最大的会议，可见在国际航空减排问题上国际民航组织取得了国际社会的巨大支持。航空减排的全球性规则制定终究离不开各国的支持与援助，这点国际民航组织在历届大会中也不断强调。

(6)ICAO第39届大会

2016年10月召开的ICAO第39届大会通过的决议在国际航空的环境保护方面取得了更加显著的成果，包括：A39-1：《国际民航组织关于环境保护的持续政策和做法的综合声明——一般规定、噪声和当地空气质量》；A39-2：《国际民航组织关于环境保护的持续政策和做法的综合声明——气候变化》；A39-3：《国际民航组织关于环境保护的持续政策和做法的综合声明——全球基于市场措施(MBM)计划》三个部分。

A39-1决议仍采用附录的形式对噪声、土地规划和对当地空气质量等方面进行审议，在此项决议中指出限制民用航空活动对环境的不利影响可以通过技术改进、高效的空中交通管理和运行程序、航空器的回收和利用、可再生清洁能源的使用以及机场和土地的规划和管理、采取基于市场的措施等多个方面综合进行。[①] 而这些环境工作也有利于实现联合国17个可持续发展目标(SDGs)中的10个。[②] 基于这些可持续发展目标国际民用航空组织正在或已实施了一系列措施包括：航空环境保护委员会针对飞机制定一项新的全球二氧化碳排放合格审定标准，附件16第Ⅲ卷——《飞机二氧化碳排放》；国际民航组织出版了对航空器噪声和发动机排放的环境指南；国际民航理事会也出版了环境管理制度的资料，制定、修改了《机场空气质量指导手册》，制定了关于非挥发性微粒物质排放的合格审定要求等。在国际民航组织大力推动限制或减少航空噪声及排放问题对空气质量所造成不利影响的同时，大会还鼓励并敦促成员方及其他组织积极通过自愿方式采取措施。

---

① ICAO, Assembly Resolution A39-1.

② 国际民用航空组织的战略目标中已经为联合国的17项可持续发展目标中的13项目标作出了贡献，单环境工作方案就为其中的10项目标作出了贡献。

A39－2:《气候变化的综合声明》中大会首先认识到由2010年第37届及2013年第38届大会确认的国际航空部门改进燃油效率的理想目标要结合2015年12月在《联合国气候变化框架公约》缔约方大会中通过的《巴黎协定》的2℃和1.5℃的理想目标,以共同探索国际航空的长期全球理想目标。[①] 而促进这一全球理想目标的实现,需要包括技术标准、可持续代用燃料,基于市场措施的“一揽子”全面减排方案。至2016年6月8日,代表全球国际航空运输量的88%的94个成员国已经编制并向国际民航组织提交了其国家行动计划,在不同国家之间适用“一揽子”减排措施时,国际民航组织根据“不让任何国家掉队”举措积极与其他国际组织开展伙伴关系为成员国采取减少航空排放的行动提供援助,促进发展中国家获得新的财务资源、技术转让和能力建设,并就取得的成果与进一步的研究建议向国际民航组织第40届大会进行报告。

作为ICAO第39届大会取得突破性进展的全球基于MBM计划的A39－3项决议,是国际民航组织制订的全球碳抵消计划发展成果的最新表现形式。大会所决定的全球基于市场的措施(Global Market－Besed Measure,GMBM)计划,将以CORSIA的形式来解决国际民用航空产生的高于2020年水平的二氧化碳排放总量,同时将考虑到各国的经济发展水平、对气候变化的抵御能力以及国际航空排放的贡献程度等方面的特殊情况,尽量减少对国内市场发展的不利影响。[②] A39－3这项决议相较于A39－1与A39－2的形式而言,规定的内容更加具体,侧重于对CORSIA的适用范围、评估计算标准以及详细的实施做法、项下机制的阐述。CORSIA采取分阶段推进的办法以照顾到各国特别是发展中国家的特殊情况和实际发展能力,此外,除了通过分阶段实施的方式来尽可能的促使不同发展水平的国家都能融入CORSIA计划中去,国际民航组织在适用主体的划定方面也对最不发达国家、小岛屿发展中国家和内陆发展中国家等航空经济发展水平较为落后、应

① ICAO, Assembly Resolution A39－2.

② ICAO, Assembly Resolution A39－3.

对气候变化影响能力较为脆弱的国家给予了充分的照顾和豁免。在以国家经济发展水平这一要素作为门槛划定适用范围的同时,CORSIA 还将排放总量、航空器质量以及航空作业的性质作为是否适用该计划的判断标准之一,将年产二氧化碳总量小于 10,000 公吨、航空器最大起飞质量小于 5700 千克、所进行航空作业的性质为人道主义、医疗、消防工作的航空器运营人作为不适用 CORSIA 计划的低水平的国际航空活动,来避免不必要的行政负担。可见,在国际民航组织所制订的全球碳抵消和减排计划中始终坚持“不让任何国家掉队”的原则,根据不同国家之间的经济发展水平及对国际航空排放的贡献分阶段、有区别的实施计划,同时设立为期 3 年的遵守周期与每年的数据报告制度,作为理事会审议实施效果并酌情进行调整的基础。国际民航组织的 GMBM 计划,实现了国际航空减排领域工作的重大进展,欧盟也为此决定暂时停止对非欧盟国家的航空器适用 EU ETS 措施,并重新对有关的法律进行修改以适应国际民用航空组织的 CORSIA 减排措施。

ICAO 2016 的环境报告详细介绍了过去 3 年内国际民航组织在环境保护方面的关键活动与取得的进展,自 2013 年起 ICAO 第 38 届大会顺利举行以及环境报告出版以来,ICAO 在环境保护领域已经取得了重大进展,先前的许多倡议草案已经制定或通过实施,这点仅通过 ICAO 发布的环境报告中所介绍的工作和成果概述就能够看出。2016 年环境报告包括:航空和环保前景、航空器噪声、当地空气质量、全球排放以及国家行动计划、航空器的报废和回收、气候变化的适应和恢复能力、伙伴关系等八个章节的内容,此外还专门介绍了 CAEP 第 10 次会议(CAEP/10)的会议内容和所取得成果。① 而航空器全球排放这一部分中又包含技术的提升、运营方式的改善、基于市场措施和可持续的替代燃料等几个具体的方面。

2016 年环境报告指出:虽然航空运输在效率和技术上取得了重大进步,但随着航空运输产业的快速发展,航空业的总排放量还会大幅增长,很难实

① ICAO,2016 Environment Report.

现 2020 年国际航空排放碳中和的理想目标,[①]而 GMBM 计划作为一项补充性、全局性政策,将促使整个国际航空部门到 2025 年抵消 1.42 亿 ~ 1.74 亿吨的二氧化碳,抵消成本从 15 亿 ~ 62 亿美元,约占国际航空总收入的 0.2% ~ 0.6%,满足"低成本、高效率"实现国际航空的减排目标。自第 38 届国际民航组织联大以来,各成员国积极落实 MBM 计划的各项要求,2014 年 3 月国际民航理事会成立了环境咨询小组负责 GMBM 计划的监督与建议工作,该小组从 2014 年 3 月至 2016 年 1 月共举行了 15 次会议;CAEP 全球基于市场措施的技术工作小组从 2014 年 3 月至 2016 年 6 月召开了 8 次会议;作为信息共享与交流论坛的国际民航组织关于基于市场措施的全球航空对话(Global Aviation Dialogues, GLADs)分别于 2015 年、2016 年举行了 5 场会议,CAEP/10 也于 2016 年 2 月召开。除此之外,2015 年 12 月 UNFCCC 缔约方会议通过了《巴黎协定》,也推动了全球碳市场的发展。[②] 在《巴黎协定》中不仅吸取了包括《京都议定书》清洁发展机制在内的经验教训,还创新地纳入了市场条款,这在很大程度上也说明了全球碳市场措施的广泛性和可行性。

为了促进国际民航组织 MBM 计划的实施,ICAO 自 2010 年第 37 届国际民航组织大会以来一直鼓励成员国自愿提交国际航空减排行动计划,并制定了一项综合措施来支持愿意采取行动的成员国,其中包括民航组织伙伴计划。[③] 这项伙伴关系计划鼓励已经提交国家行动计划的成员国与尚未提交行动计划的成员国之间形成伙伴关系,通过技术、措施等方面的资助与指导来促进国家航空减排行动计划的提交。国际民用航空组织 3 年一版的环境报告不仅是对过去 3 年中所实施工作、取得成果的概述,还是整个国际航空减排工作框架尤其是对 GMBM 计划的解读与剖析。

---

① See Michael P. Vandenbergh and Daniel J. Metzger, "Private Governance Responses to Climate Change: The Case of Global Civil Aviation", 30 *Fordham Envtl. Law Rev.* 62, 2018, p. 6.

② See Katle Sullivan, "Carbon Market, The Simple Reality", ICAO 2016 Environment Report, p. 149.

③ See Jane Hupe, "State Action Plans Overview", ICAO 2016 Environment Report, p. 179.

二、ICAO 的国际航空减排措施与安排

(一)ICAO 航空环保的机制设置

1.航空环境保护委员会

联合国中有两个机构在治理温室气体减排工作上发挥作用:一个为 UNFCCC 着眼于国内排放;另一个则是 ICAO 专门处理国际航空排放问题,致力于航空减排的全球性。[①] 而在 ICAO 项下处理国际航空排放具体问题的组织即为航空环境保护委员会。

航空环保委员会是国际民航组织理事会于 1983 年成立的技术委员会,其成立取代了航空器噪声委员会与航空器能源排放委员会,旨在帮助理事会制定有关于航空器噪声、排放以及航空对环境影响方面的新标准和建议措施。理事会审查航空环境保护委员会的建议,并以此向大会提出确定有关环境保护的相关建议。[②] 环境保护委员会由 24 名成员国以及由 5 个国家和 10 个国际组织的观察员组成,共有来自世界不同地区的 600 多位知名专家参与到活动和工作组之中。中国、印度、巴西和美国等航空发展中国家和发达国家都为该委员会的成员国。

CAEP 下设 3 个工作组,工作小组 1:航空器噪声,该小组的主要工作领域是超音速运输与航空器减噪,主要负责 ICAO 的噪声标准文件—附件 16 卷Ⅰ确保其更新且有效;工作小组 2:机场运营,该小组的工作领域则为机场的运营和地面规划、机场减噪、减排运行方案的设计以及机场环境监管与指导。工作小组 2 设立于 1991 年 CAEP 第 2 次工作会议中,工作小组 2 的独特之处在于它没有从一个 CAEP 发展到下一个 CAEP 会议的固定的工作程序,

① 参见覃华平:《欧盟航空减排交易体制(EU ETS)探析——兼论国际航空减排路径》,载《比较法研究》2011 年第 6 期。

② 资料来源:https://www.icao.int/ENVIRONMENTAL-PROTECTION/Pages/CAEP.aspx,最后访问日期:2019 年 1 月 27 日。

这就要求 CAEP 每个会议周期的成员都要确保有足够的专门知识来开展工作;①工作小组 3:排放,该工作小组主要负责航空器二氧化碳与微粒物质排放标准的界定问题,具体又包括航空器和发动机的设计以提高燃料的燃烧效率、监测当地空气质量包括不可挥发的颗粒物质、与其他工作小组共同协作达成 CAEP 的技术发展目标。

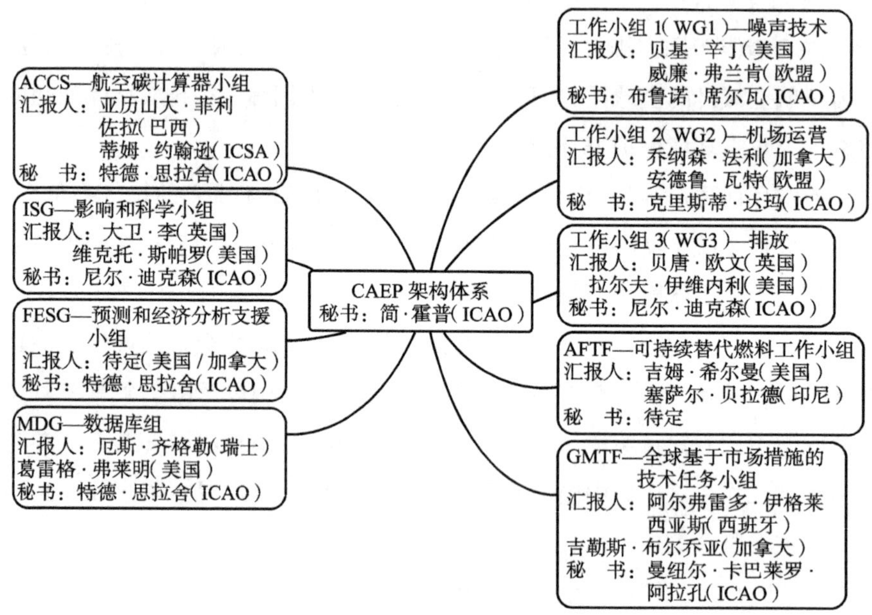

图 1 CAEP 架构设置②

CAEP 项下除了上述 3 个工作小组负责噪声、机场和排放工作外,还设立了数据库组、预测和经济分析支援小组、航空碳计算器小组、影响和科学小组、全球基于市场措施的技术任务小组以及可持续替代燃料工作小组,分别从数据库的建立和维持、经济的分析和预测、航空器二氧化碳排量的计算、航空器排放对气候变化的影响、排放的监测核查和抵消报告、可持续替代燃料

① 资料来源:https://www.icao.int/environmental-protection/Documents/CAEP/Images/WG2 - Large.png,最后访问日期:2019 年 1 月 27 日。

② 资料来源:https://www.icao.int/ENVIRONMENTAL-PROTECTION/Pages/CAEP.aspx。

的评估等几个方面对 CAEP 提供技术和数据方面的支持。

CAEP 指导小组会议每年召开一次，而正式委员会会议每 3 年召开一次，正式会议的建议由理事会批准并向大会作出报告。CAEP/10 已于 2016 年 2 月 1 日至 12 日在加拿大蒙特利尔举行。在 CAEP/10 上，理事会审查并通过了 CAEP 的建议，其中包括修改航空器噪声（附件 16 卷 Ⅰ）、发动机排放（附件 16 卷 Ⅱ）和最近建议的航空器二氧化碳排放（附件 16 卷 Ⅲ），将由理事会向大会提出报告并最终转化为大会决议。① 除此之外，CAEP/10 还在以下方面取得了重大进展：就飞机二氧化碳排放标准达成新的协议；有关于发动机所排放的不可挥发颗粒物的排放标准达成协议；就“社会参与航空环境管理”提出新的建议，以及为 2016 ~ 2019 年的 CAEP 第十一次会议（CAEP/11）提出工作计划。此外，还提出了一些新的问题：适应新的气候变化、航空器的回收利用和气候变化温度升高对国际航空产生的影响等。可见 CAEP 在 ICAO 国际航空碳减排工作中发挥着关键的作用，在航空器减噪、机场规划和限制或减少国际航空排放对当地空气质量和气候变化的不利影响方面都提供了技术和数据支持。

2. 碳排放计算器

国际民航组织的碳排放计算器是用于估算乘客在其飞行过程中所产生的二氧化碳的通用方法，可适用于碳抵消计划中。在使用过程中只需要用户提供基本的信息即可，如飞机的类型、航线的基本信息、载客或载货总量等。② ICAO 通过用户输入的航班信息与已公布的定期航班进行比较，以获得飞机的起飞次数与具体类型后，再次与 312 种等效飞机进行比对，获取燃油效率，接下来通过国际民航组织所收集的交通运营数据，可计算出所载乘客的燃油消耗总量，除以总人数即可得出每位乘客在该次航班中所

---

① ICAO, Environmental Technical Manual Volume Ⅲ— Procedures for the CO_2 Emissions Certification of Aeroplanes, Doc 9501, p. 17.

② 资料来源：https://www.icao.int/ENVIRONMENTAL-PROTECTION/CarbonOffset/Pages/default.aspx，最后访问日期：2019 年 1 月 28 日。

产出的平均二氧化碳排放量。除此之外,国际民用航空组织还开发了ICAO绿色会议计算器,其算法与碳排放计算器一致:基于对二氧化碳排放量的考虑,根据参会者的数量和始发城市等信息,可自动生成一个最佳的会议召开地点。①

为了保证民航组织此种计算方法的长期适用,各种数据信息将不断地进行更新完善,并向用户提供。其中国际民航组织交通信息和航空公司的航班表将每年进行分析和更新。

3. 国际民航组织燃油节省估算工具

国际民航组织燃油节省估算工具是秘书处在各成员国与国际组织的支持下制定的,其目的是推动各国按照CAEP和全球空中航行计划的要求节省燃料的使用,国际民航组织燃油节省估算工具本身与ICAO框架下的其他燃料节省模型和规定不存在任何的冲突关系。该工具能够分析全球各级在实施业务改进前后飞机性能方面燃油消耗的差异,②通过用户提供的必要信息计算出在运营方式、航空器性能、轨道优化等行为实施前后燃料的消耗差异,以协助未采取减排措施的国家明确业务升级的优势。

国际民航组织燃油节省估算工具将通过发布后从各成员国或其他用户处收到的反馈作为民航组织未来对该工具进行更新修改的信息来源。

4. 航空代用燃料全球框架

根据国际民航组织的统计,燃烧一公斤的传统航空燃料(Conventional Aviation Fuel,CAF)将会产生3.16公斤的二氧化碳。③ 尽管改进交通管理和基础设施是减少常规燃料使用的重要措施,但是根据CAEP的预测,随着航空运输的不断增加,仅通过管理措施的提升未来几十年航空器所产生的二氧化碳仍将大幅增加,故将代用燃料引入航空领域是十分有必要的。ICAO在

① 资料来源:http://applications.icao.int/igmc/(S(m41ukeydf2dfchrl4qujcqru))/,最后访问日期:2019年1月28日。

② ICAO,ICAO Fuel Savings Estimation Tool(IFSET Version 2.1)User Guide,2016,p.3.

③ ICAO,Environmental Technical Manual Volume Ⅱ— Procedures for the Emissions Certification of Aircraft Engines,Doc 9501,2014,p.13.

2007 年举行的第 36 届大会上通过的 A36－22 项决议中就曾鼓励理事会加深对航空代用燃料的认识；此后 2009 年 ICAO 就开展了航空和代用燃料的专题讨论会并举行了第 1 次国际民航组织航空和代用燃料会议（CAAF/1）；紧接着 ICAO 的 A37－19 和 A38－18 项决议与 2016 年通过的 A39－2 项决议都对航空代用燃料问题进行了发展；国际民航组织第 39 届大会指出引入可持续航空燃料（Sustainable Aviation Fuel，SAF）有助于 ICAO 和联合国可持续目标的实现。[①] 自 2009 年 CAAF/1 以来，SAF 产业取得了重大的发展，但同时也存在很多需要完善、进步的地方。2017 年 10 月 11 日至 13 日于墨西哥举行的 ICAO 代用燃料研讨会与第 2 次国际民航组织航空和代用燃料会议（CAAF/2）指出：会议支持 ICAO 2050 年可持续航空燃料愿景，到 2050 年工业和其他利益相关者对 CAF 适用中的很大一部分将转为对可持续航 SAF 的适用，ICAO 将不断分享信息和经验、促进金融机构和工业之间的交流、加快指导材料的编撰以支持各国开发部署 SAF。各成员国和其他利益相关者也应积极编写指导材料以促进 SAF 的适用，并为其提供资金和技术支持。此外，国家与各行业之间的交流与经验分享也是至关重要的，将对各成员国及 CAEP 的工作产生积极影响。

由于 SAF 不需要对原本适用 CAF 的飞机发动机网络进行修改便可直接进行替换或混合使用。[②] 且当 SAF 是由生物物质发展而来的时候，在理想情况下甚至不会向大气中产生额外的二氧化碳。当 SAF 产业逐步向商业化发展时，生产其所需的生物能源还能带动广泛的农村发展、创造就业机会。[③] 可见，航空代用燃料对实现限制或减少航空器排放对全球气候变化的不利影响工作会产生巨大的推动作用。

---

① 资料来源：https://www.icao.int/environmental-protection/GFAAF/Pages/ICAO-Vision.aspx，最后访问日期：2019 年 1 月 28 日。

② 资料来源：https://www.icao.int/environmental-protection/GFAAF/Pages/FAQs.aspx，最后访问日期：2019 年 1 月 28 日。

③ ICAO，Sustainable Aviation Fuels Guide，2017，p. 11.

5. 环境效益工具

国际民航组织的环境效益工具(Environmental Benefits Tool,EBT)是由制定基线、评估缓解措施与得出预期结果这三个方面组成的。① 其是对先前开发的工具,如国际民航组织碳排放计算器和国际民航组织燃料节省估算工具的补充。② 在第一部分:历史数据和基线方面,EBT 通过国家的主要航空承运人拥有的机队不超过十架飞机、可以获取五年甚至更长时间的国家数据、仅可获取一年的数据,这三种方式之一来计算截至 2050 年的基线;第二部分:EBT 将从经验、IFSET 或空中交通管理、技术的发展等方面入手带入相应缓解措施;最后第三部分:EBT 将结合基线与缓解措施的相关信息,计算出预期结果。EBT 作为 ICAO 环境效益的计算工具将为用户提供更大的灵活性和可操作性,未来会进一步将 ICAO 碳排放计算器和 IFSET 程序导入 EBT,并改善 EBT 与减排行动计划之间的连接。

以上各减排组织和工具之间相互联系、相互配合,在不同的方面为 ICAO 国际航空减排工作提供技术或者是数据支持。

(二)国际航空碳抵消和减排计划(CORSIA)

1. CORSIA 计划的发展背景

ICAO 于 2010 年第 37 届大会决议中通过了实现集体中期全球理想目标,即自 2020 年起将国际航空产生的全球净二氧化碳排放保持在相同水平;A37 - 19 项决议要求理事会在各成员国的支持下,制定一个国际航空基于市场措施的框架。基于此,在 A38 - 18 项决议中认识到制定单一的全球碳抵消机制是符合成本效益的,且这项基于市场措施的计划应避免实施做法的多重

① 资料来源:https://www.icao.int/Meetings/RS2017/Documents/S3 - % 20ICAO% 20Suppport% 20Tools% 20 - % 20part% 202.FINAL.pdf#search = EBT,最后访问日期:2019 年 1 月 28 日。

② 资料来源:https://www.icao.int/annual-report - 2016/Pages/ZH/progress-on-icaos-strategic-objectives-environmental-protection-environmental-tools.aspx,最后访问日期:2019 年 1 月 28 日。

性,大会进一步要求理事会在不影响《气候变化公约》谈判的情况下完成全球基于市场措施计划的各种可行性工作,同时应考虑有助于实现国际民航组织全球理想目标的技术、运行方式改进和可持续代用燃料的“一揽子”措施;继 A38－18 决议之后,2013 年 11 月举行的第 200 届理事会会议继续支持 CAEP 承担制订有关于 GMBM 计划的技术任务,理事会还决定设立环境咨询小组,负责监督、制订与 GMBM 计划有关的所有任务,并向理事会提出建议。① 环境咨询小组第 15 次会议于 2016 年 1 月举行,旨在为 2016 年 2 月和 4 月召开的全球 MBM 计划高级别小组会议制定大会决议草案,随后 2016 年 5 月和 8 月又分别召开了全球 MBM 高级别会议和非正式的主席之友会议。紧接着 2016 年国际民用航空第 39 届大会通过了 A39－3:《国际民航组织关于环境保护的持续政策和做法的综合声明——全球基于市场措施(MBM)计划》,在该决议中大会决定通过 CORSIA 解决国际民用航空产生的高于 2020 年水平的二氧化碳排放总量的任何年度增长量,同时采取实施监测、报告和核查制度、排放单位标准、设立登记处、国际航空碳抵消和减排计划的治理以及监管框架制度为从 2020 年起实施的 CORSIA 减排计划建立必要的配套机制。会后,CAEP 与本组织成员国进行协商后修改了《芝加哥公约》附件 16 卷四—CORSIA,并经 214 届理事会审议通过。②

2. CORSIA 减排计划的介绍

CORSIA 有助于实现全球航空理想目标,即自 2020 年起,将国际航空产生的净二氧化碳排放量保持在相同水平。③ CORSIA 依靠适用碳市场的排放单位来抵消无法通过使用技术和运营方式的改进、可持续航空燃料的适用所

① 资料来源:https://www.icao.int/environmental-protection/CORSIA/Pages/CORSIA-FAQs.aspx,最后访问日期:2019 年 1 月 29 日。

② ICAO, Environmental Technical Manual Volume IV— Procedures for demonstrating compliance with the Carbon Offsetting and Reduction Scheme for International Aviation (CORSIA), Doc 9501, p. 1.

③ Michael B. Gerrard, Edward Mc Tiernan: The Major Developments in International Climate Change, SY015 ALI-ABA 393, 2017, p. 4.

减少的二氧化碳排放量。[①] CORSIA 通过对比从 2021 年开始的二氧化碳年排放总量与二氧化碳的排放基线水平,[②]在接下来的几年中,在 CORSIA 覆盖范围下的任何国际航空二氧化碳排放量超过基线水平的部分都代表了该部门在该年度中的抵消要求。(见图 2)此外,根据 ICAO 第 39 届大会 A39 - 3 决议第 11 段(g)项,当 CORSIA 项下的航线改变时,将重新计算部门基线,为此民航组织将在每年开始时重新计算,以便考虑到自愿参加或是因为新一个阶段的开始而增加的飞往或飞离各国的航线。[③]

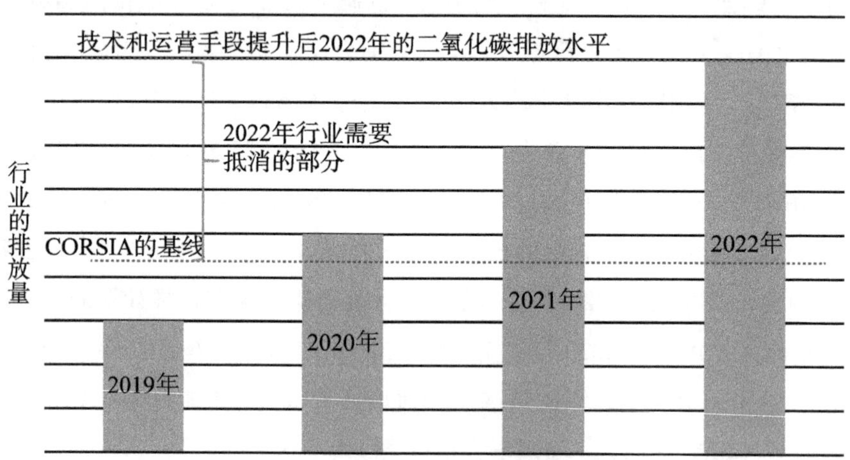

图 2 CORSIA 碳排放抵消要求[④]

CORSIA 将分为三个阶段实施,以照顾发展中国家的特殊情况,尽量缓解减排措施对国内市场的不利影响。其中,试行阶段将于 2021 ~ 2023 年实施,该阶段适用于自愿参加的国家。决定自愿参加 CORSIA 抵消计划的国家可在每年年初参加并在前一年的 6 月 30 日前将加入该计划的决定通知民航组织。另外,第一阶段将于 2024 ~ 2026 年进行,该阶段也适用于自愿参与碳

---

① 资料来源: https://www. icao. int/environmental-protection/CORSIA/Pages/CORSIA-FAQs. aspx,最后访问日期:2019 年 1 月 29 日。

② CORSIA 的二氧化碳排放基线就是自 2021 年起 CORSIA 所覆盖范围内航线 2019 ~ 2020 年二氧化碳排放量的平均值。

③ ICAO, Assembly Resolution A39 - 3 11 g).

④ 资料来源:www. icao. int/environmental-protection/CORSIA/Pages/CORSIA-FAQs. aspx。

抵消的国家,与试行阶段规定相同,仅在计算航空运营人抵消二氧化碳的排放量时既定年份的确定方面存在细微差别。[①] 2027～2035 年运行的第二阶段相较于试行与第一阶段则有所不同,第二阶段的 CORSIA 适用于所有 2018 年在以收费吨公里所表示的航空活动中其单个份额占到总份额 0.5% 以上的国家,或在以最高至最低收费吨公里数的方式排列的国家名单中累计份额达到总收费吨公里数 90% 的成员国,但最不发达国家、小岛屿发展中国家和内陆发展中国家可不适用 CORSIA 计划的第二阶段,当然大会也强烈鼓励这些受到豁免的国家能够自愿参加到该计划中。另外,国际航空业务每年排放的二氧化碳不超过 10,000 公吨的航空器运营人、最大起飞质量小于 5700 千克的航空器以及进行人道、医疗和消防作业的低水平国际航空活动都不适用 CORSIA,旨在避免对国家及行政造成负担。

在 2021 年 CORSIA 正式进入试行阶段之前,2018～2020 年的筹备阶段也发挥着相当重要的作用,具体又划分为 2018 年建议的筹备行动和 2019 ～2020 年的基线期行动两部分。从 2019 年 1 月 1 日起,所有承担国际航运任务的国家都需要制定国际航班二氧化碳排放的监测、报告和核查(Monitoring、Reporting、Verification,MRV)系统,用于计算 CORSIA 的基线和飞机运营商的抵消基础。成员国最迟应于 2019 年 4 月 30 日批准飞机运营人的排放监测计划并向国际民航组织提交本国的飞机运营人清单和经认证的核查机构清单,并最迟于 2020 年 8 月 31 日向国际民航组织提交 2019 年的二氧化碳排放数据。

3. CORSIA 框架的构成

(1)监测、报告和核查制度

CORSIA 的监测、报告和核查制度适用于 2019 年 1 月 1 日或其后使用的最大起飞质量超过 5700 千克的飞机和年二氧化碳排放量超过 1 万吨的国际

---

① 试行阶段可以在 2020 年或特定年份之间选择其一作为每年固定计算航空运营人抵消二氧化碳排放量中的年份,而第一阶段仅能通过特定年份作为计算二氧化碳排放量中的年份。

航班运营人,但低水平的国际航空活动与国家内航班除外。[①] 在2019年1月1日至2035年12月31日之前,对满足上述要求的国际航班的二氧化碳排放进行监测和核查。故在2018年的筹备期间,飞机运营人和国家应在上文所述的规定时间内提交和批准二氧化碳的排放监测计划以根据经营人的具体情况确定最为适当的二氧化碳排放监测手段和方法,以便后续排放数据的跟进。根据《芝加哥公约》附件16卷4和环境技术手册的规定,又具体分为2019~2020年期和2021~2035年期,且排放标准的界定也存在差异。

2019~2020年,通过飞机营运人国际航班产生的年二氧化碳大于、等于或者小于50万吨,来区分对其所采取的监测方法。当飞机运营人的国际航班所产生的二氧化碳排放量大于或等于50万吨时,将使用燃料使用量的监测方法;反之,当二氧化碳的排放量小于50万吨时,飞机运营人可以在燃料使用量监测方法和国际民航组织CORSIA二氧化碳核算和报告工具(CO_2 Estimation and Reporting Tool,CERT)之间进行选择;而在2021~2035年内,区分二氧化碳监测方式的排放量标准则缩减至5万吨,即当需要遵守抵消要求的国际航班产生的年二氧化碳排放量大于或等于5万吨时,飞机运营人就须适用附件16卷4附件2中的燃料使用量监测方法,当年排放量小于5万吨时则可在燃料使用量监测方法和CERT之间进行选择。值得注意的是,在2021~2035年期的监测阶段中,无须遵守抵消计划的国际航班运营人也须在燃料使用量和CERT之间进行选择。可见,对于二氧化碳排放的MRV要求是独立于CORSIA抵消计划的。在监测和计算二氧化碳排放之后,通过统一的模板和程序,飞机运营人会将必要的数据报告给国家,再由国家报告给国际民航组织,ICAO通过整理二氧化碳的排放数据,计算出部门的增长因子并通报给成员方。而二氧化碳的核查则是为了确保信息数据的准确性,即通过第三方来检验所有的操作是否准确无误。

---

① ICAO Annex 16 Vol. Ⅳ, p. 19.

(2)二氧化碳的排放监测方法

通过划分国际航班年二氧化碳的年排放量,将飞机运营人所使用的监测方法分为两类。第一种为燃料使用量监测方法,适用于不满足 CERT 要求的国际航班,其中又包含五种可选择的具体方法:方法 A、方法 B、撤轮挡/挡轮挡、燃料加注量或轮挡小时燃料分配,在此不进行赘述。本文主要介绍 CORSIA 的 CERT。

CERT 作为 MRV 系统中的一部分,旨在评估飞机操作者是否在 MRV 要求的适用性范围内以及其为支持排放监测计划所使用的燃料和监测方法,但同时也提供给国家使用,以支持数量级检查并填补任何二氧化碳排放量数据的空白。CERT 将会随着时间的推移不断地更新完善,在 2018 年版本中只包括二氧化碳的评估功能来判定是否满足适用 CORSIA 和 CERT 的资格,而改进后的 2019 年和 2020 年的版本中将包括监测和报告生成的功能,甚至在 2021 年至 2035 年的版本中还将包括受到抵消约束国家的列表。① 通过输入飞机运营信息、文件上传或手动传输飞行数据利用轮挡时间输入方法或大圆时间输入方法估算该运营人的二氧化碳排放量,最后生成排放报告,通过审查并提交的方式完成对二氧化碳的估算和报告工作,以满足灵活监测的计划要求。

(3)CORSIA 合乎条件的排放单位

一个排放单位代表一公吨的二氧化碳当量。飞机运营人须通过取消符合 CORSIA 所要求的排放单位来完成其所归属的国家计算的抵消要求。② 据此,国际航班的运营商须在符合 CORSIA 要求的排放单位所指定的登记处内取消合乎条件排放单位,这些被取消的排放单位的信息将公布在登记处的公共网站上。第一个取消排放单位报告的截止日期为 2025 年 4 月 30 日,到那时,飞机运营人和核查机构必须向国家提交 2021 ~ 2023 年排放单位的取消报告和核查报告,随后国家应通过 CORSIA 中央登记处向国际民航组织报

① ICAO, CORSIA CO_2 Estimation and Reporting Tool(CERT), p. 5.

② ICAO, Annex 16 Vol. Ⅳ 4.2.

告汇总后的信息。

而上文提到的取消合乎条件的排放单位所指定 CORSIA 中央登记系统,是国际民航组织即将开发的一个系统,①作为各国向民航组织提交数据资料的工具,这个工具将有助于实现国家提交数据的标准化和统一化,保障 CORSIA 信息透明的实现。此外,ICAO 理事会还在航空环境保护委员会的贡献下建立了技术咨询机构,②专门向理事会提供有关于排放单位的意见和建议,目前中国也加入了 TAB。

4. 符合 CORSIA 第 3 章适用程序的国家③

在《芝加哥公约》附件 16 卷 4 第 2 部分第 3 章“二氧化碳的抵消适用范围”中的国家包括:已经表示自愿参加 2021 ~ 2026 年合规期的国家、除被豁免的国家外于 2027 ~ 2035 年合规期内达到标准的国家以及虽不符合适用范围但表示自愿参加的国家。具体信息都将从 2020 年 6 月 30 日出版的国际民航组织相关文件中获取。

国际民航组织第 39 届大会 A39 – 3 决议第 9 条 d 项要求:秘书处在国际民航组织的官方网站上公布试行阶段和第一阶段国家的最新信息。截至 2019 年 1 月 15 日,已经有占国际航空活动 76.63% 的 78 个国家从一开始就打算自愿参加 CORSIA 抵消计划。但直至 2019 年 1 月 31 日,中国、印度等航空发展大国还未提交表示自愿参加 CORSIA 2021 ~ 2023 年试行阶段和 2024 ~ 2026 年第一阶段的声明报告。④ 相反,以加拿大、新加坡、日本、英国和美国为首的航空发达国家都提交了其自愿参加的声明。这 78 个国家所提

① 国际民航组织秘书处预计将于 2019 年年初启动,CORSIA 中央登记系统测试版计划在 2019 年下半年进行,据此推断,该系统将于 2020 年年初正式运作。

② 资料来源:https://www.icao.int/environmental-protection/CORSIA/Pages/TAB.aspx,最后访问日期:2019 年 4 月 7 日。

③ “CORSIA States for Chapter 3 State Pairs”这是指《芝加哥公约》附件 16 卷 4 第 2 部分第 3 章和 ICAO 环境技术手册(Doc 9501)第 4 卷—“证明符合 CORSIA 的程序”第 3 章中:“符合 CORSIA 适用程序的国家”的内容。

④ 资料来源:https://www.icao.int/environmental-protection/CORSIA/Pages/state-pairs.aspx,最后访问日期:2019 年 1 月 31 日。

交的自愿参加声明主要分为以下几种形式：欧盟国家和印度尼西亚所提交的ICAO A39－WP/414 和 A39－WP/211、以国家政府声明形式提交、国家间联合声明以及国家在 ICAO 第 39 届大会上的发言等。在上述几种声明的形式中欧盟和印度尼西亚在对 CORSIA 抵消计划表示同意的同时还提出了自己的建议供国际民航组织参考。

欧洲国家认为 GMBM 对稳定国际航空排放具有积极意义，欧盟将坚决支持 GMBM 措施使国际航空的二氧化碳净排放量保持在 2020 年的水平。只要该抵消计划所设立的自愿阶段是有限的且能够涵盖整个计划，随着时间的推移能够满足 2020 年实现碳中和增长（CNG 2020）的目标。欧洲国家认为在 ICAO 的 GMBM 计划中，必须明确关键要素：首先，该计划必须是一个真正的全球机制，即拥有一个所有国家都同意的共同标准，成员国的行为都将通过一致的非歧视方式实施；其次，GMBM 必须有效的实现气候目标，欧盟认为虽然应考虑"特殊国情和各自的能力"，但是 CORSIA 所采取的自愿参与的方式以及大量的豁免、将一部分重要排放种类排除在 GMBM 的覆盖范围之外等措施所造成的减排空白都应该尽快解决，以确保总体气候目标的实现和 GMBM 计划的可行性。欧盟进一步提出，在 ICAO 的 GMBM 计划中所给予的豁免若不按照具体情形的变化而进行调整则可能对市场造成严重扭曲。基于此可将 RTKs 作为界定标准，任何一个国家若是达到规定的 RTKs 标准都将毫无例外地列入该计划。① 但实际上在 CORSIA 的第二阶段中，除去最不发达国家、小岛屿发展中国家和内陆发展中国家可以自愿决定是否参加抵消计划外，都是通过收费吨公里来判断是否满足适用条件的。最后，欧盟还对确保计划实施的延续性与整个计划期间采取 100% 部门办法等方面提出了自己的建议和意见。不难看出，欧盟对 ICAO GMBM 计划的建议风格延续了 EU ETS 的要求模式，尽管对于 SCRC 给予了一定的重视，但

① 资料来源：https://www.icao.int/Meetings/a39/Documents/WP/wp_414_en.pdf，最后访问日期：2019 年 2 月 1 日。

仍旧刻意地强调 CORSIA 措施的统一化和标准化。[①] 这虽然对推进 CORSIA 计划和实现 CNG 目标具有很大的推动作用,但却不利于成员方的遵守、执行与全球机制的构建。

另外,代表航空发展中国家的印度尼西亚也提交了其对 GMBM 计划的建议性文件。首先,印度尼西亚强调了应在 GMBM 计划中确立有利于使用可持续替代燃料的航空器运营人的排放规定,否则将不利于采取该措施的国家和行业经营者的减排积极性。其次,印度尼西亚肯定了抵消计划的阶段性设计,认为除了发达经济体应积极自愿加入外,其他国家可以根据自己的发展情况进行决定,同时也十分赞同对于部分国家的豁免规定。此外,印度尼西亚特别强调 GMBM 项下符合要求的排放单位应与 UNFCCC 的规定保持一致。

通过对比上述代表航空业发达国家的欧盟和代表航空业发展中国家的印度尼西亚对自愿加入 CORSIA 抵消计划的声明,不难看出两方所持观点的差异。其中,欧盟认为应在肯定"共同但有区别责任"原则的同时更多的强调减排规则的无歧视统一适用,[②]主张达到一定 RTK 标准的所有国家都应无条件无豁免的适用统一的减排规范,不考虑或几乎不考虑不同国家之间航空产业的发展差异。但 ICAO 的目标是建立一个全球通用的国际航空减排体系,如不考虑国家间的经济差异将很难得到发展中国家的认可,故在 CORSIA 的抵消规则中仍旧坚持沿用了"区别责任",在此基础上也认可了无歧视的统一适用。第 39 届大会 A39 - 3 决议第 9 ~ 10 条就试图通过试行阶段、第一阶段的自愿参与以及第二阶段将 RTK 作为适用与否的判定标准这两种方式的结合来进行平衡,很大程度上也是在对发达国家和发展中国家的利益进行权衡后的产物。

可见,CORSIA 基于"共同但有区别的责任"原则设立了自愿参与的试行阶段和第一阶段,尽管再三鼓励国家尽早自愿加入抵消计划以促进本国航空

① 参见陈贻健:《共同但有区别责任原则的演变及我国的应对——以后京都进程为视角》,载《法商研究》2013 年第 4 期。

② See European Commission, "A Roadmap for Moving to a Competitive Low Carbon Economy in 2050",2011,p. 15.

运输的绿色发展,并开展了 CORSIA 伙伴关系,[①]在伙伴关系下捐助国提供的技术专家将为接受国提供现场培训,并密切跟进接受国 MRV 体系的准备和实施进程。[②] 但航空发展中国家在 CORSIA 体系下仍需承担大量的减排义务,尤其对于印度、中国等航空发展大国来说更是如此,这也是其迟迟未提交自愿参加 CORSIA 抵消计划声明的重要原因。[③]

(三) ICAO 成员国对于国际航空减排的行动计划

1. 国家行动计划的编制与提交

国家行动计划是各国向国际民航组织提交的用于说明本国处理国际航空减排所采取的措施及进展的报告。在国家所提交的有关于二氧化碳减排活动的国家行动计划中主要包括:基线设想,即在该国不采取任何二氧化碳减排措施的情形下预计到 2050 年国际航空的二氧化碳排放量;为减少国际航空运输温室气体所采取的措施一览表;采取减排措施后 2050 年国际航空可能产生的二氧化碳排放量。为此,ICAO 专门建立了网络信息公开页面和充分的技术支持,同时还制订了旨在促进国家行动计划与二氧化碳减缓措施拟定的文件《关于制定国家二氧化碳减排活动行动计划的指导》(Doc 9988)。[④] 此外,ICAO 在第 39 届大会 A39 – 2 项决议中再次鼓励各国提交自愿行动计划,并每年报告其国际航空二氧化碳的排放情况。[⑤] 国家行动计划应每 3 年提交一次,以便国际民航组织及时更新实现全球理想目标的量化资料。根据 ICAO 官网提供的数据,现阶段已经有占全球总 RTK 92.3% 的 111 个国家向 ICAO 自愿提交了国家行动计划。

---

① ICAO, Training of Trainers under the ACT-CORSIA Buddy Partnership, p. 1.

② ICAO, Transforming the Global Aviation Sector: Emissions Reductions from International Aviation, p. 1.

③ See Michael Wara, Building an Effective Climate Regime While Avoiding Carbon and Energy Stalemate, 41 *Colum. J. Envtl. L.* 313, 2016, p. 34.

④ 资料来源:https://www.icao.int/environmental-protection/Pages/ActionPlan-Questions.aspx,最后访问日期:2019 年 2 月 1 日。

⑤ ICAO, Assembly Resolution A39 – 2, Article 10.

国际民用航空组织为了促使成员方积极制定并提交国家行动计划,专门制定了《行动计划的指导》(Doc 9988)。[①] 在该指导文件中从协助编制、理解目标、促进合作和审议各国措施等几个方面入手为各国提供指导。[②] 且秘书处已经在总结国家及理事会反馈和建议的基础上出版了 Doc 9988 第 2 版,在第 1 版的基础上以更直接的方式拟订计划,各个国家甚至可以直接按照文件的章节顺序制定本国的行动计划。首先,Doc 9988 中指出成功制定国家行动计划的先决条件之一即为明确每一个利益攸关方的作用和责任,设立国家级执行机构进行具体的工作分配,并将责任细化到个人,具体负责国家与 ICAO 之间的联系和对接工作。[③] 其次,在 Doc 9988 第 3 章中秘书处专门就估计现在及将来航空燃料的消耗和二氧化碳排放的基线确定方法进行了介绍,对此 ICAO 将定期编制全球和区域客货运全球预测。再次,在第 4 章中对限制或减少国际航空运输产生的二氧化碳所采取的"一揽子"措施与如何量化措施实施后所产生的影响这两个方面提供了详细的指导,其中"一揽子"的减排措施包括:技术的提升、燃料的替代使用、机场与空中交通管理的改善、市场措施的适用等几个方面,其中不可避免的涉及 CORSIA 项下各种检测工具的适用。最后,Doc 9988 强调了在行动计划中明确援助需求的重要性及在后续实施过程中国家及 ICAO 的监督。ICAO 为了最大限度地为成员国提供指导和技术性支持,促使更多缔约国提交行动计划,还在基线的确定等方面制定了更为详细的配套文件。

2. 航空发达国家的国家行动计划

(1)巴西

在巴西所提交的国家行动计划中首先明确了将于 2025 年实现温室气体排放量在 2005 年水平的基础上减少 37%、2030 年减少 43% 的承诺。在巴西的国家行动计划中,国际航空与国内航空的区分方法与 Doc 9988 第一版中

---

① ICAO, Renewable Energy for Aviation: Practical Applications to Achieve Carbon Reductions and Cost Savings, 2017, p. 2.

② ICAO, Doc 9988, chapter1 Introduction, 1.2.2, p. 2.

③ ICAO, Doc 9988, chapter2 Action Plans, 2.6.4, p. 6.

不同，巴西认为本国航空公司运营的国际航班在本国境内阶段应被视为国内阶段，且所有外国公司均不能运营带有国内性质的起飞或目的地为巴西的航班，其整个阶段都将被视为国际阶段。① 此外，军用飞机和直升机以及地面作业等所产生的二氧化碳不适用该计划。巴西国家行动计划在划定减排范围后表示，本国的国内航空运输市场与国际航空运输相比占绝对主导的地位，大约81%的市场（按照客运量计算）都对应于国内航空阶段。② 除此之外，国际航空运输的增长速度也较为缓慢，因此，巴西对于国际航空运输的发展方式更倾向于市场的自由竞争。在国家管控力度小、市场竞争激烈的氛围中国际航空运营人就更加注重成熟的管理经验和先进的技术支持。根据巴西国家行动计划中所提供的数据，2005～2015年的这段时间内，年平均排放总量虽然仍保持增长，但同期的累计排放强度却大大降低，同时国际航空的燃油效率与2005年相比，每年能提高2.4%，甚至优于ICAO制定的每年2%的理想目标。为了实现国际航空的减排目标，巴西的国家行动计划详细介绍了本国所采取的各种减排措施，截至其递交本国国家行动计划时，其国内已经登记的机场有2643个（包括私人机场和公共机场），但实际上98%的航空运输活动都集中在其中的65个机场内，这些机场将通过赋予私营企业自主性③的方式获取更多的资金支持来实现配套设施的完善。④ 除此之外还采取了技术的提升、可替代生物燃料的适用和空中交通管理等多个方面的减排措施。⑤

通过分析巴西的国家行动计划能够看出，支持并从一开始就加入CORSIA计划对航空发达国家并不会产生太大影响。一方面巴西对于国际

① Action Plan for Green House Gas Emissions of Brazilian Civil Aviation, 2.1 Domestic Aviation and International Aviation: Concept, p. 11.

② Action Plan for Green House Gas Emission of Brazilian Civil Aviation, Chapter 3: Data of the Sector.

③ 这项计划于2011年启动，包括巴西利亚机场在内的多个机场都已获得批准。

④ ICAO, Financing Aviation Emissions Reductions, 2017, p. 1.

⑤ Action Plan for Green House Gas Emission of Brazilian Civil Aviation, Chapter 6: Measures which Contribute to the Reduction of Aviation GHG Emissions, p. 35.

航空与国内航空的区分标准使本国受到 CORSIA 抵消计划约束的国际航空运营人的范围大大减小;另一方面巴西国际航空所占比重较小且对市场冲击的抗压能力较强,甚至在部分减排领域已经领先于 ICAO 的目标和要求。

(2)英国

根据 2016 年 9 月英国提交的国家行动计划表明,航空仍然是英国旅行的首选交通工具。据统计,2013 年 72% 的外国居民通过航空运输到访英国、80% 的英国居民同样选择航空方式出国旅行。① 英国是欧洲民用航空会议(European Civil Aviation Conference,ECAC)的成员国之一,故在英国的国家行动计划中基线的确定采用了 ECAC 的标准:欧洲的航空交通包括所有起飞地点为 ECAC 领域的国际和国内的客运航班,旅客周转量也仅通过乘客的数量来进行计算,飞越 ECAC 区域的航班不包括在内。且今后一段时间内的燃料消耗与排放(2020 年、2035 年)将通过 2014 年的实际飞行距离和巡航高度来进行确定。此外,还规定了航空器的退役程序,通过这种方式确定每年所需的新飞机数量与替换飞机的服役年份。上述基线的确定方式将目的地为 ECAC 领域的欧洲航班和货运航班排除在外,影响了对航班数量和航空器排放数据确定的准确性;同时,以 2014 年的航行数据来确定未来的航空排放与燃油消耗的方式是对减排责任的逃避,毕竟国际航空运输的航行距离在不断增长且英国航空运输的排放高峰期也并非在 2014 年。

英国的气候变化委员会针对国际航空减排问题专门撰写了一份报告—《实现英国航空的目标——2050 年减排方案》,在该方案中英国表示国际航空二氧化碳的排放应通过全球部门协议或国家、地区(如 EU ETS)的减排框架进行;②在理想的情形下,所有的国际航班排放都应有一个上限,但是可能需要一个临时的过渡阶段,发达国家所有离境或抵达的航班都应进行约束,

---

① UK State Action Plan on CO_2 Emissions Reduction Activities, Chapter 2: Current state of aviation in the UK, p. 9.

② Meeting the UK aviation target-options for reducing emissions to 2050, Executive summary, p. 7.

发展中国家的国内航班可以暂时性的豁免,而这些全球或区域的减排规则都不应低于 EU ETS 的减排标准。但是,这种一个规则必须在满足另外一个规则要求的基础上才能在某一个国家或地区适用的条件,很有可能会造成两种或两种以上的规则都可以在该国家或地区适用的情形,若在各约束性规范之间欠缺一个对适用顺序的规定,则很有可能在该区域内产生双重适用的问题。

(3)美国

美国在其国家行动计划中表示从 ICAO 的 A39－19 号决议开始,美国联邦航空局与美国能源与环境办公室就始终支持着 ICAO 及 CAEP 的工作并在其中发挥着积极的作用。① 美国早在 2012 年就公布了航空温室气体减排计划,②随着 ICAO A38－18 号决议的通过,美国制订了国家行动计划作为 2012 年航空温室气体减排计划的更新,在美国的国家行动计划中不仅包括国际航空还包括了国内航空,其中国内航空将同时受到 UNFCCC 与本国减排计划的约束。美国认为航空运输的减排应强调先进的技术和国家间持续性的协商合作这两个方面,应通过本国相关管理部门、技术部门与航空公司的协作方式,共同推动航空运输低排放、低能源消耗与低噪声发展。③

但在美国的国家行动计划中,却始终未提及其作为航空发达国家应承担的区别责任和对发展中国家的援助和支持。美国作为航空强国,通过加入国际统一减排平台,以全球性对话和国家间合作的方式不仅能够把握国际性减排规则制定的主动权,还能淡化发达国家的历史性航空排放责任。毕竟从累计排放量来看,自 1850 年以来,美国就占与能源相关的二氧化碳排放量的

---

① United States Aviation Greenhouse Gas Emissions Reduction Plan, Chapter1: Background, p. 8.

② United States Aviation Greenhouse Gas Emissions Reduction Plan (2012), 资料来源: https://www.faa.gov/about/office_org/headquarters_offices/apl/environ_policy_guidance/policy/media/Aviation_Greenhouse_Gas_Emissions_Reduction_Plan.pdf, 最后访问日期:2019 年 2 月 7 日。

③ Nathan Richardson, "Aviation, Carbon, and the Clean Air Act", 38 *Colum. J. Envtl. L.* 67, 2013, p. 27.

30%,而中国则仅占7%。虽然发展中国家的排放量正在增加,但预计在今后几十年内其累计排放量都不会达到发达国家的排放总量。① 此外,仅通过美国所提交的国家行动计划,无法对其减排义务的履行起到任何保障作用,如出现美国采取类似于退出《巴黎协定》的方式拒不承担其国家减排责任的情形,凭借美国的国家行动计划不能起到任何约束或监督作用。

3. 航空发展中国家的国家行动计划

(1)印度

印度在其提交的国家行动计划中表示:作为世界人口第二大国的印度在面临着经济持续增长挑战的同时,也拥有全球第九大航空市场,航空产业具有巨大的增长潜力。且印度积极参与国际航空减排活动,尽管《联合国气候变化框架公约》及其议定书并未对作出承诺的国家规定任何约束性内容,但印度仍积极履行其减排义务、参与各项谈判。在此基础上印度认为:共同但有区别的责任应在应对气候变化等相关国际问题上得到公认,若发达国家能积极履行其技术转让等承诺,印度将会在航空减排问题上取得更大的成功。② 印度在其国家计划中强调,国际民航组织应区分发达国家与发展中国家的区别责任,而不是对所有成员国实施相同的标准和要求。发达国家的航空运输市场已经基本稳定且具有较大的市场份额,但发展中国家在市场份额、技术、管理措施与设备等方面都远远落后于发达国家,任何减少或限制排放的措施都有可能对发展中国家的航空发展造成阻碍,发展中国家也并不具有为发达国家所产生的历史排放埋单的义务。对此发达国家应主动承担起责任,《京都议定书》附件一中的航空发达国家应率先对温室气体排放作出实质性的削减并提供财政、技术等支持。③ 印度还认为,在坚持共同但有区

---

① Jeremy Richardson, "Global Warming: Climate Change and the Law Cosponsored by the Environmental Law Institute", SR039 ALI-ABA 1, 2010, p. 8.

② India's Action Plan on Reducing Carbon Emissions from Civil Aviation, chapter 1: introduction, p. 2.

③ India's Action Plan on Reducing Carbon Emissions from Civil Aviation, chapter 1: introduction, p. 5.

别责任原则的基础上，不得变相限制国际贸易的发展与扭曲成员国国内的市场经济。印度指出，航空业废气主要从航空器的排放及地面机场设施两个方面产生，对此印度一方面将定期更新和升级设备，例如，印度航空公司（Air India）购买了波音 787 Dreamliner、订购了 A 320 NEOs 和 B 737 Max，它们所配备的新型技术能够提升燃油效率；另一方面则通过适用可再生能源与改善机场管理措施的方式来减少地面废气的排放。

综上所述，印度的国家行动计划更多地关注于减少国际碳减排措施对本国经济发展与国民生活的不利影响、推动共同但有区别责任原则的指导作用与发达国家援助义务的履行等方面，采取的减排措施则集中于新型设备的购买与先进技术的引进。

（2）中国

我国的国家行动计划载明“共同但有区别的责任”与 UNFCCC 中“各自的能力”原则应被视为解决所有国家航空排放进一步行动的前提和基础。① 发达国家和发展中国家的航空运输发展历史不同，导致发展程度和历史排放量也存在差异。因此在《京都议定书》第 2.2 条、第 2.3 条中也特别强调了附件一中发达国家的减排义务。中国作为世界上最大的发展中国家，在经济发展与人民生活水平的提高方面仍然面临着严峻的挑战，航空运输作为促进经济发展的关键领域，发挥着非常重要的作用。但中国的航空产业不仅起步时间落后于发达国家，而且在市场所占份额与成熟度、技术及运营水平、历史和人均排放量、人均航空出行频率等方面都与发达国家存在差距。尽管如此，我国还将继续坚持限制和减少国际航空排放，并从国际与国内两个方面入手采取减排措施。在国内方面：我国从专门组织的设立、政策的制定、能源效率的提升、航线的优化等多方面入手推进航空减排；此外我国还积极与其他国家、国际组织进行合作，始终秉持着区别责任的承担原则，预计到 2020 年中国的航空燃料消耗率以 2005 年为基线将提高 22%。在中国民航局印发的

① China's Action Plan, Chapter2: The Position to Address the Climate Change, 2.1, p. 7.

《民航节能减排“十三五”规划》中还制定了2020年我国碳强度降低40%～45%的约束性目标。①

现阶段,发达国家与发展中国家围绕气候变化、环境保护与经济发展之间的分歧更加明显,不但国际上已成型的全球性或区域性的航空减排规则标准更倾向于保护发达国家的利益,而且在新能源的开发与先进设备的研究方面发达国家也占据着最有利的地位和最广泛的市场。在航空业高速发展与减排规则越发严格并行的情况下,对于发展中国家来讲无疑是极大的挑战。

三、国际航空减排机制中的法律问题探析

(一)减排措施间的适用冲突

从上文介绍可知,现阶段国际社会上存在多种航空减排措施,除了已经制定的国际公约、协定外,还存在区域性与全球性的减排体系。② 这些措施的建立都是为了限制或减少国际航空排放对气候变化的不利影响,故在实际适用过程中难免会产生冲突和重叠。若不及时解决规则之间的管辖冲突问题,不仅会对减排进程造成阻碍,还会对国际航空运营人带来额外的减排压力与负担,甚至会对发展中国家的航空产业带来巨大的打击。

1. 全球性与区域性减排规则之间的适用冲突

现阶段国际社会上不仅存在区域性减排体系(例如,欧盟的ETS)同时也存在着国际统一的减排规则(例如,ICAO的CORSIA减排计划),在这种情形下就会出现部分参加全球性抵消计划的成员方同时也是区域性减排计划缔约国的现象,在该成员国或该区域内也会随之产生双重适用的问题。③ 以EU ETS与CORSIA为例,当一架欧盟国家的航班从法国飞往德国时,其整个航程都位于欧盟境内,欧盟的ETS自然会依其规定对该架航班进行约束,但

① 参见《民航节能减排“十三五”规划》,载中国民航局网:http://www.caac.gov.cn/XXGK/XXGK/FZGH/201704/t20170405_43506.html,最后访问日期:2019年2月8日。

② ICAO, Regulatory and Organizational Framework to Address Aviation Emissions, 2017, p. 3.

③ IATA, Fact sheet: CORSIA & carbon pricing, 2018, p. 1.

同时国际民航组织的 CORSIA 抵消计划作为全球性的航空减排规则对于该架次的航班也当然的具有管辖权。[①] 尽管 ICAO 在第 39 届大会中强调了成员国对于制定单一性全球航空减排体系的支持,以及对分散的国家或地区市场性措施的反对,[②]但起飞地和目的地都位于欧盟境内的欧盟航班由 EU ETS 进行管辖似乎更具有正当性和合理性。

实际上,ICAO 的国际航空减排规则覆盖全球范围,故需要更多地考虑到不同国家间的发展差异,尽可能地减少减排措施对发展中国家国内市场的扭曲,所以在 ICAO 的国际航空减排措施中不仅坚持了"共同但有区别责任"原则,还规定了两个自愿加入阶段作为过渡期。而相较于全球性的减排规则,区域性的减排措施则更贴近于该区域的实际发展水平。以欧盟为例,EU ETS 规则相较于 ICAO 的 CORSIA 抵消计划来讲,减排要求更为严格,规则的设计也更贴合欧洲国际航空产业的整体发展水平。所以当欧盟国家的航空运营人在欧盟境内的国际航班面临区域性与全球性减排规则的适用冲突时,不妨在遵守 CORSIA 减排规则的基础上适用更为严格、更符合区域经济发展水平的 EU ETS 规则。这样的适用程序,一方面,并不会造成对 CORSIA 减排框架的违反;另一方面,适用更为严格的区域性减排规则也更有利于限制国际航空对气候变化的不利影响、更大程度上尊重了该区域国家的意志自由。这种应对措施也可同样适用于其他区域性与全球性减排措施之间的适用冲突中,在满足全球性减排要求的基础上允许对该区域的国际航班运营人适用标准更高的区域性减排规则,不仅更符合该区域内航空经济的整体发展水平,还能最大限度地推动国际航空减排的实施效果。但是,这就要求区域性减排措施满足国际统一减排方案的基本要求,来确保其作为符合基础规定的更严格的减排规则。

---

① Joanne Scott, Lavanya Rajamani, "EU Climate Change Unilateralism", *Eur J. Int Law*, 2012, p. 3.

② ICAO, Assembly Resolution A39 – 3.

2. 国际公约与全球性减排机制之间的冲突

除了区域性与全球性减排机制之间会产生适用冲突以外,国际公约、协定与全球性减排规则在适用过程中也会产生冲突问题。① 国际公约与全球性减排机制的适用范围都为整个国际社会、适用对象都为主权国家,且两者之间并不存在上下层关系,若一个国家在作为国际减排公约缔约国的基础上又参加了单一性的全球减排体系,那么这两种减排措施实际上都可以对该国发生效力,对于该国家来讲就可能需要履行两种不同的减排义务、承担两种不同的减排责任,这种由于减排措施之间欠缺有效的协调机制而产生的重复适用问题,对于缔约国来讲明显是不公平、不合理的。对此,可以通过以下方式进行协调:具体又分为同源性与非同源性两类,在同源性减排规则之间,可以通过规则制定主体的从属关系来确定具体的适用方式,以《巴黎协定》与CORSIA 减排计划为例:英国和美国都既为《巴黎协定》的缔约国又参加了ICAO 的 CORSIA 抵消计划,在针对这两国或这两国之间的航空活动进行规制时可以适用 UNFCCC 的相关规定,毕竟 ICAO 的国际航空减排活动仍需受到 UNFCCC 框架的制约;而针对仅参加了 CORSIA 减排计划或仅为《巴黎协定》缔约国的国家而言则不存在这样的问题,只需以其参加的减排规则进行约束即可。但是在非同源性规则之间,由于不同减排规则的制定主体之间并无从属性关系或减排主体双方各自参加了不同的减排规则的情形下,规则之间制定有效的适用方案应该是最可行的解决方式。

(二)国际航空减排体系的规划

对于未来国际航空减排的模式选择方面,首先需要明确构建全球统一减排机制的优势性:一方面,由于区域性规则在构建过程中更多的是以本区域内的航空经济发展水平作为参考来设计与之匹配的减排方案;另一方面,则是因为区域性的措施相较于全球统一减排方案而言(例如,CORSIA 抵消计

① Katherine, Bechina John, The EPA's Endangerment Finding on Aircraft Greenhouse Gas Emissions: A Preliminary Analysis, *Journal of Air Law and Commerce*, 2017, p. 10.

划)，缺乏成员方之间的配合与协作，不仅很难及时获取不同国家最新的减排信息并依此对减排方式和减排手段进行调整和完善，还容易因为缺乏体系而产生碎片化、内部规则冲突等问题。[①] 但是，在建构全球性单一减排规则的过程中也需要面临一系列的法律问题，以下将进行具体介绍。

1. 共同但有区别的责任与无歧视适用原则之间的平衡

根据上文所介绍的国家行动计划可知，在如何构建全球减排机制方面发达国家与发展中国家之间存在较大的观点差异，[②]其中发达国家认为应更多的实现规则的无歧视适用，确保减排要求的推进与减排目标的实现；[③]而与之相对的发展中国家则认为应始终坚持“共同但有区别责任”原则的基础地位，更多地强调发达国家的优先责任和援助义务。[④] 对此，笔者认为构建全球性国际航空减排规则应坚持“共同但有区别的责任”原则，充分考虑各国尤其是航空发展中国家的特殊情况，尽可能避免对其国内经济市场产生扭曲。[⑤] 因为发展中国家才是当前航空经济发展的主力军与航空器温室气体排放的主要来源，若减排规则无视广大发展中国家的发展需求与发展实际，不仅很难得到航空发展大国的支持与执行，无法实现预期的减排目标外，还不利于带动整个航空产业的发展，甚至会对国际贸易造成阻碍。而从另一个层面来讲，现阶段国际航空运输对气候环境所产生的不利后果在很大程度上是由航空发达国家造成的，从发展中国家现阶段的排放量与排放速度来讲，其在未来几十年内也很难达到发达国家的历史排放总量。若是在国际航空减排框架中迫使发展中国家在相同的标准下与发达国家承

---

① 参见杨万柳：《国际航空排放全球治理的国际视域——以国际民航组织为中心》，载《北京理工大学学报》(社会科学版)2015 年第 4 期。

② See Beatriz Martinez Romera, Harro van Asselt, “The International Regulation of Aviation Emissions: Putting Differential Treatment into Practice”, *J Environmental Law*, 2015, p. 8.

③ See Annie Petsonk, Pedro Piris-Cabezas, “Bridging the Allocation Gap in the ICAO MBM: A New Proposal”, *Carbon & Climate Law Review*, 2016, p. 3.

④ See Jae Woon Lee, “Book Reviews: Greenhouse Gas Emission from International Aviation: Legal and Policy Challenges”, *Asian Journal of International Law*, 2016, p. 386.

⑤ 参见史玉：《国际航空排放全球共同治理机制构建》，载《国际论坛》2012 年第 3 期。

担相同的责任,那么对于发展中国家来讲是十分不公平的,因为责任的主要承担主体本就不应该为发展中国家。① 即便采取有区别的责任承担方式,尽可能地减少对发展中国家航空经济的限制和压力,当前国际航空对气候环境带来的不利影响也将远小于发达国家国际航空过去对全球气候所造成的危害后果。

但是,为了促使更多的发达国家能够参与到减排体系中,带动减排进程、最大限度的实现减排目标,在照顾发展中国家国内经济的同时,也应考虑发达国家的诉求。《京都议定书》的失败、美国退出《巴黎协定》等,在很大层面上都是由于发达国家不愿意承担主要的减排责任以及对发展中国家的援助义务。② 那么,在今后国际航空减排规则的制定与完善过程中,就可以在"区别责任"的基础上,通过允许发达国家承诺援助义务或以"过渡期"、减排义务的多种履行(例如,发达国家对发展中国家的援助行为也可以视作减排义务的履行)等方式,让发达国家在履行优先减排义务的前提下享有充分的自主选择权和灵活性;与此同时,也可以在充分考虑每个国家实际情况的基础上对发展中国家采取设立"过渡期"或监测航空业整体发展水平的方式,逐步增加其减排义务的承担,缩小发达国家与发展中国家之间的责任差距,最后实现全球统一标准的减排规则。

2. CORSIA 与 UNFCCC 减排单位的一致

除了由于减排规则之间欠缺有效的实施协议而产生的适用冲突容易对缔约国或国际航班的运营人造成加重其义务和负担的双重适用问题外,各规则内减排要求和减排单位的差异性也会对参加两种或两种以上减排规则的缔约主体的国际航班运营人产生重复约束、多重施压的问题。③ 在上文提到

---

① See Michael Byers, Kelsey Franks, Andrew Gage, "The Internationalization of Climate Changes Litigation", 7 *Wash. J. Envtl. L. & Pol'y* 264, 2017, p. 17.

② See Maria L. Banda, "The Bottom-Up Alternative: The Mitigation Potential of Private Climate Governance After the Paris Agreement", 42 *Harv. Envlt. L. Rev.* 326, 2018, p. 31.

③ See Rafael Grillo Avila, Michaael Wolosin, *REDD + in ICAO: Ready for Takeoff*, Carbon & Climate L. Rev. 134, 2016, p. 4.

的印度尼西亚向 ICAO 提交的国家适用声明中重点强调了 ICAO GMBM 计划中符合标准的排放单位(Emission Units Criteria,EUC)应与 UNFCCC 规则中的保持一致。① 因为现阶段 ICAO 仅公布了《CORSIA 排放单位要求标准》的文件,而《CORSIA 满足要求的排放单位》还尚未公布,但 EUC 中至少会包括自愿减排和义务减排两个部分,在履行其义务性减排后缔约方可自愿完成进一步的减排工作,故我们对自愿排放部分可暂且不论。但在国际社会存在多种减排规则且未达成统一排放单位的情形下,义务部分的履行就很有可能产生双重计算(double counting)、双重发放(double issuance)以及双重主张(double claiming)的问题。在 ICAO 近期公布的《CORSIA 排放单位要求标准》中也针对上述问题进行了专门规定。② 根据 UNFCCC 项下《巴黎协定》第 4.2 条的规定,国家应编制、通报并保持国家自主贡献,进而采取国内减缓措施来实现贡献目标;③同时通过第 14 条"全球盘点"的方式实现监督履行情况的目的。④《巴黎协定》中规定,一些缔约国将会通过国际合作和减缓成果的转让方式来实现国家贡献,故应特别注意避免重复核算情形的发生。⑤ 进一步来看,即便通过 UNFCCC 框架与 ICAO《CORSIA 排放单位要求标准》所制定的严格的核算程序、独立的核算机构以及完善的信息公布和监督机制等方式避免了在各自减排规则下的重复适用问题,但是相同的减排单位却仍可能既在 UNFCCC《巴黎协定》的规则下由国家作为其自主贡献履行的一部分,同时又在 CORSIA 抵消计划中作为国际航班运营人所抵消的减排单位,因为在各规则之间尚未达成畅通的信息共享机制。即使通过独立的核算机构和全面的监测程序最大限度地避免了上述情形的发生,但会大大加重国家或运营人的减排负担:我们假设《巴黎协定》和 CORSIA 所要求的排放量都

---

① 资料来源:https://www.icao.int/Meetings/a39/Documents/WP/wp_211_rev1_en.pdf,最后访问日期:2019 年 2 月 1 日。

② ICAO,CORSIA Emission Unit Eligibility Criteria,Accessed April 3,2019. https://www.icao.int/environmental-protection/CORSIA/Documents/ICAO%20document%2009.pdf.

③ 《巴黎协定》第 4 条。

④ 《巴黎协定》第 14 条。

⑤ 《巴黎协定》第 6.2 条和第 6.4 条。

为A,那么,在《巴黎协定》项下国家只需履行A即可,但是当CORSIA出现后,由于《巴黎协定》与CORSIA之间欠缺统一的排放单位和相互承认机制,所以在满足《巴黎协定》所要求A值的同时还需要履行CORSIA所要求的A值,虽然在单个减排规则中排放要求仍然为A,但实际上国际航班的运营人履行了2A的义务量,这将大大增加国际航空运营人的减排压力,毕竟UNFCCC也是CORSIA抵消单位的供应来源。国际航空运输协会(International Air Transport Association,IATA)认为在这方面ICAO实际上已经超出了自己的职权范围,[①]UNFCCC应尽快提供一个明确的指导,以便有效的解决不同减排规则之间的重复计算问题。[②]

(三)国际航空减排规则的适用

即便国际民用航空减排规则在制定时尽可能地考虑发展中国家和发达国家间的不同利益,通过发达国家的自愿履行与发展中国家的自愿加入机制以及设立“过渡期”等方式,尽可能地将限制或减少国际航空排放对缔约国国内经济所造成的不利影响最小化,促使缔约国积极参加减排计划并履行其抵消义务。但是就采取国际规则的间接适用与非自动执行方法的国家而言,只有经过本国国内法的制定与补充,国际航空减排规则才能对该国实际发挥作用。而各国在对国际减排规则进行转化时,可能倾向于将规则调整为更符合本国实际主张或对本国国际航空发展更有利的模式。

1. 国际规则的生效与国内规则的制定

当国家提交从一开始就自愿加入CORSIA抵消计划的声明时,也就意味着该国认可CORSIA抵消计划对本国及本国国际航班运营人的航空减排活动产生约束效力,同意适用CORISA抵消计划。那么,是否需要将其转化为缔约国的国内规范进行适用以及所转化的国内规范是否必须与ICAO规定

① IATA, An Airline Handbook on CORSIA, 2018, p. 30.

② 资料来源:https://www.iata.org/policy/environment/Documents/paper-doublecounting.pdf,最后访问日期:2019年2月1日。

的完全相同，这些问题都可能在实际适用的过程中产生。从各国实践来看，国际条约在国内的适用主要通过两种方式—并入（又称直接适用）与转化（又称间接适用）。[①] 转化是指需要将国际规则的内容转化为国内法并将其纳入国内法律体系中；并入则是指将国际条约作为本国国内法的一部分而直接适用。[②] 但在实践中，并入常常又被区分为自动执行和非自动执行，非自动执行一般还需要经国内法进行补充后方能适用。[③] 可见，除了国际条约并入方式下的自动执行外，非自动执行及间接适用都需要补充或制定国内法。在这样的情形下可能会产生一定的时间差，即国际条约应当发挥作用与实际发挥作用之间的时间间隔。根据 ICAO 官方网站最新公布的数据来看，目前已经有 78 个国家表示自愿从一开始就加入 CORSIA 抵消计划，111 个国家已经提交了国家行动计划。而通过 A39－3 所规定的内容来看，CORSIA 抵消计划的试行阶段将从 2021 年开始启动，按照规定从 2021 年开始自愿加入 CORSIA 试行阶段及在国家行动计划中明确表示支持 CORSIA 规则的成员国的国际航班就应该受到 CORSIA 抵消计划的约束了，但是在实践中采取自动执行方式的国家毕竟是少数，大多数国家仍然采用非自动执行或是间接适用的方式。因此，当国内法补充完成或是制定出对应的国内法之前的这段时间，自愿执行 CORSIA 的成员国的国际航班运营人的减排措施应如何适用？若是直接适用 CORSIA 的规定，那实际上就采用了自动执行的方式，这又与该国所坚持的国际条约适用原则相悖；但若不直接适用 CORSIA，又与该国所提交的一开始就自愿加入 CORSIA 抵消计划的声明不符。对于如何化解这个两难问题，实际上可以借鉴美国的做法，美国专门为此制定了自愿协议（U. S. Voluntary Agreement）：美国联邦航空管理局将宣布一项自愿协议方

---

① 参见万鄂湘、余晓汉：《国际条约适用于国内无涉外因素的民事关系探析》，载《中国法学》2018 年第 5 期。

② See Hannah Chang，"International Executive Agreements on Climate Change"，35 *Colum. J. Envtl. L.* 337，2010，p. 6.

③ 参见吴晓明、罗曼：《浅析国际人权条约在中国的适用问题》，载《沈阳工业大学》2018 年第 1 期。

法,依据该自愿协议国际航班的运营人应遵守ICAO附件16卷4的内容,直到国内通过相关的立法,根据协议的规定超过90%的运营人所产生的排放将被纳入其中,但业内人士估计仍将有至少95%的覆盖率,且根据附件16卷4与美国自愿协议的规定来看,FAA也会对未提交排放数据的运营人的排放值进行估计,来弥补数据的空白和差距。实际上,美国这种通过自愿协议来解决由于时间间隔而产生的国际规则适用问题的方式具有很强的借鉴意义,在不能直接适用国际条约又欠缺相应国内法的情形下,制定这种自愿适用国际条约的协议不失为一个好办法。

2. 国际规则的转化与调整

国际条约的转化除了会产生上述问题外,还有可能产生另一个方面的问题:在将国际条约、国际规范转化为国内立法时,除了已经明确提出保留的部分,对不允许保留或未提出保留的部分,是否可以在满足规则、条约宗旨和目的的前提下,将不适合或不太适合本国实际情况的条文进行适当修改。当国际条约与本国国内法相冲突时,部分国家采取和谐解释原则,通过对法律的解释消除两者之间的冲突。① 但是,和谐解释原则能否在国际航空减排领域进行适用,如果可以适用解释的程度和范围又是多少?实际上在1944年《芝加哥公约》中就已经对该问题进行了简要的规定,《芝加哥公约》第37条规定了国际标准及程序的采用:缔约国在其所承允的规章、标准和程序范围内,应尽力求得可行的最高程度的一致。② 可见,当成员国已经采纳了国际标准的情形下,保持其在国内适用最大限度的一致性才是符合法律要求的。但是紧接着第38条就规定了背离国际标准和程序的“差异申报”制度:③任何国家认为上述国际标准和程序不能在一切方面遵守或是不能使本国的规章制度完全符合国际标准和程序时,对国际标准进行的修改应立即通知国际民航组织;此外当国际标准本身已经进行了更新和修改的情形下,任何国家未及

① 参见丁亮:《国际条约在我国的适用效力和实施问题》,郑州大学2005年硕士学位论文,第7页。

② 《芝加哥公约》第37条。

③ 《芝加哥公约》第38条。

时修改本国的国内规章和措施时，应于国际标准修正案通过后的60日内及时通知理事会。这实际上又构成了第37条的例外情形。① 以中国为例，除了我国所提交的对A39 – WP/529号文件中关于ICAO减排措施的强制约束力和A39 – WP/530号文件“决定使用EUC要求的排放单位”两部分的保留声明外，其他部分在适用过程中还能否为了贴合本国的发展实际进行一定程度的调整，根据《芝加哥公约》第38条的规定，实际上是允许成员国进行一定程度的修改的，但是在实际运用中还应考虑到国际航空减排问题本身的特殊性，以ICAO的CORSIA减排计划为例：

虽然ICAO的CORSIA抵消计划在坚持“共同但有区别责任”原则的同时，还在抵消计划第二阶段的适用条件上采用了无歧视的统一标准作为补充，且在此基础上有大量发达国家与发展中国家表示从一开始就自愿加入CORSIA抵消计划或向ICAO提交了其国家行动计划。但是，不同国家基于其本国航空产业的实际发展程度和发展特点对如何适用减排规则仍然持有不同的观点：以欧盟为代表的航空发达国家认为应以减排规则的无歧视适用为主；而以印度、中国为代表的航空发展中国家则表示，应确保区别责任原则的基础性地位。可见，不同国家在对国际减排规则进行适用时很有可能根据本国的具体主张在不违反其宗旨和目的的前提下进行一定的调整，使之更符合本国的发展实际。而这在国际航空减排领域下，实际上是不利于减排目标实现的。况且，若允许缔约国在适用过程中根据本国的实际需求对国际规则进行调整或修改的话，也很有可能会产生缔约国借此“规避”CORSIA减排义务的现象。

ICAO项下CORSIA抵消计划的试行阶段与第一阶段都设定为自愿参加的方式，缔约国可根据本国航空产业的实际发展水平决定参加与否；且在第二阶段专门针对最不发达国家、小岛屿发展中国家、内陆发展中国家以及低水平的国际航空活动规定了豁免，故缔约国没理由再对CORSIA抵消计划作出修

① Pamela Campos, “Compliance Tools for a Global Market Based Measure for International Aviation”, *Carbon & Climate Law Review*, 2016, p. 5.

改和调整。但是因为本国国内经济发生重大变化或是出现其他难以预料的情形，导致完全依据CORSIA抵消计划的规定对本国国际航班运营人进行约束是不合理、不公平的以及具备豁免资格或在CORSIA试行阶段、第一阶段自愿加入的缔约国发现在适用过程中对本国的经济发展造成了严重的阻碍且产生或可能产生无法控制的不利后果等特殊情形下，可以向ICAO提交暂时或长期修改国际减排规则的申请并说明理由，由ICAO进行审查并作出决定，待障碍消除后再进行恢复。实际上，这种方法与《芝加哥公约》的规定大体一致。

3. 减排义务履行的约束和监督

通过上文介绍可知，无论是国际公约、协定还是多边减排规则都缺乏对义务履行的监督和保障机制，虽然通过自下而上的国家承诺方式能够较大程度地取得发达国家与发展中国家的认可，但是对减排义务的履行与减排目的的实现却无法提供有效的保障，难以发挥预期效果；相反，若采取自上而下的强制性约束方式将缔约国的减排义务通过法律形式明确的规定出来，又可能会产生类似于《京都议定书》那样的尴尬局面。对此，不妨参考美国在解决国际规则的适用时所采取的签订自愿履行协议的方式，鼓励各国尤其是航空发达国家积极签订减排义务的履行协议，给予其充分的自主权以决定参加与否以及签订何种要求的减排协议；但在签订后的实施层面则更偏重于自上而下的履行约束模式，强调督促缔约国履行所签协议中的减排义务，设置完善的配套监督程序。[①] 此外，还可以鼓励各主权国家与专门性的国际组织（如ICAO）签订自愿履行协议或通过各国国家部门与本国国际航班运营人之间以及各国家之间以双边、区域的形式签订减排协议，从多种渠道共同推动减排义务的实际履行。

4. 国际减排规则的退出

2017年6月美国总统特朗普明确宣布退出《巴黎协定》，这个决定将直接增大全球应对气候变化的资金缺口，动摇世界各国应对气候变化的决心，

① See Nathan Richardson, "Trading Unmoored: The Uncertain Legal Foundation for Emissions Trading Under § 111 of the Clean Air Act", 120 *Penn St. L. Rev.* 181, 2015, p. 20.

迟滞全球低碳技术的革新。[①] 不仅如此,美国在《巴黎协定》下所承诺的减排义务也将无法实现。[②] 特朗普退出《巴黎协定》的本质原因则是美国不愿承担在"共同但有区别责任"原则下发达国家所应履行的减排责任和援助义务,认为这与其坚持的经济优先发展原则不符。基于此也引出了一个法律问题:总统是否有权力将国会排除在条约的退出或终止执行程序之外单方面作出决定,尤其是涉及环境保护等关乎世界未来发展内容的国际条约。这与镜像原则[③]不同,毕竟这些协议或条约最初投入了相当大的立法资源。[④] 即使曾经有过总统单方面终止国际协定的先例,但如此重要的问题如果过分依赖于几十年前的案例[⑤]也是不合适的,[⑥]况且两者的性质也根本不同。若美国允许仅凭如此草率的方式就可以退出国际减排公约的话,那不仅是《巴黎协定》,就连美国向 ICAO 提交的国家行动计划中承诺的减排义务与其自愿加入 CORSIA 抵消计划后所应承担的减排责任都将无法得到保障,因为在 CORSIA 抵消计划中也明确了"共同但有区别的责任"原则以及发达国家对发展中国家的支持和援助义务。美国若不及时对退出机制进行严格规制的话,将无法确保美国总统不会在未来单方面退出或宣布不履行在 CORSIA 项下的减排义务,即便出现这种情况无论是美国本国还是整个国际社会也都欠缺可以及时采取补救或惩罚措施的相应机制,这项要求也同样适用于除美国以外的其他国家。

---

① 参见罗丽香、高志宏:《美国退出〈巴黎协定〉的影响和中国应对研究》,载《江苏社会科学》2018 年第 5 期。

② See Victoria A. Arroyo, Climate Change, Sustainable Development, and Ecosystems 2016 Annual Report, SZ014 ALI-ABA 207, 2018, p. 3.

③ 镜像原则,即宪法要求退出任何特定协定的国会参与程度应于首次加入该协定时所要求的国会参与程度相一致。

④ See Harold Hongju Koh, "Presidential Power to Terminate International Agreements", 128 *Yale L. J. F* 432, 2018, p. 4.

⑤ The Court's Decision in Goldwater v. Carter.

⑥ See Harold Hongju Koh, "Presidential Power to Terminate International Agreements", 128 *Yale L. J. F* 432, 2018, p. 5.

四、中国航空减排的对策和法治化进路

中国作为世界上人口最多、规模最大的发展中国家,其航空经济的发展也十分迅速,同时航空运输产业在推动我国贸易发展、提升我国经济水平方面发挥着重要作用,但从另一个方面来讲我国也将承担更为繁重的减排任务与国际责任。2014 年 11 月 11 日我国在与美国的联合声明中表示:预计到 2030 年左右我国将实现二氧化碳的排放峰值,并尽最大努力提前实现这一峰值,且准备在 2030 年将非化石燃料的消耗比例提升 20%,[①]此外我国在 2016 年 G20 杭州峰会中也明确表示将继续为应对全球气候变化问题不懈努力。但是正如《民航节能减排"十三五"规划》所述,我国仍存在意识淡薄、基础工作薄弱以及人才匮乏、提升难度大等问题。综上所述,缓解减排压力、完善管理机制、强化法律指导、加强国际合作将是我国未来的主要任务。

(一)中国应对国际多边航空减排机制的对策

1. 国内航空碳交易机制的建立

碳交易准确来说是"碳排放权"的交易,[②]最早体现在《京都议定书》中,首先由政府确定并分配温室气体的排放总量,其次由各企业之间通过市场交易的方式自发的形成碳排放权分配和碳价格的最优模式。根据蒙哥马利(Montgomery)的研究,排放权交易方式可以实现最低的减排成本,且富有可操作性。[③] 我国从 2011 年起就开展了碳排放交易的试点工作,并批准了北京市、天津市、上海市、重庆市、深圳市、湖北省和广东省作为排放权交易的试点

---

① See Kristina Daugirdas, Julian Davis Mortenson, "United States and China make joint announcement to reduce greenhouse gas emissions, bolstering multilateral climate change negotiations", *American Journal of International Law*, January, 2015, p. 2.

② International Carbon Action Partnership, "Emission trading in practice: A Handbook on Design and Implementation", 2016, p. 16.

③ 参见荆克迪:《中国碳市场交易的机制设计与国际比较研究》,南开大学 2014 年博士学位论文,第 30 页。

地区。① 随着交易经验的不断积累,我国于2017年12月印发了《全国碳排放权交易市场建设方案(发电行业)》,该方案标志着全国碳市场的建立。但是在该方案中规定:在碳市场的建设初期,交易主体仅为发电行业年度排放达到2.6万吨二氧化碳当量(综合能源消费量约为1万吨标准煤)及以上的企业或者经济组织。② 可见航空产业并未被纳入该排放交易市场当中,但是在国际社会上航空减排规则已经初具规模,若不尽快构建国内航空碳减排规则、培养国内航空企业的减排意识和减排能力的话,将不利于我国航空产业未来的发展。

2. 构建国内航空排放碳排放监测核查体系(MRV)制度

我国作为世界上碳排放最多的国家之一,本就应注重排放数据监测结果的准确性,且ICAO的CORSIA抵消计划也要求所有承担航空运行任务的国家无论是否自愿加入试行阶段都应在规定的时间内建立MRV系统,作为飞机运营商的抵消和减排基础。所以国内MRV体系的构建应主要集中在:信息的获取和收集,即建立透明的排放数据报告制度;监测和核查的准确性,即确保排放数据的真实性两个方面。对此,我国可以通过建立透明的排放报告机制、设立独立的排放监测核查机构等方式,确保国内MRV制度的有效实施。

3. 完善排放配额的分配和价格调节机制

在我国现阶段所建立的碳交易市场中,主要通过行业基准和历史强度下降这两种方式确定排放配额。其中,对于耗能较高的产业可采用基于当年实际产量的行业基准法,而对于其他产业则可采取以历史排放强度等数据确定配额的历史强度法。③ 而航空产业则主要通过历史排放数据来确定具体的

---

① See Huizhen Chen, "Inspection and Enforcement in Chinese Carbon Emissions Trading: Progress, Problems, and Prospect", 44 *ELR* 10596, 2014, p. 1.

② 中华人民共和国发展与改革委员会:《全国碳排放权交易市场建设方案(发电行业)》,第4页。

③ 参见《我国为什么要建设全国碳市场》,载中国碳排放交易网:http://www.tanpaifang.com/tanguwen/2019/0108/62786_4.html,最后访问日期:2019年4月1日。

分配数额,这也再次强调了确保排放数据准确监测的重要性。另外,国内碳交易价格的确定可根据我国发展实际采用:以市场调节为主、政府管控为辅的方式:主要通过市场运行对价格进行自主调节,只有在出现因碳价格过高或过低而影响正常交易的情形时,政府才会出面通过发放或回收配额的方式进行调节。①

4. 加强对减排主体义务履行的监管

相较于全球性减排规则而言,在国内实施减排措施更容易对责任主体的义务履行状况进行监管。我国的碳交易措施主要通过中央政府、地方政府与企业三方主体开展:由中央政府制定总目标、确定分配总量;地方政府则主要负责具体的分配与落实工作;最后由运营人履行排放义务、清缴排放配额。②所以,加强中央、地方政府与企业之间的领导与监督关系,尤其是地方政府与各减排主体之间的联系十分重要,对此可以通过签订履行协议与提交定期报告等手段确保减排义务的履行。减排责任主体的义务履行决定了减排目标的实现,只有在构建国内航空减排机制时,加强中央政府的整体调控与地方政府的具体监督作用,才能最大限度地确保航空运营人减排义务的实际履行。

5. 促进国家间减排体系的合作与对接

正是由于航空业所具有的全球性特征,故仅通过单个国家的力量不可能实现航空产业的减排工作,也不可能不受到其他国家减排规则的影响。例如,根据CORSIA全球碳抵消计划的要求,我国国际航班所产生的二氧化碳排放数据也将被提交至ICAO并受到CORSIA计划的监管,所以我国在构建航空碳交易市场的过程中应加强与其他国家碳市场的对接与合作。通过不同国家间碳交易机制的合作,不仅能够解决未来在实施过程中可能出现的适

---

① Sarah E. Light, "The New Insider Trading: Environmental Markets within the Firm", 34 *Stan. Envtl. L. J.* 3, 2015, p. 4.

② 杨涛、李艳梅:《航空运输业碳交易机制的理论研究》,载中国环境科学学会编:《中国环境科学学术年会论文集》,中国环境科学出版社2010年版,第1177页。

用冲突问题、扩大碳交易规则的涵盖范围、促进减排目标的实现,[①]对于发展中国家来讲还能在对接过程中借鉴航空发达国家的先进技术和经验,最重要的是建立国家之间的碳交易合作机制还能最大限度地推动减排义务的履行。[②] 但是,这种合作毕竟要以国家间利益的协调一致为基础,所以可先从原则性规范入手通过协商交流的形式分阶段逐步实施。

(二)中国航空减排的法治化路径

我国航空减排领域始终缺乏统一的排放立法进行指导,不仅 2018 年修正的《民用航空法》中未进行规定,在民航局印发的《民航节能减排"十三五"规划》中对航空排放的统一立法问题也未进行明确,仅表示将会落实气候变化的相关法律法规。此外,生态环境部也表示即将出台的全国碳排放权交易管理条例和配套的管理办法前期也仅规制以发电行业为主的碳排放权交易,随着各方面条件的成熟才会进一步考虑扩展到其他行业,并以此落实《巴黎协定》、推动低碳转型。但是,包括《巴黎协定》在内的整个 UNFCCC 体系都十分注重对航空排放的限制问题,且在国际社会上对航空减排领域产生了重要影响,[③]此外航空产业的碳排放相较于其他产业来讲具有全球性和高增长性,所以更需要建立统一的航空排放立法来进行规制;[④]上文所介绍的碳排放交易体系的运行与排放信息的获取以及监测、报告和核查程序的实施都需要完善的国内法律来进行保障。因此,制定统一的减排法律是我国现阶段进行航空减排工作的关键。

---

① 参见黄以天:《国际碳交易机制的演进与前景》,载《上海交通大学学报》(哲学社会科学版)2016 年第 1 期。

② See James Chapman, "Linking a United States Greenhouse Gas Cap-and-Trade System and the European Union's Emissions Trading Scheme", 11 *Vt. J. Envtl. L.* 45, 2009, p. 24.

③ See Victoria A. Arroyo, "Chapter 25: Climate Change, Sustainable Development, and Ecosystems 2016 Annual Report", SZ014 ALI-ABA 207, 2018, p. 3.

④ 参见李汝义:《航空碳排放的法律规制:域外经验与中国实践》,载《武大国际法评论》2018 年第 4 期。

1. 减排规则的法律地位

进行统一的航空减排立法首先需要解决的就是法律定位问题,具体来讲,就是对航空减排规则在国内法律体系中的地位及其所发挥作用的界定问题。航空减排规则的定位规划需要结合航空运输产业的发展实际:我国作为航空发展大国,航空运输产业在推动我国经济增长中发挥着重要的作用,过于苛刻的温室气体减排规则不仅不利于该产业进一步的发展甚至会限制国内经济的整体增长;另外,我国在航空减排领域尚处于适应和探索阶段,减排措施的选择、减排对象的明确及减排体系的构建工作仍未完成,在这样的情形下制定过于详细的减排规则反而不符合当下的发展实际。因此,我国可采取先制定宏观、综合的减排规则,再根据各运营人的实际减排状况逐步进行细化的分阶段的方式,确保减排规则与产业发展水平相适应,尽可能地在维持航空产业发展速度的基础上开展减排工作。①

而从另外一个方面来说,航空产业相较于其他产业本就具有特殊性,因此在碳减排领域其他产业的标准和要求也未必适合航空运输产业,况且当下我国所建立的碳交易规则以及即将出台的碳交易管理条例也并未将航空产业包含在内。因此,针对航空产业进行专门立法,制定一个独立、完整的航空减排规则在现阶段更符合我国实际,同时也能为我国航空运输产业的绿色发展提供更为优质的法律环境。

2. 航空减排规则的内容设计

航空减排措施的选择、减排进程的安排以及碳交易市场的建构等都是进行航空减排工作的重要组成部分,因此在立法时也需要对此进行规制;另外在立法的制定过程中还要充分考虑不同地区航空产业之间的发展差异,以及企业的竞争地位和对风险的承受能力,②并将"区别责任"原则作为减排规则构建的前提和基础。当下,我国航空产业虽然处于高速发展阶段但与航空发

① 参见朱瑜、刘勇:《欧盟碳排放交易新政、国际航空减排谈判与中国对策研究》,载《国际论坛》2014 年第 6 期。

② 《建设统一碳市场需要制度创新》,载中国清洁发展机制网:http://cdm. ccchina. org. cn/Detail. aspx? newsId = 70195&TId = 1,最后访问日期:2019 年 4 月 4 日。

达国家相比仍存在很大的差距；除此之外，由于地理位置等原因我国不同地区航空产业之间的发展也不平衡，因此在制定规则时可采取分区域考量的方式，充分考虑不同地区之间航空运输的发展差异。在立法初期可以将减排规则和减排标准设置的较为缓和、宽松，留给国内航空运输产业充足的发展空间和适应时间。

而在具体的义务履行与责任分配方面，我国在立法过程中可以采取强制规定与鼓励措施相结合的方式，并在此基础上针对个别责任主体的履行状况附加一定的罚款、扶持或税费减免措施。例如，韩国为了保证减排措施的有效实施、缓解航空运营人在减排初期的减排责任，将从 2018 年开始逐步增大免费配额的分配，并在适当条件下启用 100% 的免费配额分配方式，在此基础上还专门设立了统一的主管部门，实现制度层面上的充分保障。① 韩国的减排机制，在排放总量的设置、排放配额的分配、义务履行时长等方面通过提升排放总量、增加免费配额比例，以及延长义务履行时间的方式，尽可能在促进我国航空产业绿色发展的同时缓解航空运营人的减排压力，毕竟我国未来的航空减排还要受到以 CORSIA 抵消计划为主的国际航空减排规则的约束，但尽早制定统一的国内减排立法则有利于我国航空产业快速满足国际减排的要求和标准。

3. 航空减排的立法保障

我国在制定航空减排立法时除了需要注重划定减排标准与分摊减排责任的内容外，还需要对减排义务履行的监督和奖惩、税费的征收以及纠纷的法律解决等程序性内容进行规定。在航空减排领域，国内规则相较于国际规则来讲更容易对责任主体进行监督和约束，也更方便根据义务的实际履行状况实施奖惩或税费的征收和减免措施。例如，日本在其本国的碳减排体系中

---

① Korea EU ETS，http://eng. me. go. kr/eng/web/index. do? menuId = 76，最后访问日期：2019 年 4 月 4 日。

就明确规定,未按照要求遵守减排目标的义务履行方需要缴纳巨额罚款。①因此,我国的航空减排规则也可根据责任主体减排义务的实际履行状况采取税收的减免或罚金的征收等措施,毕竟税费和罚金对于航空运营人来讲也是一笔不小的支出。

最后,航空减排法律的制定必然要涉及对争议和纠纷的解决问题。在适用航空减排立法的过程中,两个或两个以上的减排责任主体之间或减排义务履行方与相关管理部门之间很有可能在排放单位的归属、减排规则的约束效力、税费的缴纳与规避以及减排数据的真实性等方面产生纠纷,所以在我国的航空减排立法过程中也需要对上述问题的解决进行规制。综上所述,根据我国航空产业现阶段的发展状况以及国际社会对航空减排工作的重视,制定一部统一的航空减排法律迫在眉睫,但这也确实是一项庞大的工程,不仅需要符合我国的发展实际,同时也需要与 CORSIA 抵消计划等国际航空减排规则的标准相契合,毕竟航空运输的活动范围往往是整个国际社会。

五、结　　语

通过上文对国际民用航空减排规则的总结和介绍,不难看出国际民航组织作为由《京都议定书》授权的国际组织本就具有指导和制定有关于国际航空减排规则的法律地位。此外,全球性的减排规则相较于区域性的规则而言更能协调、兼顾不同利益主体的发展要求和发展实际。尽管国际民航组织项下的 CORSIA 抵消计划,不仅坚持了"共同但有区别责任"原则,尽可能地避免对发展中国家的国内市场和经济发展造成不利影响,而且还专门设立了两个自愿履行阶段作为过渡期。但是规则的整体设置仍未充分考虑到发达国家的历史排放,也未基于发达国家的发展历史与发展水平为其向发展中国家

① Tokyo ETS,资料来源:https://ec.europa.eu/clima/policies/ets/ets-summer-university/sites/clima-ets-summer-university/files/online_courses/Unit6_ETS_Around_the_World_JB_C.html,最后访问日期:2019 年 4 月 5 日。

的经济、技术援助提供充分的规则支撑和制度保障。发展中国家的航空经济正值发展高峰期,在这个阶段任何限制或减少航空排放的措施都有可能构成其航空产业的发展阻碍,对此,ICAO 应充分考虑到发展中国家与发达国家之间的差异,制定更为宽松、灵活、互助的减排体系。但这并不否认 ICAO 在国际航空减排问题上所具有的优势,国际航空减排问题本就涉及国家利益,也容易引起国家之间的矛盾和冲突。但综观国际航空规则的制定过程,由 ICAO 所建立的全球性减排体系相较于区域性机制来讲受到更多国家的支持,也取得了更为显著的成效。CORSIA 机制的进一步发展是肯定的,但在具体规则尚未完善,内容尚未固定的情况下,尽早解决在今后适用过程中可能产生的法律问题,最大限度地考虑发展中国家的国家利益才是重中之重。

中国作为世界上最大的发展中国家,航空贸易正处于急速上升时期,国际航空减排必然会对我国的经济发展造成阻碍,所以除了采用技术的改进、管理措施的完善、燃油效率的提升与先进设备的引进以及相应配套措施的建立等方式尽可能地缩小对我国航空经济的不利影响外,我国也可以考虑通过暂缓加入 CORSIA 试行阶段和第一阶段,寻求发达国家的技术、资金支持等方法为我国争取最大限度的发展空间;同时抓住规则制定的主动权,在谈判与协商过程中为我国为广大发展中国家争取更多的利益,提高对国际组织规则的解读能力;培养并鼓励专业人才向具有规则制定权的国际组织流动,增加我国在相关国际组织中的声音,这实际上也间接地促进了我国话语权的提升和国际权益的保障能力。

后巴黎时代国际民航碳市场立法动向及中国对策

潘晓滨[*]　王梓荧[**]

近几十年来，气候变化问题严重威胁着人类的生存和发展，联合国政府间气候变化专门委员会（International Panel on Climate Change，IPCC）第5次报告表明气候变化与温室气体排放增加的关联性在95%以上。除自然因素影响外，人为因素温室气体排放的增加对全球气候变暖产生的影响最大。在人类的生产生活中，化石燃料的燃烧、土地利用变化和农业活动等导致大气中的二氧化碳浓度大幅度增长。国际能源署在2018年报告中指出，全球与能源相关的二氧化碳排放量在2017年增长了1.4%，达到了32.5亿吨的历史最高水平，而在众多能源消耗产业当中，民用航空业是温室气体排放量增长最快的产业之一，2016年较1990年基线排放量

---

* 法学博士，天津财经大学法学院讲师，硕士研究生导师，从事国际环境法、气候变化法和碳排放交易制度研究。

** 天津财经大学法学院硕士研究生。

增长了115%。[①] 2016年各国民用航空器整体排放约为8.14亿吨二氧化碳当量,约是全球人为碳排放量的2%。[②] 随着国际航空运输总量的扩张,到2020年全球国际航空排放量预计将比2005年高出70%左右。而国际民航组织(International Civil Aviation Organization,ICAO)预测,到2050年全球航空排放量还将增长3~7倍。如何有效减少民用航空业产生的温室气体排放量,尤其是在民用航空业快速发展背景下如何以各国能够普遍接受的方式采取最小成本路径控制行业整体排放水平,成为国际社会亟须解决的重要问题。

一、国际航空碳抵消与减排机制的由来

(一)应对气候变化国际法的发展

国际社会密切关注气候变化问题,1992年达成《联合国气候变化框架公约》(以下称《框架公约》)(United Nations Framework Convention on Climate Change,UNFCCC),旨在将大气中的温室气体浓度控制在严重干扰气候系统稳定的水平之内,2015年达成的《巴黎协定》在立法目标中进一步将温控目标具体设定为2℃,并强调国际社会应将升温努力控制在1.5℃之内。但由于民用航空业这一部门的特殊性,其作为战后新兴产业发展较晚,且运输过程的排放行为并不局限在任何一个主权国家的领土范围之内,导致国际民航业的排放量不易监测和统计,因此《框架公约》没有将民航运输的控排明确纳入。直到1997年召开的联合国气候变化框架公约第三次缔约方大会,才在大会通过的《京都议定书》中对国际民航业产生的碳排放作出初步的制度

---

① IEA,"CO_2 emission from Fuel combustion:overview(2018 edition)",Accessed January 10,2019. http://data.iea.org/products/115-co2-emissions-from-fuel-combustion-2018-edition-coming-soon.aspx.

② IATA,Carbon offsetting for international aviation,Accessed November 23,2018. https://www.iata.org/policy/environment/Documents/paper-offsetting-for-aviation.pdf.

性安排,[①]但议定书并没有将其纳入具体的减排机制框架内,取而代之的是将这一问题授权给国际民航组织进行管辖。[②]《巴黎协定》确定了"自下而上"的国家自主贡献模式,尽管在协定中要求缔约方应努力在各自国家自主贡献中将人为温室气体排放与清除都包括在内,但是《巴黎协定》并没有像《京都议定书》那样明确规定将国际航空碳排放划归国际民航组织管理。在2020年《京都议定书》失效后,《巴黎协定》的实施细则谈判显得格外重要,尤其是针对航空碳排放的管辖以及涉及的贡献转让都需要在气候国际法层面加以明确。

(二)国际民航组织的立法推动

围绕国际民用航空运输减排,ICAO自2001年开始相继针对航空碳排放引起的环境问题召开了几届大会。其中富有建设性成果的第35届大会,明确了航空碳排放对气候变化产生的影响以及通过决议确认了降低碳排放的两种方式,即可采用国家自愿减排方式或将航空碳排放纳入《框架公约》机制下进行。第37届大会形成的A37－19号决议对航空碳排放与环境问题首次单独作出规定,并通过了对民用航空业的全球减排目标,即在2020年之前实现国际航空平均燃料效率提升2%,并自2020年起将国际民航业产生的全球净温室气体排放量保持在相同水平,其被称为2020年碳中和目标。第38届大会上通过了A38－18号决议,决定制订一项全球性民用航空市场计划,并考虑各成员国的特殊情况和各自能力提议解决措施。[③] 最终在2016年10

① 《京都议定书》第2.2条款中规定:"附件Ⅰ当中所列的各缔约方应该同国际民用航空组织与海事组织一起努力控制或减少飞机与船舶所用燃油产生的在《蒙特利尔议定书》中所没有管控的温室气体的排放。"

② ICAO作为政府间国际组织,根据1994年《国际民用航空公约》(《芝加哥公约》)而成立,具有独立的国际法律人格,是联合国唯一授权管理国际民用航空业的专门官方机构。资料来源:https://www.icao.int/about-icao/Pages/default.aspx,最后访问日期:2018年11月25日。

③ 《芝加哥公约》附件16第Ⅳ卷第1版 国际航空抵消与减排机制(CORSIA),资料来源:https://www.unitingaviation.com/publications/Annex－16－Vol－04－CH/#page＝6,最后访问日期:2018年11月25日。

月第39届国际民航组织大会通过了第A39－3号决议。成员国决定启动“国际航空碳抵消与减排机制”(Carbon Offsetting and Reduction Scheme for International Aviation,CORSIA),并着手实施这项全球性航空碳市场计划。[①]

(三)与欧盟航空碳市场法律制度的协调

欧盟作为全球气候变化治理的领导者,在2005年启动了全区域范围内的温室气体排放交易体系,并于2012年开始将民用航空排放纳入体系之中。[②] 根据欧盟排放交易体系(European Union Emissions Trading System,EU-ETS)的规定,[③]所有在欧洲运营的航空公司,无论其所属国是欧洲还是其他地区,都必须对航空器排放的二氧化碳进行监督、报告和核查(Monitoring、Reporting、Verification,MRV),并根据这些排放量上缴配额。截至2017年,欧盟排放交易系统已经为航空业每年减少了约1700多万吨的二氧化碳当量。针对欧盟的这一举措,不少国家都提出了反对意见,认为其违反共同但有区别责任原则(Common but Differentiated Responsibility,CBDR)以及《京都议定书》中规定的以国际民航组织解决航空碳排放为准的规则。[④] 最终,面对多个国家的不赞同意见,以及为了支持国际民航组织通过的CORSIA机制,欧盟决定从2017年起将欧盟碳市场的地域范围限制在欧盟与欧洲经济区国家的内部航班。不过欧盟在航空碳交易方面虽然做出了一定让步,但也提出了通过修订欧盟碳市场立法来实施航空碳减排的全球性措

---

① 第A39－3号决议:《国际民航组织关于环境保护的持续政策和做法的综合声明——全球市场措施(MBM)计划》,资料来源:http://www.icao.int/Meetings/a39/Pages/documentation.aspx,最后访问日期:2018年11月23日。

② See Percival Robert, *Global Law and the Environment*, *Washington Law Review* 3, 2011, p. 521.

③ 欧盟理事会2008年1月23日提出了排放交易指令修改案,出台第2008/101/EC号指令,将海运业和航空业也纳入欧盟碳市场的强制性控排范围内,以鼓励使用清洁燃料和节约燃料,保护大气环境。参见宋锡祥:《欧盟强征航空碳排放税机制及我国的法律应对策略》,载《东方法学》2013年第6期。

④ 参见郝海然:《欧盟航空碳关税引发的法律问题及中国应然立场》,载《天津法学》2018年第3期。

施。如果国际民航组织没有新的推动立法,欧盟航空碳排放交易体系将从2024年恢复到原来的全部范围,即仍然要求飞跃欧盟及经济区领空的其他国家民用航空器纳入欧盟航空排放交易体系之中。因此,2019~2024年的6年时间内,CORSIA能否实施产生实际减排效果,以及各国能否出台配套措施则显得尤为重要。

二、国际航空碳抵消与减排机制的法律制度架构

CORSIA的实施目标是将国际民用航空器产生的净温室气体排放量稳定在2020年的水平,以实现2020年后国际航空业净排放的零增长。在CORSIA机制中包括"抵消"和"减排"两个重要概念,碳减排是指参与CORSIA的民航企业要根据行业整体以及自身排放的核算方法计算排放增量,并承担与此相当的减排义务。碳抵消是指民航企业通过购买由CORSIA认可的合格碳减排项目产生的自愿减排量,来补偿自身增加的温室气体排放量。虽然碳抵消并不要求民航企业减少其内部排放,但为那些减排潜力有限或减排成本过高的航空企业提供了另一种有效的环保路径选择。

(一)国际航空碳抵消与减排机制的阶段划分及覆盖范围

CORSIA分为三个实施阶段,包括试点阶段(2021~2023年)、第一阶段(2024~2026年)、第二阶段(2027~2035年)。从2018~2020年正是筹备工作的进行期。2021~2026年,只有自愿参与试点和第一阶段的国家之间的航班接受抵消要求。从2027年开始,国际航空运输收益吨数值占比超过0.5%或者国际航空运输收益吨数值全球累计占比进入前90%的国家都需要参加。① 第二阶段成为事实上的强制性履约阶段。截至2018年10月17日,已

① 国际航空运输收益吨数值是国际航空业的技术性专有名词,特指实际运载吨数与飞行里程的乘积,是一类反映运输飞行中综合运载数量的指标。

有75个国家自愿参加。[①] 从2027年起,所有国际航班都将必须接受抵消要求的限制,但最不发达国家、小岛屿发展中国家、内陆发展中国家和占国际航空运输收益吨数值不到0.5%的国家除外,当然这些国家可以自愿参加。[②] 尽管放宽了要求,但是从2019年1月1日起,所有缔约国内的个体航空公司(包括往返非纳入国家的航班在内)都必须报告从2019年1月1日起全部国际航线的温室气体排放量。

(二)国际航空碳抵消与减排机制的主要实施规则

CORSIA各项具体制度规定于《芝加哥公约》附件16第Ⅳ卷中,各项机制的实施细则和补充文件尚在制定中,已完成的部分包括环境技术手册第Ⅳ卷以及执行所需的实施草案与辅助要素,具体规则涵盖了抵消责任划分与减排、航空碳排放的MRV、可用于抵消的合格排放单位、履约与评审、中央注册登记系统等。[③]

1. 航空碳排放的抵消责任分配与避免市场扭曲

《芝加哥公约》环境保护附件第Ⅳ卷在国际航班产生二氧化碳的抵消要求章节中专门规定了分阶段的履约要求。在CORSIA实施的第二阶段,个体

① 截至2018年10月17日,自愿加入CORSIA计划的75个国家名单:阿尔巴尼亚、亚美尼亚、澳大利亚、奥地利、阿塞拜疆、比利时、波斯尼亚和黑塞哥维那国、博茨瓦纳、保加利亚、布基纳法索、加拿大、哥斯达黎加、克罗地亚、塞浦路斯、捷克共和国、丹麦、多米尼加共和国、萨尔瓦多、赤道几内亚、爱沙尼亚、芬兰、法国、加蓬、格鲁吉亚、德国、希腊、危地马拉、圭亚那、匈牙利、冰岛、印度尼西亚、爱尔兰、以色列、意大利、牙买加、日本、肯尼亚、拉脱维亚、立陶宛、卢森堡、马其顿(前南斯拉夫共和国)、马来西亚、马耳他、马绍尔群岛、墨西哥、摩纳哥、黑山、纳米比亚、荷兰、新西兰、尼日利亚、挪威、巴布亚新几内亚、波兰、葡萄牙、卡塔尔、大韩民国、摩尔多瓦共和国、罗马尼亚、圣马力诺、沙特阿拉伯、塞尔维亚、新加坡、斯洛伐克、斯洛文尼亚、西班牙、瑞典、瑞士、泰国、土耳其、乌克兰、阿拉伯联合酋长国、英国、美国、赞比亚。See IATA, "Carbon offsetting for international aviation",资料来源:https://www.iata.org/policy/environment/Documents/paper-offsetting-for-aviation.pdf,最后访问日期:2018年11月23日。

② 《芝加哥公约》附件16第Ⅳ卷第3.1.3节b款关于可以豁免纳入CORSIA机制的国家规定。

③ Committee on Aviation Environmental Protection (CAEP), "CORSIA Implementation Elements", Accessed January 9, 2019. https://www.icao.int/environmental-protection/CORSIA/Pages/implementation-elements.aspx.

航空公司所承担的碳排放抵消责任的不同进一步划分为三个分别覆盖三年的履约期(包括 2027 ~ 2029 年、2030 ~ 2032 年、2033 ~ 2035 年)。2029 年将是重要的分水岭,在此之前,个体航空公司仅根据民航业整体增长速度计算减排责任,但在此之后航空公司必须根据个体增长速度承担比例越来越高的减排责任。这意味着民航高速发展的缔约国整体上需要承担更多的减排义务,减排责任的划分实际上是对航空排放增量赋予减排义务而非存量义务,CORSIA 采取的是一类基线信用型排放交易模式,而非总量控制与交易模型。[①] 为了避免市场竞争扭曲,只有参与 CORSIA 的国家之间的国际航线纳入减排责任分配计算,经营航线的个体航空公司需要履行抵消责任,而未参加 CORSIA 的国家之间以及只有一方国家参与机制的航线将不适用相应的分配计算与抵消责任标准。

2. 航空碳排放的 MRV

由国际民航理事会下属航空环境保护委员会(Committee Aviation Euvironmental Protection,CAEP)制定的《国际标准和推荐做法》(International Standards and Recommended Practices,SARPs),其中专门明确了航空公司如何监测、报告和核查民用航空器飞行产生的二氧化碳排放。该文件于 2018 年 6 月 27 日在国际民航组织理事会获得通过。根据标准,最大审定起飞重量超过 5700 公斤的飞机从事国际航班运营且所产生的年二氧化碳排放量超过 1 万吨的飞机运营商需要购买碳抵消信用额,但执行人道主义、医疗和灭

① 所谓总量控制与交易(Cap and trade,C & T)模式,即由政府事先设定特定时间、空间和涵盖产业范围内的温室气体排放总量,同时设定针对涵盖实体的履约期。在实施过程中,由政府部门或其指定机构按照一定标准在履约初期,将排放配额向不同排放实体进行分配,在履约期内通过节能减排降碳等方式获得剩余配额的排放实体可以将其在市场上进行出售,而超出配额分配进行排放的企业则需要从市场购买配额进行履约;而基线与信用(Baseline and credit,B & C)模式,即由政府事先设定特定时间、空间以及针对不同类型涵盖实体的排放基线,同时设定针对涵盖实体的履约期。这种排放基线既可以采用生产单位产品的温室气体排放量作为依据,也可以采用单位产量的能源消耗量,进而折算为温室气体排放量水平。参见潘晓滨:《碳排放交易配额分配制度——基于法学与经济学视角的分析》,南开大学出版社 2017 年版,第 34 ~ 35 页。

火任务的航班除外。[①] 这一要求从2019年1月1日开始实施。到2018年年底，航空运营商们需要制订一个排放监控计划，详细说明监控燃料的使用、计算排放和管理数据的程序。SARPs文件要求操作人员根据每个国际航班的实际燃料使用情况，按照五种已批准的燃料使用监测方法之一，监测各自的二氧化碳排放量。在某些情况下，操作者可以有资格使用简化监测，并使用CERT系统（国际民用航空组织开发的一种评估工具）评估其排放量。为了保证国际航空营运商向其管理机构报告数据的准确性，他们每年的排放报告在提交给国家之前，需要由一个独立的第三方核查机构进行核查，验证机构必须符合ISO 14065标准以及CORSIA机制中特定的要求。[②] 各国将向国际民航组织通报累计排放量，国际民航组织将公布各个运营商的总排放量。在每3年的达标期结束时，操作人员必须证明他们已使用符合资格的排放单位，达到了抵消要求。

3. 航空碳排放的合格碳抵消项目

CORSIA所覆盖的碳抵消包括各种各样的项目活动，风能、清洁炉灶、沼气捕获、林业或其他减少或避免排放的项目都包含在内。目前，国际民航组织正在制订评估碳抵消计划和项目类型的程序，之后国际民航组织理事会将制定一份可用于遵守的排放单位清单。这份清单将根据拟设立的技术咨询机构的建议作出，以确保各排放单位实现预期的温室气体减排量。建议的抵消项目标准目前还未确定，但可推知的是依据现行碳排放交易制度下普遍适用的原则和广为接受的碳抵消认证标准来进行。同时，为了量化抵消项目产生的温室气体减排效益，将会设定一定的基线，用来表示如果不实施CORSIA将会导致的不利后果。排放量的减少需要使用精确的测量方法，有

---

① 《芝加哥公约》附件16第Ⅳ卷第1节对国际航班与国内航班作了区分，国际航班被定义为从一个国家或其领土的机场起飞并在另一个国家或其领土的机场上降落的航空器的运行。此外，国内航班被定义为从一个国家或其领土的机场起飞并在同一个国家或其领土的机场上降落的航空器的运行。

② "ISO 14065标准"全称为对从事温室气体合格性鉴定或其他形式认可的确认与验证机构要求。参见中国质量认证中心：《企业碳排放管理国际经验与中国实践》，中国标准出版社2015年版，第205～206页。

效的协议来量化减排,并且还要接受审计。

(三)国际航空碳抵消与减排机制所应秉持的基本原则

应对气候变化国际法所秉持的 CBDR 以及国际民航组织在相关文件中多次重申的特殊情况与各自能力的原则(Special Circumstance and Respective Capability,SCRC),应当是 CORSIA 相关规则形成的重要基础。① 坚持 CBDR 要求规则的制定应当体现发达国家航空业早期高速发展所应承担的历史排放责任,并对发展中国家进行相应的资金援助和技术转让支持,在抵消责任的划分中应当对碳排放存量与增量同等重视。坚持各自能力原则,要求正视发达国家与发展中国家在航空业发展水平上的差距,尤其是两类国家在参与 CORSIA 能力上的差距,给予发展中国家适当的能力建设、缓冲期支持以及其他优惠待遇。坚持特殊情况原则,则要求规则制定必须注意到部分新兴工业化发展中国家正在经历的民用航空业高速发展的阶段性特点,统筹兼顾确定相应的国际减排标准与抵消方案,并不能在规则制定中造成对这些国家航空业发展的不利影响或变相限制。

从目前 CAEP 所采用的国际标准看,CORSIA 要求在第一阶段自愿加入国家于 2019 年 1 月 1 日起对年排放超过 1 万吨二氧化碳当量的航空公司提交排放监测报告。2018 年加入的国家既包含发达国家,也包括发展中国家,甚至还有最不发达国家与小岛屿国家,显然各个国家的发展水平不同,其国内 MRV 规则的制定标准与实施水平有很大差距,国际民航组织要求各国统一在几个月的时间来执行 MRV 工作标准,无疑会加重发展中国家的负担。②

---

① 关于"特殊情况与各自能力原则"的表述引自国际民航组织工作文件《给予市场措施成为国际民用航空部门增加温室气体排放的因素》第 5 部分"国家自愿减少排放的行动计划是表明发展中国家特殊情况和各自能力的关键要素"。文件正文第 5 部分第 1 节强调"共同但有区别责任原则"正在被特殊情况与各自能力原则所取代,但共区原则依然是绝大多数发展中国家讨论与采用基于市场措施有关问题不能妥协的起点,同时没有一个国家否认,对气候变化可能造成的灾难性后果这类全球性挑战需要所有国家做出协调一致的努力。

② 参见张芳:《我国航空业碳排放国际和国内 MRV 规则分析》,载《前沿观察》2018 年第 8 期。

从抵消责任的分配方案看,CORSIA 采用了分阶段实施路径,即在第一阶段是由航空业的行业整体平均增速分配责任,到 2027 年后将适当根据个体增速分配责任。[①] 但这样的分配方案实际上并没有体现 CBDR 的真正内涵。2020～2026 年这一阶段,属于各个国家自愿参与阶段,形式上给予了部分发展中国家一定的缓冲期,但在 2027 年之后,大多数缔约国的国际航线都要纳入其中,这一阶段由于包括我国在内的部分发展中国家正处在民航业高速增长阶段,其民用航空器的数量需求势必要远远高过发达国家,而且这一增长态势仍将持续相当长的一段时间,即使发达国家在第一阶段承诺自愿加入,总体来看其所需承担的抵消责任相比发展中国家来仍然有失公平,因而考虑到世界经济增长趋势与各个国家民航业的发展态势,CORSIA 的抵消责任分配方案与标准是否真能满足各个国家的实际需求,体现出共同但有区别责任以及特殊情况与各自能力责任仍然值得商榷。

三、中国参与国际航空碳抵消与减排机制所面临的机遇与挑战

CORSIA 是全球民用航空业应对气候变化进程的一个里程碑,如果顺利实施,不仅可以有效降低航空碳排放量,同时也为采用市场手段统一全球碳减排行动积累先行经验。[②] 但鉴于我国民航业与其他国家发展程度与需求不同,参与 CORSIA 所带来的机遇与挑战并存。

(一) CORSIA 实施对中国民航业的宏观经济影响

中国民航业正在经历高速发展。进入 21 世纪,中国民航运输总周转量年均增速达到 15%,超过全球平均增速的 5.3%,中国民航运输已经成为全

---

① 参见柴麒敏、祁悦、王任:《中国参与国际航空碳减排机制仍面临挑战》,资料来源:http://www.tanjiaoyi.com/article－22177－1.html,最后访问日期:2018 年 11 月 20 日。

② Ruwantissa Abeyratne,"Aviation and Climate Change-In Search of a Global Market Based Measure",Springer Briefs In Law,2014,pp. 79－81.

球增长的重要引擎。① 在引入可替代航空燃料或取得其他技术突破之前,航空业的碳排放增量主要取决于航空运输周转量,而 CORSIA 机制中减排责任的分配主要根据缔约国民航碳排放增量来确定,从理论上来看,我国航空运输周转量增长越快,在参与 CORSIA 机制后承担的减排责任越重。而根据美国环境保护基金会预测,中国、美国、欧盟3个主要实体将承担 CORSIA 机制下航空抵消的绝大部分责任,中国15年累计抵消总量在豁免有关国家情形下甚至要高出美国。② 由此,参与 CORSIA 机制将对中国民航业的国际竞争力带来较大负面影响。

(二)中国碳市场与 CORSIA 的衔接问题

1. 时间表的规划协调

2017年年底全国碳市场正式启动,在经历2018年的准备期和2019年的试运行期之后,2020年将只有火电行业纳入其中。根据国家总体规划,国家碳市场将覆盖包括民航运输业在内的八大主要排放行业,并在2030年之前进入成熟运行状态,民航产业何时正式纳入目前还没有清晰的时间表。③ 同时,根据 CORSIA 的时间表设定,所有《芝加哥公约》的缔约国下属国际航线在2027年第三阶段期须全部强制纳入减排管理。这意味着,在2020年之后国内民航业纳入国家碳市场需要提速推进,并让民航企业尽早适应碳约束管理,为2027年正式进入国际碳减排机制预留一定时间的准备期。在2027年之后,国内民航企业也会遇到国内与国际碳市场的双重履约问题,是否需要引入必要的选择退出制度性设计,让国内航企的国际航线豁免国内碳市场的配额履约管理,也是一个重要的衔接性问题。

---

① 参见中国民用航空局发展计划司:《从统计看民航(2017)》,中国民航出版社2017年版,第143~147页。

② 参见 EDF,"Explore emission reduction scenarios",Accessed January 10,2019. https://www.edf.org/climate/icaos-market-based-meausre,最后访问日期:2019年1月10日。

③ 参见顾阿伦:《国家航空市场减排机制对中国碳市场的影响和意义》,载《中国经贸导刊》2017年第2期。

2. MRV 规则的对标

各国所辖民用航空器的排放衡量需要对标 SARPs 文件,相对应的监测、报告与核查规则(MRV)将是我国所面临的挑战之一,其核心是要清楚知悉航空燃料的消耗以及运营排放流动中的各个环节,要确保得到的数据的真实性与准确性,并且需要建立一定的追踪机制。欧洲很多航空公司早已纳入欧盟排放交易体系,其对民航业的 MRV 规则已经十分成熟,参与 CORSIA 具有先行经验。而我国目前国家碳市场仍处在建设与完善阶段,先期只纳入了火电行业,国家碳市场覆盖民用航空业也至少要等到 2020 年之后,无论是民航管理部门还是航空公司对相关 MRV 规则掌握仍有较大差距。

3. 合格碳减排单位的衔接

国际民航组织计划通过 CORSIA 的资格标准和评估碳抵消项目,制定一项各国统一适用的排放单位清单。这意味着全球年排放超过 1 万吨的航空公司要向清单中所列项目提供者购买获得国际民航组织认可的自愿减排量(Offset Credit),这将赋予国际民航组织巨大的碳市场影响力。CORSIA 机制下可用于抵消的合格减排单位一方面将参考《巴黎协定》市场机制所建立的可转让减缓贡献成果以及部门减排的具体规则,但目前针对《巴黎协定》市场机制实施细则的谈判,2018 年年底结束的卡托维兹气候变化大会并没有取得实质性进展。① 另一方面抵消项目也可以纳入 CORSIA 排放清单,其中包括部分国际自愿抵消机制与《框架公约》下的减少发展中国家毁林、森林退化、森林保护、可持续经营、造林再造机制(Reducing greenhouse gas Emissions from Deforestation and forest Degradation in developing countries, REDD+)等。对我国而言,全国统一碳市场建设适用的自愿核证减排量如果能够纳入 CORSIA 机制下的碳抵消清单内,将为国家碳市场链接国际碳市场提供重要的机遇和平台。

---

① 参见党庶枫、曾文革:《〈巴黎协定〉碳交易机制新趋向对中国的挑战与因应》,载《中国科技论坛》2018 年第 1 期。

（三）中国参与 CORSIA 机制所遇到的法律障碍

在法律层面，《芝加哥公约》附件 16 第Ⅳ卷第 1 节明确规定了参与 CORSIA 机制的民航企业需为国际航班的运营商。但根据实施细则，适用于我国的国际航班范围将包括中国内地往返中国台湾地区、香港特别行政区和澳门特别行政区的航线。这些地区属于中国领土，任何一个国际机构都不应擅自允许其单独参与涉及主权行为的国际机制，这其中涉及的中国的主权问题不容忽视。① 另外，在 CORSIA 机制中纳入中国台湾地区、香港特别行政区、澳门特别行政区航线，也会在统计口径上显著增加我国民航业的控排负担。中国台湾地区、香港特别行政区、澳门特别行政区的民航企业固然也要纳入碳减排与抵消，但由于这些地区的航空碳交易配套机制还没有建立，对于这其产生的航空碳排放应如何抵消，也是中国与国际民航组织需共同探讨的问题。

四、我国参与国际航空碳抵消与减排机制的对策建议

习近平总书记多次强调："应对气候变化不是别人要我们做，而是我们自己要做。"作为《巴黎协定》的主要缔约方，中国业已成为全球应对气候变化的重要贡献者、参与者与引领者。在提交的国家自主贡献以及国内的应对气候变化政策行动中，中央决策层始终高度重视采取市场机制推动民航业纳入到碳排放管理。在国际民航组织推出 CORSIA 的背景下，我国不应回避而应积极融入其中，秉持国际应对气候变化法中的共区原则，坚持各自能力与特殊情况，在规则谈判中争取有利条件，同时在国内加速推进碳市场建设，提升民用航空业参与国际市场的各项能力。

---

① See Ren Wang, "The route from China to ICAO's CORSIA emissions scheme: there's still a long way to go", Accessed November 23, 2018. http://www.greenaironline.com/news.php?viewStory=2386.

(一)坚持共区以及特殊情况与各自能力原则并重的谈判立场

《巴黎协定》中所达成的国家自主贡献模式为国际气候治理展现了一条"自下而上"的减排路径,其承接了《框架公约》一直所秉持的CBDR。但是,由国际民航组织所推动的CORSIA及其实施标准,在规则形成过程中则更多采取了类似京都模式的"自上而下"减排路径,其要求的统一性多于差异性,对排放增量的管控明显多于对历史存量的考虑,其与主流应对气候变化办法所一贯坚持的共同但有区别责任原则有所背离。如前文所述,国际民航组织虽然在第37届大会以及之后的工作会议上多次提出特殊情况与各自能力原则,其初衷是想要通过新的原则概念摆脱发达国家与新兴发展中国家之间的政治分歧,并降低CBDR在航空碳市场规则形成中可能产生的潜在影响,①但我们注意到,CORSIA在规则制定过程中已经在事实上演变为一个由行业组织在发达国家主导下而建立的国际市场机制。即使CORSIA在适用范围规定中豁免了多数航空运输量较少的国家,也不能掩盖机制本身在责任分配、标准制定以及规则谈判中的不公平因素。

以中国、俄罗斯、印度等实体为代表的立场相近国家始终认为CBDR在航空减排国际法中的适用是十分必要的。一方面,特殊情况与各自能力原则并没有达到预期效果,在《京都议定书》委托国际民航组织处理国际航空温室气体排放问题近17年后,世界各国仍不清楚该原则应该如何解读,在规则制定中应该如何将其适用于具有能力的发展中国家以及可能需要应对特殊情况的国家。另一方面,包括中国在内的立场相近国家,都是《芝加哥公约》的缔约国,虽然中国谈判代表团也认为CORSIA

① See Alejandro Piera, "Addressing carbon emissions from international aviation requires the recognition of special circumstances", Accessed January 7, 2019. http://www.greenaironline.com/news.php?viewStory=2035&from=singlemessage&isappinstalled=0.

及 SARPs 可能会给部分经济高速增长的发展中国家造成过重的负担,[①]但一味回避或拒绝参与 CORSIA 将会导致违反国际法义务的被动局面。根据《芝加哥公约》第 38 条,缔约国如不同意相关国际标准和程序,需要提出相应的修改方案。[②] 对此,中国应该积极主动参与 CORSIA 的谈判,联合立场相近国家提出坚持 CBDR 以及特殊情况与各自能力原则同等重要的立场,强调发达国家对其航空存量排放所应承担的历史责任,并对特殊情况原则进行有利于我国等新兴发展中国家民航业高速发展现实的解读,为建立公平、合理、可行的国际航空减排方案摆明立场。

(二)积极争取有利于本国的国际规则

在坚持基本原则的前提下,我国应在国际谈判中积极争取有利于本国的国际规则。

一方面,针对民航企业减排责任的承担,应积极排除和否定不公平、不合理的责任设定规则。CORSIA 主要围绕国际航线中排放增量设置减排义务,由于我国特殊的国情,中国内地与中国香港特别行政区、澳门特别行政区及台湾地区之间的航线如果被认定为国际航线,将会显著增加我国民航业的排放抵消责任。因此,无论是出于维护国家主权,还是促进我国民航企业公平参与 CORSIA 的考虑,我国都应在谈判中要求国际民航组织修改相关国际航线分类规则。同时,鉴于我国具有国际航线业务的民航企业将在 CORSIA 第二阶段(2027 ~ 2035 年)被纳入强制履约期,而根据个体增长因子渐进式占

① See Green Air Communications,"China refutes reports it has withdrawn from the voluntary phases of CORSIA although its concerns remain", Accessed January 8, 2019. http://www.greenaironline.com/news.php?viewStory=2502.

② 《芝加哥公约》第 38 条,任何国家如认为对任何上述国际标准和程序,不能在一切方面遵行,或在任何国际标准和程序修改后,不能使其本国的规章和措施完全符合,应于国际标准修正案通过后 60 天内通知理事会,或表明它拟采取的行动。在上述情此项国际标准和程序,或该国认为有必要采用在某方面不同于国际标准所规定的规章和措施时,应立即将其本国的措施和国际标准所规定的措施之间的差别,通知国际民用航空组织。任何国家如在国际标准修改以后,对其本国规章或措施不作相应修改情况下,理事会应立即将国际标准和该国措施间在一项或几项上存在的差别通知所有其他各国。

比增加的抵消责任计算方法,届时经历快速成长的民航企业无疑将被赋予更多减排责任,我国应在谈判中秉持特殊情况原则为本国争取缓冲期,或修改过分偏重个体增长的抵消责任计算规则。

另一方面,为了增强国内碳市场与国际航空碳市场的衔接,我国也应当积极推动本国自愿减排市场所产生的减排单位成为国际航空碳市场认可的合格抵消单位,积极争取我国的减排项目经营者能够进入国际航空碳交易的卖方市场。根据 CAEP 测算,到 2025 年,CORSIA 机制将产生 1.42 亿~1.74 亿吨二氧化碳当量的自愿减排量需求,2035 年将产生 4.43 亿~5.96 亿吨的减排需求。① 而按照国际能源署碳价的预测估算,至 2025 年国际民航业购碳花费将达到 62 亿美元,至 2035 年进一步提升至 239 亿美元。② 巨大的商机是我国不能拒绝参与 CORSIA 的重要理由,全国碳市场正式启动后将促进国内自联合国清洁发展机制需求锐减后一直疲软的自愿减排市场回暖,如能通过参与谈判,让国内减排项目经营者具备国际航空碳市场中的碳抵消卖方资格,将进一步促进国内碳市场的增长,同时对于我国民航企业纳入 CORSIA 后不得不承受的购碳花费也起到重要的平衡作用。

(三)推进国内民航业参与国际机制的能力建设

民航业的能力建设体现在自身排放管理以及参与碳市场两个方面:首先,CORSIA 实施的重要性之一是全球各大民航企业由本国按照统一标准进行温室气体的 MRV,并以此作为计算每个国家每个航空公司减排责任的基础。SARPs 的出台对于促进国内民航业提升自身碳排放管理能力是一个重要机遇。我国应推动行业政策和配套立法推进国内民航企业建立评估与准

---

① 赵希:《国际航空碳市场打上门了,中国是继续观望还是积极挺近? 问题比想象得迫切》,资料来源:http://www.tanjiaoyi.com/article-20951-1.html,最后访问日期:2018 年 11 月 24 日。

② See IEA, "CO_2 emission from Fuel combustion Highlights (2017 edition)", Accessed January 10, 2019. http://data.iea.org/publications/freepublications/CO2EmissionsfromCombustionHighlights2017.pdf.

备工作。事实上,我国在先期全国碳市场的筹备中,也进行了民用航空运输业相关 MRV 规则的设计和筹备,CORSIA 相关实施标准的出台需要进一步融合到全国碳市场相关 MRV 技术规则的准备中,并通过建立软法性指南文件或其他推广渠道让国内民航企业尽早对标 MRV 规则。其次,CORSIA 实施的重要意义之二是将国际民航企业真正纳入全球统一行业碳市场之中,航空公司需要购买合格减排量来抵消自身的碳排放增量。我国应为全国碳市场建设的时间表提速,通过整体政策规划尽早纳入民用航空业,让其提前参与碳排放交易,熟悉交易规则和碳资产管理,对碳价波动可能带来的经营风险做好预案,加强企业内部相关的技术人员的储备,提升内部管理水平,推动国内航空业进一步的低碳转型,为后期与国际碳市场衔接做好必要准备。

五、结　语

后巴黎时代,通过部门减排推动国际碳市场发展是全球民航业应对气候变化的重要路径。在国际民航组织推出 CORSIA 机制的背景下,参与国际航空碳减排是我国民航部门不可回避的现实。作为民航产业增速最快的国家之一,我国虽然要承担更多的减排责任,但也为国家碳市场建设融入世界提供了重要机遇。为此,我国更应积极参与航空碳减排与抵消国际规则的谈判,并提速推进国内民航业的碳约束管理。通过推进民航业的低碳转型,为国家履行《巴黎协定》自主贡献项下的减排承诺,树立国家负责任的大国形象,提供重要助力。

临空经济法治

西安临空经济区军民融合发展的法治构建*

张享维**

"冷战"结束后,西方主要国家在进行国防科研投资时都采取了军民融合的发展模式,通过军民融合发展模式实现社会资源大整合,军工的市场化、产业化,以开放式和融合式发展破除军民二元体制结构,助推实现军民一体化发展。国防科工军民融合式发展是世界主要国家的成功实践,也是加快经济发展的现实需要。2015 年军民融合发展上升为国家战略,2016 年中共中央、国务院、中央军委印发了《关于经济建设和国防建设融合发展的意见》,意见着眼国家安全和发展战略全局,明确了新形势下军民融合发展的总体思路、重点任务、政策措施,是统筹推进经济建设和国防建设的纲领性文件。推进中国特色军民融合发展,深刻体现了我国经济社会发展规

---

* 本文系国家社科基金一般项目"'一带一路'背景下跨境电子商务平台法律保障机制研究"(18BFX213)阶段性研究成果。

** 西安交通大学经济学专业硕士研究生,陕西睿和律师事务所专职律师,研究方向为经济法学。

律和军事斗争变化规律,是坚持实现富国和强军统一的内在要求,既是兴国之举,又是强军之道。① 2018年4月25日国家发展和改革委员会、中国民用航空局正式批复西安临空经济示范区建设,并要求西安临空经济示范区重点推进三项任务:一是推进体制机制创新,探索临空经济发展新路径、新模式;二是推进绿色发展,培育壮大临空特色产业体系;三是推进军民融合,深化示范区与周边地区的合作互动和协同发展。同年11月7日,中国民用航空局与陕西省签署《关于推进陕西民航高质量发展战略合作协议》,协议约定双方将共同促进陕西临空经济及航空产业发展,支持西咸新区空港新城建设国家级临空经济示范区,推进陕西航空全产业链发展,将陕西省打造成具有相当规模的民用航空产业群和军民融合典范。

一、西安临空经济示范区的特色使命与军民融合发展

(一)西安临空经济区的特色使命

国家发改委、民航局联合出台的《关于临空经济示范区建设发展的指导意见》中,将临空经济区界定为,依托航空枢纽和现代综合交通运输体系,提供高时效、高质量、高附加值产品和服务,集聚发展航空运输业、高端制造业和现代服务业而形成的特殊经济区域,是民航业与区域经济相互融合、相互促进、相互提升的重要载体。依据国际上机场的空间结构模式,可将临空经济区分为四个环形:中心机场环、商业服务环、制造配送环和外围环。②

根据国家发改委、民航局的批复,西安临空经济区位于西咸新区空港新

① 参见朱慈华:《浅议推进中国特色军民融合的重要意义》,载《祖国》2014年第1期。

② 国际上机场空间结构模式以机场为中心,按照中心与周边的距离将临空经济区分为中心机场环、商业服务环、制造配送环和外围环四个环形:范围在机场周边的1千米内为中心机场环,主要包括机场的基础设施和直接与航空运输相关的产业;范围在机场周边的1千米至5千米内为商业服务环,主要是商业服务区,为空港运营及航空公司职员。旅客提供商业服务;范围在机场周边的5千米至10千米内或15分钟车程可达范围内为制造配送环,主要基于机场的交通优势和口岸所发展的高时效性、高附加值的相关产业;外围环为机场周边的10千米至15千米内。

城，规划范围南至福银高速、北至泾河、西至渭城区北杜街道行政边界、东至渭城区底张街道行政边界，管理面积144.1平方公里，其中机场规划面积26.4平方公里。批复提出西安临空经济示范区重点推进的任务之一为“推进军民融合，深化示范区与周边地区的合作互动和协同发展”，在全国多个已获批的国家级临空经济示范区中，军民融合首次被提及，既是西安临空经济示范区的特殊机遇，也是责无旁贷的挑战和使命。以创新驱动发展、军民融合发展为动力，正是西安以及关中平原城市群要重点着力的方向。

（二）军民融合的发展

第二次世界大战结束后，世界各国将发展重点转移到经济建设，采取以经济、科技竞争为主，军事力量竞争为辅的战略，倡导军民一体化，推动军民共用技术的巨大发展及进步，典型的发展模式如下。

1. 美国“军民一体化”模式

美国通过调整改革军方、军工部门和军工企业，增强军政部门间和企业间的合作，开启军用技术、民用技术和资源双向转移之门，促进国防建设与经济发展的良性互动。美国国会技术评估局1994年首次提出“军民融合”概念，国会从1990年开始通过年度《国防授权法》和制定《联邦采办改革法》等一系列重要法案和政策，积极鼓励采办民用企业的技术和产品。① 在国家颁布和制定法规政策的基础上，推广军政部门协作促进“军民融合”、实施和管理“军民融合”的科技计划、培育开放型产业链和军民结合创新主体等方式，提高了工业基础的科技创新能力、企业产业竞争力，增强了军事实力，提高装备水平和作战能力。但总体上“军民融合”尚未达到完善的水平，对个别产业竞争力拉动不足。

2. 俄罗斯“先军后民”模式

俄罗斯为充分利用过剩的军事生产能力以及将国防工业和民用企业结

---

① 参见刘果、文节、刘喜斌：《美国推进军民融合发展的经验与启示》，载《现代商贸工业》2010年第23期。

合在一起,实施“先军后民”的发展模式,既避免军民分离弊端,又无须放弃独立军工体系。通过出台法律法规将军工企业强制转为民用,然后进行优化升级,如1990年颁布《俄罗斯联邦共和国国防工业“军转民”法》,旨在积极推动“军转民”。[①] 利用成熟的军工技术进行民品研发生产,推动军民两用技术进步,加强军民两用技术的出口,带动国民经济发展,建立格洛纳斯(Glondss)全球导航定位军民两用卫星系统。这种模式的弊端在于无法充分发挥国防工业大多数综合体的生产能力,军品和民品分裂现象依然存在,军民结合发展高技术以及技术转移的政策法规无法有效落实。

3. 日本“以民掩军”模式

日本在第二次世界大战后军力发展受到种种限制的情况下,依靠民间企业发展国防科技和武器装备,实现军民融合国家创新的目标。通过政府加大对民企国防科研的投资力度,实施高度集中的管理体制与政、军、民相结合的决策运行机制,充分利用民企的技术力量和优势,大力发展两用技术,扩大民品生产,对可生产军品的民间企业优惠扶持,实现民间企业具有很强经济竞争力的同时,兼具很大的军事潜力,包括在较短时间内研发出核武器的潜力。[②] 但日本对美国的依附关系无法摆脱,其大型复杂武器系统的自主研发能力,相对世界先进国家来说仍有一定差距,大型先进装备主要依靠美国进口。

4. 我国“军民融合”模式

我国军民融合中国式发展最早可追溯至20世纪50年代,历经半个世纪的发展。2007年党的十七大报告首次提出军民融合发展概念,2015年军民融合发展上升为国家战略,2017年中共中央政治局决定设立中央军民融合发展委员会,作为中央层面军民融合发展重大问题的决策和议事协调机构,统一领导军民融合深度发展。

---

① 参见张雯、牟曦媛、王席:《“一带一路”建设中陕西军民融合创新发展路径研究》,载《西安财经学院学报》2018年第6期。

② 参见郭萍:《军民融合式发展的国际经验与启示》,载《经济研究导刊》2012年第7期。

军民融合发展,即经济建设和国防建设融合发展,将国防和军队建设融入国家经济社会发展体系,二者资源共享、协调、平衡、兼容发展,实现资源的最佳配置和充分利用,达到经济建设国防效益最大化和国防建设经济效益最大化,形成全要素、多领域、高效益发展的国家战略。军民融合主要包括两种基本含义:一是"军转民",即在民间使用军事技术发展;二是"民参军",即民营主体参与军工市场,向西方发达国家学习,将民间资本引入国防科技工业,使民营企业能够有秩序地参与军工企业的改组改制。①

(三)西安临空经济区发展军民融合产业的必要性与可行性

随着我国经济快速发展,临空经济的发展势头迅猛,对国民经济的影响越来越强,尤其在区域经济中的重要性更为明显。我国临空经济自 20 世纪 90 年代萌芽,经历了机场属地化改革之后,全国各地开始了临空经济的规划浪潮,国内临空经济进入快速发展期。② 2018 年 5 月继郑州、青岛、成都、重庆、北京、上海、广州、长沙、贵阳、杭州、宁波之后,国家发改委、民航局正式批复设立西安临空经济示范区。

根据西安临空经济区前期制定的总体方案,西安临空经济示范区将以枢纽经济、门户经济、流动经济为重点,加快打造国际航空枢纽、临空特色产业聚集区、内陆改革开放新高地、生态宜居空港城市;到 2025 年,形成以龙头企业为引领,高端产业为支撑,临空产业集群互动发展的格局,建成辐射西北、连接全国、通达世界的航空综合运输体系,跻身国家临空经济示范区"第一方阵"。航空综合运输体系及临空产业集群的发展,必然涉及西安众多国防科工及航空航天等产业的整合创新,军民融合发展作为国家战略,是时代赋予西安临空经济区的特色使命,也是实现西安临空经济区经济快速发展的必由之路。

---

① 参见张军果:《军民融合深度发展的体制机制构建研究》,载《中国军学》2016 年第 5 期。

② 参见龚峰、韩璐:《国内临空经济区的发展模式及资源禀赋的比较》,载《物流工程与管理》2017 年第 1 期。

1. 军民融合产业发展的必要性

国务院办公厅颁布的《关于推动国防科技工业军民融合深度发展的意见》中指出,国防科技工业是军民融合发展的重点领域,既是实施军民融合发展战略的重要组成部分,也是推进国家创新驱动发展战略实施、促进供给侧结构性改革的迫切需要。军民融合发展作为一项国家战略,关乎国家安全和发展全局,既是兴国之举,又是强军之策。

产业既是军民融合发展的重大领域之一,也是实施军民融合发展战略的重要抓手。发展军民融合产业,有利于在产业内实现军民间彼此融合、双向转换、互相促进、协调发展,利用一流成果为国防建设和建成世界一流军队提供支撑,利用军民两用技术培育新动能、促进经济高质量发展,在深度融合中实现经济建设的国防效益最大化和国防建设的经济效益最大化。① 西安是国家确定的全面创新改革试验区,军民融合既是西安全面创新改革试验的两大重点任务之一,也是西安临空经济区实现区域经济快速发展的最佳抓手。

2. 军民融合产业发展的可行性

陕西自贸区空港功能区是中国(陕西)自由贸易试验区的重要承载区域,总规划面积13.8平方公里。空港新城功能区临空经济示范区、跨境电商综试区获批,并成功加入世界自由区组织,综合保税区申报已报国家部委会签。国务院颁布《关于支持自由贸易试验区深化改革创新若干措施的通知》中第31~32条,以独立条款赋予西安机场行使第五航权和进一步加大对西安航空物流发展的支持力度。

西安,是中国"国际运输走廊"和"国际航空枢纽"重要城市之一,是"一带一路"核心区和内陆型改革开放新高地,西安临空经济示范区所在的空港新城是全国唯一的航空、铁路、高铁、高速公路均呈"米"字型分布的中心枢纽节点,形成了集空、铁、公、轨于一体的立体综合交通枢纽。西安地理位置优越,资源丰富,交通便利,军工企业分布密集,专业技术人才众多,科技实力

① 参见杨威、马子健、谭茂鑫:《军民融合产业概念、特征及重要意义》,载《中国经贸导刊》2018年第18期。

雄厚,西安市国防科技工业基础综合评价仅次于北京,居全国第二位,拥有全国近1/3的航天科研生产力量和近1/4的航空专业人才与高精尖设备。以上政策优惠及地缘要素为军民融合产业的深度发展提供了无可比拟的天然优势。

二、西安临空经济区发展军民融合缺乏系统完善的法治保障

(一)我国现行军民融合法律体系存在不足

军民融合发展上升为国家战略后,国家和军队都先后建立了相应工作机构,专门规划、组织和协调"军转民"及"民参军"工作,但多年来在军民融合领域,军队与地方各自为政,形成了不少人为壁垒。重复投资、重复研制、重复发展、互相封锁等现象导致军工企业封闭落后、军民结合产业支撑不足、资源共享程度不高、机制运行不畅、政策法规不够健全等问题长期存在。军民融合园区建设也出现了同质化、泡沫化的现象,整个军民融合行业的发展乱象横生,究其原因在于缺乏系统完善的法律法规制度体系的规制。虽然我国目前在军民融合产业发展方面已经制定了部分法律法规,且随着军民融合的发展也相继出台了诸多政策法规,但现有的法律体系仍存在诸多不足和问题。

1. 法律体系顶层架构缺失,立法滞后,缺少军民融合发展基本法

现有法律体系下规范军民融合发展的法律主要有《国防法》《国家安全法》《国防动员法》《国防交通法》《保守国家秘密法》《招投标法》《专利法》《公司法》《中小企业促进法》《促进科技成果转化法》《产品质量法》等,至今尚未就军民融合发展出台专门法律,军民融合发展法律体系的顶层设计中因缺失基本法,无法对整个法律制度建设提供宏观指引,对军民融合发展中涉及的主体、权责、领域等要素缺乏明确界定及规范,散见于其他法律法规的相关规定,呈碎片化,无法形成系统的法律体系。

行政法规、规章及规范性文件主要有《国防专利条例》《装备采购方式与程序管理规定》《武器装备科研生产许可管理条例》《武器装备质量管理条例》《关于建立和完善军民结合、寓军于民武器装备科研生产体系的若干意见》《关于鼓励和引导民间投资健康发展的若干意见》《关于鼓励和引导民间资本进入国防科技工业领域的实施意见》《关于推进军工企业股份制改造的指导意见》《关于推动国防科技工业军民融合深度发展的意见》等,虽然对知识产权、装备采购、市场准入、投资、税收、资源共享、科技、人才建设等方面作出相应规定,但本身法律效力层级相对较低,权威不够。因上位法缺乏,各部门权责不明晰,导致具体文件政策落实执行缺乏可操作性及协同性,而且政策文件很难系统解决体制、机制、市场主体以及相关的金融、工商税务、监督等方面的问题。

2. 现有部分法律法规之间缺乏体系性,存在冲突

军民融合发展涉及军地两大主体,而军地双方都各自具有制定部分法规的权利,一些军事法规与地方行政法规出现标准不一,甚至个别规定与军民融合发展的最新政策及指导意见出现冲突或不符情形;地方立法过程中会更倾向于地方实际情况及需要进行立法,而忽略全局及体系考虑。① 军队和国家有关行政管理部门之间也存在因职能权责的不同,难以综合全面的展开法规制定。法规政策的制定发布主体在各自部门职能模式下进行规制,难免出现立法冲突及衔接错位。

因军民融合法律体系顶层架构的缺失,现有的部分法律法规立法时间较早,且未能及时根据军民融合的发展进行更新修订,相关法律法规之间存在冲突,与现行军民融合发展要求不相匹配。1997 年颁布的《国防法》规定"国防科技工业实行军民结合、平战结合、军品优先、以民养军的方针""国家对国防科研生产实行统一领导和计划调控""国家根据国防建设的需要和社会

---

① 参见董新泉:《我国军民融合法律法规建设问题》,载《南京理工大学学报》(社会科学版)2018 年第 2 期。

主义市场经济的要求,实行国家军事订货制度"。[①] 军民融合发展要求军企进入市场,参与市场竞争,不再简单地按计划生产,按军民融合深度发展的要求及产业模式,由国家对国防科研生产实行统一领导和计划调控显然已经不合时宜。

3. 立法不完善,个别领域内容存在空白缺失

我国军民融合的发展模式主要是"军转民""民参军",而目前涉及军民融合的相关规定大多散见于国防科技工业领域的法律法规中,现有法律体系中关于军队基本建设、军事人才培养、退伍军人安置、军队或军人保障方面存在立法空白的情形,由此导致军民融合发展过程中,许多地方企业无法参与军用物品的生产与经营活动。

"民参军"方面进入门槛高、多部门交叉管理,部分法律法规年代久远,存在不完善性与滞后性问题,虽然对于民企要求办理的军工四证已经改革简化为三证,[②]但很多规定与当前的社会经济体制及市场的机制已经表现出不相适应的状态,尤其是军事订货制度方面,如何规范军品信息的发布与获取,没有指导性的法律法规,对于地方民企参与生产经营和军品采购均构成障碍。

《政府采购法》将政府采购分为民品和军品两类,其中军品采购仅规定主管部门为国防部门,具体的军事采购法规却交由中央军委另外作出规定,时至今日仍未有具体相关法律法规出台统一规范;对于采购品类的规定,未考虑军民两用技术,虽然目前从武器装备的复杂程度上来看,民营企业主要承担配套产品、部件、元器件等军选民用产品和第 3 类军品,但一些民营企业已具有进入第 1 类核心装备(武器装备总体、关键分系统、核心配套产品)研

---

① 梁毅雄:《军民融合发展问题的法律探析》,载《国防科技工业》2012 年第 5 期。

② 军工四证特指民企参军从事军工科研生产需先取得四个资质证件,主要包括:国军标准质量管理体系认证,简称国军标认证;武器装备科研生产单位保密资质认证,简称保密认证;武器装备科研生产许可证认证,简称许可证认证;装备承制单位资格名录认证,简称名录认证。2017 年 10 月 1 日正式改革实施军工三证,包括装备承制单位资格证书、武器装备科研生产单位保密资质认证、武器装备科研生产许可证。

制生产领域的能力,却因超出2007年颁布的《非公有制经济参与国防科技工业建设指南》规定进入的军品领域,而无法通过“民参军”模式发展军民融合。①

4. 现有保密管理制度缺乏一体化标准和科学灵活性

我国现行的《保守国家秘密法》《保守国家秘密法实施条例》及相关国防科技工业领域保密政策法规,明确了保密主体的职责和保密范围,强化了保密管理水平,但缺乏对军民融合保密管理法规制度体系的统一规划及军民融合保密监管有效的宏观调控和战略协同机制。保密管理程序过于复杂和严格,在一定程度上出现定密过高,或解密期后仍处于保密状态,或定密积极、解密懈怠等问题,严重制约了军民技术的双向流动,影响军民融合的发展。②解密的风险性及准入认证的复杂程序,既制约了“军转民、民参军”机制的运行,也造成了非传统军工企业因上述壁垒怠于或无法顺利参与国防市场发展,影响了民企灵活开放特性。我国现有1000余家取得生产许可证的民营企业,规模非常可观,但严格的保密管理及军品科研生产质量的高要求使企业更倾向于保守发展,最终可能使参军民企形成另一个半封闭工业体系。③这明显与军民融合发展的发展目标及政策初衷背道而驰,解密的风险性及准入认证的复杂程序,在一定程度上导致非传统军工企业及新兴民企不能或不愿迈入国防市场的壁垒问题。

5. 军民融合发展国防知识产权归属不清,利益不明

国防知识产权是指在国防科研、生产、使用以及军民两用产品研发过程中产生的创新成果,以及其他能够应用于武器装备和国防建设的发明创造及技术成果转移转化。综观当前国防专利运营流程,“重定密、轻解密”的特点

---

① 参见徐辉:《我国军民融合政策法规现状及对策研究》,载《军民两用技术与产品》2015年第11期。

② 参见宋善秋:《军民融合发展法律规制建设探析》,载《中国军转民》2018年第1期。

③ 参见徐辉:《我国军民融合政策法规现状及对策研究》,载《军民两用技术与产品》2015年第11期。

突出,很大程度上也严重影响了国防专利技术“军转民”。[①] 目前我国国防知识产权领域主要有《国防法》《武器装备研制合同暂行办法》《国防专利条例》等法律法规,但对于技术成果的研发单位或个人,享有的占有权和使用权不具有排他性,权属不清,利益不明,技术成果缺乏流动性,无法通过利益进行激励,长此以往,承担研发的单位及个人会丧失进行科技创新和成果转化的积极性。

(二)西安临空经济区发展军民融合的法治现状

近年来,依托西安地区国防科技工业资源优势,结合军民融合产业发展现状,西安市提出了构建“一区两园五基地”,[②]建设翱翔小镇、空天小镇、通航小镇、兵器小镇等一批军民融合特色的小镇,成为军民融合产业发展的新亮点。但因现有军民融合法律体系存在不足,致使军民融合产业的发展因缺乏足够的法治保障而受到制约及影响。重点推进军民融合创新发展是西安临空经济区的三大任务之一,但现行军民融合发展法律体系顶层设计缺失,导致西安临空经济区军民融合发展无法可依,法治保障基础薄弱。临空经济区并非独立的行政区域,也不等同于经济开发区,而是各种经济要素具有临空属性,以机场为地理核心,沿交通沿线向外扩张,以发展临空产业为主导,追求空港经济的最大效应。临空经济区的总体编制规划中关于军民融合发展的政策规划及相应配套法治保障因缺乏宏观指引性的法律依据成为无本之源,而临空经济区相关的政策文件又无法替代法律规范,不具备法律效力且缺乏系统性、体系性及权威性,法律体系的不完善必将直接影响西安临空经济区军民融合战略的进一步实施及产业深度融合的发展进程。

---

① 参见李俊杰、李昌胜:《军民融合知识产权转移化机制研究》,载《知识产权》2018 年第 12 期。

② 一区两园五基地指国家军民融合创新示范区;高新区军民融合产业园、经开区军民融合创新示范园;西安阎良国家航空高技术产业基地、西安国家民用航天产业基地、西安兵器工业科技产业基地、西咸新区沣西新城、洪庆军民融合基地。

三、西安临空经济区军民融合发展的法治构建

(一)我国现有军民融合发展法律体系的完善建议

党的十八届四中全会通过的《中共中央关于全面推进依法治国若干重大问题的决定》作出"加强军民融合深度发展法治保障"战略部署,2018年中央军民融合发展委员会第二次会议审议通过《关于加强军民融合发展法治建设的意见》。军民融合作为西安临空经济区的特色使命,加强军民融合法规制度建设,是建立军民融合体制的强力支撑,是军民融合机制顺利运行的可靠保障,必将有力促进国防建设与经济建设在更高层次上融合创新,助推军民融合发展水平快速提升。

1. 尽快出台《军民融合发展法》,从立法上构建军民融合法律体系

从军民融合发展法律体系顶层设计的角度上分析,应尽快出台专门用于规范军民融合发展的《军民融合发展法》①作为基本法。根据当前军民融合发展的法规政策及相关文件的要求,通过顶层基本法的立法行为,将军民融合的概念、原则、内容、机构、责任、权限等通过法律的形式进行明确界定及规范,自上而下的统筹整合现有法律体系下涉及军民融合发展的各项规定及制度,克服目前军民融合发展的法律法规碎片化及层级较低的缺陷,

我国现行《国防法》的相关规定,应按军民融合深度发展的实际要求及需要进行修订,专门增加"军民融合"章节,将相关法规政策上升为法律,将军民融合的相关原则、方针、制度作出原则性规定,为国防科工行业的深度融合发展提供明确的法律支持和依据。上述两部法律互相协调,可以破除我国军民融合发展在立法层面存在的一些障碍,为军民融合法律体系构建提供顶层支持,也为系统综合解决军民融合发展体制、机制、市场主体及相关的金融、工商税务及监督方面的问题提供明确的法律依据。

---

① 2018年8月"中国人大网"公布《十三届全国人大常委会立法规划》,将《军民融合发展法》列入69件"条件比较成熟、任期内拟提请审议的法律草案"第一类项目。

2. 加强立法统筹规划,优化军民融合发展法治环境

目前军民融合已经从初步发展进入深度发展阶段,因此在内容、领域、功能上,还是在方式、方法上都较以往有了很大变化,相关政策法规的制定从过去针对某一突出问题推出单一政策向政策制度建设体系化、结构化方向发展,表现为法规体系建设层次高、中、低全面覆盖,部分领域各层级法律法规同步推出等。① 迫切需要加强立法顶层设计和统筹规划,构建纵向到底、横向到边的法规政策体系,推进军民融合发展各项工作有序开展。② 军民融合发展要求军民技术转化,相关军用标准与民用标准的兼容性就决定了技术和装备的军民通用性,因此应通过制定、完善相关法律法规,推进军民标准和民用标准一体化改革,确保标准化体系的科学性和合理性。

严格按照《关于开展军民融合发展法规文件清理工作的通知》的范围及标准对不适应国防和军队现代化、不符合军民统筹要求等方面的全部政策法规进行清理,加快推进与军民融合深度发展不相适应的法规制度清理修订工作,重点清理陈旧过时的内容,填补空白缺失的内容,修订相互矛盾的内容,合并交叉重叠的内容,优化军民融合发展法治环境。

3. 健全完善法律法规体系,弥补立法空白

尽快出台的《军民融合发展法》和推进修订的《国防法》,作为军民融合法律体系的顶层设计,相互协调配合,从法律层面将军民融合面临的体制机制、决策机构、科研生产、人才培养、合作纲要等方面的内容,形成系统的法律法规规范,解决军民双方以前在立法层面和具体实施过程中的争议及障碍,增强军民融合法律法规的时效性和权威性。通过法律法规明确军民融合双方主体地位及融合发展产生的一系列问题,简化民企参与军民融合的审批管理手续,降低合作门槛,与当前的社会经济体制及市场机制接轨。

结合临空经济区的布局规划及国防科工行业的发展特殊性需要,必要时

① 参见徐辉:《我国军民融合政策法规现状及对策研究》,载《军民两用技术与产品》2015年第11期。

② 参见宋善秋:《军民融合发展法规制度建设探析》,载《中国军转民》2018年第1期。

制定国防科技工业军民融合专项法律规范国防科技工业的军民融合发展,就现有法律体系中尚未涉及的国防科技工业、武器装备采购、航空航天等立法空白领域通过法律法规进行明确,为具体各领域的合作提供可操作性的规范及依据,解决现行法律体系下因法规滞后及不合时宜导致的众多影响军民融合发展的体制壁垒;在法律体系中还应就军民融合发展中的基础设施建设、国防经济动员、后勤保障等多方面的综合法律问题纳入其中进行细化规范,通过立法统筹规划推进逐步健全完善。

4. 建立军民一体化的国家保密管理制度体系

在国家层面上对军民融合保密管理进行全要素、全维度、全过程监管,提升军民融合保密管理层次、拓宽保密管理范围,本着军地一致、军民一体原则,将为国防和军队建设直接服务的企业和地方人员纳入军队保密条例管理范畴;统筹协调军地保密法规衔接配套,加强法规制度的可操作性和细致性,逐步形成系统完备、衔接配套、权威高效的军民融合保密管理制度体系。

根据当前军民融合发展的政策及发展要求,对现行保密制度进行改革修订,推行适合军民融合深度发展的科学灵活的定密解密责任制度。对国防科研和生产实施保密分级制,降低军工技术保密等级、压缩军工技术保密范围,除特别核心、含重要国家安全敏感信息、威胁国家安全的技术和领域之外,应尽量放开,并根据实际情况动态调整保密事项和密级,明晰定解密工作程序和操作流程,在确保国防安全和军事利益前提下,为推进军民融合深度发展减少阻力。

5. 建立符合军民融合发展知识产权保护体系和科学激励机制

2018 年国家知识产权局与中央军委装备发展部发布通知,决定共同开展知识产权军民融合试点工作,以强化知识产权军民双向转化运用和保护为重点,不断完善知识产权领域军地组织管理体系、工作运行体系和政策制度体系,推动知识产权领域军地政策互通互利、资源共建共享、人才联培联用,实现知识产权领域军民资源整合、要素融合和优势聚合,促进更多军民融合新技术、新产品、新业态、新模式服务国防建设和经济发展,有效提高军民融合整体效益。

对于军民融合发展过程中的国防知识产权问题,在现有知识产权法律体系规定下,以强化知识产权军民双向转化运用和保护为目标,借鉴参考美国"谁创造,谁拥有"的原则,通过政策引导知识产权管理;也可根据军民一体化发展目标制定《国防科技工业成果与技术实施转化管理办法》进行规范。构建符合军民融合发展中各方利益的制度保护体系和科技进步激励机制,通过法规制度对军民融合过程中成果与技术转化的含义、转化方式、权属及利益分配、技术流动、保密与解密的法律责任进行界定,解决军民融合发展中知识产权面临的多重困境。

军民融合法律体系的构建应坚持顶层设计为先导,需求牵引为主线,深化融合为目标,全局统筹规划,从立法源头上确保政策法规与其他相关法律相融合,注重政策法规的纵向和横向衔接配套,总结我国一直以来的"军转民""民参军"的经验和做法,借鉴国内外成功实践经验,开展专项立法研究,提高立法水平及层级,增加执行力度与可操作力度,确保立法科学性、系统性和协调性。

(二)西安临空经济区军民融合发展的法治构建

西安临空经济区军民融合产业发展的法治构建,首先,依赖现行军民融合法律体系的健全及完善,从顶层设计及立法位阶上,系统化、体系化的规范军民融合产业发展,为临空经济区军民融合的深度发展及重点推进提供明确的法律规范依据。其次,根据西安临空经济区的总体编制规划及地域产业优势,针对军民融合产业发展出台专门的优惠扶持政策,在完善的军民融合发展法律体系下,按照国家发展军民融合的战略要求及临空经济区的实际需要,制定相应的法律法规实施细则替代相关政策性规定。最后,空港新城的特殊定位,决定了临空经济的发展与国际法、国际空间法密切相关,因此西安临空经济区发展军民融合产业,还需要与国际法、国际空间法接轨,充分考虑临空经济及产业融合发展在法律法规层面的协调统一。从国家法律体系及区域发展规划两个层面上,为西安临空经济区发展军民融合产业深度发展提供系统完善的法治保障。

四、结　　语

2016年中共中央政治局会议审议通过《关于经济建设和国防建设融合发展的意见》,明确要求"完善政策法规,构建军民融合法治保障体系"成为新时期推动中国军民融合发展立法的重要战略决策和制定军民融合基本法的依据。2018年中央军民融合发展委员会第二次全体会议时指出军民融合进入实质性实践阶段,审议通过《关于加强军民融合发展法治建设的意见》并明确抓好贯彻实施,推进军民融合领域立法。军民融合作为西安临空经济区的特殊使命和重点任务,随着临空经济区各项政策红利及低空空域的开放,作为国防科工大省的陕西和军工大市的西安必将迎来军民融合深度发展的新机遇。完善军民融合发展的法律法规体系,对于规范西安临空经济区军民融合深度发展,统筹区域经济与国防建设协调发展,具有重大现实意义和深远的历史意义。

首都机场临空经济区对外开放门户构建法制化探析*

张婷钰**

引　言

2019年首都机场临空经济示范区正式获批，根据前期制定的总体方案，北京首都机场临空经济示范区定位是大型国际航空枢纽、亚太地区的重要复合枢纽，服务于首都核心功能。① 在改革开放的过程中，我国的区域经济发展取得了巨大进步，为整个国民经济的发展做出了突出的贡献，从以往的经验来看，经济、市场、法律、行政政策等一系列手段在区域经济的发展中起着重要的作用，但在依法治国、依法行政的时代背景下，用法律手段来积极推进首都机场临空经济示范区的发展显得尤为重要。党的十八

---

* 本文系国家社科基金一般项目：《"一带一路"背景下跨境电子商务平台法律保障机制研究》（编号：18BFX213）阶段性研究成果。

** 贵州大学国际法学硕士研究生，研究方向为国际经济法学。

① 《首都机场临空经济示范区正式获批》，资料来源：https://www.toutiao.com/a6666964991763022339/，最后访问日期：2019年3月6日。

届四中全会提出明确要求,凡属重大改革都应于法有据,在整个改革推进的过程中应高度重视运用法治思维和法治方法,发挥法治对于改革的引领和推动作用,加强对相关立法工作的协调,确保在法治轨道上推进改革。① 当然,在强调临空经济区改革"于法有据"的同时也不能忽略改革创新的重要性。当前,首都机场临空经济示范区的发展处于试点阶段,首都机场临空经济示范区的法制化建设问题是理论界的一个前沿课题,对于该问题的研究在一定程度上可以丰富和发展我国的法学研究,希望通过笔者的浅略分析,能够引起更多学者对于这一问题的重视,起到抛砖引玉的效果,切实解决该问题。对于该问题的研究是使首都机场临空经济示范区的发展真正在法治引领下进行的前提,有利于国民经济又好又快发展。

一、国内外区域经济发展对首都机场临空经济区对外开放门户构建的启示

临空经济区是一个具有区域性、产业性和经济性的综合体,一方面,孵化培育相关产业,推动地方经济发展;另一方面,又反哺推动航空业进步,是民航业和地方经济互利共赢的纽带。② 临空经济区不是对空域的再划分,但机场这一要素是临空经济区产生的重要依托,机场是指供航空器起飞、降落和地面活动而划定的一块地域或水域,包括城内的各种建筑物和设备装置。③ 自 1959 年爱尔兰香浓国际航空港自由贸易区成立以来,国际上对航空经济的产业布局开始了持续的实践和探索。④ 从国外的发展实践来看,临空经济区的发展一般需经历成型期、发展期和成熟期三个阶段。

---

① 参见《完善自由贸易试验区"负面清单" 提速改革开放法治建设》,资料来源:http://www.moj.gov.cn/Department/content/2018-01/10/596_203617.html,最后访问日期:2019 年 3 月 6 日。

② 参见曹允春:《临空经济——速度经济时代的增长空间》,经济出版社 2009 年版,第 12 页。

③ 参见杨惠、郝秀辉:《航空法学原理与实例》,法律出版社 2011 年版,第 102 页。

④ 参见刘晓萍:《国外航空港的发展模式及启示》,载《国际交流》2015 年第 1 期。

(一)德国法兰克福国际航空城

法兰克福作为德国最大的航空枢纽,是德国乃至欧洲重要的工商业中心、金融服务中心。法兰克福临空经济区善于发挥地区比较优势,挖掘法兰克福的优势资源并致力于培育主导产业。法兰克福临空经济区以高端制造业作为配套产业,充分发挥了其高附加值、高盈利水平的功能。法兰克福临空经济区周围聚集着大量的高科技公司,这些企业的产品大都是以出口为主,例如,坐落于法兰克福的赫希斯特、德固赛和吕特格尔斯等企业的化工产品、医药、染料在全球拥有巨大的影响力。①当地政府坚持生态文明理念,坚持法兰克福的科学发展,绿色低碳健康发展,对于法兰克福临空经济区良好生态环境的形成产生了重要作用。首都机场临空经济示范区坐落于首都北京拥有着类似甚至优于法兰克福国际航空城的地缘优势,亦应发挥其比较优势,在首都机场临空经济区的发展中,逐渐由资本驱动型向创新驱动型转变,掌握高端技术、吸引高端人才,实现产业发展的高端化目标。

(二)韩国仁川机场航空城

在韩国政府2011年正式推出的仁川机场航空城的发展规划中,仁川机场经济区包括机场区、国际商务区、自由贸易及旅游开发区三大部分,力争把航空城发展成为集航运、物流、金融、高新技术于一体的具有多种产业职能的经济区域。② 仁川机场航空城的建设中非常注重对自然资源的利用和保护,尤其是对于海洋资源的利用,吸引了大量外商的投资。同时依托自由贸易区的辐射功能,促进了高新技术和高新产业的发展,也巩固了仁川机场的全球枢纽地位,极大地提升了仁川机场航空城的国际竞争力。当前,仁川机场航空城依靠对空港资源的利用已经初显三方面的发展特征:人口年龄结构以中青年为主,占人口总量的2/3以上,知识结构新、动量大;专业技术人员和工

① 参见付锦韬:《法兰克福临空经济模式分析》,载《现代商业》2016年第12期。

② 参见刘晓萍:《国外航空港的发展模式及启示》,载《国际交流》2015年第1期。

人的比例大幅度上升,空港都市区整体形成多行业均衡互补的发展态势;产业结构呈现明显的三、二、一结构,第三产业从业人口约占人口总量的60%,且保持稳定发展。①

(三)我国自由贸易区的发展

2013年上海自由贸易试验区正式成立,2013年上海市政府公布了《中国(上海)自由贸易试验区外商投资准入特别管理措施(负面清单)》(2013年),②此后该份负面清单为适应国内国际经济发展需要进行了多次调整,2018年,经党中央、国务院同意,商务部颁布了统一适用于全国的《外商投资准入特别管理措施(负面清单)》(2018年版)。③ 在自贸区的建设过程中,自贸区肩负着提供"可复制,可推广"经验的同时,也肩负着进行制度性改革试验的重任,而这种试验的核心就是推动法治理念的变化,"法治化"是贯穿中国自由贸易试验区试验过程中的关键词。在自由贸易试验区的试验改革推进过程中,推动了外商投资领域法律规范的调整,就法治领域而言,中国自贸区初步试验了一些新理念,健全完善了外商投资领域法律体制。中国自贸区的立法主要集中表现为国务院印发的自贸区政策文件,如《中国(上海)自由贸易试验区总体方案》《中国(广东)自由贸易试验区总体方案》等以及地方人大常委会或地方政府制定的自治区条例,如《中国(上海)自由贸易区条例》等。2015年修改的《立法法》第13条规定:"全国人民代表大会及其常务委员会可以根据改革发展的需要,决定就行政管理等领域的特定事项授权一定权限内在部分地方暂时调整或者暂时停止适用法律的部分规定。"该条将

① 参见吕小勇:《空港都市区空间成长机制与调控策略构建研究》,哈尔滨工业大学2015年博士学位论文,第34页。

② 参见《中国(上海)自由贸易试验区外商投资准入特别管理措施(负面清单)》(2013年),资料来源:http://www.shanghai.gov.cn/nw2/nw2314/nw2319/nw10800/nw11407/nw30984/u26aw37036.html,最后访问日期:2019年3月6日。

③ 参见《外商投资准入特别管理措施(负面清单)》(2018年版)修订说明,资料来源:http://www.ndrc.gov.cn/xwzx/xwfb/201806/t20180628_890757.html,最后访问日期:2019年3月6日。

上海自贸试验区的法治实践中所开创的在特定区域内对法律法规进行局部的、临时性的调整,即法律"因地调整"的模式正式入法。① 自贸区发展模式可以为同样肩负着提供"可复制,可推广"经验重任的临空经济示范区的发展提供一定经验借鉴。首都机场临空经济示范区亦可以并且应该主动发挥先试先行的功能,对部分法律作出临时性调整,从而作出更加有利于开放和改革的规定和解释。

二、首都机场临空经济区对外开放门户法制化建设中存在的问题

(一)法律位阶较低、法规较为分散

当前,我国临空经济发展方兴未艾,临空经济区的建设也在如火如荼地进行着,截至2017年年底,全国超过30个省、自治区、直辖市已经明确规划并进行建设的空港经济区有67个。截至2018年6月,全国已有12个临空经济示范区。为了推动临空经济区有序发展,2015年7月,国家发改委、民航局发布了《关于临空经济示范区建设发展的指导意见》,该意见指出选择若干条件成熟的临空经济区开展试点示范工作,发挥比较优势增强辐射带动作用,优化我国经济发展格局,全方位深化对外开放,加快转变经济发展方式。2019年2月27日生态环境部发布《临空经济区规划环境影响评价技术要点(试行)》,促进临空经济区与生态环境保护持续协调可持续发展。②

2019年国家发展改革委和民航局联合印发了《关于支持首都机场临空经济示范区建设的复函》(以下简称《复函》),指导北京市有序推动首都机场临空经济示范区建设。③《复函》指出首都机场临空经济示范区建设,以体制

① 参见龚柏华:《中国自贸试验区需试验法治新思维》,载《人民法治》2016年第12期。

② 参见《生态环境部:临空经济区规划环境影响评价技术要点》,资料来源:http://huanbao.bjx.com.cn/news/20190306/967027.html,最后访问日期:2019年3月6日。

③ 参见《首都机场临空经济示范区正式获批》,资料来源:https://www.toutiao.com/a666696499176302 2339/,最后访问日期:2019年3月6日。

机制创新和扩大航空服务开放为突破口,以服务京津冀协同发展为重点,进一步增强国际航空枢纽、国际交往门户和国家经贸口岸功能,提升投资与贸易便利化。综上所述,目前对于首都机场临空经济示范区的立法工作还处于探索阶段,体现了国家临空经济区立法方面的谨慎态度。

对关于临空经济区的规范进行归纳整理后可发现,除国务院的批复及地方层面的临空经济区规划外,其他规范性文件大多与临空经济区的某些具体领域及其发展密切相关,总体上缺乏系统性具有临时性、位阶低的特点,尚未出台针对临空经济区的专门性法律规范。临空经济区的设立只有政府相关部门的条例、方案,并没有相关的法律依据,也没有配套法律保证其稳定运行,如此一来,临空经济区在法律上容易处于"真空地带"。大量临时性、位阶较低的规范难以保证文件的权威性、稳定性和可持续性。"规范先行"机制有利于制度的创新性发展,特别是在首都机场临空经济示范区初期建设阶段,亟须相应配套规范的支持,以保证改革的顺利稳定推进。相对于其他临空经济示范区的发展而言,《首都机场临空经济示范区总体规划》《首都机场临空经济示范区发展规划》尚未出台,造成了首都机场临空经济示范区发展的宏观指导、规划目标、发展计划的不明确性。在改革开放初期,"破法改革"还情有可原,毕竟那时一切都处在重建阶段。① 虽然首都机场临空经济示范区担负着"先行先试"的体制机制创新的任务,然而"先试先行"不是改革开放初期阶段的"摸着石头过河",既然要实现体制机制的创新,便不宜再走"破法改革"的道路,北京市政府应尽快出台临空经济示范区发展的相关条例规范,运用法制手段推进其稳步运行。

(二)营商环境有待优化,体制机制有待创新

创新体制机制,优化营商环境是首都机场临空经济示范区建设发展的重要内容。当前,以美国为代表的发达国家出现贸易保护主义重新抬头,逆全

① 参见龚柏华:《中国自贸试验区需试验法治新思维》,载《人民法治》2016 年第 12 期。

球化思潮不断升温的现象，世界范围内的外资流动性有所降低，各国吸引外资的竞争更加激烈，再加上新兴市场国家在土地、劳动力等方面的低成本优势和更加优惠的政策措施，以及我国国内资金、劳动力、原材料等各种生产要素成本不断攀升，使我国在吸引外资方面的比较优势逐渐丧失，对外资的吸引力逐渐下降。① 因此应积极创新市场准入机制，培育竞争新优势。

从当前首都机场临空经济示范区的相关文件中可以看出，首都机场临空经济示范区的建设与发展中主要运用政策手段开展管理工作，政策手段一方面缺乏权威性，另一方面不利于发挥市场在资源配置中应有的作用。优化营商环境已然是“放管服”改革的应有之义。目前我国经济发展已步入高质量发展阶段，亟须建立适合我国国情的营商环境影响评价机制，从而厘清首都机场临空经济示范区营商环境的现状，找出经济发展中存在的问题和可借鉴之处，为营商环境的优化提供可借鉴的思路和方法。

（三）首都机场临空经济区内的涉外纠纷解决机制有待健全

投资贸易的便利化程度，不仅体现在政府行政能力与行政水平上，也体现在贸易过程中纠纷的解决机制上，商事贸易领域需要高效、便捷、经济的纠纷解决机制，但在首都机场临空经济示范区的发展中，纠纷的解决仍然主要依靠司法诉讼，诚然其具有权威性的优点，但其亦具有成本高、耗时长的缺点，这不适应贸易发展的效率性要求，同时在先试先行的法律空白领域，司法诉讼很容易造成判决缺乏法律依据的情况，赋予了法官过多的自由裁量权，可能造成同案不同判的结果，这将降低司法的权威。在国际商事贸易交往中，商事仲裁、非诉讼纠纷解决程序（Alternative Dispute Resolution，ADR）逐渐成为解决纠纷的主要途径，作为开放程度较高并承担着体制机制创新任务的首都机场临空经济示范区，需要适应国际商事贸易发展的多元纠纷解决机制以提高对外开放水平。

---

① 参见张绍乐：《中国探索建设自由贸易港的任务、障碍与对策研究》，载《郑州轻工业学院学报》2019 年第 1 期。

三、首都机场临空经济示范区对外开放门户法制化建设的完善建议

(一)加快建立完善临空经济区法律体系

当前,我国各地相继建立起临空经济区,其建设与发展已初具规模和成效。与此同时,国家"一带一路"倡议、丝路基金计划、亚洲基础设施投资银行方兴未艾,我国新一轮改革开放的战略格局正在形成,在改革创新的前提下亦应努力完善首都机场临空经济示范区的相关规范条例,为首都机场临空经济示范区的发展提供法治保障。建设首都机场临空经济示范区是国内法举措,但首都机场临空经济示范区若要进一步增强其《复函》中提到的"国际航空枢纽、国际交往门户和国家口岸功能,提升投资与贸易便利化水平",在建设过程中和制定政策法规时亦应尊重和服从国际法准则,这也是提高对外开放水平的需要。

1. 借鉴新发展的贸易便利化和投资自由化的国际法规则

贸易和环境领域被认为是国际制度最成熟、法律规范最完善、法律应用最深入、最具有规则导向的领域。[①] 其中,国际贸易法更是国际经济法中最发达、结构最为精密的部门。[②]《贸易便利化协定》是我国加入世界贸易组织(World Trade Organization,WTO)后参与达成的首个货物贸易协定,该协定规定成员方应尽可能采用风险管理和后续稽查等管理手段,加快对低风险货物的放行速度,对于经过认证的贸易商,为其提供降低单证要求和查验比例等额外的贸易便利化措施。[③]《贸易便利化协定》对成员国的口岸基础设施、管理方式以及口岸管理部门之间的协同等方面提出了较高的要求。相应地,

---

① 参见何志鹏:《WTO 体制的发展取向论》,载《国际法与比较法论坛》2010 年第 2 期。

② See Qureshi A. H., Ziegler, A. R., *International Economic Law*, 2nd ed., Sweet & Maxwell,2007,p. 267.

③ 我国接受 WTO《贸易便利化协定》议定书,资料来源:http://news.ifeng.com/a/20150907/44595107_0.shtml,最后访问日期:2019 年 3 月 6 日。

在临空经济区的建设中亦应完善相关基础设施的建设,在首都机场临空经济示范区的运营中尽快对接《贸易便利化协定》中中国已经承诺的,属于义务性的便利化程度要求,适度引入《贸易便利化协定》鼓励采用的贸易便利化措施。

中国正致力于达成高水平的双边和多边自贸安排。截至 2015 年年底,中国已实施 14 个国际自贸协定,涉及 22 个国家和地区;中国—东盟升级版经济合作也已签署。① 对于《贸易便利化协定》以及其他的双边或多边自由贸易协定、双边投资保护协定所规定的较高标准的国际贸易投资规则,在首都机场临空经济示范区的建设与发展中应加以借鉴,在首都机场临空经济示范区内先试先行高标准的国际贸易投资规则,尤其为了增强国际交往门户和国家经贸口岸功能,提升投资与贸易便利化水平,可以与自贸区《外商投资准入特别管理措施(负面清单)》(2018 年版)相对接,对于外资准入制度的简化、营商环境的优化、引导国际航空资源与高端服务功能的集聚、加快现代化经济体系的构建、港城融合的国际航空中心核心区的打造具有重要意义,从而实现引领我国临空经济区实现转型升级和创新发展的目标。

2. 遵守 WTO 协定和中国"入世"文件

中国是 WTO 的重要成员国之一。WTO 已经具备了一个框架性的宪政体系应有的因素。② WTO 形成了较为完整的法律规范体系,如普遍的最惠国待遇、国民待遇,关税、原产地规则,反倾销、反补贴、政府采购、公共健康、公共安全,农产品贸易、服务贸易、与贸易有关的投资措施、与贸易有关的知识产权、贸易与投资、贸易与环境,多边贸易自由化与区域经济一体化、争端解决机制等。③ WTO 货物贸易协定、服务贸易协定和与贸易有关的知识产

---

① 参见《中国已签署 14 个自贸协定涉及 22 个国家地区》,资料来源:http://www.chinanews.com/m/cj/2016/01-06/7704076.shtml,最后访问日期:2019 年 3 月 6 日。

② See Jackson J. H., *The Jurisprudence of GATT and the WTO: Insights on Treaty Law and Economic Relations*, Cambridge University Press, 2000, pp. 183-187.

③ See Trebilcock M. J., Howse R., *The Regulation of International Trade*, 3rd ed., Routledge, 2005, pp. 351-352.

权协定是 WTO 的实体法律内容。《中国入世议定书》中中国对于贸易制度的统一实施方面作出了相应承诺。首都机场临空经济示范区属于《中国入世议定书》中的"特殊经济区",对于与特殊经济区有关的法律、法规及其他措施应通知 WTO,同时在临空经济区内要注意遵守 WTO 关于最惠国待遇原则和国民待遇原则的规定。中国关于首都机场临空经济示范区的建设要遵守《中国入世议定书》中的义务性要求,否则就是违反 WTO,这将面临其他成员方的指控。因此,在首都机场临空经济示范区的法律体系建设中要遵守 WTO 的有关协定和《中国入世议定书》并注意不得违反最惠国待遇原则和国民待遇原则。

3. 加快完善地方立法,做好与国际国内相关法律法规的衔接工作

在首都机场临空经济示范区的建设与发展中,为及时解决试点过程中的制度保障问题,现阶段应通过地方立法,建立与首都机场临空经济示范区试点要求相适应的管理制度。虽然在临空经济区建设与发展中存在法律缺位、法律位阶较低的情形,但在现有法律体制及试点工作尚未完全结束的背景下,不宜制定《中国临空经济区法》,而应借鉴同样承担"先试先行"任务的自贸区法制建设的发展经验:各自贸区分别以颁布管理办法和条例的方式明确日常管理制度,待制度经验积累到一定程度时,再进行法律层面的立法工作,而在立法明确之前,各自贸区应当分别积极探索与国际贸易规则相衔接的政策机制,更好地完成试点工作。① 首都机场临空经济示范区的建设与发展亦应如此,在先试先行工作的进行过程中,应把握首都机场临空经济示范区的侧重点,深度挖掘自身优势,努力将天津自贸区便利政策复制、推广延伸至首都机场临空经济示范区,打造具有自身特色的临空经济示范区。完善首都机场临空经济示范区的地方立法工作,并做好与相关法律法规的协调衔接工作。例如,做好与外商投资法的衔接工作,做好与自贸区、保税区相关法律法规的协调工作;严格遵守《巴黎协定》中提出的碳排放目标,打造绿色经济,实现

① 参见崔汪卫:《自贸区知识产权司法保护制度的构建》,载《中国科技论坛》2015 年第 3 期。

临空经济区内经济的可持续、绿色健康发展,从而带动全市甚至全国经济的绿色健康发展;更好地发挥地方立法对于改革发展的引领与推动作用。

(二)创新体制机制,优化营商环境

国家发改委透露,将在放宽市场准入、规则公开透明、优化政务服务、完善评价机制四个方面发力,将优化营商环境的政策红利真正落到实处。① 对此,首都机场临空经济示范区营商环境的优化、体制机制的创新亦可从这四个方面作出努力。

首先,应放宽市场准入机制,在临空经济区内实施"负面清单"管理模式。首都机场临空经济示范区开放型经济治理体系应统筹国内国际两个市场,引导全球创新资源、高端服务和国际航空资源的集聚,打造新型外资吸引点,实现改革与开放的互利共赢。

其次,对于市场的参与者来说,市场规则的统一公开透明是进行市场参与的起码要求,因此,不能因市场主体的国籍、身份、所有制的差别而使市场参与者享有不同的待遇,应遵循 WTO 透明度原则,以行政公开原则为指导,建立透明公开的市场规则。

再次,将"放管服"改革落到实处,优化政务服务,使市场发挥在资源配置中应有的决定作用。

最后,完善营商环境评价机制,遵循科学性、合理性、通用可比、针对性、实用性和可度量等基本原则。② 为企业的发展提供方向性指引,形成可复制可推广的营商环境影响评价机制,为我国营商环境的优化提供可借鉴的发展路径。

---

① 参见《发改委将四方面发力进一步优化营商环境》,资料来源:http://www.3news.cn/redian/2019/0319/330127.html,最后访问日期:2019 年 3 月 6 日。

② 参见张景华、刘畅:《税务营商环境评价体系的构建路径》,载《税务管理》2018 年第 10 期。

(三)构建多元化涉外纠纷解决机制

当国际贸易开始进入上升通道,美国作为世界头号经济强国对国家贸易问题越发关注,于1980年通过《海关法院法案》将海关法院更名为国际贸易法庭,并将涉外贸易区案件纳入国际贸易法庭的专属管辖范围,成立了全国性法庭——国际贸易法庭,[①]可见,美国对涉外贸易案件纠纷解决机制的重视。首都机场临空经济示范区建设与发展中必然面临的外商投资争议、涉外商贸纠纷、知识产权纠纷需要适应国际贸易处理规则,建立多元纠纷解决机制。当前,各国处理经济贸易纠纷开始倾向于调解等ADR机制。ADR机制与司法审理过程并无本质差别,均由专家(法官)以事实和法律为依据作出公平合理的判决,其区别在于机构运作上的差异:前者的裁决机构是由一个5人组成的专家组,后者则由两级司法体系构成。[②] 可见,ADR纠纷解决机制具有高效性,因此首都机场临空经济示范区多元纠纷解决机制的构建应发挥ADR在中的纠纷解决作用,当然可能由于裁决机构组成人员的素质和东道国的政治政策等相关压力,得出相对不是很公平的判决,对此应积极引进培养国内外优秀法律和经贸人才进入ADR纠纷解决机制领域,这一点在一些相对自由、效率以及专业化要求较高的领域(如金融纠纷的解决)尤为显著。[③]

同时,在首都机场临空经济示范区内构建多元化涉外纠纠纷解决机制,应充分发挥仲裁机构的积极性,增设友好仲裁与临时仲裁制度,适时开放投资争端解决机制,允许当事人在穷尽东道国法律救济后,向境外仲裁机构提起投资争端仲裁。还可以引入境外仲裁等法律服务机构,与省仲裁协会开展

---

① See Scott H. S., Stephen J. O., *Playing the Zone and Controlling the Board: the Emerging Jurisdictional Consensus and the Court of International Trade*, American University Law Review, August 1995, pp. 2412 - 2415.

② See Federal Rules Decisions, *Proceedings of the Ninth Judicial Conference of the United States Court of International Trade*, New York, West Publishing Company, 1994, p. 596.

③ 参见蒋丽:《构建中国(上海)自由贸易试验区外资准入“负面清单”模式法律分析》,载《经营与管理》2014年第5期。

合作。总之,有效整合诉讼、仲裁、ADR 等多种纠纷解决机制,使当事人有多种选择,并最大限度地使纠纷得到公平合理的解决,最大限度地保护当事人的合法权益。

结　语

从以上分析可以看出,在开放型经济体制之下,首都机场临空经济示范区的发展不应被孤立化看待,首都机场临空经济示范区今后对外开放门户的法制化构建可以借鉴自贸区的发展路径,以颁布管理办法和条例的方式明确日常管理制度,待制度经验积累到一定程度时,再进行法律层面的立法工作,而在立法明确之前,首都机场临空经济示范区应当积极探索与国际贸易规则相衔接的政策机制,更好地完成试点工作,促进航空物流、临空服务、临空科创、国际商务贸易产业集群的快速发展,努力将临空经济区建设成为国际交往中心功能承载区,通过发挥首都机场临空经济示范区“先试先行”的功能不断加强与世界贸易规则接轨,在法治轨道上打造首都机场临空经济示范区高水平的对外开放门户枢纽。

第五航权

“一带一路”背景下第五航权法律制度探析*

王嘉文** 张望平***

经济全球化不断发展,我国提出“一带一路”倡议。在这一倡议下,航空业也随着沿线国家经济、文化联系日益密切的趋势不断发展变化着,航权开放成为必然之趋势。正确认识第五航权的内涵和制度现状,剖析开放第五航权所面临的问题,对比国际实践完善我国第五航权法律制度,对于推动“一带一路”建设有重要意义。

---

* 本文系2017年陕西省教育厅哲学社会科学重点研究基地项目“新加坡国际私法研究”(17JZ075)和2016年陕西省社会科学基金一般项目“空中丝绸之路经济带建设中的陕西航权开放法律问题研究”(2016F009)的阶段性研究成果。

** 西北政法大学国际法学院2016级本科生。

*** 法学博士,西北政法大学国际法学院副教授,硕士研究生导师。

一、第五航权的法律内涵

(一)第五航权定义

1. 航权

航权(traffic rights),亦称为"空中自由"(freedoms of the air)。航权的概念最早源于1944年"芝加哥会议","航权"一词一经提出,其定义莫衷一是。有学者认为航权指国际航空运输中的过境和运输业务权利,也称空中自由权或国际航空运输的业务权。① 也有学者指出,航权是指获准使用他国领空的权利。② 简言之,航权的定义可以概括为:"一国民航飞机按照约定的航线,出入对方国家领空,经停对方国家领土,并做上下旅客、装卸货物或邮件的商业活动的权利。"③

2. 第五航权

现今在国际航空法领域中,航权的类型主要发展出两种学说,即"五种自由说"(五种航权)和"九种自由说"(九种航权)。在1944年芝加哥会议上形成了《国际航班过境协定》(又称"两大自由协定"④),与之同时缔结的《国际航空运输协定》涵盖并承认了五大航空自由,⑤因此该协定又被称为"五大自由协定"。在该会议中,加拿大代表提出了四种"航空自由",即将一国民用航空器进入和途经外国的航空运输经营权利具体细分为四种。"五种航权"的说法是该会议中经美国代表补充提出得以形成的。⑥ 在五种自由说中,第

---

① 参见杨治远:《航权开放与国家经济发展及经济安全的思考》,载《中国民航飞行学报》2009年第9期。

② See Martin Bartlik, *Impact of EU Law on the Regulation of International Air Transportation*, Ashgate Publishing Company, 2007, p. 1.

③ 董箫:《航权交换研究》,知识产权出版社2010年版,第23页。

④ "两大自由"指前两种自由,即领空飞越权和技术经停权。

⑤ See Jae Woon Lee, Will Horton, "Fifth Freedom Traffic Rights: Formidable Threat or Theoretical Concern", *Air and Space Law* 43, 2018, p. 304.

⑥ 参见董箫:《航权交换研究》,知识产权出版社2010年版,第43页。

五航权最为复杂且最具经济价值。

五种航权说包括以下具体权利:第一,领空飞越权;第二,技术经停权;第三,目的地下客卸货权;第四,目的地上客装货权;第五,前站权、中间点权或以远权。

具体而言,第五航权是指双边航空运输协定的缔约国指定的民用航空公司在从事两国之间的运营时可以涉及第三国的一项权利。(见图1)

图1　第五航权示意①

(二)表现形式

第五航权可以分为三种表现形式。② (X为飞机国籍国,Y为双边协定另一缔约国,Z为第三国)

1. 前站权

在两个及以上双边协定授权下,民用航空器在与Y国的航线上位于X国前一点Z之间载运客货,即Z—X—Y。

---

① Feature-Freedoms of the Air, *The Journey* (*Cathay Pacific's monthly newsletter*), 20 Oct. 2017.

② 参见赵维田:《国际航空法》,社会科学文献出版社2000年版,第37页。

2. 中间点权

在两个及以上双边协定授权下,民用航空器从本国 X 飞往 Y 国,途中经停中间点国 Z,并在 X 国上下客货,即 X—Z—Y。

3. 以远权

在两个及以上双边协定授权下,民用航空器从本国 X 飞往 Y 国,被允许在 Y 国上下客货,同时被允许飞往第三国 Z,即 X—Y—Z。

二、国际航空法中的第五航权法律制度

法国与德国在 1913 年缔结了首例双边航空运输协定,该协定主要就两国非军用航空器在缔约另一方境内的飞越权达成协议。① 但直到 1944 年召开的芝加哥会议上《芝加哥公约》的签订,才开启了航权制度的新纪元。

(一) 芝加哥公约

在第二次世界大战末期的 1944 年,54 国政府在美国的邀请下派出代表赴芝加哥参与了国际民用航空会议,又称芝加哥会议。在该会议中,与会代表主要就各国之间是否将授权彼国享有部分或完全的五项航空自由进行了磋商。② 在美国代表的呼吁下,与会各国缔结了被誉为国际航空法的最重要渊源之一的《国际民用航空公约》,又称《芝加哥公约》(Chicago Convention)。③ 同时,会议的另一大成果就是成立了"临时国际民用航空组织",该组织便是当今国际民航组织的前身。④

---

① See P. P. C. Haanappel, *The Law and Policy of Air Space and Outer Space*, Kluwer Law International, 2003, p. 4.

② See Anthony Sampson, *Empires of the Sky: The Politics, and Cartels of World Airlines*, Hodder and Stroughton, 1984, p. 2.

③ See Ariane Debyser, EU External Aviation Policy, *European Parliamentary Research Service*, 2016, p. 2.

④ 参见赵维田:《国际航空法》,社会科学文献出版社 2000 年版,第 16 页。

(二)国际实践及发展趋势

1944 年芝加哥会议之后,国际航空运输体系也随着世界经济的发展而变化。作为传统的航空业强国,英国和美国在第五航权的实践初探和航运模式变迁中发挥着引领作用。从最初严格的双边协定模式到放宽管制的自由市场化模式,国际航权法律体系正在朝航空自由化趋势发展。

1. 欧美地区第五航权实践

(1)芝加哥标准式

芝加哥标准式指国际上以《临时航线协定的标准格式》为范本签订双边航空协定,这种双边协定被概括为两国政府的航空主管部门通过该协定建立起两国间民用航空运输服务的管理体制,主要包括互相授予过境权和业务权条款及辅助性条款两大内容。[①] 在 20 世纪四五十年代美国自由主义思想的影响下,除与加拿大外,美国在其他双边协定中均互相交换了全部的五项航空自由。

(2)百慕大模式

芝加哥会议期间,居于航空市场控制地位的两大国家——英国和美国——在商业性航空运输问题上针锋相对。美国主张依据市场经济原理的“航空自由论”,英国则主张严格管控航空运输业的“航空秩序论”,即“自由主义”和“保护主义”的交锋。[②] 尽管这两个国家的主张截然相反,他们仍在“最大让步”下缔结了双边民用航空运输服务协议,即 1946 年《百慕大协定》。(见表 1)[③]包括有较多的第五自由的百慕大模式 I 正是脱胎于该协

---

① See Paul Stephen Dempsey, *Law & Foreign Policy in International Aviation*, Transnational Publishers, 1987, p. 47.

② 参见董箫:《航权交换研究》,知识产权出版社 2010 年版,第 65 页。

③ See Paul Stephen Dempsey, *Law & Foreign Policy in International Aviation*, Transnational Publishers, 1987, p. 11.

议。[①] 在提供“充分运力”的一般原则下,缔约方可以自由地行使它的第五航权。[②]

表1 《百慕大协定》下英美第五航权部分航线

英国	伦敦—纽约—旧金山—檀香山/中途岛/威克/关岛/马尼拉—新加坡/中国香港特别行政区
	伦敦—纽约—新奥尔良—墨西哥
	伦敦—纽约—古巴—牙买加/巴拿马—哥伦比亚/厄瓜多尔/秘鲁/智利
美国	美国各航点—伦敦—荷兰/德国/斯堪的纳维亚/俄罗斯
	美国各航点—伦敦—比利时—中欧—近东—印度
	檀香山—中国香港特别行政区—新加坡—荷兰东印度群岛

国际航空业的发展深受20世纪70年代席卷全球的石油危机的波及,同时百慕大模式Ⅰ使美国在国际航空运输领域中的实力远超英国。为维护本国利益,英国宣称退出《百慕大协定Ⅰ》作为向美国发起《百慕大协定Ⅱ》谈判的筹码。《百慕大协定Ⅱ》更为凸显了英国“航空秩序论”的理念,限制了《百慕大协定Ⅰ》中的某些自由因素,[③]如对第五种航权下的以远点形式作出限制。这一模式的历史直到自由化模式诞生才告一段落。

(3)“开放天空”模式

“开放天空”协定是在国际航空自由化的背景下诞生的,其理论基础为经济学上的新自由主义。[④]《百慕大协定Ⅱ》的签订与美国航空自由化政策背道而驰,因此,国内市场自由化的大环境下,美国卡特政府在1978年8月21日颁布的《航空公司放松管制法》正式宣布取消国内市场票价、航线和时

---

① 参见赵维田:《论双边航空协定的三种模式》,载《法学研究》1988年第2期。

② See Paul Stephen Dempsey, *Law & Foreign Policy in International Aviation*, Transnational Publishers, 1987, pp. 11 – 12.

③ 参见董箫:《航权交换研究》,知识产权出版社2010年版,第117页。

④ 参见胡超容:《论航空自由的发展进程》,载《西南民族大学学报》2006年第10期。

刻表的管制。[①] 美国政府希望将这种自由开放的模式在世界范围内推广，1992 年 8 月 5 日“开放天空”政策的定义由美国运输部以官方立场作出阐释，具体包括在美国的任意航点与欧洲国家的任意航点之间对航路和航权类别不加任何经营限制。[②] 在“开放天空”模式下，中间点以及延远点的服务在缔约双方之间享有充分的自由。同年，美国与荷兰签订了第一份“开放天空”协议，20 世纪 90 年代末又同几个欧洲国家签订了双边协定。2008 年美国政府提出新的《开放天空范本》，是对传统“开放天空”模式的新发展。

(4)欧洲航空自由化和一体化

与美国航空自由化道路不同，欧洲的航空自由化和一体化进程是在欧洲经济一体化背景下同步展开的。1987～1993 年，欧共体施行三套“一揽子”自由化方案(Three Liberalization Packages)使欧洲“开放天空”得以实现。[③] 第一套“一揽子”方案规定了成员国间在运价、运力及市场准入方面的规则，第二套“一揽子”方案进一步使欧共体内部航空运输服务自由化。[④] 1992 年发布的第三套“一揽子”方案中，2407/92 号规章使欧共体内部所有航线的第五航权限制被取消，完全实现了第五项航空自由。

欧洲的航空自由化协议范畴已经超出了航权自由本身，它还包括旨在开放和公平竞争、航空安全、环境保护和航空监管等方面实现趋同的条款。

2. 航空自由之必然趋势

自 1944 年芝加哥标准式以来，国际民用航空朝着自由化的方向不断深入。在经济全球化进程中，区域内航空自由化和一体化在实践中已显有成

---

① See Ariane Debyser, “EU External Aviation Policy”, *European Parliamentary Research Service*, 2016, p. 3.

② In the Matter of Defining “Open Skies”, *Department of Transportation Order* No. 92－8－13, 1992 DOT Av. LEXIS 568. *1.

③ See Antigoni Lykotrafiti, “European Commission v. the Netherlands: A Reminder of the 2002 Open Judgment in the Light of the First EU-US Air Transport Agreement”, *European Competition Law Review* 28, 2007, p. 581; Jae Woon Lee, Will Horton, “Fifth Freedom Traffic Rights: Formidable Threat or Theoretical Concern”, *Air and Space Law* 43, 2018, p. 309.

④ See Angela Cheng, Jui Lu, *International Airline Alliances: EC Competition Law/US Antitrust Law and International Air Transport*, Kluwer Law International, 2003, pp. 31－32.

效,如欧洲航空一体化、北美运输一体化等。因此,国际航空运输模式从双边航空协定向多边航空自由化、一体化模式发展成为必然趋势。

三、我国第五航权制度现状

作为国际民航组织创始国之一,我国于1974年加入了《芝加哥公约》,之后在国际航空法领域也积极地发挥着重要作用。总体而言,我国航权法制建设尚存在一些问题亟待解决,但是从国内法到国际条约,从法律到规章,已经构建起我国特有的航权法律体系。目前,我国共批准13座城市开放第五航权,在国际航空运输领域发挥着日渐显著的作用。

(一)我国第五航权法制现状

1. 国内立法

从国内立法层面来看,我国1995年《民用航空法》(以下简称《民航法》)的颁布和施行意味着我国民用航空领域有了专门性基本法律依据,目前是我国民用航空领域地位最高的一部法律。《民航法》中规定有民用航空器国籍、民用航空器权利、航空运输涉外关系法律适用问题等。涉及航权问题,我国《民航法》以散见式对外国民航公司的指定、航线、运价、业务权等问题在具体条款中进行了原则性规定。如《民航法》第97条确定了国际航运的定价原则——依照具体双边条约执行。而从我国与别国的条约中可知目前我国仍以"双批准模式"(mutual approval)①为主流定价方式。此外,《民航法》第176条规定了与我国订立双边条约的外国民用航空公司需得到其本国的指定和我国的经营许可方可开展双边航空运输业务,而对于指定企业的数量和性质并未明确作出限制。

除法律外,我国还制定了一系列行政法规、地方法规及部门规章,如《适

① "双批准模式"指双方指定承运人向双方政府提交运价并经双方政府批准生效的审批模式。

航管理条例》《国际航权资源配置与使用管理办法》《海南省关于开放部分航权若干政策的规定》等。我国民航局和其他部委、各级人民政府也针对民用航空中的各类问题分别制定了行政规章。法律、法规和行政规章共同组成了我国的航权法律体制。

2. 国际参与

改革开放以来,在经济迅猛发展的背景下,我国航空业也随之得到了迅速的成长。我国不仅在立法领域有着突出表现,在航权交换的实践中同样取得了较大的进展。截至目前,我国共有北京、上海、西安等 13 座城市被批准开放第五航权。[①] 海南向境外航空运输企业开放了第三航权、第四航权和第五航权,海口美兰国际机场的迅速发展受益于此。目前,海口美兰国际机场的航线不仅覆盖全国,同时因其得天独厚的地理位置与东南亚各国形成紧密联系的航线网,成为事实上的航空自由港。[②] 斯里兰卡、卡塔尔和澳大利亚航空等航空公司已开通途经上海的第五航权航线。重庆机场和昆明机场也被批准向部分国家开放第五航权。[③]

早在 1946 年,中国就在与美国的双边航空协定中完成了最早的第五航权实践。中美缔结了《中美航空运输协定》,又称"中美空中协定"。该协定允许美国民用飞机在上海、天津和广州装卸客货。然而由于那个时期航空业发展极为缓慢,该协议并未给我国带来期待的经济价值。1974 年,我国加入了《芝加哥公约》。改革开放后,我国在国际航空运输领域更为活跃。值得注意的是,2007 年 7 月 9 日中美航空运输双边协定进行了第五次修订,签署了中美航空协定 2007 年《议定书》。《议定书》中提到双方未来的最终目标是实现中美航空运输市场的完全自由化(full liberalisation),有学者认为这是

---

① 我国目前开放第五航权的城市为北京、上海、广州、天津、南京、烟台、武汉、厦门、海口、银川、哈尔滨、郑州和西安。

② 参见赵晓松:《国际航空运输自由化对中国的影响及解决方案》,资料来源:http://news.carnoc.com/list/83/83501.html,最后访问日期:2019 年 3 月 16 日。

③ 参见董箫:《航权交换研究》,知识产权出版社 2010 年版,第 217 页。

中美实现"开放天空"的前兆。[①] 截至2017年年底,我国与其他国家(地区)缔结的双边航空运输协定达122个,彰显着我国在国际航空法律体系中扮演着越来越重要的角色。

通过表2中的几份航空协定可知,我国在民用航空协定的缔结中呈现以下几项发展特征:第一,第五航权的适用航线更为广泛,正在向"完全自由化"趋势靠拢;第二,第五航权的行使更为充分;对于运力、运价及班次、航空器型号等限制日渐宽松,呈现由政府介入到航空企业自由协商的变化趋势。由此,我国民用航空运输市场正在追随国际浪潮,更加自由化、国际市场化。

表2 我国缔结的第五航权协定示例

签订时间	国家/地区	航线	航权	运价规定
1966年	法国	中方:中国—巴基斯坦境内一个地点—德黑兰(可能)—巴格达或大马士革—开罗—地拉那—巴黎的往返航线; 法方:法国—地拉那或雅典—开罗—德黑兰(可能)—卡拉奇—金边—上海的往返航线	第五航权中间点权	双方航空企业协商并经民航当局审查批准
1979年	英国	中方:北京—拉瓦尔品第或卡拉奇—印度境内一个地点—海湾地区一个地点—德黑兰—布加勒斯特—雅典—罗马—苏黎世—法兰克福—巴黎—伦敦; 英方:伦敦—罗马—德黑兰—巴林—迪拜—阿曼—科威特—拉瓦尔品第或卡拉奇—孟买—德里—加尔各答—北京	第五航权中间点权,对中间点权有严格限制	双方航空企业协商并经民航当局审查批准

① 参见张恒阁、张得志:《天空开放的新进展与中美中欧新航空协议》,载《中国经贸》2007年第10期。

续表

签订时间	国家/地区	航线	航权	运价规定
2004 年	澳大利亚	中方:中国境内任意点—中间任意点—澳大利亚境内任意点—以远任意点; 澳方:澳大利亚境内任意点—中间任意点—中国境内任意点—以远任意点	第五航权中间点权、以远点权	可由缔约一方的航空企业定价,航空当局有权批准或不批准
2010 年	东盟	中方:中国境内任意点—中间任意点—东盟境内任意点—以远任意点; 东盟:东盟成员国境内任意点—中国任意点—中国境内任意点—以远任意点	充分的第三航权、第四航权; 第五航权中间点权、以远点权	在公平合理等原则基础上自由定价,除国内另有规定外无须审批

(二)当前制度之不足

虽然我国较早地参与了第五航权的国际实践,但我国对于第五航权的态度一向颇为保守。"一带一路"背景下,不仅要关注在海上丝绸之路发挥作用的东部沿海城市,更应对重要的陆上丝绸之路沿线城市加以重视和政策倾斜。目前我国仅开放了 13 个重要交通枢纽城市的第五航权,且这些城市主要分布于东南沿海及内陆沿江城市,地理分布较不平衡。

同时,我国国内立法制度也存在局限性。全球经济发展使国际航空业发生显著的变化,我国现行 1995 年《民用航空法》已经无法完全满足当今国际航空市场的需求。如第八章对公共航空运输企业和第十三章对外国民用航空器的规定,仍体现着传统的"严格管制"政策理念,与全球航空市场自由化的趋势存在矛盾。

航权问题在我国国内立法中的规定也较为模糊。在我国现行的民用航空法律、法规和规章条例中缺乏对航权问题的专篇专章的具体规定,尤其是第五航权的开放和运营限制等问题分散地存在于我国与他国的双边航空协定中。例如,在我国与英国于 1979 年签订的《中华人民共和国政府和大不列颠及北爱尔兰联合王国政府民用航空运输协定》附件的第一部分中,中英双方对双方指定航空公司的运输航线作了具体规定,同时对经停点作出较为严格的限制。① 而在我国与东南亚国家联盟(以下简称东盟)于2010年签署的《中华人民共和国与东南亚国家联盟各成员国政府航空运输协定及第一议定书》附件一中,双方明确授权缔约各成员国中间点权和以远权并载明授权航点。在该协议下,缔约各国均享有更高的自由,指定航空企业可以在中国和东盟国家境内以及航线上的中间点和以远点的任何航点享有航空自由。② 虽然考虑到不同国家和地区在实践中各具特殊性,但我国现行民用航空法律制度的确缺乏一个对航权问题的总括性规定。

四、"一带一路"背景下完善我国第五航权制度构想

"一带一路"分别指"丝绸之路经济带"和"21世纪海上丝绸之路",是我国在世界多极化、经济全球化和贸易自由化的背景下提出的一项重要倡议。"一带一路"路上和海上路线横跨亚洲、欧洲、非洲三大洲,沿线国家和地区多达65个。在区域经济一体化的进程中,国际航空客货运输量迅速增长,航空业的发展也会进一步促进"一带一路"深入发展。进一步开放第五航权,将会成为促进区域经济与贸易的重要助推力。针对目前在利用第五航权实践中面临的问题,提出制度完善建议,以更好地响应我国"一带一路"倡议的要求。

(一)"一带一路"背景下开放第五航权的经济价值

第五航权是一项复杂但极具经济价值的航空自由,被授权国的民用航班可以途径第五航权开放城市装卸旅客、货物和邮件,再飞往其他国家或地区。

① 《中华人民共和国政府和大不列颠及北爱尔兰联合王国政府民用航空运输协定》,www.caac.gov.cn,最后访问日期:2018年12月1日。

② 《中华人民共和国与东南亚国家联盟各成员国政府航空运输协定及第一议定书》,www.caac.gov.cn,最后访问日期:2018年12月1日。

在"一带一路"背景下,我国进一步开放第五航权有利于加强我国与沿线国家的区域经济与贸易联系,促进资金和人员流动,对我国以及国际社会经济发展具有十分突出的价值。

1. 刺激区域经济与国际贸易发展

交通运输在经贸活动中越来越具不可替代的作用,航空运输业的成长更是会刺激区域商贸往来和国际投资。据统计,"开放天空"协议给美欧双方带来了超 120 亿欧元的经济利益,增加了 8 万个就业岗位。① 2017 年我国民用航空运输全行业完成运输总周转量 1083.08 亿吨公里,比上年增长 12.6%;旅客运输量 55,156 万人次,比上年增长 13.0%;货邮运输量 705.9 万吨,比上年增长 5.6%。全国民航运输机场完成旅客吞吐量 11.48 亿人次,比上年增长 12.9%。②

在"一带一路"倡议下,进一步开放第五航权有利于促进中国西部内陆城市经济发展、提高国际化水平,进而吸引欧洲企业来华贸易和投资,加强沿线区域经济合作以及深入经济一体化进程。

2. 增强我国航运业竞争力

美国和欧洲诸国作为传统航空业大国,其航空公司因其更高的运力和更低廉的价格而具有更强的行业竞争力。特别是作为国际民航运输业最早发展起来的美国航空企业,奉行多元化的经营理念,在一系列竞争和改革中得以发展,目前拥有全球航空运输总量的四成③欧洲国家则在欧洲一体化背景下成立欧洲航空安全局,通过对民用航空企业的统一管理和监控,提高航空安全水平,以此推动民航企业的竞争力提升。同时,欧洲航空市场自由化建设以及"航铁联运"系统的构建极大地为民航企业注入生机与竞争力。欧洲的航空公司也根据其自身特点打造不同的经营战略以提升盈利能力,如荷兰

---

① 参见严恒元:《欧美"开放天空"协议影响深远》,载《经济日报》2010 年 7 月 10 日。

② 参见《2017 年民航行业发展统计公报》,资料来源:www.caac.gov.cn,最后访问日期:2018 年 12 月 1 日。

③ 参见杨治远:《航权开放的政策走向与我国国际航空运输的发展》,载《中国民航飞行学院学报》2006 年第 2 期。

航空公司则依靠差异式的竞争策略,以更加个性化、更为细致周到的旅客服务逐步扩大着自己的市场份额。

航权开放意味着外国具有较强市场竞争力的航空运输公司进入我国市场,与我国本土民航企业激烈竞争。这一市场竞争将会推动我国民航企业调整经营战略、优化航线和航班时间安排。同时,我国民航企业也可以充分利用第五航权,延长航线,提高运载效率,提升核心竞争力。

3. 推动旅游业发展与文化交流

第五航权的开放不仅对航空运输业本身极具价值,同时对旅游业的发展和沿线国家间文化交流起着重要作用。比如,我国海南岛在开放第五航权后旅游产业得到了极大的发展。受交通限制,海南岛的旅游产业早期并非如今这般发达,开放航权后整个旅游业迎来了新一轮的发展机遇,直达航班增加,旅客出行更为便利,入境游客人数每年均快速培长。① 进一步开放第五航权有利于降低交通成本,促进我国与沿线亚、欧、非各国的人员流动和文化交流,促进旅游业和文化产业繁荣发展。

(二)开放第五航权的法律问题

1. 领空主权问题

航权开放所涉及的领空从属于一国的国家领土之内。《芝加哥公约》第1条便规定了"领土之上的空气空间",即公约承认了主权国家对领空享有完全的和排他的主权。尊重各国领空主权是国际航空法的基本原则,有学者称:"国际航空法是与国家主权最密切相关的国际法分支。"②开放第五航权意味着将部分领空的利用权和航线运营权让渡给外国航空公司,在带来经济效益的同时,可能也会随之带来政治摩擦和国家安全隐患。

2. 空域管理与航线规划问题

我国空域资源分布极为不平衡,体现为军民空域资源分布不平衡以及东

① 参见吴川醒:《海南航权开放法律制度研究》,海南大学2012年硕士学位论文,第16页。

② 黄居正:《国际航空法的理论与实践》,台北,新学林出版股份有限公司2006年版,序言。

西部空域资源利用不平衡。根据《民航法》第 72 条的规定,我国空域资源是由中国人民解放军空军管控,军用空域占绝大部分。民用航空必须向军方申请空域和航线,主要航道上分布有较多禁飞区域,同时军方空中军事活动和临时空中管制等,导致我国超过 70% 的航班延误或取消。

从资源地域分布来看,北京、上海、广州等国际大城市拥有主要的航运资源,而西部城市空域虽广,但未能得到充分利用。深入开放第五航权对我国空域管理制度和航线规划水平的革新提出了新要求。

3. 国际航运中的环境保护问题

航空运输具有迅捷、机动和高效的特点,但它同时也会带来不可忽视的环境污染问题。资料表明一架飞机每飞行 23 小时就会产生 500 吨二氧化碳和其他污染气体,严重加剧大气温室效应。[①] 根据国际民航组织 2016 年环境报告,国际航空二氧化碳排放量约 7 亿吨,但随着国际航空运输业的迅速发展,该数额将在 2050 年增至约 26 亿吨。[②] 这对世界各国民航企业而言无疑提出了一个亟待解决的新问题。另外,民航飞机还会产生噪声污染。部分空港周边建设规划不尽合理,航班噪声污染对周边居民的生活和健康产生不良影响。

(三)第五航权法律制度探索启示

自 2003 年首次开放南京和厦门两市作为第五航权的试点以来,我国在第五航权法律制度的探索与实践中更加积极活跃,取得了一系列成果。为了更好地满足“一带一路”建设的发展需要,笔者提出以下几点完善第五航权制度的建议。

1. 完善我国第五航权法律体系

我国现行 1995 年《民航法》脱胎于我国《海商法》,因此在法律条文结构

---

① 参见《飞得快 污染得更快——飞机加剧大气层“温室效应”》,载《生态经济》2004 年第 8 期。

② 参见李汝义:《航空碳排放的法律规制:域外经验与中国实践》,载《武大国际法评论》2018 年第 4 期。

和总括性规定方面具有相似性。为进一步完善我国民用航空立法体系,航权问题应以专篇专章的形式纳入现行《民用航空法》中。由于现行《民航法》中已规定有事关指定、航线和运价等内容的法律条款,但由于《民航法》已"年代久远",相关条款应根据我国民航领域的发展现状进行相应的修订,并将条款顺序重新排列纳入"航权管理"专章。在第五航权实践中,结合我国所缔结的民用航空双边和多边协定可知,我国民用航空市场日渐自由和开放。我国对运价的法律规定体现着传统的"双批准模式",然而在近年来我国与其他国家(地区)签订的双边条约中,如《中美协定》,定价原则呈现"双不批准模式"的自由化、市场化趋势。与运价往往同时规定的还有航线问题。在实践当中,我国对航线管理逐渐从"城市—城市"的传统模式转向"任意点—任意点"的"完全自由化模式"。因此应在现行《民航法》中放宽对运价和航线等内容的政府干预和限制,将航线设计和运价的自由更多地交给民航企业。同时也要对其他单行立法中涉及民用航空的章节或条文根据航权交换实践的现状和发展趋势进行相应的调整。同时,应完善并严格执行我国《反垄断法》和《反不正当竞争法》,制定完备的反垄断体系和制止不正当竞争体系,[①]保障旅客及托运人合法权益,维护国际民用航空市场竞争秩序。

从双边条约的缔结实践来看,我国与其他国家(地区)的具体条约中存在较多共性的条款。结合我国航权管理的自由化、市场化趋势,总结几项未来谈判中的原则性基本条款如下:

(1)航空公司的指定数量依据对等原则确定;

(2)指定航空公司应在公平合理的基础上确定运价,除内国政府另有规定外无须审批;

(3)除特别商定外,缔约双方制定航空公司可在两国国境内任意点之间开展运输业务。

在双边条约谈判中,我国可以结合民航基本法以及其他法规确立的原

① 参见广林乔子:《我国进一步开放航权的法律问题及对策》,载《湖北警官学院学报》2015年第9期。

则,制订出谈判的“格式条款”作为协商的基础,再根据双方的具体情况加以调整,以增强我国第五航权法律体系的逻辑性和规范性。

2. 加强沿线重要城市航空业建设

作为一个地区所特有的特殊的“资源”,航权的利用程度与城市的长远发展和综合竞争力密切相关。[①] 2018 年 11 月 23 日国务院在对外谈判中批准并支持郑州和西安机场使用第五航权,[②]是我国第五航权的最新实践。在“一带一路”建设中,西安和郑州是两个重要的沿线枢纽城市。尤其是地处我国西北内陆的西安,既是古丝绸之路的起点,也是新“丝绸之路”经济带的路上发端,中亚、西亚、南亚对华进行贸易与文化往来的重要关口和西北部经济发展水平较高的心脏地带。但黄河艰险,缺乏海洋或江河作为水上航运依托;四面环山,地形复杂且极具封闭性,陆上交通也十分受限。在这种境况下,依托西安的高校智库资源,重点建设西安民用航空产业,才能促进西安开放程度和国际化水平的提高,发挥沿线枢纽城市的关键作用。与西安同处西部内陆地区的关键城市还有成都、重庆和兰州等,应开放西部城市第五航权,加强民用航空机场基础设施建设,结合内陆交通枢纽城市成熟的铁路、公路运输系统,努力建立多式联运体系,形成以机场为中心的综合交通网络,深度参与“一带一路”建设。[③]

3. 完善空域管理和航线规划

发挥民用航空业在“一带一路”倡议中的重要作用,必须积极完善空域管理制度和航线规划。我国的飞行管制与空域资源管理工作仍由空军掌管,民用航空受到诸多限制,这种“准战时”的军队管理体制已经无法很好地适应当今

① 参见王学林、林欣怡、杨治远:《航权放对区域产业结构优化演进的影响》,载《经济研究导刊》2010 年第 36 期。

② 参见《关于支持自由贸易试验区深化改革创新若干措施的通知》,资料来源:http://www.gov.cn,最后访问日期:2018 年 12 月 1 日。

③ 参见林茹钰、殷小丽:《“一带一路”背景下西咸空港新城航空货运发展策略研究》,载《现代经济信息》2018 年第 17 期。

飞速发展的民航经济形势。① 为促进我国民用航空业高效发展,应当对我国空域管理和航线规划问题进行专门立法,在军民空域资源配置中,军方应对空域资源向民航领域做出适当让渡。同时,在航线优化方面,应更加关注西部城市的空域资源利用,实现缓解东部航道拥挤与西部航空业深入发展双重利好。

4. 健全航空运输环境保护机制

航空业蓬勃发展对我国既是经济机遇又是环保挑战。针对该问题,欧盟于2003年提出了碳排放交易体系(European Union Emissions Trading System,EU ETS),2005年开始在欧盟内部正式实行。根据欧盟温室气体排放交易指令(Directive 2003/87/EC)及其修正案的规定,自2012年起,凡在欧盟境内起降的民用航班皆有碳排放量配额。即免费碳排放量额度有限,如在日后的运营中超出限额,必须支付相关费用。尽管该机制一经推出就遭到中国、美国等众多非欧盟国家抵制而不再对非欧盟国家产生效力,但这一体系的理念被国际民航组织吸收。2016年10月,国际民航组织第39届大会通过了《国际民航组织关于环境保护的持续政策和做法的综合声明——气候变化》和《国际民航组织关于环境保护的持续政策和做法的综合声明——全球市场措施机制》两份决议,建立了全球首个航空减排市场机制。②

我国现行《民航法》在第67条和第149条中明确了民航企业在运营管理机场以及从事运输的过程中应遵守环境保护法律法规的规定,但缺乏具体的民用航空环境保护机制。从外国法律实践经验来看,英国民用航空法案(Civil Aviation Act 2012)在原则性规定中就明确了英国航空公司在从事民用航空运输活动时必须遵循由英国民航局所确立的保护环境的基本原则,并对航空企业的运营提出具体的环保要求,如环保设施建设标准、排污标准等;

---

① 参见刘凡:《我国空域管理体制的现状分析与对策研究》,上海交通大学2012年硕士学位论文,第27页。

② 参见李汝义:《航空碳排放的法律规制:域外经验与中国实践》,载《武大国际法评论》2018年第4期;《国际民航组织第39届大会谋求达成控制碳排放历史性方案》,资料来源:http://energy.chinanews.com/ny/2016/05-15/7870893.shtml,最后访问日期:2018年12月4日。

另外,在第二章有关信息的规定第84条中确立了环境信息公开制度,要求民航企业公开一切可能会对公众产生影响的环境信息,以保障公众的知情权和舆论监督权。我国可以借鉴民航业发达的国家地区的法律规定,以使我国民航企业的发展更加符合国际环境保护的要求。

生态问题关乎全人类的生存与发展。从长远来看,我国应加强航空运输中的环境保护立法,如专门的航空碳排放法,以法律的手段制约环境污染扩大。我国民用航空企业必须加强研发投入,发展节能减排技术,如改善飞机机型、发动机及使用新型清洁能源和降噪装置来减少环境污染。

五、结　　语

作为国际民航组织的创始成员国之一,我国在国际航空领域发挥着积极作用。自2003年以来,我国不断参与并深化开放第五航权实践。随着国务院批准西安和郑州两座城市开放第五航权,我国至今共开放13座航空枢纽城市的第五航权,与122个国家和地区签订有双边航空运输协定。然而在深化第五航权实践中,我国当前制度仍存在较多不足。开放航权意味着我国民航企业将在更广阔的市场中与世界各国航运企业展开竞争,对我国企业和整个民航业的发展来说既是机遇又是挑战。为了更好地深度参与“一带一路”建设,为我国企业保驾护航,关键在于从立法、空域管理和航线规划等方面完善法律制度体系。从国内立法角度来看,应遵循当今国际航空业自由化的趋势,减少对航权管理的限制,鼓励民航企业在市场中自由竞争。从国际实践来说,我国应依据基本原则总结出一套规范性条款应用到航权开放的双边谈判中。此外,还应加强沿线城市民航基础配套设施建设,同时不能忽视航空运输中的环境保护问题,通过技术革新和谈判等方式应对欧盟碳排放交易体系对我国民航企业提出的难题。由于空域问题主要由军方管理,加之数据不足,未能在本文中展开探讨。此外仍有诸多问题有待解决,应加快制定应对措施以使开放第五航权成为我国“一带一路”建设的重要助推力。

“空中丝绸之路”建设背景下西安开放第五航权的法律思考*

刘　静**

一、第五航权的内涵与开放模式

在1944年芝加哥会议上,各国就建立国际航空运输自由市场问题达成共识,在此基础上,为避免承运人在复杂跨国航空运输活动中侵犯他国主权和威胁航空安全,各国以签订《国际航班过境协定》和《国际航空运输协定》的方式明确规定了具有国家主权

* 本文系2016年陕西省社会科学基金一般项目“空中丝绸之路经济带建设中的陕西航权开放法律问题研究”(2016F009)和2018年中国法学会部级法学研究一般项目“推进‘天空开放’的国际法治经验研究”(CLS2018C33)的阶段性研究成果。本文的写作得到了张超汉老师的悉心指导,在此表示感谢。

** 西北政法大学国际法学院2018级硕士研究生。

性质的航权的定义和种类。[①] 其中,规定在《国际航空运输协定》中的第五航权涉及的内容最丰富、调整的范围最广泛,具有显著的经济效果和极其深刻的现实意义,逐渐发展成为各国在航空运输领域中的重点关注对象。为利用第五航权提高航空运输总量和增强运输能力、构建国际航线网络和门户枢纽机场、开拓远程与运量资源不足的航线[②]以及发挥其对国家或地区的经济带动作用,各国有必要结合国际航空发展态势与国内航空运输特点深入分析第五航权的内涵与开放模式。

(一)第五航权的内涵

第五航权是指承运人前往准许其进入的国家或地区,并将从第三国载运的客、货、邮卸至该国或从该国载运客、货、邮前往第三国的权利。[③] 根据第三国所处的地理位置不同,国际社会将第五航权细化为三种情况:(1)前站权,又称航线起始点之前的航运自由,即旗国航空器飞入授权国领土并在该领土内卸下来自或装上前往规定航线上位于旗国前一点的客、货、邮的权利;(2)中停点权,又称航线过程中的中间点的营运自由,即旗国航空器飞入授权国领土并在该领土内卸下来自或装上前往规定航线上位于旗国与授权国

① 《国际航班过境协定》规定了两种过境航权。第一航权指不降停而飞越授权国领土的权利,第二航权指授权国给予被授权国制定空运企业的航空器按照协议航班飞离被授权国领土,飞至授权国领土时仅因加油、维修等其他目的而降停,不进行载上或卸下旅客、货物或邮件的作业,然后继续飞至其他国家的权利,所以也被称为"非商业性降停"。在此基础上,《国际航班运输协定》新增了第三航权、第四航权、第五航权。其中,第三航权又称"目的地下客权",指某国或地区的航空公司自其登记国或地区载运客货至另一国或地区的权利;第四航权又称为"目的地上客权",指某国或地区的航空公司自另一国地区载运客货返回其登记国或地区的权利;第五航权将在后文中作具体介绍。参见董箫:《航权交换研究》,知识产权出版社2010年版,第43页。

② 第五航权通常有三个功能:第一,第五航权可开拓远程航线,由于受到飞机航程的限制,航空公司无法为一些远程洲际航线提供不经停的直航服务,只有通过第五航权的发展才能解决此问题;第二,第五航权可开拓运量不足的航线,例如,A点到C点的运量不足以支持构建定期航线,则可借助B点的运量补充,形成A—B—C的新航线;第三,随着现代航权交换和航权合并技术的不断提高,第五航权成为提高航空运输总量和开拓国际航线网络与门户枢纽市场的重要手段。参见向吉英:《航权开放:动因、演进及其效果》,载《改革与战略》2010年第7期。

③ 参见周倜:《第五航权开放法律问题研究》,西南政法大学2012年硕士学位论文,第4页。

之间的客、货、邮的权利;(3)以远权,亦称航线终止点之后的营运自由,指旗国航空器飞入授权国领土并在该领土范围内卸下来自或装上前往规定航线上位于授权国后一点的客、货、邮的权利。①

第五航权的交换是多个国家或地区基于对本国经济利益和政治地位的考量赋予对方航空器进入本国进行装卸货物的自由与权利,通常表现在旗国、授权国与第三国签订的双边或多边条约中。具体而言,由于第五航权不仅包括旗国与授权国两个国家,而且还涉及前站点、中间点或以远点所在的国家或地区,因而只有获得第三国的许可,第五航权才有可能发生法律效力,相反,如果没有征得第三国的同意,那么第五航权将不具备实际操作的意义,显然,第五航权的实现难度要比前四种航权高得多。② 尽管如此,鉴于开放第五航权将极大地增加缔约国航空运输流量和商业利益,大多数国家都努力地为与本国具有真正和持续联系③以及由本国进行有效控制的航空承运人争取在其他国家或地区的航空运输权,从而加强旗国、授权国与第三国之间的航空联系,使各国秉承开放包容、互利共赢的原则进行航空运输活动,为构建全球“空中丝绸之路”创造契机和提供强力引擎。④ 例如,西安在 2019 年 5 月 13 日首次开放了“首尔—西安—河内”第五航权货运航线,这意味着一架获得西安第五航权的首尔飞机在西安装卸客、货、邮后,可继续飞往河内,而如果只开放前四种航权,那么首尔航空器只可以在首尔与西安或西安与河内两地之间来往,因而西安在更大程度上开放第五航权的行为加强了首尔、西安与河内三地之间的航空互动,随之西安也有可能进一步升级发展成为联通

① 参见周偶:《第五航权开放法律问题研究》,西南政法大学 2012 年硕士学位论文,第 5 页。

② 参见董箫:《航权交换研究》,知识产权出版社 2010 年版,第 46 页。

③ See A. A. Mencik von Zebinsky, *European Union External Competence and External Relations in Air Transport*, Kluwer Law International, 1996, p. 60.

④ 中国在 2018 年 3 月 22 ~ 23 日开展了以开创民航新时代共享安全和谐天空为主题的 2018 年民用无人驾驶航空器发展国际论坛,在此次论坛中,通过了《北京倡议》,主张携手共建支撑全球范围的无人驾驶航空器安全、有序和协调运行的生态系统,构建民用航空“命运共同体”。参见《〈北京倡议〉:构建命运航空命运共同体》,资料来源:http://news.carnoc.com/list/440/440527.html,最后访问日期:2019 年 5 月 21 日。

中国与世界发展的重要航空枢纽。①

通过以上分析可知，由于航权是国家主权在航空领域的重要体现，交换第五航权是国家通过让渡一部分主权的方式为本国航空器获取在其他国家航空运输市场中进行自由商业运载的权利和自由，②其涉及多重主体利益和具有丰富的表现形式，是对第三航权、第四航权的延伸和拓展。

（二）第五航权开放的历史演进

第五航权的开放经历了漫长且曲折的发展历程，虽然早在 1913 年德国与法国就通过制定双边航空协定的方式允许对方非军事用途的飞船不加限制地在本国领空内自由飞越，③但是在第二次世界大战前，国际社会还未形成航权交换的固定模式和标准，各国主要以单方面许可方式直接给予另一国内航空承运人在本国领空范围内进行商业运载的权利。④ 直到 1944 年芝加哥会议上，各国才针对航空运输管理体制问题展开激烈讨论和反思，并形成四种传统双边运输机制，随着国际竞争的进一步加剧和国际市场开放程度的提高，双边航空运输管理体制逐渐被新型多边模式所取代，因此，第五航权实现了从双边机制向多边机制的转化。

---

① 《第五航权落地西安！首尔—西安—河内全货运航线开通》，资料来源：http://www.sohu.com/a/313938181_351304，最后访问日期：2019 年 5 月 21 日。

② 学术界对第五航权的性质颇具争议，主要表现为实质权利说和互惠方式说。持实质权利说的学者主张：第五航权是主权国家通过相互开放空中运营权为手段获取他国航空运营权的一种权利，第五航权的取得使一国航空器自由进入另一主权国家的领空，并在该主权国家的同意下占用其一部分空中营运的资源，且需第三方主权国家相应的开放该国的营运资源。持互惠方式说的学者则认为：第五航权类似于私法合同中主体双方通过意思表示确定双方的权利义务，并对合同双方之外的第三人设定权利，第三方通过双方当事国的互惠自动取得对当事国的空中权利。笔者认为，第五航权是实质权利说和互惠方式说的综合。参见周倜：《第五航权开放法律问题研究》，西南政法大学 2012 年硕士学位论文，第 8 ~ 10 页。

③ See P. P. C. Haanappel, *The Law and Policy of Air Space and Outer Space*, Kluwer Law International, 2003, p. 4.

④ 20 世纪初，国家间的航空往来较少，很少通过签订航空运输协定规范国家间的航空运输关系，这种只靠国家通过许可或不许可的方式来规范国际航空运输的形式，实际上是国家依据领空主权原则，依靠国家单边主义管理国际航空运输。参见贺富永、王盛蕾：《论国际航空运输管理体制发展历程及基本走向》，载《北京航空航天大学学报》（社会科学版）2015 年第 3 期。

1. 传统双边航空运输管理体制

第二次世界大战结束前夕,美国召开并邀请多个国家参与芝加哥会议,与会国从本国民用航空产业的发展现状和国家利益出发,针对战后国际航空运输管理体制、航权交换机制以及政府对航空运输市场的管控程度等多个问题提出了不同类型的主张,其中最具代表性的两种观点,为美国主张的"航空自由论"①和英国倡导的"航空秩序论",②由于各国航空发展水平和经济政治利益存在巨大差异,国际社会很难制定完全自由和统一的多边航权交换机制,其只能在较小范围内逐步推进国际航空运输自由化目标的实现,因而各国在芝加哥会议上制定的《临时航线协定的标准格式》成为两国交换第五航权的范本,③以此形成的双边航空运输管理体制构成了国际社会对航空业最早的管理模式,同时也发展成为现代航空运输管理体系的渊源。在未来40年航空运输实践中,各国以《临时航线协定的标准格式》为指引,签订了大量双边运输协定并形成百慕大式、事先确定式、自由式以及"天空开放"四种双边航权交换机制。

《百慕大协定》是英美妥协的产物,一方面,英国放弃了事先确定运力的主张,转而接受了美国提出的运力由航空公司按照市场需求自行决定的意见;另一方面,美国被迫同意由国际航空运输协会统一拟定运费并报送两国

① "航空自由论"是美国提出的主张,美国希望所有缔约国都开放自己的领空,各国在航空运输领域开展自由竞争,各国政府对经济的管制越少越好,运力、运输班次频率、运价应当由国际市场的竞争予以决定。美国主张的"航空自由论"可从其叙述中看出:"美国的意见是在对国家领空主权无任何减损的前提下,我们应在友好国家希望从彼此那里获得的自由及权利进行充分交换的基础上,在航空运输领域展开合作"。See R. I. R Abeyratne, *Legal and Regulatory Issue in International Aviation*, Transnational Publishers, Inc. ,1996, p. 3.

② "航空秩序论"是英国提出的观点,其主张成立一个国际组织管理航空营运权,由它决定分配航线、运力等。

③ 在1944年芝加哥会议上,当以美国为首的航空大国在多边交换营运权的努力失败后,会议最后文件第8段拟定了一个"临时航路协定的标准式"作为英美妥协的产物和各国交换航权的范本。从《芝加哥公约》的缔结到1946年年初英美签订《百慕大协定》前,国际上曾参照《临时航线协定的标准格式》缔结过一批双边协定,如美国曾与加拿大、丹麦、冰岛、爱尔兰和挪威等多个国家签订这种类型的双边航空协定。凡依此范本签署的航空协定,基本上可归类于芝加哥标准式。参见董箫:《航权交换研究》,知识产权出版社2010年版,第107~108页。

政府"双批准"原则,[①]《百慕大协定》作为世界上首个双边航权交换协议,获得了大多数国家认可并一度发展成为国家间签订航空运输双边协定的样板,[②]其中,第三国家也同意该协定关于确定运价的方式,但在运力方面却采用了与其完全对立的"事先确定式"。[③] 20 世纪 70 年代,随着民用航空运输业逐步发展成为国民经济中最具竞争力的行业,以美国为首的西方发达国家又一次极力主张"航空自由论",并在卡恩提出的"减少管理"政策下[④]对国内民航体制展开了急剧变革,放松政府对国内民用航空业的管理和控制,实行航空运输业"自由式"发展,同时,美国还将此理论应用到国际民航运输业的发展中,如美国在 1978 年与一贯主张"航空自由论"的比利时和荷兰签订了双边航空运输协定以减少国家对运力、运价、航线以及第五航权的限制,形成了"比荷卢模式"。[⑤] 美国为使航空承运人获得更大限度的营运自由和灵活性,于 1992 年提出了"开放天空"新型航空运输双边模式,[⑥]其中涉及第五航

---

① 肖永平、孙玉超:《论现代国际航空法的自由化趋势》,载《法律科学》2010 年第 4 期。

② Paul Stephen Dempey,"Flights of Fancy and Flights of Fury: Arbitration and Adjudication of Commercial and Political Disputes in International Aviation",*The Georgia Journal of International and Competitive Law* 32,2004,pp. 248 – 249.

③ 1980 年国际民用航空组织第二次航空会议通过了预先确定运力模式的标准条款,对该模式的运力条款进行了较为规范化的表述:"1. 缔约双方指定的航空公司在协议航班上提供的总运力,应在经营开始前由缔约双方航空当局协议或批准,其后则应按预期营运需求确定。2. 缔约双方指定的航空公司经营协议航班的主要目的,应为按合理上座率提供充足运力,以满足缔约双方间总营运需求。3. 缔约双方应使双方指定航空公司在经营双方领土间的协议航班时,享有公平与均等的机会,原则上等分缔约双方间总运力,以实现平等互利。4. 缔约一方及其指定航空公司应考虑到另一方及其指定航空公司的利益,不影响后者的服务。5. 在检查时,如缔约双方不能就协议航班的运力达成协议,则缔约双方指定航空公司所提供的的运力不得超过原有协议的总运力(包括季节性变化在内)。"参见赵维田:《国际航空法》,台北,水牛出版社 1991 年版,第 126 页。

④ 放松管制政策始于 1975 年,卡特总统任命卡恩作为美国民用航空委员会的主席,卡恩力推减少对新航空公司进入市场的限制,鼓励航空运输业的充分竞争,主张旅客以及货主应有低价选择。See Brian F. Havel,*In Search of Open Skies: Law and Policy for a New Era in International Aviation*,Kluwer Law International,1997,p. 26.

⑤ See Paul Dempsey, *Law and Foreign Policy in Internetational Aviation*, Transnational Publication Press,1987,pp. 425 – 431.

⑥ 1992 年 8 月 5 日,美国运输部以运输部命令的方式对"天空开放"政策的目标公布了一个官方定义。See In the Matter of Defining"Open Skies",Department of Transportation Order No. 92 – 8 – 13,1992 DOT Av. LEXIS 568. *1.

权的内容规定为在美国的任一航点与欧洲国家的任一航点之间不受任何限制的经营权利,包括中间点以及延远点的服务,以及在国际门户城市上不受限制地提供旅客转至较小飞机的权利。

上述百慕大模式、事先确立式、自由化模式以及"开放天空"式的双边航空运输管理体制对航空实力悬殊和科技发展水平参差不齐的国家来说具有更大的灵活性和自主性,为国际航空自由运输市场的发展注入了活力,极大地提高了国家或地区对外开放国内航空市场的程度。然而,随着国际服务贸易的进一步推进和国际市场的深度开放,这四种传统双边体制逐渐显现出诸多弊端,①如其难以协调全部航空公司、消费者的利益;两国单独谈判的方式消耗大量的人力、物力资源以及可能阻碍自由竞争。由此,各国开始通过制定包括区域性和非区域性协定在内的多边运输管理协议的方式化解传统双边模式带来的危机。

2. 新型多边航空运输管理体制

20 世纪 70 年代以来,世界经济呈现区域化的发展态势,为使国家或地区间共享民用航空信息和航空运输市场资源,国际社会制定出与区域化经济相符的多边航空运输规则,其中最具代表性的是亚太地区和欧盟关于航空运输自由化的多边协议。首先,就亚太地区航空运输自由化而言,亚太经济合作组织成员通过在 1994 年和 1995 年分别签订了《茂物联合声明》与《大阪行动纲领》规定实现成员国之间贸易和投资开放和自由化为最终目标,该规定同样适用于航空运输领域,要求消除所有阻碍航空自由运输市场的障碍,此后,亚太地区的国家和地区对其他成员国进一步开放本国航空市场,仅在 1997 年该区域内的旅客运输量达 7.89 亿人次,占全球总运输量的 54.4%,亚太地区随之成为世界航空运输发展最为迅速和势头最为猛烈的区域。② 其次,就欧盟航空运输自由化而言,其通过三个"一揽子"方案推动航空运输向自由

---

① See Angela Cheng-Jui Lu, *International Airline Alliances: EC Competition Law/US Antitrust Law and International Air Transport*, Kluwer Law International, 2003, p. 327.

② See ICAO, Outlook for Air Transport to the Year 2001, Circular 237 – AT/96(1992). p. 3.

化方向发展,从而形成领空主权一体化的全新形态。1987 年欧共体理事会通过了第一个“一揽子”方案,允许航空公司在一定程度上自行决定运力和运费且多家航空公司的承运人可在同一条航线上进行竞争;1990 年制定的第二个“一揽子”自由化方案虽然是对第一个“一揽子”方案的继承,但其突破了成员各国与航空公司之间的特定身份关系,给予航空公司更多自由竞争的权利;1992 年第三个“一揽子”计划要求欧盟成员国之间完全开放国内航空市场,①即某一航空承运人只要属于欧盟成员国的公民,可无须征得政府的事先同意或事后批准自由进出其他成员国的领空并在该范围内从事商业运载活动,这一方案从根本上触动了传统双边航空运输管理体制的根基。以亚太地区和欧盟为代表形成的航空运输区域性协议为在世界更广范围内建立多边航空运输协议奠定了局部基础,其本质是在政治经济相似的区域范围内率先实现航空运输自由化,然后以此推动各国航空市场面向全球开放,实现全球航空运输市场自由化。

20 世纪 80 年代以来,日益增长的国际化、自由化和跨国化趋势引发各国长期探索开放程度更高的国际航空市场,各国为使航空承运人给客、货、邮提供不受政府干涉和更加便利的运输服务,协商同意将航空运输的某些方面列入《服务贸易总协定》且首次在世界贸易组织(World Trade Organization, WTO)体系下制定了涉及航空运输领域的《航空运输服务附件》,从而形成了 WTO 体制下对其他国际航空运输自由化多边协议具有参考和借鉴意义的法律性文件。②

第五航权开放的发展历程实际上是整体航权交换的缩影和表现,其从 20 世纪初单边主义管理模式发展到 20 世纪 40 年代传统的百慕大式、事先确定模式、自由式以及“开放天空”的双边管理模式,再到 20 世纪 70 年代以亚太和欧盟地区为主的区域性航空运输自由化,最后发展到 20 世纪 80 年代

① 参见张焱:《欧洲的“天空开放”:航权交换区域合作模式的新发展》,载《华东政法大学学报》2017 年第 3 期。

② 参见孙玉超:《国家航空运输自由化的法律问题研究》,武汉大学 2010 年博士学位论文,第 79 ~ 80 页。

WTO 框架下更广范围内的多边航空运输协议,终将在全球领域内实现航空运输完全自由化的目标。

二、西安开放第五航权的必要性与可能性

(一)西安开放第五航权的必要性

西安作为对外开放的重要门户和空中丝路的关键节点,①承担着重要的历史使命和职责,2019 年空港新城开放第五航权更是对西安经济转型发展、航空企业和消费者的利益平衡以及全球航空运输自由化的实现发挥着必不可少的作用。

1. 引领区域经济转型发展

航空枢纽是经济发展的"发动机"和"引擎",将西安打造为国际航空枢纽和最佳中转机场对引领区域经济跨越式发展和产业结构优化升级来说极为重要,西安开放第五航权意味着其他国家的航空承运人无须经过政府的批准即可自由进出西安上空,旗国承运人可将从授权国运载的客、货、邮卸至西安或可从西安装载客、货、邮继续飞往授权国,以此承运人可获得从西安到授权国间更广范围的客流资源,根据世界旅游组织和美国波音的最新测算,每 100 万名航空旅客平均每年为城市创造 1 亿 ~3 亿美元的经济收益,一条国际航线为地方经济创造的 GDP 相当于 3 ~4 条国内航线带来的收入,西安开放第五航权将大幅度提升客流运输总量,以此间接带动西安经济快速发展。航权交换除便利客流运输外,还可助推当地空港物流园区建设,将有利于实现陕西省政府在 2010 年《落实陕西省物流业调整和振兴规划实施方案部门工作分工》提出的目标,即"加强铁路、公路和航空集装箱中转站等物流节点的多式联运设施建设,加快发展国际物流,完善和拓展西安国际港务区、西安出口加工区等保税物流功能。以咸阳空港物流产业园为依托,建设以电子信

① 参见张义学:《陕西进入新航空时代》,载《西部大开发》2019 年第 2 期。

息、高附加值产品为主的航空物流体系"。① 西安开放第五航权还顺应2018年年底召开的《西安临空经济示范区发展规划(2018—2035)》专题研究会议的宗旨,即对建设临空开放型经济、促进空港、陆港和高铁港"三港联动"以及打造"空中丝绸之路"交通商贸物流中心至关重要,②对实现西安经济质量和速度双重飞跃、聚力发展"三个经济"和打造"追赶超越"新引擎发挥强有力的贡献。③

西安获取第五航权开放除具备前文所述对客流和物流总量的拉动效应和对区域经济平稳健康发展的促进作用外,还能极大地带动区域就业,有利于缓解公众就业压力和解决就业难的社会问题,根据国际机场协会研究资料表明,每100万名旅客可为该地区增加2500个就业岗位,④这是由于第五航权的开放将会使某一区域的运输需求急剧扩张,从而致使机场持续扩容和该区域加强对航空器空中运行的管控力度,具体包括飞行跟踪与动态监控、航班签派放行、非正常情况下航班的调配等,⑤随之必然产生与之相对应的新型产业和就业岗位,实际上,航权交换带动就业的根本原因在于产业之间具有强大的关联效应。从更深层次的角度来说,第五航权的开放可促进各国有限资源要素在全球范围内的有序流动和高效配置,尤其是在当今人工智能与网络科技创新已成为社会发展驱动力的国际背景下,第五航权的交换可加快高新技术与先进管理理念的传播与共享,强化尖端领域复合型人才的交流与互动,推动技术密集型与知识密集型产业的优化升级,从而为整个区域的产业发展注入强大动能与活力,转变经济发展方式,优化产业结构,推动区域经

---

① 参见《落实陕西省物流业调整和振兴规划实施方案部门工作分工》,资料来源:https://wenku.baidu.com/view/18ce6a629f3143323968011ca300a6c30d22f105.html,最后访问日期:2019年5月24日。

② 参见张义学:《陕西进入新航空时代》,载《西部大开发》2019年第2期。

③ 参见《省发改委召开专题会议研究〈西安临空经济示范区发展规划〉有关事宜》,资料来源:http://www.xixianxinqu.gov.cn/xwzx/xcdt/52670.htm,最后访问日期:2019年5月24日。

④ 参见彭荣国:《试论航权开放的意义及与枢纽机场建设的关系》,载《中山大学学报论丛》2007年第11期。

⑤ 参见《航空运行管理》,资料来源:http://www.taodocs.com/p-53803183.html,最后访问日期:2019年5月23日。

济朝高质量与高标准方向发展。

总之,航空运输作为国民经济的基础性和支柱性产业,对提升客流总量、构建空港物流经济区、带动就业和促进产业升级具有紧迫的理论和现实意义,对区域经济可持续和跨越式发展起着至关重要的引领作用。

2. 平衡航空企业与消费者的利益

我国市场经济体制确立以来,传统国内民航在发展和运营过程中显现出诸多先天性弊病,主要表现为资产负债率高、生产成本高、运输价位高、生产劳动率低以及竞争水平低的"三高两低"问题,①不利于保护消费者权益和充分发挥其选择权,严重制约国内民航产业的发展。为了解决这类难题和消除妨碍航空业发展的不利因素,开放第五航权具有深刻的必要性和重要的现实意义。

第五航权的开放给予其他国家航空公司承运人不受限制和自由进入本国领空的权利,极易与国内航空公司产生激烈的竞争,内航与外航之间的博弈对本国航空运输市场机制和体制提出了更高的要求,即开放第五航权的区域必须重新思考与构建更为完善和公平的航空市场环境,国内航空企业也必须率先发展航空产业,尤其是航空制造业,提升航空服务水平和降低运输价位,增强本国航空竞争能力,抢占先机,把握主动权,从而在与其他国家航空企业竞争过程中占据有利地位。

航权交换除对优化航空运输市场环境和改革航空企业发展起到极大的推动效果外,还能给消费者带来巨大的福利。第五航权的交换加剧了航空市场竞争,促使更多航空公司进入运输市场并不断提升其服务水平和降低运价,推动单一且具垄断性质的航空市场向多元化、灵活化和便利化方向转化,从而扩大消费者的选择空间和促使其消费体验不断升级,改变由航空企业主导市场的局面,扭转消费者传统被动和弱势地位,更好地保护消费者权益和平衡航空企业与消费者之间的利益。另外,由于良好的消费体验又势必带动

① 参见刘文君:《开放第五航权势在必行》,载《中国民用航空》2003 年第 12 期。

消费数量的增加和运输市场的进一步扩大,第五航权的开放利于形成供给促进消费和消费带动供给的良性市场循环。①

综上所述,西安开放第五航权对建立公平合理的航空市场环境、增强航空企业的竞争能力和平衡消费者与航空企业之间的利益极为必要。

3. 推动国际航空运输自由化

20 世纪 70 年代后,随着世界经济区域一体化趋势日益加强,国际航空运输在区域范围内有了很大的发展,为在一定区域内共享航空经济运输利益和以期获得航空政策相同国家的广泛参与,不同国家或集团缔结了区域性航空运输协定,②这种航空区域主义虽将运输活动限定在具体区域范围内,但实际上已形成全球多边航空运输体制的基础,是经济全球化和航空运输全面自由化的重要组成部分,其本质是在某一区域内率先实行自由化,以此进一步推动世界上其他更广区域航空运输自由,最终实现全球航空运输市场的全面开放。③

基于以西安为核心的西北航空板块是中国向西开放的重要门户和西北的战略屏障以及西安作为丝绸之路经济带"核心区"、"桥头堡"和"空中丝绸之路"关键节点的重要战略地位,④2019 年"首尔—西安—河内"航线的开通使西安发展成为西北 5 省第一个获得并使用第五航权的城市,有利于把西安打造为全国内陆型经济开发开放战略高地,实现西北内陆航空市场与国际航空运输市场的无缝对接,把国际航路开口引入中国内陆地区,充分利用和拓展其周边临接省区的客货和航空市场资源,促进西安和周边地区航空市场的国际化和一体化,引领西北地区和全国其他地区航空产业的联动发展,形成

① 参见王伟:《关于西安获得利用第五航权国家支持的思考》,载《空运商务》2019 年第 1 期。

② See Arnt Goppert, The Liberalisation of International Air Transport Service: Development in the US-German Bilateral Relations and their Implication on Future Regulation Approaches Toward Aviation, LL. M. Thesis, Montreal: Institute of Air & Space Law, McGill University, 1998, p. 14.

③ 参见刘功仕:《关于航空运输全球化问题》,载《民航经济与技术》1992 年第 2 期。

④ 参见高超、胡华清:《"一带一路"战略背景下我国民航建设国际航空枢纽的基础与对策》,载《中国经贸导刊》2016 年第 29 期。

以西安为核心向外辐射区域范围内的航空运输自由,从而推动全球航空运输自由化进程的加快。

基于以上分析可知,西安开放第五航权对促进产业结构优化升级和引领区域经济跨越式和转型性发展极为必要;对引入市场竞争以构建公平合理的市场机制、给予消费者更广泛的选择权与自主权以及平衡航空企业与消费者利益至关重要;对实现以西安为核心的区域航空运输自由化和以此带动全球航空市场的自由运行必不可少。总之,西安开放第五航权对经济发展、消费者权益保护和航空运输自由化均具紧迫性和必要性。

鉴于以上西安市开放第五航权具有重大的国内和国际意义,使西安必须在现有基础上实行航权交换,我们需要详细分析西安相较于其他地区在地理位置、文化底蕴和政策扶持方面开放第五航权的优势和可能性。

(二)西安开放第五航权的可能性

1. 优越的地理位置

就传统思维而言,西安地处内陆,既不靠海也不临江,不仅在国内很难打造像北京、上海和我国香港特别行政区等国际化大都市所具备的通往世界各国和各地区的直航航班,在国际上也很难建设成为类似于罗马、开罗和雅典的空港枢纽。因而长期以来西安航空企业只局限于在以本地为主的国内市场中投入和运营,缺乏通往国际航空运输市场的便捷通道和出口,极大地妨碍了西安与各航空大国、航空强国以及国际航空市场的对接和联通,限制了其在航空产业方面的对外深入交往和积极互动,不利于西安与其他国家共享航空利益和建立航空“命运共同体”。

然而,随着近年来“空中丝绸之路”倡议获得更多国家的响应和2009年国务院通过批准《关中—天水经济区发展规划》明确将西安打造为国际化大都市①的目标,以及2017年西安获准为自由贸易试验区,中国和与中国有贸

① 参见《天水市关中—天水经济区发展规划实施方案》,资料来源:http://www.tianshui.com.cn/news/tianshui/2010060317121742236.htm,最后访问日期:2019年5月23日。

易往来的国家开始重新审视西安的地理区位并认为,相较于西北和全国其他内陆地区,西安具备得天独厚的地理优势。对内来说,西安位于中国内陆腹心和版图的中心位置,连接西北内陆和东部沿海地区,是西北地区通往西南、中原、华北和华东的门户和交通枢纽,是连接东西和贯穿南北的枢纽中心,在全国区域经济结构中是承东启西、东联西进的桥头堡和依托地区;对外来说,西安是古代丝绸之路的起点和连接现代"空中丝绸之路"国家战略的重要纽带,是通向"世界上最长和最具发展潜力的经济大走廊"的起点,逐渐发展成为内陆改革开放的试验田和中国西部地区对外开放的窗口。

反观开放第五航权的国家和地区,其对外进行航权交换无一不得益于优越的地理条件,例如,韩国仁川与西海相邻,是韩国第二大贸易港口,且位于包括中国、日本、俄罗斯等国在内的东北亚经济圈的中心,①具备充足的客货资源,仅在2015年其国际旅客和货物吞吐量就分别高达近300万人次和200万吨,基此,仁川机场发展成为国际客货运航空枢纽和亚太地区最具竞争力的国际航空港。② 再看中国获得并使用第五航权的城市,如由于郑州居于中原城市群的核心位置和作为中部地区重要的物资集散地,国务院在2013年将郑州航空港定位为"国际航空货运枢纽和国内大型航空枢纽",允许其开通第五航权航线。总之,这些国家和地区都因具备良好的地理位置而享有充足的客货运资源,为承担起全球客货流"超级承运人"的角色,其通过对外开放第五航权允许更多航空公司自由进出本国上空。

在"空中丝绸之路"建设和发展如火如荼的国际背景下,同世界上开放第五航权的国家和地区类似,西安优越的地理区位将使其客货流量得到大幅度提升,从而为其开放第五航权提供巨大可能性。

2. 深厚的文化底蕴

西安作为中华文明的重要发源地之一,具有悠久的历史文化渊源和以秦

---

① 参见金政佑:《韩国仁川国际城市的开发战略研究》,青岛科技大学2016年硕士学位论文,第22页。

② 参见赵巍:《仁川机场的国际化发展道路》,载《民航管理》2015年第11期。

始皇兵马俑、大雁塔和碑林为代表的丰富物质文化,其与罗马、开罗和雅典共称“世界四大古都”和“世界历史文化名城”,早在3000年前先后有周、秦、汉、隋、唐等13个朝代在西安建都,因而西安也一度发展成为全国经济、政治和文化中心。另外,西安自古以来还承担对外交流的重要历史使命,自西汉张骞使西域后,建立起以西安为起点,贯穿中亚、西亚的古代“丝绸之路”,使西安成为东西文化交汇的中心和联系东西方通道的枢纽,在中国对外交流史上承担承上启下的作用,这类独特的历史文化资源可能引发国人对中华民族传统文化的共鸣和外国友人对“空中丝绸之路”历史踪迹的追寻,因而西安不需要过多地投入人力、物力资源即可带动本地旅游业的发展和人流量的激增,为开放第五航权提供市场保障。

除具备深厚的历史文化外,西安的高新科技和教育文化也为其交换航权进一步提供可能性。西安高科技园区、科研机构和航空产业高度密集,聚集了全国1/3的航空力量并凭此研制了包括“神舟”五号、六号火箭发动机和遥感装置等在内的先进航空工具,从而为与其他国家或地区交换第五航权提供技术和设备支持。另外,西安具有丰富的教育资源和明显的科教优势,设立专门的航空航天研究所和以航空为重点研究对象的高等院校,其高校数量位居全国第五和西北第一。2011年西安市获科技部批准“创建国家级文化与科技融合示范基地”,并在政策共享、园区建设、项目协作、平台搭建和人才交流方面取得了实质性的进展,实现了科技与文化板块的有效联动,强大的科教实力促使大批外地人才涌入西安留学,使西安航空市场需求急剧扩张,推动西安建设国际航空枢纽和拓宽国际直航覆盖范围,减少前往西安民众的负担和便利其出行。

通过以上分析可知,由于西安具有深厚的历史文化和雄厚的科教文化,吸引了大量其他国家和地区的民众前往西安旅游或留学,扩大了航空市场需求,从而为建立国际航空枢纽和航线网络提供可能。

3. 强大的政策支持

2009年6月国务院通过批准《关中—天水经济区发展规划》明确规定要

把关中—天水经济区打造为“全国内陆型经济开发开放的战略高地”，西安作为关中—天水经济区中经济最发达的核心城市，国务院进一步明确着力建设西安为“国际化大都市”，并在《关中—天水经济区发展规划》中提出“进一步强化西安咸阳国际机场枢纽功能，有序建设支线机场”。显然，国务院在较早时期就已勾勒出西安国际航空枢纽建设的路线图。近年来，在全球经济一体化、全面深化改革、扩大对外开放、加快推进“空中丝绸之路”建设和深入推进西部大开发的新形势下，基于西安作为古代“丝绸之路”起点和西部地区的中心城市地位，再次引发了国家对西安建设国际航空枢纽的高度重视，2017 年国务院在《中国(陕西)自由贸易试验区总体方案》指出，在陕西自由贸易试验区“中心片区重点发展航空物流”；“西安国际港务区片区重点发展国际贸易、现代物流、金融服务、旅游会展、电子商务等产业，建设‘一带一路’国际中转内陆枢纽港、开放型金融产业创新高地及欧亚贸易和人文交流合作新平台”；“创新航空港、陆港联动发展机制。完善集疏运体系，加密航线航班，增加国际货运航线航班。在自贸试验区内组建符合条件的本地货运航空公司，大力发展空港货运物流，打造国家航空运输枢纽”。① 该文件从战略定位到具体执行方案中多次提到将西安建设成为国际中转枢纽航空港和运输枢纽，以凸显国家对西安开放第五航权的支持和将其建设成为国际航空中转中心的决心。2018 年，国务院出台《关于支持自由贸易试验区深化改革创新若干措施的通知》，其中第 31 条和第 32 条对航空运输作了专门的规定，即“在对外航权谈判中支持西安机场利用第五航权，在平等互利的基础上，允许外国航空公司承载经西安至第三国的客货业务，积极向国外航空公司推荐并引导申请进入中国市场的国外航空公司执飞西安机场”和“进一步加大对西安航空物流发展的支持力度”。② 这些都成为推动西安开放第五航权和建设国际航空枢纽的政策红利，成为西安空港新城建设再上台阶的坚实基础，

---

① 参见《中国(陕西)自由贸易试验区总体方案》，资料来源：https://www.yidaiyilu.gov.cn/zchj/zcfg/10490.htm，最后访问日期：2019 年 5 月 23 日。

② 参见《国务院支持自由贸易试验区深化改革创新若干措施的通知》，资料来源：http://www.zzx.gov.cn/c1876/20190314/i847158.html，最后访问日期：2019 年 5 月 23 日。

西安开放第五航权面临着千载难逢的机遇。

当前,西安开放第五航权已经获得了国家的政策支持,其在获批开放第五航权半年内实现了航线落地,2019 年 5 月 13 日,西北首条第五航权货运航线“首尔—西安—河内”正式开通,且空港新城正在持续加大与外国航空公司的对接力度,积极争取开通“莫斯科—西安—阿拉木图”和“伊斯坦布尔—西安—中亚国家”等第五航权货运航线,[①]标志着西安拥有了进入国际航空运输市场的“通行券”,开启了西安打造国家航空货运枢纽的新篇章。在“空中丝绸之路”逐渐发展成为世界经济和社会发展巨大推动力的新型国际背景下,目前西安仅开放货运第五航权无法应对客、邮流量的攀升趋势,这就对西安第五航权的开放提出了更高的要求,西安应在已有的航权基础上,凭借其优越的地理条件、深厚的文化底蕴和强大的政策扶持,进一步思考深度开放第五航权的法律路径。

三、“空中丝绸之路”建设背景下西安开放第五航权的法律路径

现阶段,“空中丝绸之路”倡议得到了越来越多国家和国际组织的积极响应并受到国际社会的广泛关注,其在全球的影响力和号召力日益扩大,各国和各地区之间的交流和互动也随之更加频繁,在此背景下,各国对航空市场的需求也与日俱增,其中以作为“空中丝绸之路”关键节点的西安航空市场尤为明显。然而,西安在航权和运力投入及竞争力等方面存在许多不足,如其航空公司尚未充分利用航权与“空中丝绸之路”的沿线国家建立全面的航线网络,且与中东、西亚和北非等欠发达地区之间的航班和通航点较少,导致西安与这些地区间的通达通畅水平低下和航空市场极度萎缩。除西安自身航空竞争力不足外,外国航空枢纽对这部分市场分流较为严重,与周边的

---

① 参见《陕西省首条第五航权货运航线“首尔—西安—河内”首航》,http://www.caacnews.com.cn/1/5/201905/t20190515_1273687.html,最后访问日期:2019 年 5 月 28 日。

仁川、曼谷和成田等国际机场相比,西安航空枢纽建设处于劣势地位,加之迪拜和伊斯坦布尔等机场的迅速崛起,给西安进一步开放第五航权造成巨大冲击和影响。[①] 结合西安开放第五航权的现状,为化解以上困境和提高西安航空竞争能力,为建设国际航空中转市场和枢纽,西安可拓展国际航空协作和积极开拓市场资源,大力开发新航线和航班,特别是国际客货航线;根据西安航权开放的种类,相应提升航空港基础设施保障能力和加强机场体系建设,从而进一步强化西安在航空运输网络尤其是国际航空运输网络中的中转功能和组织功能,使西安与世界、世界与西安直接相连。

(一)积极开拓市场资源

就开放第五航权的国家或地区而言,由于开放第五航权的目的在于分散人流和集疏货物,广阔的客货市场是交换航权的先决条件和决定性因素。如果要将某一机场打造成为国际航空枢纽,那么必须具备充足的客货资源与有效的航空市场;相反,如果前往该地的客货流量不足而未达开放航权的标准,那么开放第五航权则无法发挥其应有的效果和实质的经济意义。就同西安类似深处国家内陆的郑州而言,2017 年新郑机场的旅客吞吐量为 2430 万人次,位居中部地区第一名;货邮吞吐量突破 50 万吨,跻身全球前 50 强,客货运规模在中部区域范围内实现了"双第一",[②]为郑州开放第五航权提供了广泛的市场资源,基此,国家在同年 6 月 17 日支持郑州—卢森堡"空中丝绸之路"的建设,卢航执飞的货机在卢森堡装载货物后可根据郑州开放第五航权继续在郑州机场进行二次装卸,再直飞芝加哥机场;同样地,返程时卢航在芝加哥机场完成装卸任务后,在郑州机场拥有再次集疏和调整货物的权利,从而为航空公司和实际承运人安排货源提供了更大的选择余地和更灵活的操

① 参见高超、胡华清:《"一带一路"战略下我国民航建设国际航空枢纽的基础与对策》,载《中国经贸导刊》2016 年第 29 期。

② 参见郭军峰:《河南打造"空中丝绸之路"的优势及对策研究》,载《对外经贸》2019 年第 1 期。

作空间。[①] 再从国际视角来看,2016 年羽田机场和成田机场国际旅客吞吐量分别为 1357 万人次和 3124 万人次,全球大型国际航空枢纽承载的客运量均在 500 万人次以上,每日进出港国际航线可达 293 条,因而开放第五航权对拓宽国际航空市场具有重要意义。[②]

通过对郑州和全球国际航空枢纽的分析可知,丰富的市场资源是国际机场赖以产生和发展的关键因素。在共建"一带一路"和"空中丝绸之路"倡议的提出为中国航空企业"走出去"提供新发展机遇的国际背景下,为实现将西安打造为国际航空中转机场的目标,西安应在已开放第五航权和旧有市场的基础上,与沿线国家开展全方位的航空协作,在南线以南亚和东南亚国家为主要合作对象,在北线以中亚、西亚和独联体国家为重点,[③]积极寻找在航空领域的全球合作伙伴,不断开拓市场资源,持续扩大旧航路和开辟新航线。

为将上述举措具体落实到实践中,作为拓宽市场和航线主导力量的航空公司可通过与外国航空企业合作形成国内外企业联动机制,针对沿线和更远国家与地区的不同航空实力和需求,采取"共商、共议、共建"方式尊重各大航空集团的利益诉求,使更多国家愿意在友好协商前提下扩大与西安间的旧航线和开辟新航路。具体而言,国家和地方政府应高度重视航权开放工作,政府应充分调查各国旅客的出行目的和货物的运输走向,了解当地市民旅游、公民出差、探亲访友和出国留学等公民出行原因,并据此加大与交往密切的国家和地区双边谈判的力度,从而通过这种方式有针对性的扩大旧航线并为旅客出行和货物运输提供便利。在此基础上,为进一步扩大本地航空市场和与更多国家进行合作,开辟新型航线,陕西省和西安市政府还可积极做好航权开放的对外宣传和营销工作,共同出资设立新开航线发展培育基金,从

① 参见《究竟是什么让郑州成为全球航空"中转站"的第五航权》,资料来源:http://www.zzsz.net.cn/news/zhengzhou/19708.html,最后访问日期:2019 年 5 月 29 日。

② 参见姜巍:《国际航空枢纽发展特征分析及对我国的发展建议》,载《价值工程》2018 年第 19 期。

③ 参见梁晓英、马宁:《促"一带一路"航空合作 享"空中丝路"共赢发展》,载《中国航空报》2018 年 9 月 15 日,第 2 版。

资金上给予专项补助，培育现已开通暂时亏损且具有发展潜力的重点国际航线和新引进的基地航空公司。另外，国家外交和民航等部门也可根据国内航权开放的实际情况和航运市场的发展程度，并结合西安经济发展现状，在1944年《芝加哥公约》以及与日本、韩国等国成功达成的双边航空运输协定的框架和经验下，与巴黎、伦敦和纽约等一些国际化大都市所在国进行积极有序和对等的双边航权交换谈判，争取与这些国际城市实现直航。当然，在条件成熟时，还可以进行多边谈判并适时加入一些多边协定。

除选择和开辟航线外，西安还应注重航线开辟之后的运营管理工作。在航空公司开辟出一条新航线后，如何使其投入运营、快速占领市场和为本地创造经济效益成为各航空公司了解的重点，西安航空企业在准确了解此类信息后，应把握契机，采取相应措施使新航线尽快适应市场需求，如可通过收益管理模式和科学合理的在线订座系统提高旅客客座率；针对不同国际航线差别定价、超售和控制座位存量，将产品适时销售给更多旅客，从而达到航空企业经济利益最大化的效果。①

综上所述，西安应通过政府对外宣传和经济补贴开辟新航线，并将其快速投入市场运营以获取经济效益，从而在旧有航线的基础上进一步扩大本地航空市场，促进西安国际航班的良性循环和实现可持续发展，有力推动西安发展成为国际航空大都市和国际航空枢纽。

（二）优化配套基础设施

机场的配套基础设施对提升航空服务水平和扩大对外开放程度具有极大的影响和促进作用，任何外国航空企业和具体承运人在进入西安航空市场前，势必会事先调查和了解西安本地机场的配套基础设施，因此，西安第五航权的推动和实际效益的实现，在很大程度上与机场基础设施建设密切相关。综观世界上开放第五航权的国家与地区，其开放航权无一不得益于国际机场

---

① 参见薛琳琳：《中国二线城市国际航线开拓策略研究》，载《空运商务》2017年第2期。

的优质基础设施。如韩国仁川机场有针对性地设有33个登机门供韩亚航空、日本航空和中国东方航空等航空公司使用,在机场周围设有众多餐饮、购物和娱乐设施供候机的旅客消遣;日本成田机场发达的交通体系和租车服务为来往旅客提供巨大便利,这些机场因与其他交通方式联动构成综合交通运输枢纽,具有较为全面的配套基础设施和高水平服务质量以及强大的机场安全监管保障能力和完善的航空救援体系而逐步发展成为国际化航空运输中转中心并在更大程度上与其他国家交换航权。为扩大航权开放范围和程度,西安可在对照其他国际机场的基础上完善集疏运体系建设和统筹协调多种运输方式的发展,不断提高服务水平和促进航空枢纽建设与网络技术、智能化时代的对接,强化航空安全保障能力和风险救助机制,从而将西安机场建设为国际航空枢纽。

1. 联动多种交通和多区域机场群发展

当前机场不再是单纯为航空运输提供服务的终端,而是已逐渐从满足旅客航空出行的单一节点向集民航、公路、铁路和轨道等多种交通运输方式于一体的综合枢纽转化,世界旅客转乘量最大和最繁忙的亚兰特国际机场通过城市快速运输系统实现了机场航站楼和城市中心火车站的快速对接,配合多条州际高速公路组成了高速公路环线,形成了高效快捷的机场交通系统;法兰克福机场附近建有长途和地区火车站以及高速公路,实现了“空铁联运”和“空路联运”,①以此满足旅客对航空枢纽多样化和系统化的要求。为通过建立便捷高效的综合运输体系向更多国家开放第五航权,西安应强化机场交通枢纽地位,注重以轨道和高速公路为重点的集疏运网络体系建设,实现机场与公路、铁路和城市轨道等多种运输方式的无缝衔接,尤其是与具有速度快、运能大和安全系数高等特点的轨道交通对接。其中,最主要和有效的方法是建设综合交通的统一信息服务平台与便捷换乘通道,以此建立一个以轨道交通为主轴、以公共交通为主体、多种交通方式相互协调发展的综合交通

---

① 参见汪祝君:《大型机场集疏运体系发展经验启示》,载《综合运输》2018年第9期。

系统。[①] 具体而言,为缩短旅客在路途中的周转时间和便利其出行,西安应在距离机场较近的位置规划铁路、高铁、公共汽车甚至专门的网约车线路,还应为公共汽车与网约车设置独立通道和特殊的上下车点,从而实现客运“零换乘”和货运“零运转”,推动航站楼与其他交通站点紧密结合和一体化衔接;另外,民航与其他交通方式还可突破地理层面的联系,建立更深层次的多式联运机制和综合交通的统一信息服务平台,主要可采取以下几种做法:

第一,支持空铁、空轨客票的混合查询、销售、生成订单,完善联程、往返和异地等票务服务,简化支付、退改签和清算等流程;第二,健全旅客身份查验制度,提高其入站、通关和安检效率;第三,完善旅客服务系统,推行跨运输方式的异地候机候车、行李联程托运等配套服务;第四,全面考虑可能出现的异常情况,如出现延机和航班取消等情况时,可为旅客提供更灵活多样的行程选择和多维度组合路线建议。[②]

除要加强航空与其他多种交通方式的联动外,西安还应注重地区间机场群的协同发展,以此强化航空运输功能、提升机场国际影响力以及与更多地区施行航权交换。例如,法国戴高乐、奥利和勒布尔热机场因共同构成巴黎机场集团而扩大了客货中转量,仅在 2017 年戴高乐和奥利机场合计客运量就超过 1 亿人次,货运量接近 230 万吨和飞机起降数超过了 70 万架;作为国际客货枢纽的肯尼迪机场和与国内旅客为主、国外旅客为辅的纽瓦克机场以及主飞加拿大的拉瓜迪亚机场联合发展成为纽约机场群,极大地扩大了纽约航空市场容量,有利于将纽约打造为全球经济中心和旅游中心。[③] 为响应 2017 年《民用运输机场建设“十三五”规划》中“强化区域性枢纽机场功能”[④]

---

① 参见陈洪波、金勇、曹喆懿:《一市两场背景下北京机场综合交通提升研究》,载《民航管理》2019 年第 2 期。

② 同上。

③ 参见徐翀宇:《建设世界级城市群背景下的京津冀机场群协同发展研究》,中国民航大学 2018 年硕士学位论文,第 23 页。

④ 参见《十三五机场建设规划》,资料来源:http://www.chinabgao.com/freereport/78136.html,最后访问日期:2019 年 5 月 30 日。

的规定和通过区域机场良性互动增加旅客运输量,西安应从区域间多个机场的实际情况出发,以市场导向为合作基础,找准符合区域现实情况和具备区域特色的发展路径,主动构建统一管理机构,加强其与郑州和新疆等机场的互动联通,强化各机场在信息和资源共享、航班备降以及应急救援等多方面的合作力度,补齐短板,消除“瓶颈”,全方位提升区域内多机场体系的航空运输和可持续发展能力。①

总之,如果西安要面向更多国家开放第五航权和获取更丰富的市场资源,那么有必要加强机场在距离、票务信息、服务流程和技术系统上与其他交通方式的对接,建立全面高效的国际航空枢纽,并在区域内部建立一体化和综合化机场群。

2. 提升优质和智能化服务水平

服务水平是考量某一机场是否符合国际机场标准的关键因素。西安应通过设置中转捷运系统、中转休息室和中转专用通道为旅客提供优质中转服务;开辟国内和国际的快速中转通道,实现无缝转接;制定高效顺畅的中转流程,在各个航站楼和中转通道上设立引导指示牌,提升空港软件建设。另外,西安还应加大对空港硬件基础设施的资金投入和政策扶持,强化机场附近餐饮和住宿、娱乐设施、医疗设备和救援体系建设,从而为旅客提供必要的生活保障或方便其消遣漫长候机时间。

除通过上述传统方式优化服务质量外,在人工智能和网络科技的创新发展已成为社会发展的强大驱动力背景下,国际社会对国际航空枢纽的建设提出了更为严苛的要求,近年来国内外大型中转机场高度重视“智慧机场”的建设,如希斯罗机场斥巨资引进了个人捷运和轻轨系统;2018 年,昆明长水机场推行“无纸化”便捷出行服务,旅客只需出示手机订票二维码即可快速通过安检;中国南方航空公司在 2019 年正式宣称将以网上值机方式代替人

① 参见周子钦、应杰、冯建忠:《区域机场协同发展的探讨》,载《民航管理》2019 年第 2 期。

工值机。[①] 为顺应智能时代和新型高科技的发展,西安可借鉴这些国家和地区的先进实践经验,对接"互联网+"技术,充分发挥互联网在机场生产要素配置中集成和优化作用,推动网络技术在安全防范、生产运营和旅客服务环节的应用。具体而言,机场可推动人工服务逐步向网络服务方向转化,在航空公司官网和航旅服务提供商等多种网络平外上发布航班信息、提供购票服务和值机程序,使旅客可通过网络自助模式快速完成查询、订票、值机和登机等全流程个性化服务,需要托运行李的旅客也可通过这种自主模式完成行李托运,从而缩短了周转时间并满足了旅客高效化和便捷化要求。另外,西安机场还可通过大数据、新技术收集旅客信息,运用人脸识别技术核准旅客身份,即旅客只需在航显屏前"刷脸"就可出现其乘坐航班的信息,并自动指引旅客前往指定登机口。当然,除利用人脸识别技术查验航班动态和快速通过安检外,机场还可利用该技术实时统计机场旅客流量,并通过为特定人群提供专门化服务的方式分散人流和方便其出行,例如,对怀孕妇女、幼童、老人和行动不便者可设置专门的通道和舱位,真正实现"一张脸畅行机场"。

通过以上分析可知,国内外大型枢纽机场都具有极其广阔的航空市场资源和优质基础设施,为通过将西安打造为国际中转机场使其进一步开放第五航权,西安应积极参鉴国内外机场的先进经验和有效启示,在"空中丝绸之路"背景下寻找更广泛的合作伙伴和拓宽市场,联动多种交通方式与多区域机场发展,构建全面综合的交通运输体系,在不断提升传统机场服务的前提下,尽可能扩大智能化技术在机场建设中的应用范围,从而推动西安在已开放航权基础上与更多国家更深入全面地交换航权。

---

① 参见毕晓青:《浅谈智慧机场之昆明长水国际机场的发展对策研究》,载《中国商论》2019 年第 8 期。

四、结　　语

在“空中丝绸之路”倡议从理念转化为行动、从愿景转化为现实以及国际影响力逐步提升的背景下,各个国家和地区开始重新审视其在航空领域中的开放程度,并对处在 WTO 框架下的多边航空管理模式进行了深刻的反思。为顺应国际航空自由化趋势,西安在 2019 年正式开通了“首尔—西安—河内”航线,标志着西安在开放第五航权上实现了重大突破且为进一步开放航权指明了方向。

由于开放第五航权可引领区域经济跨越式发展和推动产业结构优化升级,加剧国内外航空企业竞争,为消费者提供更加灵活化和多样化的选择,平衡航空企业和处于“弱势”地位消费者之间的利益以及通过率先实现区域航空自由化的方式推动国际航空运输自由化,这就对西安开放第五航权提出了更为严格的要求。反观西安航权交换现状和条件,其作为古代“丝绸之路”起点和“空中丝绸之路”的重要依托城市,具有优越的地理位置;作为“十三朝古都”和科教大省的省会城市,具有深厚的文化底蕴;作为国家重点关注和扶持的航空集团,具有强大的政策支持,这些因素使西安拥有丰富的市场资源,为西安开放第五航权提供了巨大可能性。为面向更多国家和地区开放第五航权,西安应在借鉴其他国际航空枢纽发展经验的基础上,不断扩大旧航路和开辟新航线,积极寻求更多合作伙伴和拓宽市场;推动多区域机场和多种运输方式的联动建设,提升优质和智能化服务水平,从而在全球范围内构建航空“命运共同体”。

航空法基础理论

航空器之法律地位与航空器之国籍

吴光平*

一、前　言

1783年6月5日法国孟戈菲兄弟(约瑟夫—米歇尔·孟戈菲(Joseph-Michel Montgolfier)与雅克—艾蒂安·孟戈菲(Jacques-Étienne Montgolfier)首次将可用于运送之热气球升空,开启了人类的航空活动。由于航空活动既不受海洋分隔,也无高山阻挡,此为船舶、火车、汽车等交通工具所不能者,故以航空器从事运送遂逐渐发展,尤其是今日,因航空运送较海上运送更具机动性且更为快速便捷,航空旅客运送更已取代绝大部分海上旅客运送之功能,成为跨国旅客运送最主要的运送方式。

因应1783年孟戈菲兄弟的热气球升空,法国于1794年颁行法令,规定未经警察核准,禁止热气球升空,是为第一个航空法令。但航空法真正开始快速发展,则是1919年《关于飞航管理的公约》(Convention

* 法学博士,台湾开南大学法律学系暨研究所专任副教授。

Relating to the Regulation of Aerial Navigation),简称《巴黎公约》(Paris Convention)之后的事。由于航空运送起步甚晚,相较于海上运送之悠久历史,海上运送在发展演进之过程中海商法渐次建立起诸如船舶国籍制度、船舶权利登记制度、船舶所有人责任限制制度、海事优先权制度、船舶抵押权制度、海上运送人单位责任限制制度等完整而独自之法律体系,①到 20 世纪才起步之航空运送,依循着海上运送之足迹,乃为合理,故航空法乃仿海商法建立航空器国籍制度、航空器权利登记制度、航空器营运人责任限制制度、航空器优先权制度、航空器抵押权制度、航空运送人单位责任限制制度等法律体系。航空法之制度建构参酌甚至移植海商法之制度,实乃自然之事,盖二者都是利用交通工具从事运送,只是一个在空中另一个在海上,故 20 世纪才开始发展的航空法,当然会见贤于公元前 3 世纪《罗地海法》(*lex Rodhos*)开始就已发展的海商法。②

鉴于此,本文乃就航空器抵押权制度、航空器权利登记制度及航空器国籍制度出发,就此等制度所涉及之基本问题——航空器法律地位之问题,加以探讨,并适时与此等制度所源之船舶抵押权制度、船舶权利登记制度及船舶国籍制度,分析其间之同异。

二、航空器之定义

(一)从《巴黎公约》到《芝加哥公约》

为因应航空活动之勃兴,且因第一次世界大战时,航空器普遍运用于军事上,故于战后即有需要召开国际会议,制定国际公约以规范航空活动。于 1919 年 10 月 3 日在法国巴黎召开的会议上,通过了 1919 年《关于飞航管理

---

① 关于此等有别于民法之海商法上制度之由来与功能,以及以此等制度为元素所形成之海商法固有性(或独自性),参见吴光平:《海商法与海事国际私法研究》,台北,台湾财产法暨经济法研究协会 2007 年版,第 20~43 页。

② 关于自公元前 3 世纪《罗地海法》开始,海商法发展之历史演进过程,参见吴光平:《海商法与海事国际私法研究》,台北,台湾财产法暨经济法研究协会 2007 年版,第 5~20 页。

之公约》(Convention Relating to the Regulation of Aerial Navigation,以下简称《巴黎公约》),为第一个规范航空活动之国际公约法。《巴黎公约》本文并未就航空器之定义加以规定,但于附件A,则规定"航空器为借由大气层中以空气之反作用力为支撑之任何器物"(Le mot aéronef désigne tout appareil pouvant se soutenir dans l'atmosphère grâce aux reactions de l'air)。依此,《巴黎公约》上的航空器范围较广,既包括重于空气的飞机、滑翔机、直升机,亦包括轻于空气的热气球、阻塞气球(barrage balloon,有时亦称为飞船)等器械,[①]但以自身动力上升而不以空气反作用力支撑的火箭,则不包括在内。此定义,意味航空活动仅限于大气层中,盖航空器既须以空气之反作用力飞行,则航空器自无从在无空气之大气层以外飞行。而《巴黎公约》此一对航空器之定义,完全为1944年《国际民用航空公约》(Convention on International Civil Aviation,以下简称《芝加哥公约》)所继受。

由于第二次世界大战期间,航空器在战争中更加被大大利用,且破坏力强大,使人们对空战有很大的恐惧,故认为无论是军事航空器抑或是民用航空器,都应置于国际控制下。但是,各国却又相当重视国际航空运送所蕴含的经济利益,故而于国际控制与维护航空运送经济利益之二大思维背景下,有了重新制定符合当前时代需求之国际公约的酝酿,此即为《芝加哥公约》之制定背景。时任美国总统罗斯福于1944年11月1日邀请同盟国与部分中立国于美国芝加哥召开国际民用航空会议,并于同年12月7日通过了《芝加哥公约》,并有52国签署,同时依《芝加哥公约》第43条之规定于1947年4月4日成立国际民用航空组织(International Civil Aviation Organization,ICAO)并于同年10月成为隶属于联合国经济及社会理事会(Economic and Social Council,ECOSOC)下的组织。《芝加哥公约》目前有191国加入,是当前协调世界各国于民用航空领域内各种经济与法律事务、制定航空技术国际标准之最重要的国际组织。而《芝加哥公约》本文亦未就航空器之定义加以

① Isabella Henrietta Philepina Diederiks-Verschoor, an Introduction to Air Law, 8th ed., Kluwer Law International, 2006, p. 5.

规定,但于附件 6 与附件 7,则完全继受《巴黎公约》附件 A 对航空器之定义,规定为“航空器为大气层中以空气之反作用力为支撑之任何器械”(Any machine that can derive support in the atmosphere from the reactions of the air)①。但国际民用航空组织于 1967 年 11 月 6 日修正了这一定义,将空气对地球表面反作用力之情况排除在外,而重新定义为“航空器者,借由大气层中以空气之反作用力,但并非以空气对地球表面之反作用力,为支撑之任何器物”(Any machine that can derive support in the atmosphere from the reactions of the air other than the reactions of the air against the earth's surface),依此修正后之定义,可以缩小航空器之范围,将气垫船、气垫车等不适当之器械排除于外。而现今《芝加哥公约》对航空器之定义,则可见于关于“航空事故及事故调查”(Aircraft Accident and Incident Investigation)的附件 13 中。②

由于《芝加哥公约》成员国众多,因此《芝加哥公约》对航空器之定义,已成为国际习惯法的一部分。各国航空法关于航空器的定义,大多实行此一定义,例如,1988 年澳洲《民用航空法》(Civil Aviation Act)第 3 条规定:“航空器者,借由大气层中以空气之反作用力,但并非以空气对地球表面之反作用力,为支撑之任何器物。”③但仍有非实行此一定义者,例如,1952 年日本《航空法》第 2 条第 1 款规定:“本法所称航空器,指人所支配供飞行所用之飞机、直升机、滑翔机、飞船及其他法令所规定供飞行所用之机器。”④1958 年美国

---

① Isabella Henrietta Philepina Diederiks-Verschoor, an Introduction to Air Law, 8th ed., Kluwer Law International, 2006, p. 5.

② See “International Investigation Standards”, Accessed January 1, 2019. http://www.iprr.org/manuals/Annex13.html.

③ Section 3: “‘*aircraft*’ means any machine or craft that can derive support in the atmosphere from the reactions of the air, other than the reactions of the air against the earth's surface.”

④ 第二条 この法律において「航空機」とは、人が乗つて航空の用に供することができる飛行機、回転翼航空機、滑空機及び飛行船その他政令で定める航空の用に供することができる機器をいう。

《联邦航空法》(Federal Aviation Act)[①]第101条第5款规定:"现有或日后所发明、使用或专供用于空中航行、飞行的任何机器。"[②]

(二)民用航空器与国家航空器

航空器具有不同之用途,不同的部门使用或不同之目的使用,将决定其不同之法律地位。《芝加哥公约》第3条第1款规定:"本公约适用于民用航空器,不适用于国家航空器。"[③]即将航空器区别为民用航空器(civil aircraft)与国家航空器(state aircraft),此一区分,不但呼应了《芝加哥公约》之名称,更界定了《芝加哥公约》之适用范围,显示出《芝加哥公约》系适用于民用航空活动,盖民用航空器乃是用于民用航空活动之航空器。质言之,《芝加哥公约》并不适用于国家航空器,[④]故其第3条第2款:"用于军事、海关与警察任务之航空器,为国家航空器。"[⑤]所定义之国家航空器,即不受《芝加哥公约》规范。

按国家航空器之界定,并非单一标准,可以所有权作为标准,亦可以使用目的作为标准,如为前者,则国家航空器可理解为国有的航空器,如为后者,则国家航空器可理解为公共任务的航空器。《芝加哥公约》并非采取前者,其第79条:"一国得由其政府或由政府指定一间或数间航空公司,参加联营

---

① 已收录于《美国法典》(United States Code)第四十九编"运送"(Transportation)第七章"航空计划"(Aviation Programs)第一节"航空商业与安全"(Air Commerce and Safety)中。

② Section 101:(5)"Aircraft" means any contrivance now known or hereafter invented, used, or designed for navigation of or flight in the air.

③ Article 3:(a) This Convention shall be applicable only to civil aircraft, and shall not be applicable to state aircraft.

④ 但《巴黎公约》亦适用于国家航空器,其第七章即为"国家航空器"之专章,其中第32条规定:"(第1项)缔约国之军事航空器,未经特别授权,不得飞越另一缔约国领土上空或降落于该国领土。经授权后,若未有特别约定,军事航空器享有如外国军舰般习惯上之特权。"(Article 32:1. No military aircraft of a contracting State shall fly over the territory of another contracting State nor land thereon without special authorisation. In case of such authorisation the military aircraft shall enjoy, in principle, in the absence of special stipulation, the privileges which are customarily accorded to foreign ships of war),更规定了军事航空器之特权。

⑤ Article 3:(b) Aircraft used in military, customs and police services shall be deemed to be state aircraft.

组织或合营协议。航空公司,国家可决定为国营、部分国营或私营。”①将国营航空公司纳入适用范围,而国营航空公司所有之航空器乃国有航空器,故可知《芝加哥公约》应系采取后者,盖纵为国有航空器,其用于民用航空活动者,亦为民用航空器。因此,《芝加哥公约》对于民用航空器与国家航空器之区别,乃是采取功能取向,民用航空器系用于民用航空活动,而国家航空器系用于公共任务的航空活动。

《芝加哥公约》第 3 条第 2 款对于国家航空器“用于军事、海关与警察任务”之规定究系列举规定抑或例示规定,将影响第 3 条第 3 款“缔约国之国家航空器,未经特别协议或其他方式之授权并依照其中之规定,不得飞越另一缔约国领土上空或降落于该国领土”②之适用。③ 若认为系列举规定,则国家航空器仅限定于从事军事、海关与警察任务之航空器,除非该航空器从事国际定期航班而依第 6 条“国际定期航班,未经特别许可或其他方式之授权并依照其中之规定,不得飞越或进入另一缔约国领土上空”④之规定亦受相类之限制,否则航空器属于不定期国际航班而依第 5 条“(第 1 项)缔约国同意其他缔约国之所有不从事定期国际航班飞行的航空器,于遵守本公约所规定之条件,无须事先获得可,有权飞入或飞越其领土而不降停,或为非商业性降停,但飞经国有权令其降落。为飞航安全,航空器欲飞经之地区不得进入或无当航行设施,缔约国保留令其依照规定航路或获得特别许可后方许飞行之

---

① Article 79: A State may participate in joint operating organizations or in pooling arrangements, either through its government or through an airline company or companies designated by its government. The companies may, at the sole discretion of the State concerned, be state-owned or partly state-owned or privately owned.

② Article 3:(c) No state aircraft of a contracting State shall fly over the territory of another State or land thereon without authorization by special agreement or otherwise, and in accordance with the terms thereof.

③ 当然,本款规定于逻辑上似乎与同条第 1 款有所矛盾,盖同条第 1 款既然表明了国家航空器不在《芝加哥公约》之适用范围,那何以本款要规定国家航空器之权利与义务,而使本款显有适用于国家航空器之意。

④ Article 6: No scheduled international air service may be operated over or into the territory of a contracting State, except with the special permission or other authorization of that State, and in accordance with the terms of such permission or authorization.

权利。(第2项)此航空器所从事者为获取报酬或出租而载运旅客、货物、邮件但非从事定期国际航班飞行,于依照第七条规定之情况下,亦有上下旅客、货物或邮件之特权,但上下地点所在之国家有权规定其认为需要之规则、条件或限制"①之规定,得以不经许可而飞入、飞越或非商业性降停于一国,若认为系例示规定,则其他从事于邮政、地理勘察、灾难救助、载运国家元首、载运政府官员等公共任务之航空器,亦为国家航空器,而适用第3条第3款。质言之,《芝加哥公约》第3条第2款为列举规定抑或例示规定,关系到"领空主权"(airspace sovereignty or sovereignty over airspace)与"飞航自由"(freedoms of the air)②之拉锯。本文认为,该公约第3条第2款应为列举规定,理由有三:(1)《巴黎公约》第30条第1项规定:"下列为国家航空器:一、军

① Article 5:1. Each contracting State agrees that all aircraft of the other contracting States, being aircraft not engaged in scheduled international air services shall have the right, subject to the observance of the terms of this Convention, to make flights into or in transit non-stop across its territory and to make stops for non-traffic purposes without the necessity of obtaining prior permission, and subject to the right of the State flown over to require landing. Each contracting State nevertheless reserves the right, for reasons of safety of flight, to require aircraft desiring to proceed over regions which are inaccessible or without adequate air navigation facilities to follow prescribed routes, or to obtain special permission for such flights. 2. Such aircraft, if engaged in the carriage of passengers, cargo, or mail for remuneration or hire on other than scheduled international air services, shall also, subject to the provisions of Article 7, have the privilege of taking on or discharging passengers, cargo, or mail, subject to the right of any State where such embarkation or discharge takes place to impose such regulations, conditions or limitations as it may consider desirable.

② "飞航自由"包括飞越领空而不降落之领空飞越权(又称为第一航权 first freedom of the air)、飞往外国途中因技术需要而在协议国降落但不得上落客货之技术经停权(又称为第二航权 second freedom of the air)、本国飞到另一国之目的地卸载权(又称为第三航权,third freedom of the air)、另一国飞到本国之目的地装载权(又称为第四航权,fourth freedom of the air)、航程由开始或结束而有权途经两个外国并载卸客货之中间点权(又称为第五航权,fifth freedom of the air)、在本国以非技术原因作中转停留之桥梁权(又称为第六航权,sixth freedom of the air)、在境外接载客运而不返回本国完全第三国运送权(又称为第七航权,seventh freedom of the air)、在另一国内的二或以上机场间可载卸客货航线而须以本国为起点或终点之境内运送权(又称为第八航权,eighth freedom of the air)、在另一国内的两个或以上机场间的航线而无须涉及本国之完全境内运送权(又称为第九航权,ninth freedom of the air)。参见国际民用航空组织官网:http://www.icao.int/Pages/freedomsAir.aspx,最后访问日期:2019年1月1日。

用航空器。二、专门用于例如邮政、海关、警察等国家部门之航空器。”①对于邮政、海关、警察有“例如”(such as)之用语,但《芝加哥公约》第3条第2款并无类似用语,很明显《巴黎公约》第30条第1款第2项为例示规定,而《芝加哥公约》第3条第2款为列举规定。(2)军事、海关与警察任务,具有高度之国家主权象征,故依第3条第3款须经特别协议或其他方式之授权方可飞越或进入一国领空,以维护领空国之主权,至于军事、海关与警察以外之公共任务,则较与国家主权较无关联,故并无划归为国家航空器而依第3条第3款之必要,故将第3条第2款解为列举规定,使军事、海关与警察以外公共任务之航空器划归于民用航空器,而能适用《芝加哥公约》,可扩大《芝加哥公约》适用范围,而符合《芝加哥公约》之宗旨和目的。(3)《巴黎公约》较大程度接受“飞航自由”。故其第2条第1项规定:“缔约国应接受其他缔约国之航空器于和平时期有无害通过其领土上空之权利,且公约中所规定之条件应予保留。”②赋予外国航空器无害通过权,但《芝加哥公约》则较大程度维护“领空主权”而限制“飞航自由”,从其第3条第3款针对国家航空器及第6条针对定期国际航班之规定可知,以经同意后(协议或许可)方可飞越或进入一国领空为原则,以不经同意为例外(第5条之不定期国际航班),而从事军事、海关与警察以外公共任务之航空器,因其任务与国家主权较无关联,故应将该公约第3条第2款解为列举规定,使此等航空器划归于民用航空器,而能依其任务之性质为不定期(例如,地理勘察、灾难救助)抑或定期(例如,邮政)而分别适用该公约第5条或第6条,一方面可扩大《芝加哥公约》之适用范围,另一方面又兼顾“领空主权”与“飞航自由”。

1958年美国《联邦航空法》并未采取民用航空器与国家航空器之区别,而系采取民用航空器与公共航空器(public aircraft)之区别,并于第101条第

---

① Article 30:1. The following shall be deemed to be State aircraft:(a) Military aircraft. (b) Aircraft exclusively employed in State service, such as Posts, Customs, Police.

② Article 2:1. Each contracting State undertakes in time of peace to accord freedom of innocent passage above its territory to the aircraft of the other contracting States, provided that the conditions laid down in the present Convention are observed.

36 款将公共航空器定义为:"公共航空器意指政府或政治分支部门,包括任何州政府、领地、美国属地或哥伦比亚特区,专用于从事任务之航空器,但不包括政府所有而以商业目的从事客货运送之航空器。本款所称专用于从事任务,意指除了联邦政府外,政府实体所基于非商业目的而所有及营运之航空器,或专用于租赁予此等政府实体不少于连续九十日。"①此之公共航空器类同于国家航空器,但兼所有权标准及使用目的标准。1988 年澳洲《民用航空法》第 3 条将国家航空器之定义为:"国家航空器意指:一、任何军队之航空器(包括任何受军队成员基于其职责所命令之航空器);及 二、为外国从事军事、海关与警察任务之航空器。"②采取使用目的标准,且亦采列举规定,但范围较《芝加哥公约》第 3 条第 2 款广,多了军队之航空器。1995 年《中华人民共和国民用航空法》未明文定义国家航空器,但由其第 5 条:"本法所称民用航空器,是指除用于执行军事、海关、警察飞行任务外的航空器。"对民用航空器之定义可知,执行军事、海关、警察飞行任务的航空器即为国家航空器,③此系采取使用目的标准,且亦采列举规定,而范围则与《芝加哥公约》第 3 条第 2 款相同。

附带一提者,航空刑法之国际公约皆采取与《芝加哥公约》相同区别民用航空器与国家航空器之规定,例如,1963 年《关于在航空器内犯罪和其他某些行为的公约》(Convention on Offences and Certain Other Acts Committed on Board Aircraft,以下简称《东京公约》)第 1 条第 4 项、1970 年《制止非法劫

---

① Section 101:(36)"Public aircraft" means an aircraft used exclusively in the service of any government or of any political subdivision thereof, including the government of any State, Territory, or possession of the United States, or the District of Columbia, but not including any government-owned aircraft engaged in carrying persons or property for commercial purposes. For purposes of this paragraph, "used exclusively in the service of" means, for other than the Federal Government, an aircraft which is owned and operated by a governmental entity for other than commercial purposes or which is exclusively leased by such governmental entity for not less than 90 continuous days.

② Section 3:"*state aircraft*" means:(a) aircraft of any part of the Defence Force (including any aircraft that is commanded by a member of that Force in the course of duties as such a member); and (b) aircraft used in the military, customs or police services of a foreign country.

③ 参见黄涧秋:《国际航空法研究》,中国法制出版社 2007 年版,第 53 ~54 页。

持航空器之公约》(Convention for the Suppression of Unlawful Seizure of Aircraft,以下简称《海牙公约》)第3条第2项、1971年《制止危害民用航空安全的非法行为之公约》(Convention for the Suppression of Unlawful Acts Against the Safety of Civil Aviation,以下简称《蒙特利尔公约》)第4条第1项等,均规定"本公约不适用于用于军事、海关与警察任务之航空器"(This Convention shall not apply to aircraft used in military, customs or police services)。至于航空私法之国际公约,则未采取民用航空器与国家航空器之区别,但依1929年《统一关于国际航空运送某些规则之公约》(Convention for the Unification of Certain Rules relating to International Carriage by Air,以下简称《华沙公约》)第2条第1项"本公约适用于国家或其它公法人于第一条规定之条件下所为运送"①之规定国家航空器从事旅客、货物、行李之运送者,亦适用《华沙公约》,②而1999年《统一关于国际航空运送某些规则之公约》(Convention for the Unification of Certain Rules Relating to International Carriage by Air,以下简称《蒙特利尔公约》)第2条第1项亦全文移植《华沙公约》第2条第1项之规定,此系出于功能性之考虑,盖航空私法之国际公约

① Article 2:1. This Convention applies to carriage performed by the State or by legally constituted public bodies provided it falls within the conditions laid down in Article 1.

② 1971年《修正由1995年9月28日海牙议定书所修正之1929年10月12日于华沙所签署统一关于国际航空运送某些规则之公约之议定书》(Protocol to Amend the Convention for the Unification of Certain Rules Relating to International Carriage by Air signed at Warsaw on 12 October 1929 as Amended by the Protocol done at The Hague on 28 September 1955,以下简称《危地马拉议定书》)第23条规定:各国得于任何时间向国际民用航空组织声明修正华沙公约之1955年海牙议定书及1971年危地马拉议定书不适用于于该国登记之航空器为该国军事单位载运人员、货物及行李,且该机之全部载运量已为该单位包用。(Article XXIII:1. Only the following reservations may be made to this Protocol:(b) a State may at any time declare by a notification addressed to the International Civil Aviation Organization that the Warsaw Convention as amended at The Hague 1955, and at Guatemala City, 1971 shall not apply to the carriage of persons, baggage and cargo for its military authorities on aircraft, registered in that State, the whole capacity of which has been reserved by or on behalf of such authorities.)系沿袭自1955年《修正1929年10月12日于华沙所签署统一关于国际航空运送某些规则之公约之议定书》(Protocol to Amend the Convention for the Unification of Certain Rules Relating to International Carriage by Air signed at Warsaw on 12 October 1929,以下简称《海牙议定书》)第26条之规定,此等规定让缔约国得声明保留,使从事军事运送之航空器不适用《海牙议定书》及《危地马拉议定书》。

主要系处理民事责任之问题,因航空运送所生民事责任之归责,当无区别民用航空器与国家航空器之必要。

三、航空器为具有不动产性之动产

由上述可知,“航空器为大气层中以空气之反作用力为支撑之任何器械”此一定义为多数国家所接受,纵不是采取此一定义之国家,也至少认为航空器为机器,故毫无疑问的,航空器为动产。然有鉴于航空器于航空活动中之地位,与船舶之于海上活动相同,故而航空法对于航空器物权之制度,移植了海商法之船舶物权制度,将海商法上之船舶抵押权制度与船舶权利登记制度,转用到航空法,而于航空法上形成了航空器抵押权制度与航空器权利登记制度,此乃重视航空器与船舶之高昂经济价值,及其于航空活动与海上活动中无可取代之活动核心地位所为之设计,而赋予二者不动产性,使二者成为具不动产性之动产,提升二者于法律上之重要性,而与一般动产有别。以下即分析使航空器具有不动产性之航空器抵押权与航空器权利登记制度。

(一)抵押权制度之适用

日本《民法》第 369 条规定:“(第 1 项)抵押权人,就债务人或第三人不移转占有而供债务担保之不动产,有先于其他债权人受自己债权清偿之权利。(第 2 项)地上权及永佃权得为抵押权之标的,于此情形准用本章之规定。”①但属于动产之航空器与船舶却得设定抵押权,实将之以不动产对待。

中世纪以来,日耳曼法一直视船舶为“浮动岛屿”(floating island),而将之定性为不动产,直至公元 16 世纪受罗马法影响后方将船舶改定性为动产,

① 第 369 条　抵当権者は、債務者又は第三者が占有を移転しないで債務の担保に供した不動産について、他の債権者に先立って自己の債権の弁済を受ける権利を有する。2 地上権及び永小作権も、抵当権の目的とすることができる。この場合においては、この章の規定を準用する。

但因为受到曾一度将船舶定性为不动产之历史发展过程影响,故仍遗存有不动产之特性,且船舶经济价值高昂,甚至高出不动产之土地及其定着物甚多,故使之适用不动产方适用之抵押权制度及权利登记制度等,除了有将之以不动产对待之意义,更具有鼓励取得资金以从事海上活动(抵押权制度)、维护交易安全(权利登记制度)之功能,而1926年《统一关于海事优先权与船舶抵押权某些法律规则之国际公约》(International Convention for the Unification of Certain Rules of Law relating to Maritime Liens and Mortgages)、1967年《统一关于海事优先权与船舶抵押权某些规则之国际公约》(International Convention for the Unification of Certain Rules relating to Maritime Liens and Mortgages)、1993年《船舶优先权与抵押权国际公约》(International Convention on Maritime Liens and Mortgages)等国际公约法,1993年《中华人民共和国海商法》第11~20条、1899年日本《商法典》(最后一次修正为2014年)第848条等,亦皆实行船舶抵押权制度。而航空法自海商法移植了船舶抵押权制度,于航空法上实行航空器抵押权制度,实乃因航空器与船舶类同,皆具有高出不动产甚多之经济价值,且亦须鼓励取得资金以从事航空活动,故将之以不动产对待,而适用抵押权制度,1948年《国际承认航空器权利公约》(Convention on the International Recognition of Rights in Aircraft,以下简称《日内瓦公约》)即为规范航空器抵押权之国际公约法,[①]其第1条第1项第1段本文第4款规定:"缔约各国承允,承认:(四)为担保清偿债务而合意设定之航空器抵押权、质权及类似权利"[②]1953年日本《航空器抵押法》(最后一次修正为2004年)、1995年《中华人民共和国民用航空法》第16~17条等,亦皆实行航空器抵押权制度。中国台湾地区"民用航空法"亦实行航空器抵押权制度,于第19条第1项规定航空器得为抵押权之标的,但须注意的是,同条第2项:"航空器之抵押,准用动产担保交易法有关动产抵押之规

---

① 关于《日内瓦公约》之介绍,see Brian F. Havel & Gabriel S. Sanchez, *The Principles And Practice of International Aviation Law*, 2014, pp. 347 – 351.

② Article 1:1. The Contracting States undertake to recognise: (d) mortgages, hypotheques and similar rights in aircraft which are contractually created as security for payment of an indebtedness...

定。”使航空器抵押权之设定准用“动产担保交易法”动产抵押之规定，故“民用航空法”并无再就航空器抵押权实质制度内容加以规范。

（二）权利登记制度之实行

依大陆法系民法体制，不动产因价值较为高昂，为保障交易安全，其权利之得、丧、变更须经登记，此即不动产权利登记制度，例如，日本《民法》第177条规定：“不动产物权之取得、丧失及变更者，非经不动产登记法（平成16年法律第123号）之规定登记，不得以之对抗第三人。”①虽属于动产之航空器与船舶却适用权利登记制度，实将之以不动产对待。

按船舶适用权利登记制度，除了赋予不动产性之结果外，更为维护交易安全之目的，盖船舶造价高昂，且船舶之多寡攸关一国国力，故其权利归属状态实有加以公示之必要，以维护船舶静的安全。1986年《船舶登记条件联合国公约》（United Nations Convention on Conditions for Registration of Ships）即为规范船舶权利登记制度之国际公约法，1993年《中华人民共和国海商法》第7条及第13条与2007年《中华人民共和国船舶登记条例》第5～6条、1899年日本《商法典》（最后一次修正为2014年）第687条与2005年日本《船舶登记规则》第21～30条等，亦皆实行船舶权利登记制度。而航空法自海商法移植了船舶权利登记制度，于航空法上实行航空器权利登记制度，实乃因航空器与船舶类同，皆具有高出不动产甚多之经济价值，其权利归属状态实有加以公示之必要，以维护航空器静的安全，故将之以不动产对待，而适用权利登记制度。在国际公约法方面，《日内瓦公约》第1条第1项规定：“缔约各国承允，承认：（一）航空器所有权；（二）以买卖并占有而取得航空器之权利；（三）依租赁期限为六个月以上之租赁而占有航空器之权利；（四）为担保清偿债务而合意设定之航空器抵押权、质权及类似权利；但此等权利须符合下

---

① 第177条　不動産に関する物権の得喪及び変更は、不動産登記法（平成十六年法律第百二十三号）その他の登記に関する法律の定めるところに従いその登記をしなければ、第三者に対抗することができない。

列条件:1. 权利之设定符合该航空器进行国籍登记之缔约国于设定该权利时之法律,且 2. 经合法地登记在该航空器进行国籍登记之缔约国的公共登记簿内。于不同缔约国中进行连续登记之合法性,依每次登记时该航空器进行国籍登记之缔约国法律予以确定。"①第 2 条规定:"(第 1 项)同一航空器之登记事项应记载于同一登记簿内。(第 2 项)除本公约另有规定外,登记本公约第一条第一项所列权利对第三人之效力,依该项权利登记地之缔约国法律确定。(第 3 项)缔约国得禁止登记依其国内法不能有效成立之权利。"②均为航空器权利登记之规定,而 1999 年《移动设备国际利益公约》(Convention on International Interests in Mobile Equipment,以下简称《开普敦公约》)系就航空器、铁路车辆(railway rolling stock)及太空设备资产(space assets)等移动设备之营业性租赁、融资性租赁、售后租回与附条件买卖等担保交易加以规范,其第四章"国际登记制度"(the international registration system)(第 16 ~ 17 条)及第五章"其他登记事项"(other matters relating to registration)(第 18 ~ 25 条)为包括航空器在内之移动设备的、国际利益、预期国际利益、可登记之非约定权利或利益、国际利益之转让与预期转让、依准据法而通过法定或约定方式代位取得国际利益、国内利益之通知、前述各项利益之从属

---

① Article 1:1. The Contracting States undertake to recognise:(a) rights of property in aircraft;(b) rights to acquire aircraft by purchase coupled with possession of the aircraft;(c) rights to possession of aircraft under leases of six months or more;(d) mortgages, hypotheques and similar rights in aircraft which are contractually created as security for payment of an indebtedness; provided that such rights(i) have been constituted in accordance with the law of the Contracting State in which the aircraft was registered as to nationality at the time of their constitution, and (ii) are regularly recorded in a public record of the Contracting State in which the aircraft is registered as to nationality. The regularity of successive recordings in different Contracting States shall be determined in accordance with the law of the State where the aircraft was registered as to nationality at the time of each recording.

② Article 2:1. All recordings relating to a given aircraft must appear in the same record. 2. Except as otherwise provided in this Convention, the effects of the recording of any right mentioned in Article 1, paragraph 1, with regard to third parties shall be determined according to the law of the Contracting State where it is recorded. 3. A Contracting State may prohibit the recording of any right which cannot validly be constituted according to its national law.

利益①登记之规定;②外国立法方面,1952 年日本《航空法》第 3 - 3 条及 1953 年《航空器抵押法》第 2 条、1995 年《中华人民共和国民用航空法》第 14 条及第 16 条等,亦皆实行航空器权利登记制度。

四、航空器之国籍

除了抵押权制度与权利登记制度之外,航空法亦移植了海商法之船舶国籍制度,而实行了航空器国籍制度。一般动产并无所谓国籍之问题,而航空器国籍制度,则使航空器成为有别一般动产之特殊动产。以下即分析航空器国籍制度之相关问题。

(一)拟人化之减弱

航空法虽然广泛移植海商法之制度,但也尚非全盘移植而全部接受,航空法仍有所调整,盖航空运送与海上运送虽皆利用交通工具从事运送,但仍有相异之处。以海上运送言,海象难测,而船舶只能停靠于港口,船舶一旦离开出发港出航,于未到达目的港或于中途停靠于中途港时,在广阔的海面上形单影只,于发生海难时,更因他船救援不及而使全船沉没,故而海上航行具有高风险、孤立性、风险发生之全损性三项特质;而航空运送,虽天象亦难测,但航空器并非只能降落于航空站,只要条件适当即得随时降落,而发生空难时,倘地面救援得宜,尚非即为全损。由此可知,就风险性而言,海上活动之风险性显然仍颇高于航空活动,且与陆地之连结性,航空活动更因航空器得随时降落于陆地且空难损害亦有可能发生于陆地,而显然有与陆地较

① Article 16: 1. An International Registry shall be established for registrations of: (a) international interests, prospective international interests and registrable non-consensual rights and interests; (b) assignments and prospective assignments of international interests; (c) acquisitions of international interests by legal or contractual subrogations under the applicable law; (d) notices of national interests; and (e) subordinations of interests.

② 关于《开普敦公约》之介绍, see Brian F. Haveil & Gabriel S. Sanchez, *The Principles and Practice of International Aviation Law*, 2014, pp. 351 - 380。

高之连结性。也因此,航空法于移植海商法之制度时,仍有必要就相异之处,加以调整,而海商法对船舶之拟人化,即为航空法于移植海商法制度时所加调整者。

以海上活动言,船舶为海洋世界之主角,为海上航行之主体,因此14世纪之《康索拉度海法》(*le Consulato del mare mer*)将船舶拟人化,赋予船舶人格性,而英国法亦将船舶拟人化,而发展出以船舶为被告之对物诉讼(*action in rem*),此种拟人化之措施,使船舶成为权利主体,而与一般之物为权利客体有别。现代法制原则上仍将船舶定性为权利客体,但以船名制度、船舶国籍制度、船籍港制度等,将船舶拟人化,使船舶成为拟人化之物,而与一般之物有很大的差异。以船舶国籍之国际公约法言,1982年《联合国海洋法公约》(United Nations Convention on the Law of the Sea)第91条"(第1项)每一国家应确定给予船舶国籍,船舶于其领土内登记及船舶悬挂该国旗帜权利之条件。船舶具有其有权悬挂的旗帜所属国家之国籍。国家和船舶间须有真正联系。(第2项)每一国家应向其给予悬挂该国旗帜权利的船舶颁发给予该权利之文件"①为船舶国籍之规定,1986年《船舶登记条件联合国公约》(United Nations Convention on Conditions for Registration of Ships)亦规范了船舶国籍制度;以船舶国籍之规定言,1993年《中华人民共和国海商法》第5条与2007年《中华人民共和国船舶登记条例》第3~4条、1899年日本《商法典》(最后一次修正为2014年)第686条与1899年日本《船舶法》(最后一次修正为2014年)等,皆规范了船舶国籍制度。而船舶之拟人化,尚有如同自然人姓名之船名以及如同自然人住所之船籍港,2007年《中华人民共和国船舶登记条例》第10条、2005年日本《船舶登记规则》第24条等皆规范了船名;而2007年《中华人民共和国船舶登记条例》第9条、1899年日本《船舶

① Article 91:1. Every State shall fix the conditions for the grant of its nationality to ships, for the registration of ships in its territory, and for the right to fly its flag. Ships have the nationality of the State whose flag they are entitled to fly. There must exist a genuine link between the State and the ship. 2. Every State shall issue to ships to which it has granted the right to fly its flag documents to that effect.

法》第4~5条与2005年日本《船舶登记规则》第37条等,皆规范了船籍港。

航空法自海商法移植了船舶国籍制度,但并未移植船名制度与船籍港制度,使航空器仅有国籍制度,而未有航空器名制度与空籍港制度,在一定程度上减弱了航空器拟人化之效果。此系航空法有意不全盘接受海商法之船舶拟人化,盖航空器与陆地较高之连结性,不因起飞即与陆地失去连结而成为形单影只之航空活动独角戏主角,此与船舶因发航即与陆地失去连结而成为形单影只之海上活动独角戏主角,有很大的不同,故航空器并无强大之拟人化需求,仅须借由国籍制度使航空器国籍国对航空器为行政管理以及领空国对领空为管制,而无须实行航空器名制度与空籍港制度。

(二)国籍登记制度

航空活动发展初期,航空活动人员之国民地位问题比航空器地位更为重要,当时视航空活动人员为航空活动之唯一支配者,航空器仅为被支配之交通工具。但自20世纪开始,航空运送快速发展,航空器地位开始受到关注,渐认为航空器在航空活动中具支配性地位,故自海商法移植了船舶国籍制度,于航空法确立了航空器国籍制度。航空器国籍为航空法重要的基础要素,借由国籍制度,一国对于具该国国籍之航空器实施管理(见诸各国之航空法规),一国对于他国国籍之航空器是否得进入其领空实施管制,例如,《芝加哥公约》第9条:"(第1项)各缔约国基于军事需要或公共安全之理由,得限制或禁止其他国家之航空器于其领土内之某些区域上空飞行,但对该领土所属国从事定期国际航班飞行之航空器与其他缔约国从事同样飞行之航空器,就此不得有所区别。禁区之范围与位置应合理,以免空中航行受到不必要之阻碍。缔约国领土内禁区之说明及其随后之任何变更,应尽速通知其他缔约国及国际民用航空组织。(第2项)于非常情况、紧急时期,或为公共安全,各缔约国也保留暂时限制或禁止航空器于其全部或部分领土上空飞行之权利并立即生效,但此限制或禁止应不分国籍适用于所有其他国家之航空器。(第3项)各缔约国得依其制定之规章,令进入前二项所指地区之任何航空器尽速于其领土内一指定之机场降落。"[①]此显示国家于航空法上之权利义务,乃是以其为航空器之国籍国、飞入国、经停国等不同法律地位予以确定。

航空器国籍以登记加以确定。1919 年《巴黎公约》第 6 条即已规定航空器具有其登记国家之国籍,[②]并为《芝加哥公约》第 17 条"航空器具有其登记国家之国籍"[③]继受。《芝加哥公约》第 17 条未直接规范何主体得拥有航空器,除了隐含应由一国自行决定其本国航空公司(国民)之权利(授予国籍),亦体现了《芝加哥公约》认为商业航空服务与某特定"国籍运送人"(flag carrier)之"本国"应具有密切联系。[④] 而《芝加哥公约》并未建立确定国籍登记之国际标准,其于第 19 条"航空器于任何缔约国登记或转移登记,应依该国之法律与规章办理"[⑤]规定了国籍登记之标准由各缔约自行决定(登记条

---

① Article 9:(a) Each contracting State may, for reasons of military necessity or public safety, restrict or prohibit uniformly the aircraft of other States from flying over certain areas of its territory, provided that no distinction in this respect is made between the aircraft of the State whose territory is involved, engaged in international scheduled airline services, and the aircraft of the other contracting States likewise engaged. Such prohibited areas shall be of reasonable extent and location so as not to interfere unnecessarily with air navigation. Descriptions of such prohibited areas in the territory of a contracting State, as well as any subsequent alterations therein, shall be communicated as soon as possible to the other contracting States and to the International Civil Aviation Organization. (b) Each contracting State reserves also the right, in exceptional circumstances or during a period of emergency, or in the interest of public safety, and with immediate effect, temporarily to restrict or prohibit flying over the whole or any part of its territory, on condition that such restriction or prohibition shall be applicable without distinction of nationality to aircraft of all other States. (c) Each contracting State, under such regulations as it may prescribe, may require any aircraft entering the areas contemplated in subparagraphs (a) or (b) above to effect a landing as soon as practicable thereafter at some designated airport within its territory.

② Article 6: Aircraft possess the nationality of the State on the register of which they are entered, in accordance with the provisions of Section I(c) of Annex A.

③ Article 17: Aircraft have the nationality of the State in which they are registered.

④ Kirsten Bohmann, "The Ownership and Control Requirement in US. And European Union Air Law and US. Maritime Law-Policy, Consideration, Comparison", *Journal of Air Law and Commerce* 60, 2001, p. 692.

⑤ Article 19: The registration or transfer of registration of aircraft in any contracting State shall be made in accordance with its law and regulations.

件国内法主义),[①]并于第21条要求各缔约国应提交其本国航空器登记与所有权情形给他缔约国或国际民用航空组织。[②] 但合观其第17条与第19条可以得知,《芝加哥公约》阻止任一缔约国就于另一缔约国依该国法律与规章登记之航空器国籍争执。

至于航空器国籍之登记条件,立法例上有积极条件主义与消极条件主义:前者系直接规定航空器登记为该国国籍须具有之条件,1958年美国《联邦航空法》第501条第2项规定:"航空器符合下列情况,且唯有符合下列情况,方适合于登记:一、1. 航空器为美国公民或依法准许于美国长期居住之外国公民所有;或 为依法组织并依美国或美国任一州法律从事营业之法人(仅有一个美国公民之法人除外)所有,且该航空器之基地在美国并主要用于美国国内。2. 未依外国法律登记。二、航空器属于美国联邦政府、州政府、领地、美国属地、哥伦比亚特区或政治分支部门。依本项,运输部经'判断基地

---

① 此与1982年《联合国海洋法公约》第91条:"(第1项)每一国家应确定对船舶给予国籍,并确定船舶于其领土内登记及船舶悬挂该国旗帜的权利之条件。船舶具有其有权悬挂的旗帜所属国家之国籍。国家与船舶间须具有真正联系。(第2项)每一国家应向其给予悬挂该国旗帜权利的船舶颁发给予该权利之文件。"(Article 91:1. Every State shall fix the conditions for the grant of its nationality to ships, for the registration of ships in its territory, and for the right to fly its flag. Ships have the nationality of the State whose flag they are entitled to fly. There must exist a genuine link between the State and the ship. 2. Every State shall issue to ships to which it has granted the right to fly its flag documents to that effect.)关于船舶国籍所实行登记条件国内法主义相同。

② 第21条:"关于登记的报告,各缔约国承允,如经要求,应将在该国登记的某一航空器之登记及所有权情形提供给他缔约国或国际民用航空组织。此外,各缔约国应依国际民用航空组织制定之规章,向国际民用航空组织报告有关在该国所登记经常从事国际航行之航空器所有权与控制情形的可提供之有关数据。如经要求,国际民用航空组织应将所得数据提供给他缔约国。"(Article 21:Each contracting State undertakes to supply to any other contracting State or to the International Civil Aviation Organization, on demand, information concerning the registration and ownership of any particular aircraft registered in that State. In addition, each contracting State shall furnish reports to the International Civil Aviation Organization, under such regulations as the latter may prescribe, giving such pertinent data as can be made available concerning the ownership and control of aircraft registered in that State and habitually engaged in international air navigation. The data thus obtained by the International Civil Aviation Organization shall be made available by it on request to the other contracting States.)

在美国并主要用于美国国内'后方予以登记。"①1995 年《中华人民共和国民用航空法》第 7 条规定:"(第 1 款)下列民用航空器应当进行中华人民共和国国籍登记:(一)中华人民共和国国家机构的民用航空器;(二)依照中华人民共和国法律设立的企业法人的民用航空器;企业法人的注册资本中有外商出资的,其机构设置、人员组成和中方投资人的出资比例,应当符合行政法规的规定;(三)国务院民用航空主管部门准予登记的其他民用航空器。(第 2 款)自境外租赁的民用航空器,承租人符合前款规定,该民用航空器的机组人员由承租人配备的,可以申请登记中华人民共和国国籍,但是必须先予注销该民用航空器原国籍登记。"二者皆采此制。后者系规定航空器登记为该国国籍不能具有之条件,1952 年日本《航空法》第 4 条规定:"(第 1 项)航空器所有人该当左列各款情况者,不得为登记:一、不具日本国籍者。二、外国或外国公共团体或类似机构。三、依外国法令或规章设立之法人或其他团体。四、任何法人,其代表为符合前三款情况之人员时,其三分之一以上之高级职员或三分之一以上之表决权为此等人员所有者。(第 2 项)具外国国籍之航空器,不得登记。"②即采此制。

由上述可知,无论积极条件主义抑或消极条件主义,皆以航空器所有人之国籍作为决定航空器国籍之登记条件,但此有可能会产生"权宜国籍"

---

① Section 501:(b) An aircraft shall be eligible for registration if, but only if—(1)(A) it is—(i) owned by a citizen of the United States or by an individual citizen of a foreign country who has lawfully been admitted for permanent residence in the United States; or (ii) owned by a corporation (other than a corporation which is a citizen of the United States) lawfully organized and doing business under the laws of the United States or any State thereof so long as such aircraft is based and primarily used in the United States; and (B) it is not registered under the laws of any foreign country; or (2) it is an aircraft of the Federal Government, or of a State, territory, or possession of the United States or the District of Columbia or a political subdivision thereof. For purposes of this subsection, the Secretary of Transportation shall, by regulation, define the term "based and primarily used in the United States".

② 第四条 左の各号の一に該当する者が所有する航空機は、これを登録することができない。一 日本の国籍を有しない人 二 外国又は外国の公共団体若しくはこれに準ずるもの 三 外国の法令に基いて設立された法人その他の団体 四 法人であつて、前三号に掲げる者がその代表者であるもの又はこれらの者がその役員の三分の一以上若しくは議決権の三分の一以上を占めるもの 2 外国の国籍を有する航空機は、これを登録することができない。

(flag of convenience)之问题,亦即具有登记国国籍之航空器与航空器国籍国(登记国)间欠缺真正或有效之联系(genuine link or effective link)。航空器与其国籍国欠缺真正或有效之联系时,国籍国对航空器即无法有效地管理与控制,此将引发现行以航空器国籍为基础而划分国家管辖权体系之混乱,而国际公约法以航空器国籍为基础相互授予他方国家权利亦会产生权利过度之结果,故“权宜国籍”应加以防止。按“权宜国籍”之问题于海商法亦存在,但至少1982年《联合国海洋法公约》于第91条第1项“国家和船舶间须有真正联系”之明文已有所宣示,而《芝加哥公约》却连类似宣示之明文也没有,所幸各国间所缔结双边航空协议中,一般都载有航空公司“实质性所有权与有效控制”(substantial ownership and effective control)之条款或类似条款,因此对大部分航空公司为国有或为其本国国民具有主要所有权,此一要求加载双边协议后,应能够防止“权宜国籍”之发生。

(三)重国籍之禁止

《芝加哥公约》第18条规定:“航空器于一个以上国家登记不得认为有效,但其登记得由一国转移至另一国。”①明文禁止航空器之双重国籍,但允许航空器变更国籍。1952年日本《航空法》第4条第2项“具外国国籍之航空器,不得登记”、1958年美国《联邦航空法》第501条第2项“未依外国法律登记”、1995年《中华人民共和国民用航空法》第9条前段“民用航空器不得具有双重国籍”皆为禁止航空器双重国籍之规定。

国际航空运送实务中大量之租机、包机、互换航空器等经营现象与需求,挑战了禁止航空器双重国籍之原则,只允许航空器具有一国籍之规定将导致航空器国籍与实际经营人国籍之分离,而产生“权宜国籍”之问题,对航空器民事责任、航空犯罪、航空事故调查等问题之处理,带来了困扰。因此,国际民用航空组织于1980年10月6日第23届大会上通过了一项修订《芝加哥

---

① Article 18:An aircraft cannot be validly registered in more than one State,but its registration may be changed from one State to another.

公约》之 A23－2 号决议,决议增订第 83－1 条:“(第 1 项)虽有第十二条、第三十条、第三一条、第三二条第一项之规定,于一缔约国登记之航空器由在他缔约国有主营业所或永久居所之经营人依租用、包用或互换航空器之协议或其他类似协议经营时,登记国得与该他缔约以协议,将第十二条、第三十条、第三一条、第三二条第一项赋予登记国对该航空器之职责与义务转移至该他缔约国。登记国应被解除对已转移职责与义务之责任。(第 2 项)前项协议未依第八三条之规定向理事会登记并公布前,或该协议之存在与范围未由协议当事国直接通知各有关缔约国,转移对其他缔约国不发生效力。(第 3 项)前二项规定对第七七条所规定之情形亦适用之。”①并已于 1997 年 6 月 20 日生效。依此,于租机、包机、互换航空器之情形,依航空器国籍国与经营人营业地国之协议,航空器国籍国于《芝加哥公约》下所应负的某些职责与义务,包括空中飞航规则、无线电设备、适航证、人员执照等,得以转移给经营人营业地国,此对因禁止航空器双重国籍原则对租机、包机、互换航空器,所生“权宜国籍”现象所导致对航空器即无法有效地管理与控制问题之解决,有所帮助。

(四)联营所生之国籍问题

国际航空运送实务中,除了产生租机、包机、互换航空器等经营现象,同

---

① Article 83 bis:(a)Notwithstanding the provisions of Articles 12,30,31 and 32(a),when an aircraft registered in a contracting State is operated pursuant to an agreement for the lease,charter or interchange of the aircraft or any similar arrangement by an operator who has his principal place of business or,if he has no such place of business,his permanent residence in another contracting State, the State of registry may,by agreement with such other State,transfer to it all or part of its functions and duties as State of registry in respect of that aircraft under Articles 12,30,31 and 32(a). The State of registry shall be relieved of responsibility in respect of the functions and duties transferred. (b)The transfer shall not have effect in respect of other contracting States before either the agreement between States in which it is embodied has been registered with the Council and made public pursuant to Article 83 or the existence and scope of the agreement have been directly communicated to the authorities of the other contracting State or States concerned by a State party to the agreement. (c)The provisions of paragraphs(a)and(b)above shall also be applicable to cases covered by Article 77.

时也产生了航空运送联营组织(joint air transport operating organizations)之现象,最著名之例,为1946年7月31日由瑞典、丹麦、挪威3国之航空公司依一定资金比例联合组成之斯堪的那维亚联合航空公司系统(Scandinavian Airlines,SAS),总部设于瑞典的斯德哥尔摩,并为星空联盟(Star Alliance)之创会成员,主要经营北、南大西洋航班。

联营组织依相互间协议经营,每一航空器于一个或其他参加国登记国籍,但如于两个或两个以上参加国登记航空器国籍,虽不会产生"权宜国籍"现象所导致对航空器无法有效地管理与控制之问题,但无疑抵触了禁止航空器双重国籍原则,故《芝加哥公约》第77条规定:"本公约不妨碍二或二以上缔约国组成航空运送联营组织或国际性经营机构,以及于任何航线或地区合营航班。但此组织或机构之合营航班,应遵守本公约之一切规定,包括将协议向理事会登记之规定。理事会应决定本公约关于航空器国籍之规定以何种方式适合于国际经营机构所用之航空器。"①乃因应此所为之规定国际民用航空组织理事会并因此通过决议,决定联营组织或国际性经营机构之航空器应具有共同之标志、每一航空器应具有组成该联营组织或国际经营机构每一个国家之国籍,此无疑为禁止航空器双重国籍原则之例外。所面临之问题,例如,于国际私法上,航空器物权应以登记国法为准据法,则联营组织或国际性经营机构所有之航空器,其物权之准据法,即难以确定。

1970年《制止非法劫持航空器之公约》受到《芝加哥公约》第77条规定之影响,于第5条规定:"若各缔约国成立航空运送联营组织或国际经营机构,而其所用之航空器需进行联合登记或国际登记时,等缔约国应以适当方法就其为每一航空器指定一个国家,该国为本公约之目的,应行使管辖权并

① Article 77: Nothing in this Convention shall prevent two or more contracting States from constituting joint air transport operating organizations or international operating agencies and from pooling their air services on any routes or in any regions, but such organizations or agencies and such pooled services shall be subject to all the provisions of this Convention, including those relating to the registration of agreements with the Council. The Council shall determine in what manner the provisions of this Convention relating to nationality of aircraft shall apply to aircraft operated by international operating agencies.

具有登记国之性质,并应将此指定通知国际民用航空组织,由该组织将上述通知转告本公约所有缔约国。"①复依同公约第 3 条第 4 项"对于第五条所规定之情况,如在其内发生犯罪的航空器之起飞地或实际降落地于同一国领土内,且此国为该条所规定国家之一,则本公约不适用"②之规定,倘航空器之起飞地或实际降落地位于航空器登记国领土外,应适用该公约。相较于《芝加哥公约》,1970 年《制止非法劫持航空器之公约》明确规定航空运送联营组织或国际经营机构所用之航空器可以分别进行联合登记或国际登记,但应为航空器指定一个登记国,使禁止航空器双重国籍原则得以维持,此种做法较国际民用航空组织理事会破坏禁止航空器双重国籍原则之决议为妥。

五、结　　论

本文作为航空法之论文,主题为航空法中最基础但也最重要之航空器之法律地位与航空器之国籍,期能以此航空法之基础研究,为抛砖引玉之效,使航空法之研究能够更为精进。

---

① Article 5: The Contracting States which establish joint air transport operating organizations or international operating agencies, which operate aircraft which are subject to joint or international registration shall, by appropriate means, designate for each aircraft the State among them which shall exercise the jurisdiction and have the attributes of the State of registration for the purpose of this Convention and shall give notice thereof to the International Civil Aviation Organization which shall communicate the notice to all States Parties to this Convention.

② Article 3: 4. In the cases mentioned in Article 5, this Convention shall not apply if the place of take-off and the place of actual landing of the aircraft on board which the offence is committed are situated within the territory of the same State where that State is one of those referred to in that Article.

The Cape Town Treaty and Aircraft Lessor's Repossession Rights

Jin Zhe *

1. Introduction to the Cape Town Convention

The international legal system prior to the Cape Town Convention is inadequate to protect the interests of aircraft lessors and financiers and consequently impedes the flow of investments into the aircraft leasing industry. In 1988, Canada first proposed to study the possibility of developing an international framework of security laws for mobile equipment. The work was undertaken by the International Institute for the Unification of Private Law (UNIDROIT) and the Aviation Working Group (AWG), with the assistance of the International Air Transport Association (IATA)

---

* LL. M. , Partner at Grandall Law Firm (Beijing).

and the International Civil Aviation Organization(ICAO).①

A decade later, the working group came up with a draft instrument and presented it to UNIDROIT and ICAO for scrutiny. The final versions of the Cape Town Convention and the Aircraft Protocol (Cape Town Treaty) were agreed upon by 53 countries on 16 November 2001② and have now been ratified by 79 and 76 states respectively.③

The objective of the new framework is to facilitate the financing of internationally mobile assets by creating certain proprietary rights to be recognised in all member states and to offer creditors recourse to specified and pragmatic remedies. To that end, the Cape Town Treaty has been devised with the following features.

1.1 Creation of international interest

The right in rem istypically regulated by domestic laws. In breaking national boundaries, the Cape Town Convention creates, without referring to any national laws, certain rights in rem regarding high-value movable objects and define them as the international interests. Deriving solely from the operation of the convention and to be recognised in all contracting states, the international interests serve to dispel the uncertainty over the recognition of rights under the laws of different jurisdictions.

Broadly, international interestsinclude those granted to the creditor under a security agreement, a title reservation agreement or a lease agreement.④ Some

---

① See Donald G. Gray and Auriol Marasco, "The Cape Town Convention: Where is Canada?", *The Air & Space Lawyer* 24, 2011, p. 18.

② See AWG, "Cape Town Convention 2001: Implementation Resource Materials", see www.awg.aero/assets/docs/Implementation%20Resource%20Materials%20(April2016).doc.

③ See www.unidroit.org/status - 2001capetown and see www.unidroit.org/status - 2001capetown-aircraft.

④ Art. 2, the Cape Town Convention.

minimum procedural and substantive requirements should be satisfied though, for the creation of international interests, such as the agreement providing for such interests shall be in writing.

The international interests are registered with an independent international registry managed by an Irish company under the supervision of ICAO. The international registry operates electronically via internet-based service and has witnessed about 650,000 registrations and 720,000 searches during the first ten years of operation. ①

The Cape Town Convention also specifies the order of priority of these interests. A registered international interest ranks higher than an unregistered interest and a subsequently registered interest, to the exception that it is subordinate to certain non-consensual liens as a contracting state may declare, even if the lien itself has not been registered. ② This simple but effective rule of priority gives "greater certainty to a creditor who registers its interest in the International Registry". ③

1.2 Default remedies

One major issue that the Cape Town Treaty seeks to address is the divergence in default remedies available to creditors in different jurisdictions. Some countries are more creditor-friendly, while the others are quite stringent in enforcing a remedy. Consequently, in order to facilitate financing arrangements, the convention drafters adopt a pro-creditor approach, but as a compromise,

---

① See Roy Goode, "Private commercial law conventions and public and private international law: the radical approach of the Cape Town Convention 2001 and its Protocols", *International and Comparative Law Quarterly* 65, 2016, pp. 523 – 529.

② Art. 29 and 39, the Cape Town Convention.

③ Michel Deschamps, "The Perfection and Priority Rules of the Cape Town Convention and the Aircraft Protocol: A Comparative Law Analysis", *Cape Town Convention Journal* 2, 2013, pp. 51 – 57.

allow contracting states to exclude certain remedies by way of declarations. For example, a default on the part of the lessee under a lease agreement may entitle the lessor to terminate the lease and reclaim the aircraft through self-help or court assistance;① however, a contracting state may ban the self-help approach by declaring that leave of that court must be obtained in order to exercise such remedies.

Other remedies, including interim relief and use of Irrevocable De-registration and Export Request Authorisation (IDERA), are also available insofar as the acceding states have elected to apply the same.

1.3 Insolvency protection

The provision regarding insolvency protection is viewed as the most essential part economically because the rights of creditors and their protections are most needed in the event of bankruptcy of the debtor.② In principle, an international interest validly registered before the insolvency proceedings will rank ahead of any claims of unsecured creditors,③ which gives assurance to its holder. One of the advantages of international interest is that even if such interest is void under the domestic law, it may still work in insolvency proceedings provided being duly registered under the Cape Town Treaty.

The Protocol sets forth two alternative remedies on insolvency that each contracting state may opt for. Alternative A, also known as the "hard version", is more creditor-friendly in that it provides a waiting period within which the debtor or insolvency practitioner must return the aircraft object to the creditor unless all defaults have been cured and a promise to observe future obligations

---

① Art. 10, the Cape Town Convention.

② Roy Goode, "Cape Town Convention and Aircraft Protocol—Official Commentary", Unif. L. Rev. Vol. 7, 2002(2), p. 354.

③ Art. 30, the Cape Town Convention.

has been given. Such waiting period is to be specified by each state when it opts for this alternative. While under Alternative B, the "soft version", the local court has much discretion in whether to permit the repossession of the aircraft by creditors and, if so, on what terms. In all the 71 states that have acceded to the Protocol, 48 have adopted Alternative A and only 1 has chosen Alternative B.① The remaining countries who decide not to make any declarations will apply their national insolvency rules.

In the vast majority of cases, an insolvency event also qualifies as a default under the lease agreement. Therefore, the exercise of rights under Alternative A or Alternative B or, if neither is chosen, a state's domestic insolvency rules would be supplemented by default remedies available to creditors.

1.4 Use of declaration options

Finally, in recognition of the vast disparity between common law and civil law countries with respect to their basic legal doctrine in creating and executing proprietary rights, the Cape Town Treaty innovates a scheme of declarations that provides each acceding state the opportunity to decide which provisions shall apply to it and which shall not. For instance, a contracting state may choose to apply IDERA provisions② while declaring that the convention shall disapply to its "internal transactions".③ These rights are referred to as "opt-in" and "opt-out" rights.

The use of declarations can be critical in determining the true value of the Cape Town Convention. For example, Mexico is the only country that has opted for Alternative B as an insolvency remedy whereby the repossession of aircraft by

---

① Mexico has opted for Alternative B.

② Art. Ⅷ, the Protocol.

③ Art. 50, the Cape Town Convention.

creditors would be subject to judicial discretion. In its 2010 crisis, Mexicana, one of Mexico's oldest airlines, declared insolvency. Prior to the insolvency proceeding, most creditors, in fear of a long and costly repossession process, simply terminated their lease agreements, which in turn exacerbated the airline's financial difficulty. If Mexico had opted for the more creditor-friendly Alternative A, creditors would likely have had more assertive confidence in the success of recovery of their assets, which would have allowed Mexicana to continue operating those aircraft. After this unpleasant experience, Mexico has been reconsidering its insolvency option under the convention. ①

It is undeniable that the aggressive use of declarations② under the Cape Town Treaty gives maximum flexibility to the contracting states and consequently leads to a widely accepted instrument, albeit on bespoke terms for each state. This may also cause some problems, notably in the accession process and in the implementation of the treaty. As the Legal Advisory Panel of the AWG suggests, "A thorough analysis of the declarations made by a Contracting State is required to obtain an understanding of the rights of the parties to a transaction in that Contracting State". ③

2. Aircraft Lessor's Repossession Rights under the Cape Town Treaty

The Cape Town Convention and the Protocol grant access to certain default

① Donald G. Gray and Auriol Marasco, "The Cape Town Convention: Where is Canada?", *The Air & Space Lawyer* 24, 2011, pp. 19 – 20.

② There are more than 20 types of declarations under the Cape Town Treaty, some of which are mandatory.

③ AWG, "Practitioners'Guide to the Cape Town Convention and The Aircraft Protocol", 2015. See www. awg. aero/assets/docs/VED-Practitioners-Guide – 9 – 9 – 15. pdf.

remedies that are indispensable to "provide the certainty and stability needed to reduce financing costs for aircraft." ① The most substantial remedy relates to the repossession of aircraft, which entitles a creditor, such as an aircraft lessor, to retrieve its aircraft in a way stipulated by the Cape Town Treaty. It is worth mentioning that these remedies crafted by the treaty are not exclusive. One can always avail itself of any other domestic remedies as long as they are not in contradiction with the mandatory treaty provisions. ②

Aircraft repossession may involve physical recovery, de-registration and exportation of an aircraft. Each part of the process will be addressed respectively in the following sections from the perspective of an aircraft lessor.

2.1 Physical Recovery

The Cape Town Convention recognizes the fundamental right of a lessor to physically take back its property in the event of default by a lessee. Article 10 of the Cape Town Convention provides that a lessor may "terminate the (lease) agreement and take possession or control of any object to which the agreement relates" if a default occurs under the lease agreement. The lessor may also turn to a court to exercise these remedies. ③

2.1.1 Default

The availability of repossession remedies is conditional on the occurrence of a default, which in most if not all cases, will be clearly defined in a lease agreement. Typically, the event of default may refer not only to a lessee's failure

---

① Brian F. Havel and Gabriel S. Sanchez, *The Principles and Practice of International Aviation Law*, Cambridge University Press, 2014, p. 366.

② Art. 12, the Cape Town Convention. See also Sandeep Gopalan, "Securing Mobile Assets: The Cape Town Convention and Its Aircraft Protocol", N. C. J. Int'l L. & Com. Reg. Vol. 29, 2003, pp. 59 – 75.

③ Art. 10, the Cape Town Convention.

to perform its payment obligations or any other contractual obligations, but also to its breach of representations, warranties or covenants. The binding nature of parties'agreement on the scope of "default" is affirmed by Article 11(1) of the Cape Town Convention.

If in some unusual cases where the parties are silent on what constitute an event of default, the Cape Town Convention establishes that a "default" has to be "serious in the sense of substantially depriving the creditor of its legitimate contractual expectation."① In the absence of an express agreement, such substantial defaults may include the non-payment of rents, disposal of aircraft without the consent of the lessor or failure to keep the aircraft registration, etc.

2.1.2 Extra-judicial Remedies

Extra-judicial or self-help remedies are welcomed by creditors who demand commercial expediency whereas resisted by many states who strive to maintain the integrity of their legal systems. As a result, a scheme of declaration is used to address the divergence, leaving each state freedom to decide whether a court order is required in exercising the convention-based remedies. Indeed, this is the only mandatory declaration that every contracting state must make at the time it ratifies the Cape Town Convention.② Among all the contracting states, only eight, namely China, Colombia, Côte d'Ivoire, Cuba, Egypt, Saudi Arabia, Spain and the United Arab Emirates, insist on the intervention of courts.③

The declaration of a state is decisive in conferring extra-judicial remedies. In other words, if a state declares the requirement for the authorisation of the court under the Cape Town Convention, then no matter what the local law may otherwise provide, extra-judicial remedies are not permitted in this state.

---

① Art. 11, the Cape Town Convention.

② Art. 54(2), the Cape Town Convention.

③ UNIDROIT, see www.unidroit.org/depositary-2001capetown? id=446.

Similarly, if a state declares that exercise of such remedies does not require any court interference, creditors are free to resort to extra-judicial remedies though the possible absence of sufficient substantive laws and procedural rules to accommodate such relief may give rise to pragmatic problems.

2.1.3 Judicial Interim Relief

If the lessor and the lessee have a dispute over the default remedies, it may take the court years to reach a final decision with respect to the dispute, during which time the status of the aircraft in question may deteriorate, thus increasing the lessor's risk of losses. To tackle this matter, the Cape Town Convention vests the right to seek interim relief in a lessor if it wishes to request "possession, control or custody of the object",① subject to the following conditions and qualifications.

a. The lessor must present evidence of default on the part of the lessee. The court will not grant any orders unless it is satisfied with the form and substance of such evidence.

b. The lessee must agree to such interim relief either before or after the occurrence of the default. The lessee's consent may be given in the lease agreement or in any other form, oral or in writing. Such consent does not have to make specific reference to the interim relief; it can refer to any remedies available at law or under the Cape Town Convention.

c. The court has the discretion to set such preconditions as are necessary to ensure that the rights of interested parties are not prejudiced if the lessor fails to obtain a final court decision in its favour.② Nevertheless, the interested parties may, by written agreement, waive the requirement for such protective measures,

---

① Art 13, the Cape Town Convention.

② Roy Goode, "Cape Town Convention and Aircraft Protocol: Official Commentary", *Unif. L. Rev* 7, 2002, p. 354.

provided that the forum state has made qualifying declarations. ①

Furthermore, the states are also free to specify in their declarations the number of working days within which the interim relief sought will be granted, subject to "applicable aviation safety laws and regulations" though. ②

The interim relief regarding the repossession of an aircraft may be sought, at the option of the lessor, in a contracting state before (i) the courts decided by the parties; or (ii) the courts of the territory where the aircraft is located; or (iii) unless the parties have chosen an exclusive jurisdiction, the court of the state of registry of the aircraft. ③ The second forum (the *situs* of the object) cannot be excluded by party autonomy. ④ Besides, the forum from which the interim relief is sought may be different from the court or arbitration tribunal issuing the final decision on the claim. ⑤ A state party, however, may declare that it will not apply these jurisdiction rules about the interim relief, wholly or in part. ⑥

2.2 De-registration and Export

The mere recovery of the aircraft will bear little benefit if the next operator or buyer is in a country other than the one where the aircraft is previously registered and if the creditor is not permitted to de-register and export the aircraft from its current location. This concern is addressed by the Protocol, which mandates two additional remedies, i. e. "de-registration of the aircraft" and "export and physical transfer of the aircraft object from the territory in which it is

---

① Art. Ⅹ, the Protocol.

② Art. Ⅹ, the Protocol.

③ Art 43, the Cape Town Convention and Art. XXI, the Protocol.

④ Roy Goode, "Cape Town Convention and Aircraft Protocol: Official Commentary", *Unif. L. Rev.* 7, 2002, pp. 354 - 392.

⑤ Art. 43, the Cape Town Convention.

⑥ Art. 55, the Cape Town Convention.

situated". ①

2.2.1 Extra-judicial Remedies

These two remedies available to lessors can be exercised without the assistance of the court, subject to the following conditions:

a. An event of default, as defined in Article 11 of the Cape Town Convention, has occurred.

b. The lessee has agreed to such remedies at any time, orally or in writing, specifically or in general.

c. The holders of such registered interests ranking prior to those of the lessor have given written consent to these remedies. In practice, any non-consensual interests specified by a state declaration, registered or non-registered, may also need to be discharged. ②

The extra-judicial mechanism must operate in accordance with the local procedural rules, and the registry is obligated to respect such requests for de-registration and export if certain conditions specified by the convention are met. ③

Alternatively, creditors may exercise the de-registration and export remedies using convention-based approaches, namely the judicial interim relief and IDERA, which are specially designed to expedite such process, as long as the states concerned have made the opt-in declarations.

2.2.2 Judicial Interim Relief

In addition to making feasible the physical recovery of the aircraft, the Cape Town Treaty provides, subject to the opt-in declarations, for a further relief with respect to the de-registration and export of the aircraft with the assistance of the

---

① Art. IX, the Protocol.

② AWG(n 29)129.

③ Art. IX, the Protocol.

court. The government agencies responsible for the de-registration and approval of the export of aircraft shall cooperate with each other with a view to the expeditious exercise of such remedies within the time frame (five working days) upon the presentation of a valid court order. ① If a relief is given by the court of another jurisdiction, it may be subject to the recognition by a local court. ②

The purpose of the court route is to avoid further investigation of facts by the aviation authorities and accelerate the de-registration process. Again, the three conditions for the exercise of self-help remedies specified in the above section also serve as prerequisites for this approach. ③

2.2.3 IDERA Route

The Protocol also devises, provided a ratifying state has so declared, a dedicated mechanism which allows a designated creditor (lessor, financier or, indeed, any party) to request for the de-registration and export of an aircraft by using an IDERA.

Under this approach, the debtor, such as the lessee, will be required to issue an IDERA substantially in the form provided by the Protocol in favour of an authorised party, who shall become the sole person empowered to have the aircraft in question de-registered. The IDERA will then be submitted to the aviation authority for recordation. When the authorized party so recorded makes a de-registration and export request, the relevant government agencies shall enforce

---

① The original language of the Protocol refers to a court ordering granting de-registration and export. However, this has been widely viewed as a drafting error. As Sir Roy Goode clarifies that the reference should be to an order granting relief under Article 13(1) of the Cape Town Convention (i. e. possession). See Dean N. Gerber and David R. Walton, "De-Registration and Export Remedies under the Cape Town Convention", *Cape Town Convention Journal* 3, 2014, pp. 49 – 55.

② Art. X, the Protocol.

③ Dean N. Gerber and David R. Walton, "De-Registration and Export Remedies under the Cape Town Convention", *Cape Town Convention Journal* 3, 2014, pp. 49 – 55.

these remedies expeditiously, without the need for leave of the court or the debtor's agreement. ① An IDERA, once given, is irrevocable unless removed by the authorised party. ②

The purpose of this IDERA route is to restrict the power of discretion of the relevant aviation authorities and to provide more certainty and predictability to creditors who wish to exercise their fundamental rights under the Cape Town Treaty. However, the power conferred by an IDERA may only be exercised without contravening any applicable safety laws. ③

Technically speaking, the IDERA route works as a self-help mechanism④ to the effect that no court involvement is required, although this is not made explicit in the text of the convention. If, for some reason, leave of a court is required under the local procedural rules, an interim relief given under Article 13 of the Cape Town Convention shall suffice. ⑤

2.2.4 Export

The availability of remedies regarding the "export and physical transfer of aircraft" is expressly provided for in Article IX of the Protocol, subject to the same provisos applicable to the exercise of the de-registration remedies. While de-registration of an aircraft may concern only the aviation authority, export involves at least one more government authority which is the Customs.

The Cape Town Treaty does not touch upon any customs issue, as it could

---

① Roy Goode, "Cape Town Convention and Aircraft Protocol: Official Commentary", *Unif. L. Rev.* 7, 2002, p. 354.

② Art. XIII, the Protocol.

③ Art. XIII, the Protocol.

④ Iwan Davies, "The New Lex Mercatoria: International Interests in Mobile Equipment", *The International and Comparative Law Quarterly* 52, 2003, pp. 151 – 171.

⑤ AWG, "Model Implementing IDERA Regulation", Version 2, May 2015. See www.awg.aero/assets/docs/IDERA%20Regulation%20 – %20AWG%20Model%20 – %20%20FINAL%20NOV2014X%20(2)%20(revised%20May%202015)%20final.pdf.

be too sensitive for any sovereign country. However, it does prescribe that the duties of government authorities to procure the export(including in circumstances of IDERA) shall be subject to " any applicable aviation safety laws and regulations",[①] which means exporting the aircraft to some destinations may be barred.

2.3 Repossession on Insolvency

The most significant invention developed under the Protocol should be the remedies on insolvency, which offers each state party the freedom to choose among Alternative A, Alternative B and its domestic insolvency rules.[②] However, no matter which option a state chooses, it must be applied in its entirety given the fact that each option is a set of integrally linked rules which, if used partially, may result in loopholes.

Since Alternative B renders little comfort to creditors and only Mexico has chosen this regime, for the purpose of this paper, Alternative A will be examined in further details.

2.3.1 Remedies under Alternative A

Under Alternative A, unless the insolvency officer or debtor has corrected all defaults and agreed to observe the contractual terms within a "waiting period" (to be specified by a contracting state), they must surrender the aircraft by the end of the waiting period. In the meantime, the insolvency officer or debtor must take active steps to maintain the aircraft in compliance with the relevant agreement.[③]

The waiting period specified in Alternative A is the maximum period that

---

① Art. X(7) and Art. XIII(3), the Protocol.

② Roy Goode, "The Cape Town Convention on International Interests in Mobile Equipment: a Driving Force for International Asset-based Financing", *Unif. L. Rev* 7, 2002, pp. 3 – 14.

③ Art. XI, the Protocol.

gives aircraft lessors " the assurance of a clear and unqualified rule ". ① Notwithstanding any contrary provisions in the local insolvency laws or the Cape Town Convention, ②the court, or the insolvency administrator, or the aviation authority may not suspend the exercise of such repossession rights by any creditor entitled to the same, or modify the debtor's contractual obligations without the agreement of the creditor. No second waiting period is permitted if the insolvency officer or debtor defaults again after curing all the defaults under the agreement.

Furthermore, Alternative A requires that the de-registration and export process be completed by the government authorities in a speedy manner without breaching the applicable safety regulations. It also stipulates expressly that registered interests shall have priority over any rights or interests in insolvency proceedings other than non-consensual rights or interests prescribed by a state declaration. ③

2.3.2 Conditions for Alternative A

The application of Alternative A will be triggered upon the satisfaction of the following conditions.

a. The occurrence of an " insolvency-related event " as defined in the Protocol. This includes the initiation of insolvency proceedings or, if such action is restricted by law, the debtor's failure to make payments when due.

b. The creditor holds a valid international interest, or other rights or interests which are equally protected by the Cape Town Convention, ④in each case where (i) the registration of such interests has been completed before the start of the

---

① Roy Goode, "Cape Town Convention and Aircraft Protocol: Official Commentary", *Unif. L. Rev* 7, 2002, p. 354.

② Local law procedures to which Article 14 of the Cape Town Convention refers is also overridden by this Article XI.

③ Art. XI, the Protocol.

④ Such as registrable non-consensual right, or a notice of national interest.

insolvency proceedings; or (ii) such interests will be recognized as having priority over other unsecured debts. ①

c. A contracting state 'in which the centre of the debtor's main interests is situated' has made the applicable declaration. ②

d. The parties have not agreed to disapply or modify these insolvency remedies. ③

2.3.3 Jurisdictions under Alternative A

The Cape Town Convention does not confer any jurisdiction regarding insolvency proceedings, "which are a matter for the relevant insolvency jurisdiction". ④ That being said, a contracting state may agree to offer all possible assistance in accordance with its laws to foreign courts or foreign administrative officers in protecting a creditor's rights under Alternative A. ⑤

2.4 General Requirements onthe Exercise of Remedies

The above remedies available to creditors must be exercised in conformity with certain general requirements as set out by the Cape Town Treaty.

2.4.1 Procedural Requirement

The Cape Town Conventions substantive in nature and, instead of seeking to harmonize national procedural laws, it requires that any remedies exercised thereunder shall conform to the procedural requirements of the place where the remedy is to be enforced. ⑥ For example, if written consent from the aviation

---

① Roy Goode, "Cape Town Convention and Aircraft Protocol: Official Commentary", *Unif. L. Rev* 7, 2002, p. 354.

② Art. I and XI, the Protocol.

③ Art. IV, the Protocol.

④ Roy Goode, "Cape Town Convention and Aircraft Protocol: Official Commentary", *Unif. L. Rev* 7, 2002, p. 354.

⑤ Art. XII, the Protocol.

⑥ Art. 14, the Cape Town Convention.

authority is a legal requirement for the repossession of aircraft in a member state, a lessor may not take possession of its aircraft without such consent even though self-help remedies are granted by the Cape Town Convention and are allowed in that state.

This is a mandatory requirement that cannot be altered by the parties' agreement. ① Nonetheless, if there is a direct conflict between the local procedural laws and the Cape Town Treaty, the latter shall prevail. ②

2.4.2 Reasonableness Test

Furthermore, remedies under the Cape Town Convention, judicial or non-judicial, concerning an aircraft must be exercised in a "commercially reasonable manner". Though the reasonableness test may base on the particular circumstances of each case, a remedy is deemed commercially reasonable if it is exercised in accordance with the written agreement of the parties except where such agreement "is manifestly unreasonable". ③ The "established commercial practice" and "accepted international practice" may also play a role in the determination of reasonableness. ④

Being an international private law convention, the Cape Town Treaty has innovated in the creation of a notion of interest beyond national borders for the protection of creditors such as a lessor. It has also brought assurance, confidence and cost cuttings to enforcing a lessor's repossession right in an event of default or bankruptcy on the part of the lessee in a jurisdiction where the interests of lessors are otherwise not well protected.

---

① Art. 15, the Cape Town Convention.

② Donald Gray, Jason MacIntyre and Jeffrey Wool, "The Interaction between Cape Town Convention Repossession Remedies and Local Procedural Law: a Civil Law Case Study", *Cape Town Conventional Journal* 4, 2015, pp. 17 – 29.

③ Art. IX, the Protocol.

④ AWG(n 29)114.

However, the adoption of an international instrument is only halfway to its success.① It is always vital to procure an effective implementation. While the lessor's repossession right under the Cape Town Convention and its Protocol has never been tested in a Chinese court, with the continuous expansion of the aircraft leasing sector in the country, eventually, the solution will find its way to both the Chinese judicial authorities and the market players in due course.

---

① Roy Goode, "Private commercial law conventions and public and private international law: the radical approach of the Cape Town Convention 2001 and its Protocols", *International and Comparative Law Quarterly* 65, 2016, pp. 523 – 540.

航空法热点前沿

陆空货物多式联运合同法律适用问题研究

——以国际公约的适用为视域*

张丝路**

自2013年3月7日国务院批准郑州航空港经济综合实验区以来,我国目前已有12个获批的临空经济示范区。临空经济围绕着航空运输而展开。而由于航空器自身的特殊性,航空运输通常需要与其他运输方式相结合,才能实现货物从接收到交付或者人员从出发地到目的地的运输全过程。而航空运输通常结合的运输方式就是公路运输。考虑到发生人身损害时,法律适用问题并不是需要优先考察的问题,以及在国际航空运输结合国际公路运输

---

* 本文系2015年陕西省教育厅哲学社会科学重点研究基地科研计划项目"中国航空法治改革研究"(15JZ080)和2017年陕西省教育厅哲学社会科学重点研究基地科研计划项目"'一带一路'国际多式联运法律问题研究"(17JZ074)的阶段性研究成果。

** 法学博士,西北政法大学博士后研究人员,讲师,从事国际私法和航空法研究。

的情况下,[①]多运输区段导致的法律适用问题的复杂性。因而,研究陆空货物多式联运合同的法律适用问题,有助于保障航空货物运输业的有序发展,进而促进临空经济的发展,以便最终实现临空经济示范区促进民航业发展、优化我国经济发展格局、全方位深化对外开放、加快转变经济发展方式的目标。而考虑到航空运输以及公路运输有各自广泛适用的国际运输合同公约(以下简称运输公约),因此,本文以国际公约的适用为视角,研究陆空货物多式联运合同的法律适用问题。

一、陆空货物多式联运合同法律适用的概念及特殊性

(一)陆空货物多式联运合同的概念

依据我国《海商法》第102条第1款的规定,货物多式联运合同是指:“多式联运经营人以两种以上的不同运输方式,其中一种是海上运输方式,负责将货物从接收地运至目的地交付收货人,并收取全程运费的合同。”类推而言,陆空货物多式联运合同应是指,多式联运经营人以两种以上的不同运输方式,其中一种是航空运输方式,另一种是公路运输方式,负责将货物从接收地运至目的地交付收货人,并收取全程运费的合同。

需要指出的是,应通过货物运输合同的实际履行情况,认定货物运输合同是否属于陆空货物多式联运合同。现今运输实践中,承运人与托运人多数情况下,并不对运输方式作具体规定。更关注的是承运人能不能及时以及安全地将货物运输到目的地。[②] 基于此,必须从货物运输合同的实际履行情况判断是否使用了航空运输以及公路运输这两种运输方式,进而判断是否属于陆空货物多式联运合同。

---

① 为行文简洁,下文以航空运输和公路运输代指国际航空运输和国际公路运输。

② See Ralph De Wit, *Multimodal Transport-Carrier Liability and Documentation*, Lloyd's of London Press, 1995, p. 308.

(二)陆空货物多式联运合同法律适用的概念

合同法律适用通常是指通过冲突规则确定准据法的过程。但对于陆空货物多式联运合同来说,其法律适用的概念不应仅包括确定准据法的过程,而还应包括考察运输公约是否适用的过程。

国际私法的最终任务是确定涉外民商事关系当事人之间的权利和义务。[①] 基于此,法律适用应是指调整涉外民商事关系当事人之间权利义务规则的确定。[②] 从我国学者对于合同法律适用的理解来看,无论如何定义其范围,都不包括依据统一实体法公约确定当事人之间的权利义务关系。这种理解是将调整当事人之间权利义务关系的规则,仅视为通过冲突规则确定的准据法。这种理解对于受到统一实体法公约调整的合同来说,显然是片面的。受到统一实体法公约调整的合同,确定当事人之间权利义务关系的规则,不仅包括准据法,还包括统一实体法公约中的规则。故而,在运输公约普遍存在的国际运输领域,合同法律适用不应仅指通过冲突规则确定准据法,还应包括通过运输公约确定当事人之间的权利义务关系。此外,如果将运输公约的适用范围条款视为一条单边冲突规则,也即在满足公约适用条件时,公约缔约国法院应适用公约,[③]即便坚持合同法律适用仅指通过冲突规则确定准据法,陆空货物多式联运合同法律适用也应包括考察运输公约适用与否。因而,讨论陆空货物多式联运合同法律适用问题,不仅需要考察依据冲突规则如何确定陆空货物多式联运合同准据法,还需要考察运输公约能否适用于陆空货物多式联运合同。

(三)陆空货物多式联运合同法律适用的特殊性

就运输公约能否适用的角度而言,货物多式联运合同法律适用的特殊性

---

① 参见刘想树:《国际私法基本问题研究》,法律出版社 2001 年版,第 59 页。

② 参见肖永平:《国际私法原理》,法律出版社 2007 年版,第 16 页。

③ See Malcolm Clarke, *International Carriage of Goods by Road: CMR*, 6th ed., Informa Law from Routledge, 2014, p. 19.

在于,应适用规则的确定与实体问题的解决具有关联性。尽管解决法律适用问题,通常并不与实体问题的解决相互关联,但在货物多式联运合同法律适用中,确定货物灭失、损坏或者造成迟延交付(以下统称货损)发生的运输区段,这一实体问题却对法律适用产生了影响。对于定域性损失,[①]无论是运输公约的缔约国法院还是非运输公约的缔约国法院,都需要考察该运输区段应适用的规则,比如,运输公约或者具有强制适用性的国内运输规则。而对于非定域性损失,非运输公约缔约国需要通过冲突规则确定准据法,而运输公约缔约国法院则需要首先考察涉诉货物多式联运合同是否满足运输公约扩张适用的条件,如果运输公约不适用,则也需要通过冲突规则确定准据法。

基于以上分析,下文首先讨论发生定域性损失时,调整航空运输的1999年《统一国际航空运输某些规则的公约》(以下简称《蒙特利尔公约》)以及调整公路运输的《国际公路货物运输合同公约》(以下简称《公路公约》)分别适用于陆空货物多式联运合同航空运输区段和公路运输区段的条件,而后考察发生非定域性损失时,《蒙特利尔公约》扩张适用于陆空货物多式联运合同的条件。

二、定域性损失时运输公约的适用

(一)《蒙特利尔公约》的适用条件

《蒙特利尔公约》第38条第1款明确规定,除第18条第4款规定外,公约只适用于陆空货物多式联运合同中的航空运输区段。因此,《蒙特利尔公约》的适用取决于以下两个问题:第一,陆空货物多式联运合同约定的航空运输区段是否属于《蒙特利尔公约》的调整范围;第二,《蒙特利尔公约》关于航空运输区段规则适用的起止。

---

① 通常以导致货物灭失、损坏或者造成迟延交付的事由能否被证实发生在某一特定运输区段,将多式联运运输过程中发生的货损,划分为定域性损失以及非定域性损失。See Hugh Kindred, Mary Brooks, *Multimodal Transport Rules*, Kluwer Law International, 1997, p. 32.

1.《蒙特利尔公约》的调整范围

《蒙特利尔公约》第 1 条规定:"本公约适用于所有以航空器运送人员、行李或者货物而收取报酬的国际运输。本公约同样适用于航空运输企业以航空器履行的免费运输。"需要指出的是,《蒙特利尔公约》第 1 条第 2 款对于国际运输的定义中包含了当事人约定(agreement between the parties)的要求。一般认为,这一要求等同于当事人之间需要存在合同关系。而依据《蒙特利尔公约》第 1 条第 3 款的措辞,①该合同一般也应被认为是航空运输合同,而非其他类型的合同。② 但仅就措辞本身而言,笔者认为,当事人约定并不意味着当事人之间必须达成一个完整的合同,也不意味着当事人之间的合同必须是航空运输合同,只要当事人之间存在关于国际运输的约定即可。

依据《蒙特利尔公约》第 1 条第 2 款,③公约所适用的国际运输主要包括两种情况:

第一,运输的始发地以及目的地在两个不同缔约国的单程运输。对于单程运输来说,如果始发地或者目的地不在《蒙特利尔公约》的缔约国,或者始发地以及目的地都不在公约的缔约国,则不属于公约所规定的国际运输。始发地与目的地应通过当事人之间的合同,而不是实际发生的运输地点判断。《蒙特利尔公约》没有对单程运输中的经停地作出要求。因而,在单程运输中如果存在约定的经停地,或者由于天气原因、技术故障或者为了飞行安全而迫降,或者在未约定的地点经停,都不影响《蒙特利尔公约》的适用,只要

---

① 《蒙特利尔公约》第 1 条第 3 款规定:"运输合同各方认为几个连续的承运人履行的运输是一项单一的业务活动的,无论其形式是以一个合同订立或者一系列合同订立,就本公约而言,应当视为一项不可分割的运输,并不仅因其中一个合同或者一系列合同完全在同一国领土内履行而丧失其国际性质。"

② Malcolm Clarke, *Contracts of Carriage by Air*, 2nd ed., Lloyd's List Press, 2010, p. 43.

③ 《蒙特利尔公约》第 1 条第 2 款规定:"就本公约而言,'国际运输'系指根据当事人的约定,不论在运输中有无间断或者转运,其出发地点和目的地点是在两个当事国的领土内,或者在一个当事国的领土内,而在另一国的领土内有一个约定的经停地点的任何运输,即使该国为非当事国。就本公约而言,在一个当事国的领土内两个地点之间的运输,而在另一国的领土内没有约定的经停地点的,不是国际运输。"

单程运输本身的始发地和目的地满足公约的要求即可。① 需要指出的是,由于《蒙特利尔公约》与其他运输公约一样,也认可缔约承运人以及实际承运人的分野以及连续运输。因而,只要运输整体上被认为是航空运输,即便合同中的一个航段属于国内运输,无论该国是否属于《蒙特利尔公约》的缔约国,该航段仍受公约的调整。② 但与其他运输公约不同,《蒙特利尔公约》不仅允许当事人通过一个合同来完成连续运输,还允许当事人通过一系列合同来实现连续运输。在当事人通过一系列合同实现连续运输时,关键的判断标准在于,运输合同各方认为几个连续的承运人履行的运输是一项单一的业务活动,也即必须存在客观的证据显示,一系列合同的所有当事人都将多个连续的航段视为一项单一的运输。

第二,运输的始发地以及目的地在同一缔约国内,但在另一国有约定经停地点的往返运输。《蒙特利尔公约》不适用于发生在非缔约国内的往返运输,或者在缔约国发生的没有约定经停地点的往返运输。约定的经停地点是否属于缔约国、约定的经停地点的数量以及经停的目的在所不问。往返运输的约定通常发生在旅客运输合同中。尽管在货物运输中,在特殊条件下,也有可能发生往返运输,比如,货物运达目的地而无人接收,承运人依据托运人的指示而将货物运回始发地。但由于《蒙特利尔公约》是以当事人之间约定的运输而不是实际发生的运输判断公约是否适用,故而公约是否适用于这种实际发生的往返运输,需要考察当事人之间的合同。

此外,依据《蒙特利尔公约》第 1 条第 1 款,公约同样适用于免费运输。尽管货物运输合同在通常情况下是有偿的,但《蒙特利尔公约》并没有排除公约适用于免费货物运输的可能。

---

① See Elmar Giemulla eds. ,*Montreal Convention*,Loose Leaf ed. ,Kluwer Law International,2006,Article 1,para. 5.

② 参见[美]乔治·汤普金斯:《从美国法院实践看国际航空运输责任规则的适用于发展》,本书译委会译,法律出版社 2014 年版,第 74 页。

2.《蒙特利尔公约》适用的起止

由于华沙体系在一定范围内仍有适用的可能,[①]并且该体系的规定对于理解《蒙特利尔公约》的规定仍具有指导意义。因而,本部份一并讨论华沙体系以及《蒙特利尔公约》适用范围的起止。

依据《华沙公约》第 18 条第 2 条的规定,[②]航空运输公约适用的起止是以航空站或者说机场为界限。由于《华沙公约》没有规定机场的概念,应遵循 1944 年《国际民用航空公约》规范机场的附件 14,将机场界定为:"全部或部分用于航空器进场、离场和地面活动的陆上或水上的一划定区域(包括建筑物、设施和设备)。"从划定区域的措辞来看,应有必要的边界、围墙或者其他措施,以便区分机场与周边区域的界限。

随着航空运输业的发展,在一些繁忙的机场,与货物装卸以及交付有关的某些行为,如仓储,只能在机场边界之外完成。为了将发生在航空承运人掌管之下,但发生于机场边界之外的货损,纳入《华沙公约》的调整范围之内,一些学者试图从功能的角度认定机场。这种观点认为,机场边界之外的仓库如被用于仓储从机场运来或者准备运往机场进行航空运输的货物,并且靠近机场边界,就能使机场边界之外的仓库被认为如同在机场之中。[③] 由于从功能的角度认定机场,不可避免的需要在个案中,针对不同机场的情况分别认定,并且该方法只适用于一些特殊情况。与之相比,通过机场边界认定《华沙公约》适用的起止,不仅清晰、明确,而且符合《华沙公约》条款的规定。因此,机场边界应是通常意义上认定《华沙公约》适用起止的方法。

---

① 华沙体系是对历次修订 1929 年《统一国际航空运输某些规则的公约》(以下简称《华沙公约》)的公约、议定书的统称。关于华沙体系内有关国际航空货物运输的规则,参见师怡:《国际航空货物运输承运人责任制度研究》,吉林大学 2014 年博士学位论文,第 8 ~ 13 页。

② 《华沙公约》第 18 条第 2 款规定:"上款所指航空运输的期间,包括行李或货物在承运人保管下的期间,不论是在航空站内、在航空器上或在航空站外降落的任何地点。"航空站外降落通常是指迫降,因而,在通常的航空运输中,并不讨论此种情况。

③ See George Leloudas, "Door-to-Door Application of International Air Law Conventions: Commercially Convenient, but Doctrinally Dubious", *Lloyd's Maritime and Commercial Law Quarterly*, 2015, p. 377.

《蒙特利尔公约》第 18 条第 3 款对航空运输期间的规定,[①]去除了《华沙公约》在机场内的限制,仅规定航空运输期间系指货物处于承运人掌管之下的期间。仅从字面意思来看,该款将《蒙特利尔公约》变为了一部调整门到门运输的公约,即从承运人接收货物开始,到交付货物为止,都应由《蒙特利尔公约》调整。但从《蒙特利尔公约》第 38 条的规定来看,[②]除非存在例外情况,公约只适用于航空运输。因此,不能仅从字面意思理解第 18 条第 3 款的措辞。

虽然不能仅从字面意思理解第 18 条第 3 款的措辞,但该款措辞却带来了一个实践上的问题,如果承运人从机场向其在机场之外的仓库运输货物,该段运输处于机场之外,依据《蒙特利尔公约》第 18 条第 4 款,不应适用公约的规定,但当货物在承运人掌管的仓库时,依据第 18 条第 3 款,公约应当适用。也就是说,《蒙特利尔公约》从货物运出机场后不再适用,当货物运到机场外仓库时,又开始适用。

对于这种碎片化地适用《蒙特利尔公约》的方式,司法实践中有两种解决途径:第一,将前述从机场到机场外仓库的地面运输视为航空运输的一部分。比如,美国法院在一些涉及《华沙公约》第 18 条第 2 款的案件中指出,只要航空承运人依据航空运输合同对货物仍保持实际或者推定占有,航空运输期间就没有结束。[③] 如果将这种认定方式适用于《蒙特利尔公约》,当然能避免前述碎片化地适用《蒙特利尔公约》,但这种方法显然忽视了《蒙特利尔公约》本身只调整航空运输的目的。同时,这种认定不仅与公约第 18 条第 4 款第 1 句的规定相违背,也即将公约调整的货损发生的地域范围扩大到了机场之外,而且与公约第 18 条第 4 款第 2 句的规定相违背。因为只有发生非定

---

① 《蒙特利尔公约》第 18 条第 3 款规定:"本条第一款所称的航空运输期间,系指货物处于承运人掌管之下的期间。"

② 《蒙特利尔公约》第 38 条第 1 款规定:"部分采用航空运输,部分采用其他运输方式履行的联合运输,本公约的规定应当只适用于符合第一条规定的航空运输部分,但是第十八条第四款另有规定的除外。"

③ Magnus Electronics, Inc. v. Royal Bank of Canada, 611F. Sup 436, 440(N. D. Ill. 1985).

域性损失时,从机场到机场外仓库的地面运输才能被认为构成航空运输的一部分。第二,限制解释掌管的含义。上述碎片化地适用《蒙特利尔公约》主要源于对承运人掌管货物的理解包括货物在仓库由其照管期间。尽管《蒙特利尔公约》没有排除这种解释的可能,但这种理解方式显然会导致上述实践中的问题。因而,更可取的方式是,基于《蒙特利尔公约》不调整仓储行为,将承运人掌管理解为其在机场范围内掌管。据此,由于《蒙特利尔公约》对航空运输期间措辞上的修改,导致了公约可能适用于其不调整的行为。因而,笔者认为,更好的方式是在解释公约适用范围之起止时,将公约所删除的《华沙公约》对机场的规定添加进来,也即将调整《蒙特利尔公约》的适用范围限制在机场边界之内。

综合来看,如果陆空货物多式联运合同实际履行的航空运输区段,满足《蒙特利尔公约》规定的国际运输,那么公约应适用于发生在机场范围内的定域性损失。

(二)《公路公约》的适用条件

《公路公约》第 1 条第 1 款规定:"本公约适用于任何为了取得报酬而通过车辆在道路上运送货物的合同,当合同约定的接收货物和指定交货地点位于两个不同的国家,而至少其中一个是缔约国时,不考虑当事人的居住地和国籍。"显然,《公路公约》的适用取决于以下条件:其一,承运人与托运人之间应存在通过车辆有偿运输货物的合同,《公路公约》不适用于无偿运输或者旅客运输;其二,判断接收地或者交付地应以承运人与托运人的意图为准,并且接收地或者交付地之一应为缔约国。① 在航空货物运输实践中,当事人通常将调整航空运输的公约,通过约定的方式,扩张适用于非航空运输区段。此时,如果公路运输区段满足《公路公约》的适用条件,受诉法院应以当事人约定优先,还是直接适用《公路公约》是需要考察的问题。

---

① See Malcolm Clarke, *International Carriage of Goods by Road: CMR*, 6th ed., Informa Law from Routledge, 2014, p. 52.

在司法实践中,对于上述情况,英国和德国法院却有不同见解。在量子案(Quantum Corp. Ltd. v. Plane Trucking Ltd.)中,原告将涉案货物从新加坡发往爱尔兰都柏林,该案第二被告法国航空公司作为承运人,负责将该批货物从新加坡运往都柏林,法航将该批货物用飞机从新加坡运至巴黎戴高乐机场后,将之交给了该案另一被告,以公路运输的方式将该批货物从巴黎运往都柏林,该批货物在运往英国的途中被盗。该案涉及的航空货运单规定,1955年《修订华沙公约的议定书》(以下简称《海牙议定书》)调整陆空货物多式联运合同。因而,该案的核心问题是《公路公约》还是当事人约定的《海牙议定书》适用于巴黎到都柏林之间的公路运输。

英国上诉法院认为,审查《公路公约》能否适用于量子案中的公路运输区段,关键在于考察两个问题。第一,《公路公约》是否只适用于明确约定通过公路进行运输的合同。上诉法院区分了四种情况:合同约定只进行公路运输;合同约定进行公路运输,但承运人可以选择其他运输方式履行全程或部分运输区段;合同没有对运输方式作出规定或者约定使用不特定的几种运输方式,其中之一是公路运输;合同约定通过其他运输方式进行运输,但承运人可以选择公路运输方式履行全程或部分运输区段。就第一种情况而言,《公路公约》的适用是显而易见的。但由于在现今运输实践中,多数合同对运输方式不作规定或者交由承运人选择,因而,如果将《公路公约》的适用仅限于第一种情况,无疑会严重地限制公约的适用范围,这就与公约本身的目的,标准化调整公路运输合同的规则相违背。因此,上诉法院的法官认为《公路公约》的适用,应取决于依据承托双方之间合同而实际发生的公路运输,而不仅只适用于约定进行公路运输的合同。① 第二,如何认定《公路公约》适用范围条款所规定的接收与交付货物。由于上诉法院认为《公路公约》的适用取决于依据承托双方之间合同而实际发生的公路运输,故而,该法院认为,公约同样调整陆空货物多式联运合同中的公路运输区段。据此,进一步的问题在

① Quantum Corp. Ltd. v. Plane Trucking Ltd. [2002] C. L. C. 1002,1008 - 1009.

于,如何认定《公路公约》适用范围条款规定的接收货物以及交付货物。上诉法院认为,应将之视为承运人以公路运输承运人的身份接收和交付货物。①

然而,德国最高法院在2008年的一起判决中认为,《公路公约》并不适用于陆空货物多式联运合同所包含的公路运输区段。该案涉及从日本东京通过海运,经荷兰鹿特丹港到德国门兴格拉德巴赫的陆空货物多式联运合同,当事人在陆空货物多式联运合同中选择日本东京地方法院管辖,适用日本法律。由于货损发生在鹿特丹港到门兴格拉德巴赫之间的公路运输区段,德国上诉法院认为,应当适用《公路公约》,因而德国法院具有管辖权。但德国最高法院却推翻了上诉法院的判决,认定不能适用《公路公约》,其理由主要有两个方面:其一,德国最高法院认为,《公路公约》适用范围条款中的措辞,"在道路上运送货物的合同",说明公约仅适用于公路运输合同。其二,《公路公约》第2条以及签署议定书中的规定,说明《公路公约》只在满足第2条规定的情况下,②才有限度的扩张适用于背负式陆空货物多式联运合同。除此以外,其他类型的陆空货物多式联运合同,无论是合同自身还是合同包含的单式运输区段都不由《公路公约》调整。③

① Quantum Corp Ltd. v. Plane Trucking Ltd. [2002] C. L. C. 1011.

② CMR Article 2:"1. Where the vehicle containing the goods is carried over part of the journey by sea, rail, inland waterways or air, and, except where the provisions of article 14 are applicable, the goods are not unloaded from the vehicle, this Convention shall nevertheless apply to the whole of the carriage. Provided that to the extent it is proved that any loss, damage or delay in delivery of the goods which occurs during the carriage by the other means of transport was not caused by act or omission of the carrier by road, but by some event which could only have occurred in the course of and by reason of the carriage by that other means of transport, the liability of the carrier by road shall be determined not by this Convention but in the manner in which the liability of the carrier by the other means of transport would have been determined if a contract for the carriage of the goods alone had been made by the sender with the carrier by the other means of transport in accordance with the conditions prescribed by law for the carriage of goods by that means of transport. If, however, there are no such prescribed conditions, the liability of the carrier by road shall be determined by this Convention."

③ See Peter Laurijssen, "Quantum Corporation Inc. v. Plane Trucking Ltd. Revisited by German Supreme Court: Consideration on the German Federal High Court's Decision of 17 July 2008", *European Transport Law* 44, 2009, pp. 143 – 145.

通过分析英国以及德国法院的判决以及《公路公约》的适用范围条款,笔者认为,公约基于以下三点理由应适用于陆空货物多式联运合同包含的相应公路运输区段:(1)对于适用范围条款,不应施加仅通过某种运输工具进行运输的限制。这不仅是对《公路公约》适用范围条款的不当限制,而且忽视了现今运输实践中,不对运输方式作出规定或允许承运人选择的现状。(2)基于《公路公约》的目的,其也应适用于陆空货物多式联运合同包含的公路运输区段。一方面,公约的目的是统一调整公路运输合同,陆空货物多式联运合同包含有公路运输合同,且在满足公约适用条件时,当然应由《公路公约》调整。另一方面,由于《公路公约》具有强制适用性,如果陆空货物多式联运合同中的公路运输区段不由公约调整,则实际上为承运人提供了通过合同手段避免公约适用的可能,这同样与公约的目的相背离。(3)就法律适用的角度而言,适用《公路公约》能够带来法律适用上的确定性以及可预见性。如果公约不适用于陆空货物多式联运合同包含的公路运输区段,那么必将由受诉法院通过冲突规则确定应适用的国内法。这势必会导致应适用规则的多样性。而由于公约相对容易查明,并且存在它国判例可供参考,适用公约显然能带来应适用规则的确定性以及可预见性,实现法律适用结果的公正性。

三、非定域性损失时《蒙特利尔公约》的适用

《蒙特利尔公约》第 18 条第 4 款①规定了公约扩张适用于陆空货物多式联运合同条件。而如果不满足第 18 条第 4 款的规定,则需要通过受诉法院的冲突规范,确定应适用于陆空货物多式联运合同的规则。前已述及,由于

① 《蒙特利尔公约》第 18 条第 4 款规定:"航空运输期间,不包括机场外履行的任何陆路、海上或者内水运输过程。但是,此种运输是在履行航空运输合同时为了装载、交付或者转运而办理的,在没有相反证明的情况下,所发生的任何损失推定为在航空运输期间发生的事件造成的损失。承运人未经托运人同意,以其他运输方式代替当事人各方在合同中约定采用航空运输方式的全部或者部分运输的,此项以其他方式履行的运输视为在航空运输期间。"

航空器自身的特殊性,航空运输通常需要与其他运输方式相结合,才能实现货物从接收到交付的全过程。因而,在约定进行航空运输的合同中规定其他运输方式(以下简称辅助运输)是非常常见的。但有学者认为在前述运输模式中,由于辅助运输不具有独立性,因而不应被认为是陆空货物多式联运合同。① 因此,在考察如何适用第 18 条第 4 款之前,应首先明确辅助运输是否具有独立性,进而判断是否属于陆空货物多式联运合同。

(一)辅助运输的独立性

从《蒙特利尔公约》的规定来看,公约没有否定辅助运输的独立意义,进而使得规定了辅助运输的货物运输合同,至少在《蒙特利尔公约》的调整的范围内,应被认为是陆空货物多式联运合同。

第一,《蒙特利尔公约》没有否定辅助运输的独立性。从法律上否定辅助运输独立性比较典型的例子就是《国际铁路货物运输合同统一规则》(以下简称《铁路规则》)第 1 条第 3 款:"当依据一个运输合同进行的国际运输包含作为补充跨境铁路运输的缔约国国内公路或者内河运输时,该规则应适用。"可以看出,《铁路规则》否定的独立性的条件主要有三点,运输合同规定了国际铁路运输以及辅助运输、辅助运输作为国际铁路运输的补充以及《铁路规则》的规定扩张适用于这种特殊类型的合同。与《铁路规则》相比,尽管《蒙特利尔公约》在第 38 条第 2 款不排除在约定航空货物运输的合同中规定其他运输方式。② 同时,在规定辅助运输的情况下,该运输也应被认为是航空运输的补充。但依据《蒙特利尔公约》第 1 条,公约只适用于满足条件的国际运输,而不扩张适用到其他运输方式。从这个角度来看,《蒙特利尔公约》没有与其他单式运输公约一样,从法律上否定辅助运输的独立性,进而将之纳入公约的调整范围内。

---

① See Elmar Giemulla eds. , *Montreal Convention*, 6th ed. , Kluwer Law International, 2006, Article 38, para. 9.

② 《蒙特利尔公约》第 38 条第 2 款规定:"在航空运输部分遵守本公约规定的条件下,本公约不妨碍联合运输的各方当事人在航空运输凭证上列入有关其他运输方式的条件。"

第二,《蒙特利尔公约》认可约定航空运输以及辅助运输的合同是陆空货物多式联运合同。一方面,《蒙特利尔公约》第 38 条第 1 款明确规定,①合同约定部分采用航空运输,部分采用其他运输方式的构成陆空货物多式联运合同,但该条并没有要求其他运输方式必须具有独立性,进而使约定进行航空运输结合辅助运输的合同也应构成公约认可的陆空货物多式联运合同。另一方面,由于《蒙特利尔公约》适用范围的限制,公约只适用于陆空货物多式联运合同中的航空运输区段,进而使该公约第 38 条第 1 款但书的规定,实际暗含了第 18 条第 4 款构成公约不适用于陆空货物多式联运合同的例外。基于此,应认为第 18 条第 4 款规定的运输模式应是陆空货物多式联运合同。因而《蒙特利尔公约》的规定或明确或暗示了公约认可,约定航空运输结合辅助运输的合同应构成陆空货物多式联运合同。

此外,还需指出,尽管《蒙特利尔公约》第 18 条第 4 款明确提到了"履行航空运输合同",但基于《蒙特利尔公约》第 38 条第 2 款,如果认为规定了其他运输方式的航空运输单证,仍可被认为是航空运单,那么规定了其他运输方式的陆空货物多式联运合同,在航空运输区段,也应被认为航空运输合同。②

(二)《蒙特利尔公约》扩张适用的条件

从《蒙特利尔公约》第 18 条第 4 款第 2 句本身的措辞来看,其类似于一个证据规则,即除非有证据证明损失发生在辅助运输区段,航空运输结合辅助运输这种模式的陆空货物多式联运中所发生的所有损失,应被认为发生在航空运输期间,进而由航空运输承运人承担,由《蒙特利尔公约》调整。③

---

① 《蒙特利尔公约》第 38 条第 1 款规定:"部分采用航空运输,部分采用其他运输方式履行的联合运输,本公约的规定应当只适用于符合第一条规定的航空运输部分,但是第十八条第四款另有规定的除外。"

② See Marian Hoeks, *Multimodal Transport Law-The Law applicable to the multimodal contract for the carriage of goods*, Kluwer Law International, 2010, p. 247.

③ See Elmar Giemulla eds., *Montreal Convention*, 6th ed., Kluwer Law International, 2006, Article 18, para. 92.

因而,该条的适用除了发生非定域性损失外,关键的认定标准在于如何界定《蒙特利尔公约》所要求的辅助运输,即为了履行航空运输合同而进行的装载、交付或者转运。美国第二巡回上诉法院在"商业联盟诉意大利航空案"(Commercial Union v. Alitalia Airlines)中,考察了与《蒙特利尔公约》第18条第4款第2句措辞一致的《华沙公约》第18条第3款第2句的适用条件。[①] 因而,该案能为理解如何认定辅助运输提供一定的启示。第二巡回上诉法院在审查了《华沙公约》的起草背景后指出,公约规定的辅助运输对于航空运输而言并不重要。但《华沙公约》本身以及公约的起草过程中,并没有规定如何认定相对于航空运输重要与否的标准。因而,法院作出了自己的认定,其认为如果合同约定的运输主要是航空运输,但也履行了辅助运输,无论辅助运输是否规定于合同中,在发生非定域性损失时,《华沙公约》第18条第3款的规定都应适用。[②] 显然,这一判断将实际履行作为了认定辅助运输的标准,但这种认定方式显然存在问题。以量子案为例,如果该案中发生的是非定域性损失,按照这一标准,《华沙公约》应当适用,但量子案中涉及的公路运输明显不应被认为是辅助运输。因此,这种认定方式完全忽视了运输距离,尽管不是判断辅助运输的唯一标准,但在判断是否构成辅助运输时,也是需要考察的。

因此,从上述案件来看,可以从运输的目的结合运输距离共同判断何为辅助运输。辅助运输实际是为了完成不能通过航空器完成的,从托运人所在地到始发机场的运输区段、目的地机场到收货人所在地的运输区段以及两个机场间不能通过航班进行的转运。因此,装载应被认为是,从托运人所在地收集货物运送到最近的机场,该机场应具有开始计划的航空运输所必要的运输设备以及航班。交付应是指从航空运输所能到达的,距离最终目的地最近的机场到最终目的地的运输。而转运应是指,在两个机场间不存在直达航班

---

① 《华沙公约》第18条第3款规定:"航空运输的期间不包括在航空站以外的任何陆运、海运或河运。但是如果这种运输是为了履行空运合同,是为了装货、交货或转运,任何损失应该被认为是在航空运输期间发生事故的结果,除非有相反证据。"

② Commercial Union Ins. Co. v. Alitalia Airlines, S. A., 347 F. 3d 448, 469(2003).

或者由于技术原因不能通过航班连接时,必须进行的地面运输。①

四、结　　语

考虑到运输公约的宗旨和强制适用性,以及适用运输公约能够带来的法律适用方面的确定性和可预见性,运输公约缔约国在审理有关陆空货物多式联运合同的争议时,在满足运输公约的适用条件时,应当适用运输公约,而不应通过冲突规则确定应适用的规则。基于此,通过分析《蒙特利尔公约》以及《公路公约》的文本、有关案例以及学术著作,本文试图澄清公约适用于陆空货物多式联运合同航空运输区段、公路运输区段以及合同本身的条件,以期为陆空货物多式联运合同争议的解决提供智力支撑。

① See Marian Hoeks, *Multimodal Transport Law-The Law applicable to the multimodal contract for the carriage of goods*, Kluwer Law International, 2010, pp. 248 - 249.

论国际航空安保法中的管辖权立法模式

——以国家对危害民航安全行为的管辖为视角*

张　政**

一、导　　言

民用航空运输业具有天然的国际性,这一特征使危害民用航空安全的有关犯罪和其他行为也产生了国际性,进而推动了国际规则的制定。① 从是否构成刑事犯罪的角度划分,危害民用航空安全行为的种类可分为“危害民航安全的犯罪”和“尚不构成犯罪的扰乱性行为”;从行为种类的角度划分,可分为

---

* 本文系2019年教育部人文社会科学研究基金青年项目“冲突地区民航飞行风险预防机制及中国对策研究”(19YJC820070)的阶段性研究成果之一。

** 华东政法大学国际法学博士,现供职于中国东方航空集团(股份)有限公司法律合规部,主要研究领域为航空法。

① 参见刘承汉、蔡喆生:《民用航空法论》,中国交通建设学会1954年版,第3页。转引自董玉鹏:《国际航空运输法律适用研究》,浙江大学出版社2012年版,第13页。

"严重影响民航安全的非法干扰行为"和"破坏机上和机场良好秩序或纪律的扰乱性行为"。对这些特征有别、种类迥异的危害民航安全行为实施规制的国际公约和其他非公约类国际性规则被概括称为国际航空安保法律规则,并日渐为各国认可和重视。各国以国际航空安保法律规则为依据实施管控时,首先需要判别并适用国际公约和国际规则针对不同类别的危害民航安全行为所设立的管辖权规则。国际民航安保立法的核心任务之一即是创设一套对于各个缔约国而言,针对处于不同方位和状态的航空器内部发生的行为和针对航空器本身均可适用的管辖权规则。

二、危害民航安全行为的类别及对应的管辖权规则

不同类型的危害民用航空安全行为会导致不同的法律和现实后果,故由不同的国际航空安保法律规则予以规制,进而适用不同的管辖权规则。其行为类别主要规定在 1944 年《国际民用航空公约》(以下简称《芝加哥公约》)等国际公约和国际民航组织(International Civel Aviation Organization,ICAO)发布的《芝加哥公约》附件等国际航空公约和规则中,既包括劫持(seize)和破坏(sabotage)航空器及国际机场等行为,亦包括通过其他手段干扰国际民航正常运营的犯罪和行为。

(一)构成犯罪的非法干扰行为

除少数国际罪行外,危害民航安全的犯罪主要由各国的国内刑事法律制度予以规范并惩治。为统一各国对此类犯罪行为的认识,国际航空安保公约对多项十分严重的犯罪行为进行了规定,其中典型的是劫持和破坏航空器的行为。此类行为随着航空运营逐渐商业化而出现,并一直威胁国际航空业的安全。首次劫持国际商业航班的记录发生在 1948 年,劫机者劫持了香港国泰航空公司的航班并最终导致航班坠落在中国澳门特别行政区附近的海域。[①] 自

---

① See Paul Stephen Dempsey, *Public International Air Law*, Montréal McGill University, Institute and Center for Research in Air & Space Law,2008,p. 229.

1948 年起劫持航空器行为进入了多发时期,仅当年就发生了 7 起劫持事件。至 1968 年,劫持航空器事件的发生频率达到巅峰——1968 年至 1969 年就发生了 76 起航空器劫持事件。①

如此高频率发生的劫机事件促使联合国将制止劫持航空器问题列入大会议程,并在国际民航组织的主持下制定了由 1963 年《关于航空器内犯罪和其他某些行为的公约》(以下简称《东京公约》),1970 年《关于制止非法劫持航空器的公约》(以下简称《海牙公约》),1971 年《关于制止危害民用航空安全的非法行为的公约》(以下简称《蒙特利尔公约》)这 3 个国际公约为主体的国际航空刑法公约体系。② 学者们又将其称之为国际"反劫机公约"体系,这一系列国际公约为缔约国构建了对航空器上犯罪行为的管辖权框架。③ 此后,航空安保立法逐渐从相对广义的"航空安全"概念中分离,形成针对严重危害民航安全行为(又称"非法干扰行为")的独立法律体系。

1971 年《蒙特利尔公约》主要针对的是除《海牙公约》规定的非法劫持或控制飞行中的航空器的行为之外的其他犯罪行为。公约规定了实施暴力行为可能危及航空器安全、破坏或损坏航空器或导航设备从而危及航空器的安全,以及传递虚假情报危及航空器安全的诸多行为都属于公约上的罪行(offense)。④《蒙特利尔公约》的意义在于将非法干扰航空飞行的行为种类从单一的暴力或暴力威胁劫持航空器行为加以扩展,囊括了多种破坏和干扰航空器正常飞行的行为,行使管辖权的范围得以相应扩大。

在《蒙特利尔公约》的指引下,1988 年 2 月 24 日《制止危害用于国际民用航空机场的非法暴力行为的议定书》(以下简称《蒙特利尔补充议定书》)

---

① See Evans, Alona E., "Aircraft Hijacking: Its Cause and Cure", *The American Journal of International Law* 63(4), 1969, pp. 695 – 710.

② 参见王虎华:《危害国际航空安全犯罪的理论与中国的实践》,载《犯罪研究》2002 年第 5 期。

③ 参见赵维田:《论三个反劫机公约》,群众出版社 1985 年版,第 7 页。

④ See Paul Stephen Dempsey, *Public International Air Law*, Montréal McGill University, Institute and Center for Research in Air & Space Law, 2008, p. 246.

在加拿大蒙特利尔签署,并于 1989 年 8 月 6 日生效。[①] 在当时雅典、罗马、法兰克福、维也纳和以色列特拉维夫机场发生的多起袭击事件的背景下,[②]《蒙特利尔补充议定书》将破坏国际民用航空服务的机场及机场设施或民用航空器的行为列为公约下的罪行,反劫机公约体系所规范的危害民航安全罪行构成了国际航空安保工作的主要对象。各缔约国应根据公约规定,通过国内立法对此类罪行确立刑事管辖权。

分别在 2018 年 7 月 1 日和 2018 年 1 月 1 日生效的 2010 年《制止与国际民用航空有关的非法行为的公约》和 2010 年《制止非法劫持航空器公约的补充议定书》(以下简称 2010 年《北京公约》,以及 2010 年《北京议定书》)分别对 1971 年《蒙特利尔公约》和 1970 年《海牙公约》进行了修正和延续。两部新近制定的公约虽没有增加新的管辖权种类,但在行为和主体上都作了扩张,侧重规制带有恐怖主义色彩的新型危害民航安全犯罪。公约和议定书通过纳入多种新型危害民航安全行为和行为主体,并增加了公约罪名和适用条件,以期能够避免管辖权存在的空缺和改变国家消极行使管辖权的情势。

(二)尚不构成犯罪的扰乱性行为

扰乱性(disruptive)行为,亦称不循规(unruly)行为,是指发生在航空器上或机场的破坏机上和机场良好秩序或纪律的行为。其本身并非一个全新的法律概念,甚至早于劫持航空器罪行即已在国际公约中有所规定。1950 年"美国诉科尔多瓦案"(United States v. Cordova)引出了国家如何规制扰乱

① Protocol for the Suppression of Unlawful Acts of Violence at Airports Serving International Civil Aviation, Supplementary to the Convention for the Suppression of Unlawful Acts Against the Safety of Civil Aviation (Montréal Supplementary Protocol), ICAO Doc. 9518/1589, 1988.

② 在 20 世纪 80 年代发生了针对特拉维夫和雅典机场的袭击,在 20 世纪 90 年代又出现了多起针对罗马、慕尼黑、维也纳、法兰克福等地民用机场的袭击。

航空器内正常秩序的行为的问题,并催生了 1963 年《东京公约》。[①]《东京公约》制定的主要目的之一即是规范在机上扰乱性行为发生时,如何分配对行为人的管辖权并维护机长对航空器的控制权,以及到达航空器的目的地或经停地时对行为人的后续处理事宜。[②]

因此,《东京公约》虽然规定了非法控制航空器的行为而被列为反劫机公约之一,其立法的核心却在于分配国家对危害民航安全行为的管辖权和处置权,对管辖权的行使范围则尽量予以扩展。可以说《东京公约》是首个同时规范航空器内非法干扰行为和扰乱性行为的国际公约,无论扰乱性行为是否被航空器降落地国或行为人母国的国内法认定为罪行或是不构成犯罪的违法行为,《东京公约》均可在其规定范围内予以适用。

2002 年 6 月国际民航组织理事会发布了《不循规旅客法律问题的指引性材料》(以下简称 288 号通告),意图通过公布示范法的模式使成员国将规制不循规/不轨旅客的规则纳入国内法体系中。[③] 这也是机上扰乱性行为首次被单独列为国际航空安保法律的规制对象。但由于各国立法的巨大差异,288 号通告并没有得到成员国的接受。国际民航组织随后于 2014 年 3 月 26 日在蒙特利尔国际航空法外交会议上审议并通过了《修正〈关于在航空器内犯罪和犯有某些其他行为的公约〉的议定书》(以下简称 2014 年《蒙特利尔议定书》)[④]和更新后的 288 号通告,旨在重点加强对扰乱性行为的规范,以期对《东京公约》进行全面的修正。同时,附件 17 第 8 版中也首次提出了扰

---

① 该案发生在 1948 年 8 月 2 日,科尔多瓦在圣胡安飞往纽约的 DC－4 No. NC－90911 次航班上殴打了飞行员马切达和一名圣地亚哥的空乘人员。但受理该案的美国纽约东区联邦法院认为航空器不属于国内法上规定的"船只",因此美国海事法律所规定的管辖权无法适用于在公海上空飞行的航空器内发生的犯罪。See United States v. Cordova(U. S. District Court E. D. New York,1950. 89 F. Su,p. 298).

② Convention on Offences and Certain Other Acts Committed on Board Aircraft, Signed at Tokyo, on 14 September 1963(Tokyo Convention 1963), ICAO Doc. 8364, 1963, Chapter 4.

③ See ICAO, Guidance Material on Legal Aspects of Unruly/Disruptive Passengers, Circular 288, LE/1, Jun. 2002.

④ Protocol to Amend the Convention on Offences and Certain Other Acts Committed on Board Aircraft, done at Montréal on 4 April 2014(Montréal Protocol, 2014), ICAO Doc. 10034.

乱性旅客的概念。① 虽然目前2014年《蒙特利尔议定书》尚未达到生效所要求的加入国数量,②但在288号通告和附件17的指引下,应在国内立法和实践中对扰乱性行为实施规制已逐渐成为各国的共识。

三、国家对航空器内部行为的管辖

在国际航空安保法更加细致地将罪行和行为纳入规制范围的同时,首先需要解决缔约国对此类罪行和行为的管辖权问题。根据《芝加哥公约》对国家领空主权原则这一习惯国际法的确认,发生在国家领空和国际机场的犯罪和行为,在理论上可以由国家行使属地管辖权予以管辖。而飞行中的航空器在高速移动的过程中,难以确定犯罪行为实施地,传统的属地管辖权无法有效作为国家司法机关据以管控危害民航安全行为的连接因素在国际航空运输活动中得以适用,故国际航空安保法律体系中规定了特殊的管辖制度。

(一)《东京公约》创建的并行管辖制度

在飞行中的航空器内发生犯罪和违法行为时,航空器所在的具体位置通常难以确定,即便可以确定发生在国家管辖外的空域,国际航空法领域也缺失类似"船旗国管辖"的管辖权分配规则,国家同样难以行使管辖权。在这一前提下,由于国际航空运输常跨越多国国界,如多个国家依据各自国内的法律规范对同一行为实施管辖,则势必产生管辖权的争夺,形成国家管辖权之间的"积极冲突"。积极冲突如出现在国家对危害民航安全行为处罚力度不均时,处罚力度较轻的国家可能引起处罚力度较重国家的不满。如国家依据本国法律审查案件事实后均发现无法律依据行使管辖权时,则会形成管辖权的"消极冲突",不利于惩治危害民航安全行为。前文所述的"美国诉科尔

① See Security: Safeguarding International Civil Aviation Against Acts of Unlawful Interference, 8th edition, 2017.

② ICAO, Current Lists of Parties to Multilateral Air Law Treaties, Accessed Aug. 15, 2017. https://www.icao.int/secretariat/legal/Lists/Current%20lists%20of%20parties/AllItems.aspx.

多瓦案”就是管辖权消极冲突的典型表现。国际航空安保公约的立法目的之一就是从国际法的角度对管辖权进行分配和统一,从而消弭管辖权的积极冲突和消极冲突,使破坏国际民航安全运行秩序的行为得到恰当的预防和惩治。

《芝加哥公约》中未涉及对航空器内部人员和行为的管辖问题,而现实中越来越多的劫持事件要求国际社会尽快制定对发生在航空器内行为行使管辖权的规则。1963 年《东京公约》作了首次尝试,从 1958 年的蒙特利尔稿,1959 年的慕尼黑稿,1962 年的蒙特利尔修订稿到 1962 年的罗马稿,起草者针对管辖的实施方式讨论了是否采用航空器注册国管辖或行为发生地国管辖,亦讨论了行使管辖所依据的法律是否应以注册国法或行为发生地国法为准来判断行为是否构成犯罪等问题。[①] 最终,1963 年通过的《东京公约》适用于一切在航空器上发生的危害或可能危害航空器和所载人员的犯罪行为(offences)和其他行为(acts)。[②] 公约确立了“并行管辖”(concurrent jurisdiction)制度,首次对飞行中的航空器内部行为确立了国家的管辖权。

并行管辖是指航空器登记国(State of registration)和各公约当事国均有权依本国法对航空器内的人和行为行使管辖权。[③] 公约在国际航空法领域明确了自“荷花号案”以来持续存在争议的国家管辖权域外效力问题。长期以来,国家主权原则所引申的刑法域内原则一直是英美法系所恪守的传统,即便大陆法系的法国,在“荷花号案”中也拒不承认土耳其刑法具有域外效力。“荷花号案”的法官穆尔(Moore)明确表示,刑法的域内性是绝对的。[④] 根据常设国际法院(Permanent Court of International Justice, PCIJ)的这一判决,除非有例外情况,否则国家不能对域外行使刑事管辖权。《东京公约》对“荷花号案”确立的国家管辖权域内效力进行了突破,即使行为发生时该航

---

① International Conference on Air Law, August-September 1963 at Tokyo, ICAO Conference Doc. No. 5.

② Tokyo Convention, 1963, Art. 1.

③ 参见刘伟民:《论国际航空法中的刑事管辖权》(下),载《法学研究》1983 年第 2 期。

④ See the Judgement of S. S. Lotus (Fr. v. Turk.), P. C. I. J. (ser. A) No. 10, Sept. 7, 1927.

空器在别国领空或不属于任何国家领空的空域飞行,航空器登记国均有权依公约规定管辖在本国登记的航空器内发生的犯罪行为。《东京公约》基于《芝加哥公约》确立的航空器国籍制度,为航空器登记国管辖发生在航空器内部的行为创设了公约依据,在理论上实现了对飞行中的航空器内发生的犯罪或行为不存在管辖空缺的目标。①

《东京公约》的意义之一,在于明确了航空器登记国行使管辖权的空间范围,即管辖权是对航空器内部"空间"发生的行为行使。由于并非针对某项"罪行"行使管辖权,从而避开了各国国内法对行为是否构成犯罪存在不同认定标准的问题,同时使国家管辖的对象囊括了非法干扰行为和扰乱性行为。然而,公约的管辖规定未能完全消弭管辖权消极冲突的问题。公约仅要求当事国通过"必要措施"确立管辖权,但对管辖权的行使却仅作了授权性规定,即当事国"有权行使"(competent to exercise)其作为航空器登记国的管辖权。这一规定赋予了当事国自由决定是否行使管辖权的权利——包括依据本国法律规定不予行使某些类型管辖权的权利,②从而给当事国逃避管辖留下了较大的空间。

同时,为确保管辖权得以恰当行使,《东京公约》第 3 条第 3 款规定:"将不排除当事国依据本国法规定的任何刑事管辖权。"也就是说,任何公约的当事国——而非仅限于航空器登记国——均可以依据本国刑事法律的规定,对航空器内的人和行为行使从属地管辖权到保护性管辖权中的任意一种管辖权,这一管辖权与航空器登记国管辖并行行使。并行管辖建立的初衷在于避免因登记国怠于管辖航空器内发生的犯罪行为,或因为法律未能规定某些特定的管辖权而导致的管辖权空缺。但不可避免的问题是,并行管辖引发了管辖权的积极冲突乃至过度管辖的问题,管辖权的积极冲突还可以通过国家间

---

① 郑斌(Bin Cheng)教授将其称为准属地管辖权(quasi-territorial jurisdiction),这一管辖权由《芝加哥公约》授权设立,管辖权行使的依据基于《芝加哥公约》第 12 条的规定。See Stephen Hobe, *Cologne Commentary on Space Law*, Carl Heymanns Verlag, 2009, p. 157.

② International Conference on Air Law, Tokyo, 20 August – 14 September 1963, ICAO. Doc. 8565/Lc/152 – 1.

司法协助等方式来解决,但过度管辖可能引发更加严重的事件。韩国 KE007 次航班被击落就是一种极端情形,苏联认为大韩航空的 KE007 次航班内存在间谍活动,而根据本国法行使的对航空间谍活动管控虽然严苛,但其属于国家主权权利的行使,并不构成国际法上的不法行为。故苏联拒绝承担国家责任,最终只对死难者承担了人道主义赔偿义务。① 《东京公约》的制定和实践表明,公约目的在于解决如何对航空器内犯罪行使刑事管辖权这一新型法律问题,重点在于消弭管辖空缺。而随着航空技术的发展和国家对航空安全的日益重视,国家针对航空器内发生的行为行使管辖权有扩张的趋势,其管辖权的冲突也日渐加剧。

(二)《海牙公约》确立的有优先级的并行管辖制度

《东京公约》的保守之处与其制定背景分不开,公约制定的目的并非是创建完整的制约航空犯罪的国际刑法体系,而是填补管辖权的空白。公约本身也并没有明确管辖权行使的对象是一般违法行为还是罪行,也没有对罪行的种类和构成要件进行明确定义或列举,而是笼统的称为对航空器所载人员的犯罪和行为,整体而言稍显粗陋。而 1970 年《海牙公约》则真正地将劫持航空器行为作为一种犯罪行为来对待,在管辖权的立法上也对《东京公约》作了较大突破。首先,《海牙公约》通过第 1 条和第 2 条规定了犯罪行为以及对犯罪行为的严惩原则,②规定各国均应以国内惩治刑事罪行的程度对待劫持航空器犯罪。其次,公约在第 4 条中确立了"有优先级的并行管辖"原则,试图修正《东京公约》中对管辖权并行行使时存在积极冲突且无法确立权利行使序位的问题。

有优先级的并行管辖原则是《海牙公约》的创造性规定,公约第 4 条第 1

---

① See McCarthy, Gerard Michael, "Limitations on the Right to Use Force against Civil Aerial Intruders: the Destruction of KAL Flight 007 in Community Perspective", *New York Law School Journal of International and Comparative Law* 6(1), 1984, pp. 177 – 209.

② See Convention for The Suppression of Unlawful Seizure of Aircraft, 1970, (Hague Convention, 1970), Arts. 1 & 2.

款规定了受到劫机犯罪行为损害的当事国的优先管辖权,并增添了降落地国管辖和航空器干租时,[①]承租人主营业地或常住地的管辖两个新的管辖权。该公约第4条第1款中所列的国家和地区往往会受到劫持航空器行为最为直接的影响,损失也最大,因而对行使管辖权有着最积极的态度。公约第4条第2款则规定了被指犯罪的行为人在当事国境内时,在与犯罪行为本身没有实质联系的情况下,当事国仍需要承担公约第7条规定的"或引渡或起诉"(*aut dedere aut judicare*)的刑事管辖义务。[②] 此时当事国并非公约第4条第1款中列举的国家,而是与犯罪行为不存在直接联系,行为人可能只是因为将航空器迫降至一国而流窜而进入了另一当事国境内而被扣押,此时当事国同样(likewise)有权依据公约行使对此类犯罪的管辖权。但由于不存在直接联系,此时当事国行使的管辖权类似普遍管辖权,在不将行为人引渡至其第4条第1款中受到劫机犯罪影响最大的国家时,方得以行使。

这一带有优先行使次序的并行管辖体制,为各当事国制裁跨国犯罪但又难以一概适用普遍管辖的情形提供了一种新的立法模式,并提供了一种可能解决管辖冲突的方式。这一立法模式由随后的1971年《蒙特利尔公约》继承,后者只是对公约的适用范围作了修改,增加了犯罪行为地国的管辖权并取消了对某些类型犯罪的普遍管辖权。[③] 随后生效的其他国际航空安保公约和国际反恐怖条约都或多或少地借鉴了1970年《海牙公约》所创设的这一管辖模式。[④] 因此《东京公约》和《海牙公约》创设的管辖体系是国际航空法上对航空器内行为行使管辖权的基本模式,其他公约或多或少的发展了这一管辖体系,在这一基础上增添了管辖权的类型或管辖对象的种类。

2010年《北京公约》是对1971年《蒙特利尔公约》和1988年《蒙特利尔

① 干租又称光机租赁,即由出租人仅提供航空器租赁,而不附带机组、航油或备件及维修。此时出租人与航空器之间的关联十分薄弱,航空器与承租人之间反而有密切的联系。

② Hague Convention, 1970, Art. 4.

③ 参见刘浩:《论国际民用航空保安公约中的管辖权条款》,载《社会科学家》2014年第5期。

④ 参见赵维田:《国际航空法》,社会科学文献出版社2000年版,第463页。

补充仪定书》的全面修订,进一步填补了管辖权的缺失,并将联合国缔结的一些反恐怖主义公约中存在的某些管辖规定纳入航空安保公约中,扩展了公约的普遍性管辖的范围,体现了反恐怖主义立法的趋势。① 但《北京公约》和《北京议定书》并未对管辖权实现突破,其所增设的以扩大管辖权行使为目标的"犯罪是由该国国民实施的"强制性管辖理由,和"犯罪是针对该国国民实施的、犯罪是由其惯常居所在该国境内的无国籍人实施的"两项任择性管辖理由的规定则难以获得预期的效果。如1981年巴基斯坦航空公司的客机被劫持至阿富汗首都喀布尔机场,当时的苏联和其控制的阿富汗当局则并未对犯罪分子实施惩罚。② 可见犯罪分子所在的国家有可能以本国司法主权为由不遵守公约规定,从而架空公约规定的刑事管辖权。

四、国家对航空器本身的管辖

反劫机公约体系创设的法律制度规范了对发生在航空器内部行为的刑事管辖权,但国际航空法还包含对航空器本身的管辖。《芝加哥公约》附件17下规定的标准和建议措施(Standards are Recommended Practices, SARPs)中,就包含多项国家对受到非法干扰行为影响的航空器的管控措施。当航空器遭受劫持或被作为武器使用时,航空器本身也构成对空中规则的违反,与航空器内发生的非法干扰行为都属于国际航空安保法的规制对象,故国家对航空器本身行使的管辖也是安保立法的重要问题。

(一)国家管辖航空器本身的现实原因

对航空器本身的管辖是指当航空器被劫持或用作武器使用时,国家为保护更大的社会法益,避免航空器对地面人员或财物造成巨大威胁,主动对此

---

① See Acts or Offences of Concern to the International Aviation Community and not Covered by Existing Air Law Instruments, ICAO Doc. A36 – WP/12, Aug. 14, 2007.

② 参见林欣:《论对危害国际民用航空安全罪的刑事管辖权》,载《法学研究》1981年第5期。

类航空器实施干预性管辖。在国际航空安保法的语境下,不符合自身用途的航空器通常指因为遭受非法干扰行为影响而无法以正常状态飞行的非正常航空器,其飞行状态无法预测。

传统的航空器内犯罪或扰乱行为的实施者通常无意影响航空器自身的安全飞行。例如,早期的劫持航空器行为,大多数都出于逃离某国管辖范围的目的而改变航空器的飞行方向,①行为人并无意对航空器本身的安全造成影响。然而自美国"9·11"事件之后,恐怖主义犯罪成为危害民航安全犯罪的主要表现形式之一。行为人既不区分攻击目标,亦不顾及造成毁伤的规模,其本身的目的就是通过劫持行为摧毁航空器,杀害人质,乃至使用航空器造成尽可能大的地面财物破坏,杀伤平民。在此背景下,非正常航空器已经转化为一种攻击性武器,对此实施管辖,保护地面人员和财物不受毁伤是国际航空安保法中的一项重要内容。

2010 年《北京公约》就明确列入了"任何人如果利用使用中的航空器造成死亡、严重人身伤害,或对财产或环境的严重破坏",该人即构成犯罪这一条款,对扩展了传统反劫机系列公约所规定的罪行。② 然而,恐怖主义犯罪利用民用航空器作为武器的现实使传统对行为人的刑事管辖权难以行使。国家可以对停留在机场的航空器实施管控,进而抓捕航空器内的犯罪行为人。但对于已被恐怖分子掌控的"使用中"的航空器通常处于飞行中,此时国家无法登临航空器,因此对航空器本身实施管辖成为惩治航空器内犯罪行为的现实原因。

(二)国家管辖航空器本身的法律依据

对航空器实施管辖的权力源于航空活动与国家安全的天然关联。领空主权原则早在第一次世界大战前即有相关国家实践,并最终由 1919 年《巴黎

---

① 参见刘昊阳:《试析我国劫持民用航空器犯罪的类型及防范》,载《政法学刊》2009 年第 6 期。

② See the Convention on the Suppression of Unlawful Acts Relating to International Civil Aviation(Beijing Convention)2010,Art. 1.

公约》所确立。国家基于领空主权原则对领土上空的空域行使管辖权,任何试图脱离或拒绝接受国家管辖的航空器都会被视为对领空主权的侵犯,以及对国家安全的重大威胁。

1919 年《巴黎公约》确认了国家对其领土上空具有完全和排他的主权这一原则之后,国际航空法在领空主权原则的基础上进行发展。主权是国家具有的独立自主的处理自己的对内和对外事务的最高权力。[①] 1944 年《芝加哥公约》承继了 1919 年《巴黎公约》确认的领空主权原则,并围绕这一原则制定现代航权、空中规则、航空器国籍和注册等规则体系。按照《芝加哥公约》的规定,当事国对本国领土的上空和降停于本国领土上的航空器的属地管辖是主权排他性的直接体现。需要明确的是,公约规定的管辖对象是民用航空器且仅限于民用航空器,任何国家航空器或不属于航空器的其他飞行装置均不受公约约束。

国际航空法下对航空器行使管辖权的法律依据主要是属地管辖权(territorial jurisdiction),适用于发生在该国国家领土内的一切行为。此外,由于航空器在三维空间中运行,具有高度高、速度快、方向复杂多变的特点,对航空器实施管辖的时间窗口非常狭窄,国家难以等待航空器进入领空内才实施管辖。并且,待遭受非法干扰尤其是劫持行为的航空器进入国家领空后,其有很大可能性可以轻易摆脱管控并在短时间内即对地面人员和财产造成重大损害。因此国家对航空器的识别和管控是国际航空安保法实施的现实需要。

《芝加哥公约》赋予了国家对在域外飞行的民用航空器实施管辖的权力。该管辖权与属地管辖权均规定于《芝加哥公约》第 12 条中,根据公约规定,当事国有权在公海和国家管辖外区域上空对不遵循《芝加哥公约》中空中规则的民用航空器实施管辖,以确保航空器的商业运营在世界范围内安全有序地开展。

---

① 参见周鲠生:《国际法》(上册),商务印书馆 1976 年版,第 74 页。

公约第12条集中规定了对航空器的飞行作业管辖,包括:(1)对领土上空飞行或在其领土内运转的每一航空器的属地管辖权;(2)对具有当事国国籍标志的航空器在任何地区飞行和运转的管辖权;(3)对在公海和不属于任何国家管辖区域上空飞行的航空器,依据公约规则实施的管辖权。① 该管辖权是航空法上的一项独特的管辖权,指根据《芝加哥公约》的授权,国家对航空器在公海和国家管辖外区域上空飞行时不遵守公约空中规则的行为实施的管辖权。② 其法律特征在于:(1)该权利由公约规定设立,准属地管辖权行使以《芝加哥公约》规定的航空器国籍制度为基础,依据公约规定对本国领土外的航空器实施管辖。(2)该管辖权可在公海和国家管辖外区域上空行使,但不能涉及其他国家的领空,在其他国家领空飞行的航空器应由该国行使属地管辖权。(3)国家对公海和国家管辖外区域上空飞行的民用航空器,根据《芝加哥公约》制定的空中规则进行运行管控。此处的空中规则主要指《芝加哥公约》附件2空中规则中规定的国际标准,全世界民航国家必须遵循且不得任意予以变更。一旦民用航空器未按照空中规则进行飞行活动,国家即可认为该航空器已经属于非正常航空器,进而有权对此类航空器行使管辖权。

(三)《芝加哥公约》对国家管辖"航空器本身及其内部行为"的统一

《芝加哥公约》第12条规定涉及公约当事国对民用航空器本身和对航空器内部人员和行为的管辖,并非仅规定对航空器的管辖或仅规定对航空器内部人员与事件的管辖。在民用航空器遭受非法干扰且不正常飞行时,对其内部人员的犯罪行为实施管辖必须要通过对航空器本身的管辖来实现。劫持航空器或其他非法干扰行为的行为人在控制航空器后,已然实际控制航空器的人员破坏了民用航空器的正常飞行程序和本应遵循的空中规则,航空器超

---

① Chicago Convention, 1944, ICAO Doc. 7300, Art. 12.

② See Stephen Hobe, *Cologne Commentary on Space Law*, Netherland, Carl Heymanns Verlag, 2009, p. 157.

出了国际航空法为航空器正常运行的所制定的各项规范，公约当事国有必要对航空器实施管辖从而使空中规则恢复正常。

而对于航空器内部发生的非法干扰或扰乱性行为，公约并未区分是否已经对航空器的正常飞行造成影响。行为人可能实施了劫持航空器犯罪，并破坏空中规则，亦可能行为人仅实施了航空器内的非法干扰或扰乱，却未能夺取航空器控制权，空中规则本身没有被破坏。对此，公约则规定了当事国有权起诉（prosecution）不遵守空中规则的一切人员（all persons）。[①] 这一规定赋予了当事国对航空器内的人员进行管辖的权力。公约采用了明显具有刑法意义的“（刑事）起诉”措辞，公约当事国应当据此规定对干扰正常飞行的行为人行使刑事管辖权。《芝加哥公约》之所以未列明当事国对航空器内犯罪的刑事管辖权，是因为在公约制定当时劫持航空器还不是一个严重现象，而且公约本身也不是一个国际刑法公约。刑事管辖权的具体行使，对航空器内的行为是否认定为犯罪以及是否有必要对此类犯罪进行追诉的问题，被认为应当交于当事国国内法予以规定。[②]

《芝加哥公约》的规定在航空安保的语境下，同时覆盖了当事国对民用航空器本身和航空器内的人员的管辖。公约虽然未能对当事国采取何种方式对航空器内的人员和行为进行管辖，亦缺失实施管辖的程序性规定，但公约明确了管辖权实施的法律要件。即在航空器本身违反空中规则时——当这一违反是由非法干扰或扰乱性行为导致的——当事国有权对航空器本身行使管辖权。对机内非法干扰或扰乱行为实施管辖时，则不论航空器本身的状态，任何公约的当事国均应当对行为人实施刑事管辖。具体的管辖权在当事国之间的分配和管辖权行使的对象，则由专门的国际航空安保公约来进行细化。

---

① Chicago Convention, 1944, Art. 12.

② See Alona E. Evans, Aircraft Hijacking: Its Cause and Cure, *American Journal of International Law* 4, 1969, pp. 695 – 710.

五、结　　论

国际航空安保法语境下的管辖权问题是实施国际民航安保公约的前提和基础。对具体的危害民航安全行为,如非法干扰行为或扰乱性行为实施管辖时,需在正确理解各项国际航空安保公约及规则中对国家管辖权规定的基础上,制定符合公约规定的国内法,避免出现管辖权的积极冲突和消极冲突,阻碍对危害民航安全行为的惩治。此外,国家对民用航空器本身的管辖和对航空器内部人员和行为的管辖也应在国际航空安保法语境下作出明确区分。《芝加哥公约》第 12 条以空中规则为基础,为国家制定了对民用航空器在国家领空、公海上空以及国家管辖外区域上空飞行时,出现破坏空中规则的情况下国家管辖的行使,同时对航空器内部人员和行为的追诉进行了规定,从而统一了这两种既有区别又密切相关的管辖权。

GNSS Liability in the Context of International Air Law: *Status Quo*, Inadequacies and Solutions

Qiu Ruiyan *

1. Introduction

The aviation market continues to grow worldwide with the reliance on global navigation satellite systems (GNSS) increasing. ① According to the definition given by ICAO, GNSS refers to "a worldwide position and time determination system, that includes one or more satellite constellations, aircraft receivers and system integrity monitoring augmented as necessary to support the required navigation performance for the actual phase

---

* 丘瑞雁(Qiu Ruiyan),女,荷兰莱顿大学航空法与空间法硕士,国际民航组织航空运输局实习生。

① European GNSS Agency, "GNSS Market Report Issue 5", 2017, p. 43.

of operation". ① In the aeronautical area, GNSS is regarded as a key element of the Communications, Navigation, and Surveillance/Air Traffic Management (CNS/ATM) systems, upon which the States can deliver air services with enhanced accuracy and availability.

Along with the advantages that it has brought to air industry, the broad application of GNSS services also introduces some legal challenges to aviation lawyers, as the legal framework for GNSS liability is inadequate. At present, a uniformed legal framework for GNSS liability does not exist. The global nature of GNSS in technology requests a unitary nature in international law. Without the convergence of national legal systems in addressing a global service, conflicts of law will occur and ultimately bring legal uncertainty. The GNSS liability issue is worthy of examining rigorously, as GNSS is an essential component of air navigation activities. A faulty signal of GNSS may cause a disastrous loss of human lives in an air accident.

A GNSS consists of three components: the ground stations, the satellites and the receivers. Through the coordination and collaboration between different parts, GNSS can improve the efficiency of air transport services. Since different components are often controlled by different parties, there are a number of participators in a GNSS service chain. It is difficult for a victim involved in a GNSS liability case to know which one is the proper compensator without sufficient professional knowledge. Furthermore, the public character of GNSS service providers induces the problem of sovereign immunity.

The circumstances mentioned above indicate that the *status quo* of the legal regime for GNSS liability is far from satisfactory. Therefore, the international society has raised many concerns in respect of the allocation of liability in case of

---

① Annex 10 to the Convention on International Civil Aviation: Aeronautical Telecommunications, Vol. 1, 2006, section 3.7.1.

damage caused by GNSS services.

2. GNSS Liability Under International Conventions

To have a comprehensive perception of the GNSS liability issues in the context of air law, it is useful to discuss some pertinent provisions in the Chicago Convention 1944, the Warsaw Convention 1929 and the Montreal Convention 1999. Although none of them directly address the GNSS liability issues, the principles and general obligations laid down there have shed light on the completion of the legal framework for GNSS activities.

2.1 Chicago Convention 1944

The Convention on International Civil Aviation (hereinafter referred to as the "Chicago Convention"), adopted in 1944, is generally considered as the *Magna Carta* of international air law since it stipulates the most prominent principles to maintain the safety and efficiency of international air transportation. At the time of its adoption, GNSS services were not in existence, as the earliest launch of a global navigation satellite was conducted in 1978.① Therefore, the Chicago Convention does not directly address the application of GNSS services. While as GNSS turns to be an aid of air navigation facilities, it has to follow relevant provisions contained in the Chicago Convention.

Among many articles, article 28 is most relevant to the operation of GNSS services. This article imposes obligations on member States, stipulating that each State should provide air navigation facilities in accordance with the ICAO Standards and Recommended Practices (SARPs). Therefore, GNSS is subject to

---

① Wikipedia English, "Global Positioning System", Accessed January 5, 2019. https://en.wikipedia.org/wiki/Global_Positioning_System.

article 28 of the Chicago Convention. However, the mechanisms by which a State may fulfil its obligations have not been prescribed by the Chicago Convention. ① Neither are they covered by any other international conventions, so these specific questions fall under applicable national laws. States will certainly be held liable if they fail to fulfil its responsibilities as a part of the GNSS system due to their commitments under article 28 of the Chicago Convention, while to what extent these responsibilities must be carried out was not defined and still raises arguments. ②

2.2 Warsaw Convention 1929 and Montreal Convention 1999

The Convention for the Unification of Certain Rules Relating to International Carriage by Air of 1929, commonly known as the Warsaw Convention, is an international convention that applies to "all international carriage of persons, luggage or goods performed by aircraft for reward". ③ The Warsaw Convention, together with its subsequent amendments and supplement, ④ forms the Warsaw System that resolves the liability issues of international carriage. It provides a bottom line of compensation for consignors, consignees and passengers in case their rights are infringed.

As the aviation business began to expand on a large scale, it was widely felt that the Warsaw System no longer met the requirements of modern air transport

---

① Alessandra A. L. Andrade, *Navigating into the New Millennium: The Global Navigation Satellite System Regulatory Framework*, New York, Ashgate Publishing, 2001, p. 124.

② Francis P. Schubert, "An International Convention on GNSS Liability: When Does Desirable Become Necessary", *Annals Air & Space Law* 24, 1999, p. 255.

③ Convention for the Unification of Certain Rules Relating to International Carriage by Air, 137 L. N. T. S. 11, 1929, art. 1.

④ The Warsaw System includes the following instruments: the Warsaw Convention 1929, the Hague Protocol 1955, the Guatemala Protocol 1971, the Guadalajara Convention 1961, the four Montreal Protocols 1975 (No. 1, No. 2, No. 3 and No. 4).

system taking care of enhanced passenger protection. ① Moreover, the "patchwork" of the Warsaw System had deviated from the intention of the drafters of the Warsaw Convention. ② It follows that there was a need to modernize and consolidate the Warsaw System and replace it by another uniform instrument. Consequently, the Montreal Convention 1999 was adopted world-wide. Under article 55 of the Montreal Convention, this convention prevails over any rules which apply to international carriage by air. ③ Therefore, in case where both the Warsaw System and the Montreal Convention apply, the latter prevails.

The aforementioned legal instruments give us an insight of GNSS liability from a perspective of private air law. The Warsaw Convention introduced a limited liability regime while relieved the passengers and the shipper of goods from the burden of proof. ④ The Montreal Convention created a two-tier liability system of compensation by combining the principles of strict liability and fault liability in article 21. ⑤

At a glance, the GNSS liability issues, as a form of liability, shall also be subject to the Montreal Convention or the Warsaw System, provided that the concerned States are the parties to these treaties.

However, both conventions only oblige the air carrier to pay for the damage, remaining silent on the damages that the air carrier suffers from the malfunction of GNSS services.

---

① I. H. Philepina Diederiks-Verschoor, *An Introduction to Air Law*, Alphen aan den Rijn, Kluwer Law International BV, 2012, p. 219.

② Ibid.

③ Convention for the Unification of Certain Rules for International Carriage by Air, 2242 U. N. T. S. 30, 1999, art. 55.

④ Convention for the Unification of Certain Rules Relating to International Carriage by Air, 137 L. N. T. S. 11, 1929, art. 17.

⑤ Convention for the Unification of Certain Rules Relating to International Carriage by Air, 137 L. N. T. S . 11, 1929, art. 21.

In the context of private air law, strict liability and the two-tier approach apply to the case as long as the damage is qualified as the "damage" prescribed by the conventions, even if the damage is *de facto* caused by the faulty signal provided by GNSS. Nevertheless, the principle of strict liability and the two-tier approach laid down in the conventions only partially resolve the legal relief for passengers. When the air carrier does not commit wrong for the damage, and the compensation has exceeded the amount set in the Warsaw System and the Montreal Convention, it could be difficult for a victim to complain extra compensation as no legal instruments regulate the liability of the GNSS service provider. Furthermore, no legal instruments ensure the legal remedies for an air carrier to claim its rights against the GNSS service provider. Therefore, either from the perspective of passengers or air carriers, the current legal regime for GNSS liability is ambiguous and leaves uncertainty for resolving disputes.

3. Civil Liability Regime for GNSS

The damage scenarios stemming from the global characteristics of GNSS may occur everywhere on the earth, resulting in conflicts between various jurisdictions. Since the chain for GNSS services involves State-owned participators as well as private entities, the liability issues involve both the international law and domestic laws. The civil liability regime for GNSS cannot overlook the importance of the choice of law, as it serves as a bridge to transform an international dispute to a down-to-earth domestic matter, and ultimately leads to the applicability of substantive laws.

Generally speaking, liability can be divided into three forms, which includes criminal liability, administrative liability, and civil liability. Concerning the former two kinds of liability fall out of the scope of private air law, only civil liability will be discussed here, namely, the contractual liability and non-contractual liability.

3.1 Contractual Liability

The contracting parties' will dominates the conclusion of a contract. Contractual liability attributes to contractual obligations and reflects the constitutional function of a contract. In a case related to GNSS, contractual liability usually happens between the GNSS service provider and the direct users. In terms of aviation, the direct users of GNSS services are air carriers. When the GNSS service causes damages, in general, the contractual obligations are not fulfilled duly by the service providers. As victims of a breach of a contract, air carriers are entitled to seek for legal remedies, usually in the form of compensation for damages.

In practice, contracts may contain agreed damages clauses which expressly set an agreed sum of a recoverable nature. This sort of clauses is particularly necessary in commercial contracts, as it enables contracting parties to reach a satisfactory result shortly after the damage happens. The binding force of a contract is universally recognized all over the world. For example, articles 8 and 9 of Contract Law of the People's Republic of China reaffirmed that a party shall perform its obligations in accordance with the contract and that the law protects the contracts formed in accordance with it.① Provisions on contractual

① Contract Law of People's Republic of China, 1999, arts 8&9.

obligations can be found in volumes of written law in a number of countries. ①

The contractual legal framework is specifically initiated by the ECAC States at the 35th ICAO Assembly, which mainly aims to provide for a number of legal and institutional provisions that are deemed necessary for addressing GNSS at a regional level. ② It creatively harmonized the public and private elements of the GNSS issues and introduced a two-dimensional approach to regulating the contractual liability arising from the use of GNSS. This legal regime includes two contracts: the private law contract concluded between the parties involved in the chain of implementation, operation, provision and use of GNSS signals and systems and the public law agreement between the States involved. By this way, States can ensure essential provisions concerning the certification, liability and jurisdictional matters are harmonized and unified.

The framework agreement contains a section about liability issues, in which it addresses the principle of allocating liability. Under this section, each entity or person involved shall be liable to the extent it has contributed to the occurrence of the loss or damage arising out of a failure, malfunction or improper use of GNSS. ③ This section reaffirms the applicability of existing international and national laws to a GNSS liability case. ④ In the event that a loss or damage cannot be clearly traced to a specific defendant, this section declares that the

---

① For instance, section 311 (1) of the German Civil Code reads that: "In order to create an obligation by legal transaction and to alter the contents of an obligation, a contract between the parties is necessary, unless otherwise provided by statute." See more information at http://www.gesetze-im-internet.de/englisch_bgb/englisch_bgb.html#p0439. Art. 1194 of the French Civil Code reads that: "Contracts create obligations not merely in relation to what they expressly provide, but also to all the consequences which are given to them by equity, usage or legislation." See more information at https://www.trans-lex.org/601101/_/french-civil-code-2016/.

② ICAO A35 - WP/125, ECAC States, "GNSS Development of a Contractual Framework Leading Towards a Long-Term Legal Framework to Govern the Implementation of GNSS", 2004.

③ Ibid., Appendix B, section 12.

④ Ibid.

defendants involved in the chain of events shall be jointly liable for the entire amount of the loss or damage. ①

Although the contractual regime seems to satisfy the needs of contracting parties to clarify their obligations and rights, it fails to deal with non-contractual liability issues. In aviation cases, passengers are the third party to the contract between the GNSS services provider and the air carrier. It follows that a contractual regime cannot help passengers claim compensation based on a contract against the GNSS services provider directly.

3.2 Non-contractual Liability

Non-contractual liability encompasses all liability attributable to damages that are caused other than breach of contracts. It can also be understood as the third-party liability. The qualification of non-contractual liability should meet two requirements simultaneously. First, someone has sustained a loss or harm as the result of some act or failure to act by another. Second, no contracts regulate the obligations and rights of the involved parties. In a GNSS liability case, the third-party liability may occur between the GNSS service provider or GNSS manufacturer and the passengers who do not use the service directly. The passengers suffered from harm or loss caused by the defaulting GNSS service are victims of torts.

In general, there are two principles of allocating liability ina tort case, which are principles of strict liability and fault liability. Strict liability refers to liability without fault while fault liability, as its name indicates, is based on commitments of faults. Both principles can be found in international law and

---

① ICAO A35 – WP/125, ECAC States, "GNSS Development of a Contractual Framework Leading Towards a Long-Term Legal Framework to Govern the Implementation of GNSS", 2004, Appendix B, Section 12.

domestic laws.

3.2.1 Non-contractual Liability Under International Law

In the view of international law, space law forms an essential part of the legal framework for GNSS liability because GNSS consists of a number of satellites in outer space. The principle of strict liability contained in art. 4 of the Convention on International Liability for Damage Caused by Space Objects 1972 (hereinafter referred to as the "Liability Convention") provides valuable guidance to allocate the GNSS liability in aviation.

GNSS can harm the operation of aircraft through two ways. One refers to the event where a GNSS satellite collides with an aircraft in flight and causes damage. The other refers to the circumstance in which a GNSS signal causes damage to an aircraft.

In the first case, the strict-liability principle under art. 4 of the Liability Convention is applicable. Art. 4 establishes a strict-liability principle to deal with the collision between a space object and an aircraft, and therefore launching States are absolutely liable to the third States if their space objects cause damages on the surface of the Earth or to the aircraft in airspace. ① Since a GNSS satellite is a space object and it collides with an aircraft, the principle of strict liability applies. The strict-liability principle laid down in this article is conscious of the abnormally dangerous nature of space activities. In the second case, the strict-liability under art. 4 does not apply because a GNSS signal is not considered as a space object.

The Liability Convention also contains a fault-liability principle, but it is not applicable to the two cases abovementioned since it does not apply to the damage caused to aircraft. ② In other words, the Liability Convention is silent

---

① Convention on International Liability for Damage Caused by Space Objects, 24 U. S. T. 2389, 1972, art. 4.

② Ibid., art. 3.

upon the issue concerning the damage caused by a GNSS signal to an aircraft.

From the perspective of general international law, international liability entails the obligation of a State to pay compensation or make reparations for injuries that non-nationals suffer outside its territory attributing to activities within its national boundary or under its control. ① Since GNSS services are under the control of the operating States, the operating States engage international liability if the services cause damage outside its territory. It is affirmative that a State shall bear international liability if its GNSS satellites collide with aircraft of another State, as it has been explicitly stipulated by the Liability Convention. However, the damage caused by a faulty GNSS signal to an aircraft is not ruled by specific provisions in international conventions. In this regard, the international law does not provide satisfactory resolutions to solve the non-contractual liability issues.

3.2.2 Non-contractual Liability Under Domestic Law

In the view of domestic law, a complete legal system regarding GNSS liability cannot be found within any jurisdictions. In the U. S., there have been some cases where traffic accidents happened as a result of the failure of GPS signals or malfunction of GPS services. ② Although those cases were not brought to the court up to the date, the U. S. tort law did not deny in principle the possibility for liability claims. ③ Even with the most mature system at this time, no case law concerning GPS can provide an definitive answer to how to allocate liability. In the Tort Liability Law of China, if an actor, through his own fault,

---

① Sompong Sucharitkul, "State Responsibility and International Liability Under International Law", *Loyola of Los Angeles International and Comparative Law Journal* 18, 1996, p. 822.

② John E Woodard, "GPS Manufacturer Liability under A Strict Product's Liability paradigm when GPS Fails to Give Accurate Direction to GPS End-users", *Dayton Law Review* 34, 2006, p. 441.

③ Frans von der Dunk, "Liability for Global Navigation Satellite Services: A Comparative Analysis of GPS and Galileo", *Space, Cyber, and Telecommunications Law Program Faculty Publications* 3, 2004, p. 30.

infringes upon the civil rights or interest of another, he shall bear tort liability. ① Since Chinese law does not specifically address the GNSS liability, the general principle of fault-liability is applicable to a GNSS liability case in China.

Therefore, it can be concluded that the domestic laws of tort will be applicable in case non-contractual liability issues occur, resulting in conflicts between diversified laws in multi-jurisdictions towards the completion of the legal framework for GNSS liability.

4. Legal Inadequacy of GNSS Liability Regime

4.1 Identification of the Proper Defendants

Since many participators are involved in a GNSS service chain, it is hard for victims to determine whom to sue without professional knowledge. Basically, the multiple actors in a GNSS service chain include the signal-in-space provider, augmentation provider, air carrier, ATC agency, aircraft operator, State of registry of the aircraft, equipment and components manufacturers, third parties interfering with the signal, pilot-in-command, ② the victim may become puzzled at whom to blame in a case.

4.2 Multi-jurisdictions

Besides, following a universally recognized maxim *actor sequitur forum rei*, it raises the problem of multi-jurisdictions, ③ which may bring much legal uncertainty as whenever a claimant wants to sue someone, he or she needs to

---

① Tort Liability Law of People's Republic of China, 2009, art. 6.

② European GNSS Agency, GNSS Market Report Issue 5, 2017, p. 141.

③ Ulrich Magnus, "Civil Liability for Satellite-Based Services", *Uniform Law Review* 13, 2008, p. 947.

solve the first question that which court is competent to hear the case. Since each defendant can be sued at the place of its seat or domicile, the victim may go forum-shopping and choose the court where the legislation will benefit his claims to the maximum extent. Indeed, it provides the victims with more chances to get the most amount of compensation, which is in consistence with the interest of the victims. Yet, it is not always an adorable instrument for two reasons:

First, not all the victims have the possibility to get the full compensation amount even if they have chances for forum-shopping. In consideration of the high risk of the aviation industry, when an accident occurs, the number of victims is usually very huge, and the first claimant may go to the court to take action, with his benefits most likely to be satisfied, leaving the other victims a negative position to claim their damages.

Second, multi-jurisdictions increase the costs for both the plaintiffs and the defendants to go through legal proceedings. Due to the variety of legal systems and conflicts of laws in different States, the recognition and enforcement of judgment can become impediments for victims to realize their claims.

4.3 Diversified Substantive Laws

As a result ofthe multi-jurisdictions and the lack of unified rules, various substantive laws may be applied to a case concerned with GNSS liability, which makes it an open question for determining which kind of instrument may help to give resolutions to this issue in the best way.

4.3.1 GPS

Global Positioning System (hereinafter referred to as "GPS"), ① as the

① Global Positioning System (GPS) is a GNSS consisting of 33 satellites operated by the U. S. government. It provides geolocation and time information to a GPS receiver and help people pinpoint the location. The first launch of a GPS satellite was conducted in 1978. It is a GNSS with the widest application around the world. See more information at https: //www. gps. gov/.

earliest GNSS in the world, was developed by the U. S. government. In the U. S., the government would be held liable for tort damages if it were established that the failure or malfunctioning of the GPS signal was the proximate cause of an accident. ① In other words, it means that the U. S. government has waived its right to claim sovereign immunity in GNSS, forming a victim-oriented system in the liability regime for GNSS. This practice is in consistence with the report of the ICAO on the legal aspects of CNS/ATM Systems, which states that the doctrine of sovereign immunity must not constitute an obstacle to bringing all parties into legal proceedings before the court where the victim has brought an action. ②

4.3.2 GLONASS

In Russia, all indemnification and legal liability issues associated with the operation of GLONASS③ are within the national law of torts. In the case of the international regime, non-contractual liability comes into effect. ④

Interestingly, the Russian government concluded an agreement with India in 2007, which is considered as the most successful international cooperation that Russia has achieved. ⑤ The unique agreement stands out as a contract between States for uninterrupted, unrestricted, and non-deteriorated provision of

---

① Alessandra A. L. Andrade, *Navigating into the New Millennium: The Global Navigation Satellite System Regulatory Framework*, New York, Ashgate Publishing, 2001, p. 135.

② ICAO C-WP/Ⅲ90, Report of the Second Meeting of the Secretariat Study Group on the Legal Aspects of CNS/ATM Systems, 1999.

③ GLONASS is a GNSS consisting of 26 satellites operated by the Russian government. It provides an alternative to GPS. The first launch of a GLONASS satellite was conducted in 1982. It is the second navigational satellite system in operation with global coverage. See more information at https://www.glonass-iac.ru/en/.

④ Sergey Maltsev, "'Global Satellite Navigation and International Law' GLONASS Herald", http://vestnik-GLONASS.ru/en/news/articles/global-satellite-navigation-and-international-law/, Jan 5, 2019.

⑤ Ibid.

GLONASS signals with the only exceptions related to Russia's national security. ① This agreement sets a bilateral liability regime but only falls within the scope of contractual liability. In reference to the legislation in India, the private individual's rights to sue the Russian government are excluded unless the person has been obtained special permission granted by the Indian government. ②

4.3.3 Galileo

When it comes to the EU, things become more complicated, because Galileo③ raises double doubts of immunization, concerning Eurocontrol④ and the EU respectively, with the former as the service provider and the latter as the owner of Galileo.

The first doubt is whether the navigation service provider, namely Eurocontrol, has the right to claim for immunity. In reference to the definition given by the International Law Commission (ILC), "International organization" means "an organization established by a treaty or other instrument governed by international law and possessing its own international legal personality. International organizations may include as members, in addition to States, other entities". ⑤ Since Eurocontrol was established upon the enforcement of Eurocontrol Convention and has been playing an intergovernmental legal

---

① Rishiraj Baruah, "An interpretation of lex lata versus lex ferenda in the Indian legal system as applicable to satellite navigation services", *Uniform Law Review* 21, 2016, p. 371.

② Ibid.

③ Galileo is a GNSS consisting of 30 satellites operated by the EU through the European GNSS Agency. The first launch of a Galileo satellite was conducted in 2011. The completion of the Galileo system is expected by 2020. Up to date, it is the only GNSS that does not include military part. See more information at http: //ec. europa. eu/growth/sectors/space/galileo/.

④ Eurocontrol is a European organization for the safety of air navigation. It aims to achieve safe and seamless air traffic management in Europe. It was founded under the Eurocontrol Convention in 1960. Currently, it has 41 member States. See more information at http://www. eurocontrol. int.

⑤ International Law Commission, Draft Articles on the Responsibilities of International Organizations, 2011, art. 2, Accessed January 5, 2019. http: //legal. un. org/ilc/texts/instruments/english/draft_articles/9_11_2011. pdf.

personality, with an independent status in legal proceedings, it shall be considered as an international organization under international law. Therefore, it enjoys the privileges and immunity under public international law. Even if Eurocontrol was not established under a treaty, it could still invoke the privileges and immunities for it functions to achieve safe and seamless air traffic management, which is the common aim for all the member States, and this particular function is based on the consensus of all the member States and performed as the will of the States. The Second doubt is whether EU can invoke privileges as an international organization. Certainly, it is an international organization established under the Treaty on European Union. If the absolute immunity is granted to the EU, the victims will have no remedies.

To sum up, if both Eurocontrol and the EU invoke privileges as international organizations to enjoy immunity, it seems that claimants' appeal for remedies cannot be justified.

4.3.4 BDS

In China, there is no legislation covering the liability regime of BeiDou Navigation Satellite System (hereinafter referred to as "BDS"), ① as the draft of Satellite Navigation Act is still under discussion among the CAAC, military department and scholars. ② Although BDS has not yet completely emerged into the aviation industry in China, it is initiated by the State Council to promote the application of BDS into aviation. ③ Besides, as the Belt and Road Initiative moves forward, BDS will be applied to building emergency service platform for

---

① BeiDou Navigation Satellite System (BDS) is a GNSS consisting of 35 satellites operated by the Chinese government. The first launch of a BDS satellite was conducted in 2000. BDS started to provide global service on 27 Dec 2018. See more information at http://en.beidou.gov.cn/.

② Xinhua Net News, China finished its first draft on GNSS regulations, Accessed January 5, 2019. http://m.xinhuanet.com/2017-05/23/c_1121021804.htm.

③ Chinese State Council, Medium and Long Term Development Plan of National Satellite Navigation Industry, 2013, p. 97.

the neighboring States along the route, ① which means that cross-border legal issues will involve in GNSS liability in the very near future. Hence, the legislation of BDS is of great importance.

Whereas no special regulations have been established to solve BDS liability, two paths can be proposed for the claimant: contractual liability arrangement under the Contract Law of the People's Republic of China, and third-party liability including product liability under the Tort Law of the People's Republic of China. ②

The substantive laws in the U. S., Russia, the EU and China illustrate various approaches to solve a GNSS liability case and forms a fragmentized picture of legal system for GNSS. It brings obstructions to mitigate the legal conflicts between laws and jurisdictions.

4.4 The Principle of Sovereign Immunity

As briefly touched above, the principle of sovereign immunity raises doubts in jurisdictions and the enforceability of a judgement in foreign jurisdictions. This principle is of interest to the GNSS liability regime due to the public nature of GNSS services. GNSS are under the control of sovereign States, and thus the principle *par in parem non habet imperium*-which forms the basis of State immunity-applies.

Sovereign immunity is a principle founded upon the principles of sovereign equality and independence of States. ③ It involves the immunity from jurisdiction

---

① Chinese State Council, Medium and Long Term Development Plan of National Satellite Navigation Industry, 2013, p. 97.

② Dejian Kong, "Shaping a legal framework for China's BeiDou Navigation Satellite System", *Space Policy* 42, 2017, p. 29.

③ Alina Kaczorowska, *Public International Law*, Abingdon Oxon, Routledge Cavendish, 2005, p. 147.

and the immunity from enforcement. States are entitled to waive the immunity from jurisdiction in which case the municipal courts of the other State may exercise jurisdiction. ① Even so, States may invoke the immunity from enforcement to escape being bound by the judgments.

GNSS services are performing governmental functions operated by States. Since sovereign immunity provides that States cannot commit a legal wrong and are immune from civil suits, the providers of GNSS services receive immunity unless this has been waived by the States themselves. As a corollary, without States' consent, it is impossible for a victim to sue a State before a court to request remedies.

ICAO also acknowledged the legal obstructions that the sovereign immunity may bring to the allocation of liability in a GNSS case and has marked it in its documents for many times. ② As ICAO stated, "the principle of sovereign immunity renders court actions against States or governmental entities providing ATC services by making use of GNSS signals, facilities and services difficult or impossible, when such action is brought abroad." ③ Even though the same tone was repeated frequently in ICAO documents, ④ the international community have not developed corresponding measures to exclude the application of sovereign immunity in a GNSS liability case.

---

① Alina Kaczorowska, *Public International Law*, Abingdon Oxon, Routledge Cavendish, 2005, p. 147.

② See ICAO A35 – WP/75, Report on the Establishment of a Legal Framework with Regard to CNS/ATM Systems Including GNSS, 2004; See also ICAO Doc 9750, AN/963, Global Air Navigation Plan, 2007.

③ ICAO A35 – WP/75, Report on the Establishment of a Legal Framework with Regard to CNS/ATM Systems Including GNSS, 2004, Appendix, section 3.3.1.

④ Ibid.

5. Recommended Solutions

The Panel of Legal and Technical Experts on the Establishment of a Legal Framework with Regard to GNSS (hereinafter referred to as the "LTEP") ① has formulated some recommendations concerning the legal framework of GNSS liability. ② The LTEP stresses that the studies on the liability regime of GNSS should take into account that "appropriate methods of risk coverage should be utilized so as to prevent frustration of legitimate claims". ③ Furthermore, the LTEP notes that it is necessary to pay due regard to the doctrine of sovereign immunity in liability claims based on GNSS services. ④ To solve two matters mentioned above, there are two proposed mechanisms in existence, which respond to the need of assuring risk coverage and clarifying the exclusion of sovereign immunity in GNSS liability claims.

5.1 International Compensation Fund for GNSS Liability

5.1.1 Original Model of the Fund

The first proposed mechanism is to establish an International GNSS Liability Compensation Fund (hereinafter referred to as the "IGLC Fund"). The proposed IGLC Fund is envisaged along the line with the International Oil Pollution Compensation

---

① The LTEP was established by the ICAO Council in 1995. It has been given the mandate to consider the different types of the long-term legal framework for GNSS.

② See generallythe LTEP was established by the ICAO Council in 1995. It has been given the mandate to consider the different types of the long – term legal framework for GNSS.

③ ICAO Doc 9750, AN/963, Global Air Navigation Plan, 2007, section 2 – C – 4.

④ Ibid.

Funds(hereinafter referred to as the "IOPC Funds")[①] which were initially established under the International Convention on the Establishment of an International Compensation Fund for Oil Pollution Damage.[②] The LTEP suggests that the IGLC Fund should be established in case the GNSS signal provider is not sufficient to satisfy the claims for compensation for damages sustained in relation to GNSS.[③]

5.1.2 IGLC Fund's Proposed Mechanism

For the IGLC Fund to be verifiable, further questions need to be answered, including: Who should be the members of the IGLC Fund? How should the fund be financed? What roles should the international or regional organizations play? Similar to the regime of its original model, the IOPC Funds, the IGLC Fund should be established under a specific international convention whose members are the States instead of private entities. The finance of the IGLC Fund comes from contributions paid by GNSS service providers.

However, that envisagement of its financing needs further examinations as it overlooks the differences between liability caused from oil pollution and GNSS. The IOPC Funds are financed by contributions paid by entities that benefit from sea transport. These contributions are based on the amount of oil received in the relevant calendar year, and cover expected claims, together with the costs of administering the Funds. Oil pollution is attributable to the sea transport where merchants do business and chase interests, while the provider of GNSS signal,

---

① The IOPC Funds used to include the 1971 Fund, the 1992 Fund and the Supplementary Fund. The 1971 Fund was dissolved in 2014. The IOPC Funds continues to provide financial compensation for oil pollution damage resulting from spills of persistent oil from tankers. See more information at http://www.iopcfunds.org/about-us/.

② International Convention on the Establishment of an International Compensation Fund for Oil Pollution Damage, Brussels, 18 December 1971, United Nations Treaties, Vol. 1110, No. 17146, Accessed January 5, 2019. https://treaties.un.org/doc/Publication/UNTS/Volume% 201110/volume-1110-I-17146-English.pdf.

③ See Alessandra A. L. Andrade, *Navigating into the New Millennium: The Global Navigation Satellite System Regulatory Framework*, New York, Ashgate Publishing, 2001, p. 137.

does not charge for using the service. Compared with business relying on sea transport, GNSS is more likely to be considered as a public service since the provider does not aim to make profits directly through the application. The military nature of GNSS cannot be neglected. In terms of GPS, it was first developed by the military department of the U. S., though the U. S. government implied that it has commercial usage, the civil part of GPS is still free and open to the public without fees. In the same manner, no fees are charged to the application of GLONASS, Galileo and BDS. Hence, the people who benefit from using of GNSS should be obliged to pay a sum of money to the international compensation fund. In the aviation area, both air carriers and airports should contribute to the IGLC Fund on the basis of their margins from running business.

5.2 International Liability Convention for GNSS

5.2.1 Stagnation of Concluding an International Convention

Another proposal to deal with the legal inadequacy of GNSS liability regime is to conclude an international liability convention for GNSS.① Since the application of GNSS not only concerns with aviation industry, but also the maritime and the space segments, the legal regime of GNSS should be coordinated with the above three segments in order to foster a uniformed legislative framework. Therefore, the proposed international convention should be advanced by International Civil Aviation Organization, International Maritime Organization (IMO)② and the United Nations Committee on the Peaceful Uses of

① ICAO A35 - WP/125, ECAC States, GNSS Development of a Contractual Framework Leading Towards a Long - Term Legal Framework to Govern the Implementation of GNSS, 2004, Appendix C.

② International Maritime Organization (IMO) is a United Nations specialized agency with responsibility for the safety and security of shipping and the prevention of marine and atmospheric pollution by ships. See more information at http: //www. imo. org/en/About/Pages/Default. aspx.

Outer Space(UNCOPUOS).①

However, in 1998, the ICAO Council, the Legal Committee, and the LTEP exhaustively examined the issues concerning GNSS, without coming into a consensus that any major changes are needed at the point.② ICAO asserted that the implementation of GNSS did not face fundamental legal obstacles.③ In 2004, another ICAO Secretariat report held that it was premature to conclude an international convention.④ Until now, this proposal has been at a standstill.

5.2.2 Reasons to Push Forward the Proposal

Although there are voices against developing an international convention, the paper submitted by African States, the European Community and Japan demonstrated that many States are in favor of developing an international convention.⑤ Furthermore, the pattern of GNSS has turned from a GPS-monopolized world into a situation where GPS, GLONASS, Galileo and BDS co-exist. It follows that the conflicts between laws will be aggravated, leaving GNSS services in a frustrating legal environment. The context by which ICAO concluded as premature has changed to a great extent. The legal inadequacy of GNSS liability regime is impeditive for the development of GNSS industry so there is an urgent need to improve the situation.

Moreover, the concept of "right time", as the antonym to "premature", should be rigorously scrutinized before it is introduced into the completion of

---

① The United Nations Committee on the Peaceful Uses of Outer Space(UNCOPUOS) was set up by the UN General Assembly in 1959 to govern the exploration and use of space for the benefit of all humanity: for peace, security and development. See more information at www.unoosa.org/oosa/COPUOS/copuos.html.

② ICAO WW/IMP WP/74, *Information-Legal Implications of CNS/ATM*, 1998, p. 1.

③ Ibid.

④ ICAO A35 - WP/125, ECAC States, GNSS Development of a Contractual Framework Leading Towards a Long - Term Legal Framework to Govern the Implementation of GNSS, 2004, p. 4.

⑤ Ibid.

legislation. In human history, the completion and improvement of legislation are always motivated by some incidents. There have been no cases directly related to GNSS liability until now, which decreases the society's concern on it. As lawyers, however, it is crucial to bear in mind that, law should be forward-looking, trying to overcome the hysteresis quality which is inherited from itself. Furthermore, an international convention can be amended with multiple practices responding to the development of technologies. The interpretative documents can also serve as supplements to the provisions.

6. Conclusions

GNSS services can influence the aviation industry to a great extent. The legal regime for GNSS liability issues, therefore, constitutes an essential part of air law. However, the Chicago Convention, Warsaw System and Montreal Convention, as vital legal instruments in air law, do not deal with the GNSS issues with a satisfactory focus on the complex characteristics of this technology. Legal ambiguity exists in the current civil liability regime for GNSS. The contractual regime for allocating liability, which can clarify the obligations and rights in advance, is nevertheless inadequate to solve the liability issues due to the relativity of contracts. The third-party liability issues can only be solved in a non-contractual regime. Even though the principles of strict liability and fault liability seems to provide general guidance in solving the non-contractual liability issues, no specialized legislation has yet been found in either international or domestic law with regard to the damage caused by a faulty GNSS signal to an aircraft, leading to the aggravation of legal uncertainty. The inadequacy of the legal regime for GNSS liability also reflects in the difficulty to identify the proper defendants, multi-jurisdictions and the possibility to invoke sovereign immunity, which impede the completion and perfection of such legal regime. To remove the legal barriers, it is therefore highly recommended to establish an international fund on GNSS liability and conclude an international convention to eliminate the legal uncertainty as well as to maintain the integrity of the legal regime.

Foreign Investment Protection of the Business of Aviation: Can the Air Carriers' Operation be a Protected Investment for the Purposes of Foreign Investment Protection in the host State?

DANIELA MARÍA ROJAS GARCÍA*

This paper aims at analyzing the possibility of an airline to frame its operation as a protected investment for the purposes of foreign investment protection within a foreign host State. This, given that the traditional remedies provided by the public air law regime appear to provide less efficient and effective legal avenues, which is commercially and financially unsustainable. This paper was researched and written under the

---

* LL. M Candidate of the Advanced Programme of Air and Space Law of Leiden University, a Colombian-Qualified Attorney Specialised in International Transport Law and International Dispute Resolution.

mindset that an airline is no more and no less than a commercial undertaking that operates to make healthy revenues and profits, just as much as any other industry in the world.

1. INTRODUCTION

The business of airlines is known to be an inherently international commercial and cross-border operation that fosters economic development and purports for commercially viable and sound performance. However, the avenues that airlines have traditionally sought to demand compensation from negative economic consequences derived from the action of States, have mostly proven ineffective to protect the financial interests of a multimillion-dollar enterprise.

The violation of the State's obligations derived from the aviation law regime, is not only capable of engaging the States liability towards other States but should also suffice to trigger full compensation towards affected airlines as commercial undertakings. The aim of this paper is, therefore, to analyse if an airline can make recourse to the investment law regime to receive appropriate compensation for such damages, on the basis of the breach of the air law obligations but from the standpoint and under the protections of the investment law regime. To this end, this paper studies the protection of the airlines' business from the air law regime; and the business of an airline from and investment law perspective, to then come to some conclusions.

2. The Protection of the Airlines' Business from the Air Law Regime—The Chicago System

The legal regime created to harmonize and unify civil aviation through the

Convention on International Civil Aviation (hereinafter, the "Chicago Convention"), created an underlying intent: to protect the commercial undertaking that is an airline, considering that airlines, just as any other business, are focused on making healthy profits and returns.① The Contracting States of the Chicago Convention put the international interests of aviation above the purely regional and individual State interests in air transportation,② agreeing to limit their sovereignty over their airspace "to plan the future development of international aviation, to help create and preserve friendship and understanding among the nations and peoples of the world".③

This underlying intent is found throughout the text of the Chicago Convention, starting with its Preamble,④ to the more specific and economically focused provisions such as those found in Articles 9,⑤ 15,⑥ or 79,⑦ where it is evident that the Contracting States aimed at providing for sound financial

① McGeorge(1994), at 305, 309 -310.

② Macintosh(2008).

③ McGeorge(1994), at 305, 309 -310

④ Chicago Convention, 1944, Preamble: "(...) that international civil aviation may be developed in a safe and orderly manner, and that international air transport services may be established on the basis of equality of opportunity and operated soundly and economically."

⑤ Chicago Convention, 1944, Article 9 (a)—Prohibited Areas: "Each Contracting State may, for reasons of military necessity or public safety, restrict or prohibit uniformly the aircraft of other States from flying over certain areas of its territory, provided that no distinction is made in this respect between the aircraft of the State whose territory is involved, engaged in international schedule airline services and the aircraft of the other contracting States likewise engaged."

⑥ Chicago Convention, 1944, Article 15—Airport and Similar Charges: "Every airport in a Contracting State which is open to public use by its national aircraft shall likewise, subject to the provisions of Article 68, be open under uniform conditions to the aircraft of all the other contracting States (...) Any charges that may be imposed or permitted to be imposed by a Contracting State for the use of such airports and air navigation facilities by the aircraft of any other Contracting State shall not be higher[as to other aircraft in similar conditions](...)"

⑦ Chicago Convention, 1944, Article 79—Participation in Operating Organizations: "A State may participate in joint operating organizations or in pooling agreements, either through an airline company or companies designated by its government. The companies may, at the sole discretion of the State concerned, be State-owned or privately owned."

conditions for "airline companies" worldwide. The Chicago Convention created a system of rights which are further developed by the States themselves[①] through bilateral[②] or plurilateral[③] treaties (hereinafter, the "Chicago System") for air carriers to operate free of common taxes, duties and fees, generally imposed to any other domestic of foreign commercial undertakings, creating beneficial conditions for "sound economic operation".

From a purely operational perspective, the business of an airline is inherently cross-border, and usually international.[④] Simultaneously, airlines are seen as a special public interest where transportation is the apex of globalization and interconnection.[⑤] Yet, historically, airlines' recourse to settle disputes and claim damages derived from them operating in a foreign country, remains exclusive to either a State-to-State rationale, where States settle aviation disputes on the basis of the Chicago System,[⑥] by means of exhausting local remedies or by using the more traditional options of diplomatic channels. Despite the international and global operation that is natural for the aviation enterprise, airlines remain strictly adhered to the stringent national regulation of their State of Registration and to their dispute settlement provisions.[⑦]

This exclusivity, which is not only found in the dispute resolution provisions, but also on the outdated ownership and control clauses,[⑧] imposes an unnecessary market barrier for airlines to claim compensation for financial losses

---

① Macintosh (2008).

② See for example, Costa Rica-Germany ATA, 2004; Colombia-Mexico ATA, 1975.

③ See for example, The Fortaleza Agreement, 2001; EU-US Open Skies, 2007.

④ Steinberg & Kotuby (2011), at 460.

⑤ Dempsey (2003), at 235, 241.

⑥ Chicago Convention (1944), Articles 84 Settlement of Disputes and 85 Arbitration Procedure.

⑦ Steinberg & Kotuby (2011), at 459.

⑧ Havel & Sánchez (2011), at 648.

derived from the action of a host State (or State of Destination), whenever such action tampers, interferes or jeopardizes the operation of the airline and affects its rights and obligations towards third parties including its users.

The aviation industry, just as much as any other industry, has suffered the negative consequences of foreign State action, but was not provided with legal standing to directly claim appropriate compensation. This State-to-State exclusivity makes sense from a traditional public international law perspective, where only States are subjects of international law and therefore, only States have legal standing against other States. ① This is precisely the exclusivity that Air Canada has attempted surpass in its most recent claim against the Republic of Venezuela, where the action of the State *de facto* prevents the airline to repatriate its capitals from Venezuela to Canada. As far as the publicly available information shows, on 13 January 2017, Air Canada filed a Request for Arbitration before the International Centre for the Settlement of Investment Disputes (ICSID) under the ICSID Additional Facility Rules to claim compensation for such action. ②

Should any industry be excluded from ordinary regimes of investment protection? Instinctively, the answer is that there is no reason for such an exclusion. Yet, the authentically global enterprise—the airline—remains excluded from the "fully liberalized trade and investment rules" ③ with no justification for this segregation. Provided that airlines are "doing business" abroad, just as any other business or enterprise, ④ airlines have or should have

---

① Miles (2008); Steinberg & Kotuby (2011), at 461.

② Air Canada v. Venezuela, on IPH (2018). According to the publicly available information, by 14 December 2018, the Claimant had filed a reply memorial on the merits, as well as a counter-memorial on jurisdiction. For more information at https://icsid.worldbank.org/en/Pages/cases/casedetail.aspx? Case No = ARB (AF)/17/1.

③ Havel & Sánchez (2011), at 647.

④ IATA, Agenda for Freedom.

full access to the protections available to all other businesses. Airlines should be able to find legal standing to directly claim against the foreign State—the State of Destination—whenever its action negatively impacts its operation as a commercial air services provider. The only regime that provides precisely for that standing is the foreign investment law regime, to which most States are parties. ①

This argument is not to be understood as an attempt to circumvent the, rather exclusive, public aviation law regime, nor to ignore or disregard the rules, rights and obligations contained in the Chicago System. On the contrary, it should be understood as an attempt to find an additional and sometimes better, more efficient legal avenue to claim compensation and to recover rightly quantified damages and economic losses, on the basis of the negative consequences that the State's breach of an international air law obligation has over the airline enterprise.

With this reasoning, the following Section of this paper will find the common ground between public air law and international investment law, to determine if the business of an airline can in abstract, constitute a protected investment for the purposes of foreign investment protection.

3. The Business of an Airline from an Investment Law Perspective

International investment law, just like public air law, is contained in bilateral or multilateral treaties that provide private entities with legal standing to directly claim against a foreign State, the host State of their investment. These

① Robbins(2006), at 406, 413.

legal instruments, known as international investment agreements (IIAs), have eliminated the difficulties of recourse to diplomatic protection and of the State-to-State exclusivity of public international law, by conferring international law rights directly to individual investors; in this manner, private entities gained access to both substantive and procedural rights and obligations—and ultimately, autonomous legal standing—for them to take legal action directly against the host State in binding Investor-State Arbitration. ① With this regime, the Claimant/Airline is free from requiring its home State's involvement, and therefore, of other burdens that generally come from setting into motion the traditional diplomatic channels. IIAs contain their own dispute settlement provisions for Investors to bring claims against the host State, which constitutes the State's consent to arbitrate all disputes that arise from a Protected Investment as regulated by the treaty itself. ②

Recourse to investment arbitrationregarding air transit services is usually not expressly included, nor excluded in IIAs. The subject of investment protection (the element of jurisdiction *ratione personae*), is a natural or legal person, commercial undertaking, firm or association, national of the home State. ③ The object of protection of IIAs (the element of jurisdiction *ratione materiae*) is usually any and/or all forms of assets derived from an operation performed by the "protected investor" inside the territory of the host State. ④ Save for the very few exceptions where the air transit sector is expressly excluded, airlines and their operation can be encompassed in the definition of "investor" and of

---

① Steinberg & Kotuby (2011), at 403, 415.

② Ecuador v. Chevron (2011), at 384, 393.

③ Nationality for the purposes of corporations includes considerations such as the principal place of business, the domicile of the central administration, the registered office, the place of substantial business, etc. See for example, Colombia-UK BIT, 2014 Article 1.

④ See for example, Venezuela-Netherlands BIT, 1991, Article 1.

"investment" for the purposes of foreign investment protection. Of course, whenever such express exclusion is present in an IIA, the airline could be *prima facie* prevented from accessing foreign investment protection, but that is merely the exception to the general rule. This is the case of the US-Argentina BIT, where the United States expressly reserved the right of maintaining limited exceptions to foreign investment protections in the air transport sector. ①

These express carve-outs are not very common and even when they are present, they do not completely isolate the entire field of aviation from the entire foreign investment regime. ② The US-Argentina BIT, for example, maintains limitations to the investment protection of National Treatment, but does not make reservations in respect to the obligation to provide Full Protection and Security③ and Fair and Equitable Treatment. ④

This Section will address, in abstract, the generalities of the two main issues of an investment case from the perspective of and airline, dealing with (3.1) the jurisdictional grounds of the case, and (3.2) the merits of the case:

3.1 The Jurisdictional Grounds of the Case

For a commercial entity to benefit from foreign investment protections, it must be able to successfully argue that it falls under the definition of "protected

---

① US-Argentina BIT, 1991, Protocol, Sections 2 and 5.

② Steinberg & Kotuby(2011), at 415.

③ *Asian Agricultural Products v. Sri Lanka*, ¶79: In this case involving the battle between the security forces of Sri Lanka and the insurgents that destroyed a shrimp farm during the Tamil Insurrection, the arbitral tribunal found that a promise to provide full protection and security can mean an absolute standard imposing strict liability. The basis of this case was the Sri Lanka-United Kingdom Bilateral Investment Treaty, from which the arbitral tribunal declared that Sri Lanka had violated its obligation of providing full protection and security by not taking all possible measures to prevent the destruction of the investment, event in the State had had no part in the insurrection and the violence itself. See also: Malik(2011), at 5.

④ US-Argentina BIT, 1991, Article Ⅱ.2(a)

investor" (*ratione personae*); however, the analysis of this element of jurisdiction falls outside of the scope of this paper. Be it sufficient to say that the jurisdiction *ratione personae* for an airline will face its own different interpretations even despite the existence of the national ownership and control clauses of the majority of bilateral and multilateral air transit agreements, because in the context of foreign investment, the character of a "protected investor" related to air services suppliers will not only be the airline, but a case could be made to find that the financiers, the lenders, the special purpose vehicles of an aircraft finance transaction, to name a few examples, could seek protection of their (direct or indirect) "investment" in a foreign State. ①

The question of whether the operation of an airline falls under the definition of "protected investment" relates to the element of jurisdiction *ratione materiae*, which simply put, refers to the subject-matter of the dispute that is capable of being submitted to international investment arbitration. ②

Both the definition of "investor" and of "investment" are found in the text of the applicable IIA and are different for each agreement, as they are the result of the States' negotiations. It is not possible to make a cross-cutting analysis to determine if, in all cases, airlines and the rights and obligations contained in the air law regime, can be subjects of foreign investment protection. This conclusion can only be reached on a case-by-case basis.

However, for the purposes of this paper, the analysis is based on the presumption that the airline complies with the jurisdiction *ratione personae*, *i. e.*, it is a "protected investor". Therefore, this paper will touch on the possibility of framing the airline's operation under the jurisdiction *ratione*

① For a general analysis of the nationality and ownership and control clause on aviation law, see Havel & Sánchez (2011).

② Sornarajah (2008), at 872.

materiae. The analysis can be made through the most common definition of "investment", as found in Article 1(a) of the Venezuela-Netherlands BIT:

"The term 'investments' shall comprise very kind of asset and more particularly though not exclusively: (i) Movable and immovable property, as well as any other rights in rem in respect of every kind of asset; (ii) Rights derived from shares, bonds and other kinds of interests in companies and joint ventures; (iii) Title to money, to other assets or to any performance having an economic value; (iv) Rights in the field of intellectual property(...); (v) Rights granted under public law(...)" ①

The quoted provision is a common one mostly found in the first generation of IIAs, and has been broadly interpreted by arbitral tribunals, as encompassing quite literally "every kind of asset". Tribunals such as the *Fedax v. Venezuela*,② and *ČSOB v. Slovakia*③ have found in favour of the Claimant investors, providing protection to their investments in the territory of the host States. These interpretations were based precisely on the "wide-opening phrases" of the provisions of the relevant IIAs, where the tribunals found that the *intent of the parties* was not to limit the scope of the definition of "investment".④

It cannot be denied that the operation of the airline is, by its very nature, structured to extend above and beyond any national border, and to "spread over the entire surface of the earth",⑤ which is why it could be possible for a Respondent State to challenge the jurisdiction *ratione materiae* of an investment tribunal, on the grounds that the operation is not entirely performed within the territory of the host State. However, an airline can just as well make its case based

---

① Venezuela-Netherlands BIT, 1991, Article 1(a).

② *Fedax v. Venezuela*, ¶¶ 1, 16, 19, 31-32.

③ *ČSOB v. Slovakia*, ¶ 77.

④ Campbell, Shore & Weiniger(2007), ¶ 6.31.

⑤ Boyer(2010), at 93, 110.

on the broader interpretations of territoriality that many investment tribunals have made when they have dealt with cross-border economic operations. The fact that the operation of the airline is not entirely performed within the territory of one State, or that a portion of the operation is performed outside of it, should not automatically prevent it from foreign investment protection. ①

One of the most notable examples of this broad interpretation of the territoriality of an investment is found in the *SGS v. Philippines* case: the Swiss investor demanded compensation for its claims to cash derived from a service contract to perform import services and associated customs revenue, performed both within and outside the Philippines. ② SGS' cross-border operation closely resembles that of a foreign airline: in that case, the investor/airline, will not only be exercising traffic rights derived from the bilateral air transit agreements (*i. e.* inside and outside the granting State/host State), but it will also acquire additional rights and obligations with third parties, ③ closely intertwined with the provision of air services, all of which can be partly performed abroad, without such character depriving the airline of its link with the host State. The object of analysis and protection for these purposes should be the entire web of rights and obligations derived from the *operation* of the airline in a foreign territory, which will ultimately impact the quantification of damages in the merits' stage of the case.

3.2 The Merits of the Case

Broadly put, the majority of IIAs contain mostly unrestricted foreign

① Steinberg & Kotuby(2011), at 471.

② *SGS v. Philippines*, ¶¶ 99 – 103. See also: *SGS v. Pakistam*, ¶¶ 133, 143.

③ These rights and obligations range from mere licenses, permits and authorizations issued by the host State and often contingent to the payment of the foreign airline for local usage charges for en-route and terminal area services as well as charges for meteorological and aeronautical information, to commercial deals with suppliers of connected services, such as hotels, travel agencies, fueling, maintenance and repair, catering, baggage handling and cargo related services, etc.

investment protections that provide for substantive rights, as opposed to merely procedural rules, allowing foreign investors to claim compensation in a host State whenever a dispute that arises from the "protected investment", carried out within the territory of the host State, and in accordance with its laws. These substantive rights are naturally paired with compulsory arbitration clauses, that do not usually exclude aviation from its scope. ①

Companies from all industries, including those that provide air-related services, have sought compensation for direct and indirect expropriation, ② for adjudication of breaches of contracts with foreign national governments (the umbrella clauses), ③ and for protection from the imposition of unreasonable and discriminatory measures by the host State. ④ This tendency, appears to be only present in undertakings that provide additional goods or services related to the air transportation industry, but the air service providers continue to shy away from this beneficial procedural and substantive law regime. Airlines thus, continue to seek assistance of their home governments—through diplomatic channels or through the ICAO dispute settlement system—to tackle purely commercial issues that could be better and more efficiently dealt with, directly between the airline and the host State.

One of the most relevant benefits that any foreign investor enjoys

---

① Steinberg & Kotuby(2011), at 471.

② See for example: *Fraport v. Philippines* (case related to the expropriation of contract rights in an international air terminal); *Teinver v. Argentina* (claims raised under the Argentina-Spain Bilateral Investment Treaty for the alleged expropriation of the national airline by the government of Argentina).

③ See for example *Austrian Airlines v. Slovakia*(claim derived from the breach of contract of Slovakia in relation to the dents of the airline acquired and operated by the protected investor).

④ See for example *EDF v. Romania*(where the UK investor, an operator of the duty-free stores in the Romanian airports, sought compensation from the Romanian government for the enactment of new strict regulations for the operation of those types of stores. Such strict regulations led to the revocation of the investor's operating license in Romania. The Claimant sought protection through appropriate compensation on the basis of unreasonable, arbitrary and discriminatory measures).

through the investment law regime, in the form of protections such as national treatment, ① most favoured nation, ② full protection & security and fair & equitable treatment, ③ expropriation, ④ free capital transfer⑤ and currency

① See for example: NAFTA, Section A—National Treatment: "Article 301: National Treatment: 1. Each Party shall accord national treatment to the goods of another Party in accordance with Article Ⅲ of the General Agreement on Tariffs and Trade (GATT), including its interpretative notes, and to this end Article Ⅲ of the GATT and its interpretative notes, or any equivalent provision of a successor agreement to which all Parties are party, are incorporated into and made part of this Agreement. 2. The provisions of paragraph 1 regarding national treatment shall mean, with respect to a state or province, treatment no less favorable than the most favorable treatment accorded by such state or province to any like, directly competitive or substitutable goods, as the case may be, of the Party of which it forms a part. 3. Paragraphs 1 and 2 do not apply to the measures set out in Annex 301. 3."

② German Model BIT, Article 3: "National and most-favored-nation treatment (1) Neither Contracting State shall in its territory subject investments owned or controlled by investors of the other Contracting State to treatment less favorable than it accords to investments of its own investors or to investments of investors of any third State. (2) Neither Contracting State shall in its territory subject investors of the other Contracting State, as regards their activity in connection with investments, to treatment less favorable than it accords to its own investors or to investors of any third State(...)"

③ Colombia Model BIT, Article Ⅲ: 3: "Each Party shall accord fair and equitable treatment in accordance with customary international law and full protection and security in its territory to investments of investors of the other Contracting Party."

④ Switzerland-Colombia BIT, 2006, Article 6: "Expropriation and Compensation: Neither of the Parties shall take, either directly or indirectly, measures of expropriation, nationalization or any other measures having the same nature or the same effect against investments of investors of the other Party, unless the measures are taken in the public interest, on a non-discriminatory basis and under due process of law, and provided that provisions be made for prompt, effective and adequate compensation. Such compensation shall amount to the market value of the investment expropriated immediately before the expropriatory action was taken or became public knowledge, whichever is earlier. The amount of compensation shall include interest at a normal commercial rate from the date of dispossession until the date of payment, shall be settled in a freely convertible currency, be paid without delay and be freely transferable. The investor affected shall have a right of review, under the law of the Party making the expropriation, by a judicial or other independent authority of that Party, of his case and or the valuation of his investment in accordance with the principles set out in this Article."

⑤ Australia-Argentina BIT, 2005, Article 5. 1: "Each Contracting Party shall grant to an investor of the other Contracting Party the unrestricted right to transfer abroad funds related to an investment."

convertibility,① among others, is that the regime itself creates the objective criteria to appropriately quantify damages in order to seek and get full compensation. These protections are triggered whenever the host State breaches an obligation or violates a right of private entity, including international air law obligations. There is no reason to exclude the substantive air law rules derived from the public air law regime, such as the obligation of not imposing discriminatory measures in relation to air navigation services, ② or charges and duties on airports,③ from the investment law regime in order to seek award for suitable financial compensation.

In fact, the Chicago Convention contains similar goals to protect the industry from discriminatory treatment,④ to provide an environment of strong economic operation,⑤ and a unified set of rules for international civil aviation. ⑥

4. The Aviation Industry is Moving Towards Investment Protection

Indeed, as of the date of writing of this paper, only Air Canada has initiated

① EU-Japan IIA 2018, Chapter 9 – Capital Movements, Payments and Transfers and Temporary Safeguard Measures: "Article 9.1. Current Account: Without prejudice to other provisions of this Agreement, each Party shall allow, in freely convertible currency, and in accordance with the Articles of Agreement of the International Monetary Fund, as applicable, any payments and transfers with regard to transactions on the current account of the balance of payments which fall within the scope of this Agreement. For the purposes of this Chapter, "freely convertible currency" means a currency that can be freely exchanged against currencies that are widely traded in international foreign exchange markets and widely used in international transactions. For greater certainty, currencies that are widely traded in international foreign exchange markets and widely used in international transactions include freely usable currencies as designated by the IMF in accordance with the Articles of Agreement of the International Monetary Fund."

② Chicago Convention, 1944, Article 28.

③ Chicago Convention, 1944, Article 15.

④ See for example, Chicago Convention, 1944, Articles 9 and 44.

⑤ Chicago Convention, 1944, Preamble.

⑥ See for example, Chicago Convention, 1944, Article 33.

arbitration under the investment law regime. Other players of the aviation value chain, mostly entities on airport infrastructure, have submitted investment protection claims against host States; for example, the Claimant in *ADC v. Hungary* claimed that against the host State on the basis of its rights under a contract entered into with the Hungarian State Agency ATAA for the renovation, construction and operation of two air terminals in the Budapest-Ferihegy International Airport in Hungary. ① Amongst the different challenges on jurisdiction, Respondent argued that the tribunal was prevented from hearing the case because the Claimant's claims were purely contractual in nature; ② however, after analysing the substance of the transaction, ③ the tribunal found that the legislation passed by the government severely diminished the rights and the legitimate expectations of the investor. ④

Likewise, in *Aeroport Belbek and Kolomoisky v. Russia*, the investor claimed against Russia on for the alleged expropriation of the commercial passenger terminal operated by the claimant in the airport, following the annexation of Crimea; ⑤ in *Flughafen Zürich v. Venezuela* the dispute arose from the Government's alleged expropriation, through governmental action, of the Claimant's concession to operate the Isla Margarita Airport under a contract with the State of Nueva Esparta. ⑥

---

① *ADC v. Hungary*.

② *ADC v. Hungary*, ¶¶234, 301.

③ *ADC v. Hungary*, ¶325. For this, the tribunal relied in the findings of the arbitral tribunals in *CMS Gas Transmission Company v. The Republic of Argentina*, *ICSID Case No. ARB*/01/8, ¶27, and *Enron Corporation*, *et al.* *v. The Argentine Republic*, *ICISD Case No. ARB*/01/03, ¶60.

④ *ADC v. Hungary*, ¶304.

⑤ *Aeroport Belbek and Kolomoisky v. Russia*.

⑥ *Flughafen Zürich v. Venezuela*. Other examples include: *Frapport v. Philippines* (Ⅲ), derived from direct and indirect shareholding in a project company that held certain rights under a concession agreement for building and operating an airport terminal; *Mailcorp v. Egypt*, where the Claimant raised claims against the Respondent derived from the State's rescission of the contract for the construction and operation of Ras Sudr international airport in Sinai.

There does not seem to be a significant difference on whether or not the undertaking is an operative airline or the construction of an airport terminal, as long as the foreign commercial operation is, in itself, entitled to rights and obligations derived from the conduction of its business in the territory of a host State with which the host State has an IIA providing for their protection.

5. Conclusion

From a legal perspective the investment law regime gives airlines legal standing to directly claim against a foreign government, without such recourse meaning that the aviation law regime is discarded. On the contrary the public air law obligations are to be used as the legal grounds to apportion liability to the breaching State, which is why an investment case related raised by an airline undisputedly requires both the air law and the investment law regimes. Simply put, the international air law obligations of the States provide the legal basis of the airline's claims, whereas the investment protections provide the legal avenues to quantify the damages and justify full compensation.

From a commercial standpoint it appears that recourse to this strategy would allow airlines to directly enforce the rights that the Chicago System envisioned to protect.

Bibliography

Doctrine	
1. Boyer M. Christine, *Aviation and the Aerial View: Le Corbusier's Spatial Transformations in the* 1930*s and* 1940*s*, Diatrics, Volume 33, No. 3/4, New Coordinates: Spatial Mappings, National Trajectories, The John Hopkins University Press, 2010	Boyer(2010)

续表

Doctrine	
2. Campbell McLachlan, Shore Laurence and Weiniger Matthew, *International Investment Arbitration, Substantive Principles*, Oxford University Press, 2007	Campbell, Shore & Weiniger(2007)
3. Dempsey Paul Steven, "Transportation: A Legal History", *Transportation Law Journal* 30, 2003	Dempsey(2003)
4. Havel Brian, Sάnchez Gabrial S., "The Emerging Lex Aviatica", *Georgetown Journal of International Law* 42, 2011	Havel & Sάnchez (2011)
5. Macintosh Andrew, "Overcoming the Barriers to International Aviation Greenhouse Gas Emissions Abatement", Australian National University Center for Climate Law and Policy, Working Paper Series 2008/2, 2008	Macintosh(2008)
6. Malik Mahnaz, "The Full Protection and Security Standard Comes of Age: Yet Another Challenge for States in Investment Treaty Arbitration?", *International Institute for Sustainable Development, Best Practices Series*, 2011	Malik(2011)
7. McGeorge Robert L., "An Introduction and Commerntary: Revisiting the Role of Liveral Trade Policy in Promoting Idealistic Objectives of the International Legal Order", *Northern Illinois University Law Review* 14, 1994	McGeorge(1994)
8. Miles Katie, "A Political Juncture for International Investment Law: Breaking from the Past or Reproducing Economic Imperialism?", No. 3, 2008	Miles(2008)
9. Robbins Joshua, "The Emergence of Positive Obligations in Bilateral Investment Treaties", *University of Miami International and Comparative Law Review*, 2006	Robbins(2006)
10. Sornarajah M., *The International Law on Foreign Investment*, Third Edition, Cambridge University Press, New York, 2010, p. 308; see also *Jurisdiction and Admissibility* in Oxford Handbook of International Investment Law, Oxford University Press, 2008	Sornarajah(2008)

续表

Doctrine	
11. Steinberg Andrew B., Kotuby Charles T. Jr., "Bilateral Investment Treaties and International Air Transportation: A New Tool for Global Airlines to Redress Market Barriers", *Journal of Air Law and Commerce* 76, 2011	Steinberg & Kotuby (2011)
International Conventions	
1. Agreement Between the European Union and Japan for an Economic Partnership, signed on 17 July 2018	EU-Japan IIA, 2018
2. Agreement Between the Government of Australia and the Government of the Argentine Republic on the Promotion and Protection of Investments, signed on 23 August 1995	Australia-Argentina BIT, 2005
3. Agreement Between the Republic of Colombia and the Swiss Confederation on the Promotion and Reciprocal Protection of Investments, signed on 17 May 2006	Switzerland-Colombia BIT, 2006
4. Agreement on the Encouragement and Reciprocal Protection of Investments Between the Kingdom of the Netherlands and the Republic of Venezuela, of 22 October 1991	Venezuela-Netherlands BIT, 1991
5. Agreement on Subregional Air Navigation Services signed by the Republics of Chile, Argentina, Bolivia, Brazil, Paraguay and Uruguay of 16 February 2001 – The Fortaleza Agreement	Fortaleza Agreement, 2001
6. Air Transit Agreement between the Republic of Costa Rica and the Federal Republic of Germany signed on 14 October 2004	Costa Rica-Germany ATA, 2004
7. Air Transport Agreement between the Republic of Colombia and the United Mexican States, signed on 9 January 1975	Colombia-Mexico ATA, 1975
8. Colombian Model Treaty for Bilateral Agreement for the Promotion and Protection of Investments of the Republic of Colombia, of August 2007	Colombian Model BIT
9. Bilateral Agreement for the Promotion and Protection of Investments Between theGovernment of the United Kingdom of Great Britain and Northern Ireland and the Republic of Colombia, of 17 March 2010, Treaty Series No. 24(2014)	Colombia-UK BIT, 2014

续表

International Conventions	
10. German Model Treaty Concerning the Encouragement and Reciprocal Protection of Investments, Federal Ministry of Economics and Technology, 2008	German Model BIT
11. International Civil Aviation Organization-ICAO-*Convention on International Civil Aviation*, ICAO Doc. No. 7300/9, Ninth Edition(2006), signed at Chicago on 7 December 1944	Chicago Convention, 1944
12. North America Free Trade Agreement between the United States of America, the United Mexican States and Canada signed on 1 January 1994	NAFTA
13. Open Skies Agreement between the European Union and the United States of America, signed on 25 and 30 April 2007	EU-US Open Skies, 2007
14. Treaty Between the United States of America and the Argentine Republic Concerning the Reciprocal Encouragement and Protection of Investment, of 14 November 1991	US-Argentina BIT, 1991
International Case Law	
1. *ADC Affiliate Limited and ADC & ADMC Management Limited v. Republic of Hungary*, ICSID Case No. ARB/03/16, Award of the Tribunal, 2 October 2006	*ADC v. Hungary*
2. *Aeroport Belbek LLC and Igor Valerievich Kolomoisky v. The Russian Federation*, PCA Case No. 2015 – 07, 24 February 2017	*Aeroport Belbek and Kolomoisky v. Russia*
3. *Asian Agricultural Products Ltd. v. Republic of Sri Lanka*, ICSID Case No. ARB/87/3, Final Award, 27 June 1990	*Asian Agricultural Products v. Sri Lanka*
4. *Austrian Airlines v. The Slovak Republic*, UNCITRAL, Final Award, 9 October 2009	*Austrian Airlines v. Slovakia*
5. *Československa Obchodni Banka, A. S. (ČSOB) v. The Slovak Republic*, ICSID Case No. ARB/97/4, Decision of the Tribunal on Objections to Jurisdiction, 24 May 1999	*ČSOB v. Slovakia*

续表

International Case Law	
6. *EDF (Services) Limited v. Romania*, ICSID Case No. ARB/05/13, Award, 8 October 2009	*EDF v. Romania*
7. *Fedax N. V. v. The Republic of Venezuela*, Decision of the Tribunal on Objections to Jurisdiction, 11 July 1997	*Fedax v. Venezuela*
8. *Flughafen Zürich A. G. and Gestión e Ingenería IDC S. A. v. Bolivarian Republic of Venezuela*, ICSID Case No. ARB/10/19, 18 November 2014	*Flughafen Zürich v. Venezuela*
9. *Fraport AG Airport Services Worldwide v. Republic of the Philippines*, ICSID Case No. ARB/03/25, Annulment Proceeding, 23 December 2010	*Fraport v. Philippines*
10. *Mailcorp Limited v. Arab Republic of Egypt*, ICSID Case No. ARB/08/18, 7 February 2011	*Mailcorp v. Egypt*
11. *SGS Société Générale de Surveillance S. A. v. Republic of the Philippines*, ICSID Case No. ARB/02/6, Decision of the Tribunal on Objections to Jurisdiction, 29 January 2004	*SGS v. Philippines*
12. *Societé Génégale de Surveillance S. A. v. Islamic Republic of Pakistan*, ICSID Case No. ARB/01/13, Decision on Jurisdiction, 6 August 2003	*SGS v. Pakistan*
13. *Teinver S. A., Transportes de Cercanías S. A. and Autobuses Urbanos del Sur S. A. v. The Argentine Republic*, ICSID Case No. ARB/09/1, 21 July 2017	*Teinver v. Argentina*
National Case Law	
Republic of Ecuador v. Chevron Corporation, Texaco Petroleum Company, United States Court of Appeals, Second Circuit, 638 F. 3d(2011)	Ecuador v. Chevron, 2011
Internet Sources	
1. International Air Transport Association-IATA-*Agenda for Freedom*, https://www.iata.org/policy/Pages/agenda-freedom.aspx, last visited: 25 November 2018	IATA, Agenda for Freedom

续表

Internet Sources	
2. Investment Policy Hub, Air Canada v. The Bolivarian Republic of Venezuela[ICSID Case No. ARB(AF)/17/1], last visited: 25 November 2018	Air Canada v. Venezuela, on IPH (2018)

航班时刻分配制度比较研究

原菊豆*

一、引　　言

航空法是“调整民用航空活动及其相关领域中产生的社会关系的法律”，①其具有国际性，是国际法的一个分支，且越来越多地与宪法、贸易法、竞争法、行政法、民法等诸多领域的法律制度相互交织在一起。航班时刻分配法律制度是民用航空法律体系的重要组成部分，其关系着整个航空业的安全、高效、有序发展。

随着突飞猛进的科学技术进步和航空运输业的高速发展，航班时刻逐渐成为航空法调整的重要客体。航班时刻作为航空运输领域一种具有使用价值的稀缺资源，由于具有巨大的经济效益，引起了航空公司、机场还有国家竞相争夺。从国家层面讲，航班

---

* 西北政法大学国际法硕士，北京惠诚东方知识产权代理有限公司职员。

① 刘伟民主编：《航空法教程》，中国法制出版社2001年版，第52页。

时刻分配法律制度事关航空强国战略的布局,事关各地区航空基础建设和经济发展;从中间层面讲,航班时刻分配法律制度事关航空公司、机场等各相关主体的切身利益;从个人层面讲,航班时刻分配制度事关消费者权益的保障。

国内关于航班时刻分配制度的研究大多数从经济管理学角度进行,且自2018年我国颁布的《航班时刻管理办法》以来对航班时刻的研究较少。同时,我国法学理论界关于航班时刻这一资源的法律属性探讨较少,多数国家一般从公共资源的广义范畴出发认为航班时刻资源属于国家所有。大多数国家的法律对航班时刻的属性没有明确的规定,仅是认为航班时刻分配是一种行政许可权。澄清航班时刻法律性质和权利归属,事关航班时刻是否可流转进行市场化运作,事关航班时刻分配和管理的顺利实施。

目前,国际上各国家在航班时刻资源分配方面主要存在两种基本模式,即行政性分配模式和市场化分配模式。大多数国家采用行政性分配模式配置航班时刻资源,美国、英国等少数国家采用行政性分配和市场化配置相结合的方式配置航班时刻资源,还没有任何一个国家采用完全市场化方式配置航班时刻资源的。

二、航班时刻分配制度的学理探析

(一)航班时刻的概念界定

1.时刻的定义和特点

时刻是指极短的时间,[①]是时间里的短暂一段或某一点。[②] 从物理学上定义,时刻是指某一瞬间,是具体的某一时间点,表现为时间轴上的一个节点,它在运动中对应的是位置、速度、动量等状态量。时刻是衡量一切物质运

① 参见中国社科院语言所编:《新华字典》,商务印书馆2011年版,第269页。

② 参见字词语辞书编研组编:《新编现代汉语词典》,湖南教育出版社2016年版,第1137页。

动的先后顺序,它没有长短只有先后,是一个序数,把短暂到几乎接近于零的时间叫即时,即时表示时刻。

时刻与时间不同。时间具有三种含义,“时间是物质存在的一种客观形式,由过去、现在、将来构成的连续系统,是物质运动及变化的顺序性、持续性的一种表现;时间表示从起点到终点的一段时间;在时间里的某一点也可以表示为时间”。[①] 从时间的三种内涵可知,时间不仅包含时刻概念,它还表示时段的意思,时段是两时刻之间的一段距离间隔,是时间轴上的一条表示距离的线段,在运动中对应的是位移、静量等过程量。时间只有长短,没有方向,其具有持续性、单向性、变化性、序列性等特点。

从时刻的含义可知,其具有瞬间性、不可逆性、非序列性和物质性等的特点。与时间相比,时刻是不能延续的动作,动作一发生即代表结束,表示一个短暂的具体的时间状态,因此其具有短暂性、一次性、瞬间性;根据自然科学规律,自然界的时间是一个不断向前发展的过程,正因时刻是时间轴上的一个节点,随着时间不断地向前推进,一旦某特定时刻经过,在自然状态下该时刻不会自发地反演逆转并恢复到原来的时刻状态,只能进入下一个时刻,时间的单方向性决定了时刻具有不可逆性;在数学上,序列是被排成一列的对象或元素,如果将序列中的每个对象或元素比作序数,那么序列就是一个遵循顺序性的序数的集合体,这是一个排列组合。而时刻只是这个序列上的一个序数,无须讨论顺序性,因此时刻具有非序列性的特点。

时间是一个极其抽象笼统的事物,我国古代发明了日晷、圭表等天文仪器来计算预测的时间,表明时间是客观存在的事物。从唯物主义哲学理论出发,时间表示一切物质不断变化或发展所经历的过程,其不以人的意志为转移,具有客观物质性,是人民为了生产生活便利而创设的一种工具,因此时间和时刻都具有物质性。

---

① 字词语辞书编研组编:《新编现代汉语词典》,湖南教育出版社2016年版,第1137页。

2. 航班时刻的源起和定义

航班时刻的英文表达为"slot"。"slot"的英文释义之一为"an assigned place and time in a sequence or schedule",[①]将其翻译为中文是"在序列或时间表中的一个指定地点和时间",在航空领域引申为专业术语"机场航班时刻"。航班时刻最早出现于1966年的美国华盛顿国家机场,各相关方协议将飞往华盛顿国家机场的航班起降时刻限定为最大每小时60架次,这在当时被视为解决机场拥堵和航班延误的临时性措施。现今,航班时刻分配制度已经成为全球各国家甚至国际组织普遍接受的一种航班协调制度,而关于航班时刻的定义其各自规定的并不一致。

美国最早在其《美国法典》(The United States Code)第41714节中规定,"航班时刻被定义为在航空运输中航空器所属的航空公司所保留的以仪表飞行规则运行的起飞和着陆"。[②] 该定义是美国法律中对航班时刻的最早定义,且规定的较为简单,明确了航班时刻包含起降时刻,且指出飞机的时刻运行只与使用机场跑道设施有关,没有提及航班时刻需要使用除跑道外的其他机场基础设施的情形。在最新的《美国联邦法规汇编》(Code of Federal Regulations,C. F. R)第14卷第Ⅰ章第F子章第93部分第S子部分第93.213节中对航班时刻的有了新的定义,该定义为"航班时刻是指在某一高密度机场的特定每小时或每半小时内,执行以仪表飞行规则运行的航班起飞和着陆的运营许可权"。[③] 与美国最早对航班时刻的定义相比,该定义的内容更为丰富,增加了使用机场设施的权利,限定了航班时刻只在美国的高密度机场运行,明确了航班时刻既包含航班的起降时刻,又包含使用机场必要基础设施的权利。

欧盟最早于1993年1月18日在其立法文件中颁布了第(EEC)95/93号

---

① 孙复初主编:《汉英科学技术辞海》,国防工业出版社2003年版,第2825页。

② [德]阿基姆·泽尼等编:《航班时刻——改革的国际经验与借鉴》,王利亚译,中国民航出版社2011年版,第44页。

③ Code of Federal Regulations, § 93.213 Definitions and general provisions. ,14 C. F. R. § 93.213.

规章《通勤机场时刻分配一般规定》[Council Regulation(EEC)No. 95/93 of 18 January 1993 on common rules for the allocation of slots at Community airports],该规章中第2条第a款将航班时刻定义为"航班时刻是指根据本规章条款规定,在协调机场的某特定时间内,由时刻协调人分配给航空公司执行飞行的预定起飞和离开时间",①鉴于该规定在实践操作中的局限性,欧盟对该定义进行了修订,形成欧盟第793/2004号规章[Regulation(EC)No. 793/2004 of the European Parliament and of the Council of 21 April 2004 amending Council Regulation(EEC)No. 95/93 on common rules for the allocation of slots at Community airports②]。欧盟第793/2004号规章对航班时刻的定义为,"航班时刻指的是在协调机场某个特定日期某个特定时间基于起飞或降落的目的,航空公司所拥有的使用必要的各种机场设施以开展航空运营服务的权利"。③ 与第(EEC)95/93号规章的规定相比,航班时刻的定义在欧盟第793/2004号规章中彰显得更为全面具体,尤其是在航班时刻的定义中增加了航空公司为执行飞行活动而使用其所需的机场基础设施的权利,包括使用跑道、廊桥和全体服务人员提供的服务。欧盟对航班时刻的定义更接近于国际航空运输协会(International Air Transport Association,IATA)对航班时刻的定义,都规定的较为精准细致,具体内容参见下文IATA对航班时刻的定义。

我国在2018年颁布的《民航航班时刻管理办法》(以下简称《办法》)第2条中对航班时刻的定义为"航班时刻是指航空器在指定日期和时间,为抵离某个机场而使用相关基础设施与服务的权利,航班时刻的时间基于挡轮挡时间和撤轮挡时间",该定义中包含飞机执行飞行的起抵时间、使用机场基础设

① Council Regulation(EEC)No. 95/93 of 18 January 1993 on common rules for the allocation of slots at Community airports, Celex No. 31993R0095.

② Regulation(EC)No. 793/2004 of the European Parliament and of the Council of 21 April 2004 amending Council Regulation(EEC)No. 95/93 on common rules for the allocation of slots at Community airports, Celex No. 32004R0793.

③ Regulation(EC)No. 793/2004 of the European Parliament and of the Council of 21 April 2004 amending Council Regulation(EEC)No. 95/93 on common rules for the allocation of slots at Community airports, Celex No. 32004R0793.

施与服务的权利等内容，从字面上看，此定义并没有就使用航班时刻的机场种类进行说明，但从《办法》中其他条款规定可以明确其指代的机场包括主协调机场和辅协调机场，即机场地面容量不够充裕的机场，也即在某一时间段内航班时刻需求大于供给的机场。

IATA 在 2019 年 1 月 1 日生效的《世界航班时刻准则》（Worldwide Slot Guidelines，WSG）英文版第 9 版中对航空时刻的定义为“An airport slot（or ‘slot’）is a permission given by a coordinator for a planned operation to use the full range of airport infrastructure necessary to arrive or depart at a Level 3 airport on a specific date and time”。① 在《世界航班时刻准则》中国语言版本第 8 版（2017 年 1 月 1 日生效）中关于航班时刻的定义是，“机场航班时刻（或“航班时刻”）是指由协调人给出的计划运营许可，凭此与特定日期和时间在三级机场使用到港或离港所需的一切机场基础设施”。② IATA 官网上显示英语语言版为官方正式版本，其他语言译本与英文版本所述意思不一致时以英语语言版本优先适用，③上述两种语言表述的航班时刻定义的内容几乎没有实质出入，因此无须考虑因语言翻译等技术问题造成的理解误差。IATA 对航班时刻的定义至少明确了以下四点内容：申请航班时刻的前置条件是获得协调人的行政运营许可权利；航班时刻包括到港和离港时刻，该两个时刻对应的是飞机上轮挡（到达）和撤轮挡（起飞）的时间点；执行航班时刻需要使用因飞行所需的包括但不限于机场跑道、机坪和航站楼等的一切必要机场基础设施的权利；航班时刻只能在三级机场进行分配和运营。IATA 发布的《世界航班时刻准则》中在术语和缩略语下对协调人和三级机场的解释分别为：协调人是负责三级机场航班时刻分配，且具有一定专业知识的组织和个人；关于“三级机场”的解释，相当于我国和欧盟法律规定中的“协调

---

① See International Air Transport Association, *Worldwide Slot Guidelines*, 2019, Edition 9, p. 14.

② 参见国际民航运输协会编：《世界航班时刻准则》（简体中文第 8 版），第 13 页。

③ 参见国际民航运输协会官方网：https://www. iata. org/policy/slots/Pages/slot-guidelines. aspx，最后访问日期：2019 年 4 月 2 日。

机场”概念,通俗来讲其是指因机场尚未建设足够的基础设施,或政府对机场施加条件限制,从而无法满足需求的机场。相比较来讲,IATA 对航班时刻的定义较为全面且更为具体。

学术界关于航班时刻定义的争论主要有两种:第一种主张航班时刻仅指飞机起飞和降落的时刻,①该种主张只是从表面上对航班时刻进行定义,没有理解航班时刻的本质要义。第二种主张航班时刻包括航班的起飞和降落时刻,以及机场基础设施和空域航路的使用权利。随着实践的深入发展与检验,各国和国际组织对航班时刻的概念界定逐渐清晰且完善,实践证明了航班时刻要在综合考虑具体航线上空运需求的时间分布特征、飞机的充分利用、航班之间的衔接以及机场和航路的合理使用等因素的基础上进行安排。从经济学角度讲,航空公司获取航班时刻权利,其本质是为了获取与航班时刻相对应的特定时间特定空间上存在的便利的机场基础设施与服务的权利,以便在航空运输中占据优势地位赢得更大的经济效益。因此,本文赞同第二种主张,认为航班时刻不仅指飞机的起飞时刻和降落时刻,还包含航空公司、机场、协调人等利益相关方因共同执行航班时刻而必然产生的使用机场基础设施和相关服务的权利,甚至有可能还对执行航班时刻的机场性质作出限定。

3. 航班时刻的特点

航班时刻的稀缺性是其最主要的特点。航班时刻的数量和价值取决于它所连接的空域航路状况和机场设施状况,机场容量和空域容量决定了航班时刻的供给量。② 机场的基础设施决定了机场的容量,机场终端区、跑道、滑行道、停机坪、登机口以及停机位、摆渡车、候机楼、车辆环行路、空港道路系统等基础设施的数量越多、布局越合理,可供分配的航班时刻就越多。而实际情况是,民航运输机场起降架次逐年上升对应的是市场需求的快速增长,

---

① See Margherita Colangelo, *Creating Property Rights*: *Law and regulation of Secondary Trading in the European Union*, Martinus Nijhoff Publishers, 2012, p. 55.

② 参见中国民航局政策法规司、中国民航大学编:《民航航班时刻管理的理论与实践——一种稀缺资源的应用研究》,中国民航出版社 2009 年版,第 7 页。

航班需求过剩和供给不足的不平衡现状是全球范围内大多数机场面临的一个长期待解决问题，且该问题在人们活动频繁的经济发达地区显得更为严重。与此同时，任何一家航空公司想要开辟新的航线，必须申请可以开航的空中航线经营权和航班时刻使用权，但可申请的空域容量是有限的，空中进出口航道数量基本固定，这在一定程度上影响航线对应的航班时刻数量。全球各国经济的快速发展使航班客货流量不断加大，这也对陈旧的机场基建设施和空域资源提出了更高的容量需求，这使航班时刻资源在当下显得异常的稀缺和紧张，且这将会是一个较为长期的过程。

航班时刻具有依附性的特点。虽然航班时刻的分配独立于双边航空服务协议规定的航权分配，但在一个国家的民航体系中，时刻、航线和空域是最核心又互相联系不可分割的三类资源。一方面，执行航班时刻离不开使用机场基础设施与服务；另一方面，在没有航线经营权的情况下即便航空公司申请到了黄金航班时刻也无法进行运营，只有在航空公司、机场管理机构、空中交通管理单位和其他利益紧密相关方等人力、物力协同配合的基础上才能保证航班时刻的正常使用，脱离航班运营的协同条件航班时刻无法发挥其应有的价值。因此，航班时刻的使用依附于航线和空域等其他配套权利的使用。

航班时刻具有差异性的特点。航班时刻存在好坏优劣之分，这与消费者的出行偏好、自然环境、社会环境等众多不确定影响因素具有直接关系。在一条航线上，乘客购买不同时间的航班，票价也是不同的，好的时刻也即处于黄金时段的航班时刻对应的票价会更高，通常分布在一天中的早晨10时至下午的5时①（具体时刻所属的时间段跟季节、机场容量等变化因素有关，一般集中在白天早晨6时至晚8时。例如，据统计，2006年夏季巴黎机场从早晨5时至晚7时的时刻都超出机场的最高保障能力，已经难以满足机场使用

① 参见《天空之争：起底中国民航航线争夺现状》，载瞭望东方周刊网：http://app.myzaker.com/news/article.php?pk=55ed0b9a9490cb624200005f，最后访问日期：2019年3月21日。

者的需求[①]),且在一年中的旅游、节假日、国家或地区的重大活动前后等的时间段内航班客流量最大,带来的经济利益也最高,因此黄金航班时刻成为各航空公司竞相追逐的对象。

(二)航班时刻的法律属性和权利归属

1. 航班时刻的性质

(1)航班时刻是否属于自然资源

《现代汉语词典》对资源的解释为:指"资财的来源,一般指天然的来源,如煤炭资源、石油资源",[②]指出资源是具有经济价值的要素,资源包括自然资源和社会资源两大类,那么自然资源同样是具有经济价值的要素。我国《辞海》对自然资源的解释为:"指天然存在的自然物(不包括人类加工制造的原材料)并有利用价值的自然物,如土地资源、矿藏资源、水利资源、生物资源、气候资源、海洋资源等,是生产的原料来源和布局场所",[③]这个定义指出了自然资源具有天然性的这一根本特点。联合国环境规划署从人类利用的角度对自然资源的定义为:"自然资源是在一定的时间和技术条件下,能够产生经济价值,提高人类当前和未来福利的自然环境因素的总称",[④]这一定义同样肯定了自然资源的经济价值,还指出了自然资源的天然性和可开发利用性。我国《宪法》和《民法通则》中规定矿藏、水流、森林、山岭、草原、荒地、滩涂等属于自然资源,我国法律上所说的自然资源指的是天然存在的具有经济价值的环境要素。[⑤] 在学术界,环境法学者一致认为,"自然资源指客观存在于自然界中,能够为人类所直接利用或转化利用的作为生产资料和生活资料

---

① 参见中国民航局政策法规司、中国民航大学编:《民航航班时刻管理的理论与实践——一种稀缺资源的应用研究》,中国民航出版社2009年版,第13~14页。

② 字词语辞书编研组编:《新编现代汉语词典》,湖南教育出版社2016年版,第1696页。

③ 辞海编辑委员会编:《辞海》,上海辞书出版社1981年版。转引自郑昭佩:《自然资源学基础》,中国海洋大学出版社2013年版,第22页。

④ 郑昭佩:《自然资源学基础》,中国海洋大学出版社2013年版,第22页。

⑤ 谈萧:《环境资源法》,华中科技大学出版社2015年版,第3页。

来源的自然因素,包括土地、水、矿藏、森林、草原、野生动植物、阳光、空气等"。①

综合以上各定义可知,"自然资源是能够为人类开发利用,满足其当前或未来需要的在自然界中的空间、空间内天然存在的各种物质、物质存在形式及运动形式所含的能量以及物质运动变化所提供的各种服务功能"。② 以往对自然资源的诸多解释中几乎没有将"时间"或"时刻"直接列入自然资源的列举范围内,但从以上各定义及自然资源的特点出发可知,由于自然资源的概念是人为界定的,且其本身需要具备天然性这一根本属性。当航班时刻代表飞机起降时刻时,抽象化来讲航班的起飞或降落时刻属于时间上的某一时间节点,是运动中的某一静态点形式及自然界中一种物质存在形式,因此从物质性这一角度讲,航班时刻具有天然性,属于自然资源。此外,航班时刻也只有与机场设施和航线运营权结合在一起时,才能发挥其价值,因而航班时刻本身并无单独价值,但是其具有使用价值。正如前文所论述的航班时刻的定义内容一般,除飞机的起降时刻外,航班时刻还包括因执行起飞活动而使用机场基础设施的权利,权利是人为要素,机场的基础设施等硬件或软件属于人类社会活动的产物,因而从这一层含义上显示,航班时刻并不符合自然资源的定义和特点,其不完全属于自然资源。综上得出以下结论:航班起降时刻是人类社会赋予其使用价值的自然资源,但从航班时刻的整体内涵上讲,航班时刻并不是纯粹意义上的自然资源。

(2)航班时刻是否属于公共资源

"Public Resources"和"Common Resources"都可以被翻译成"公共资源",二者所属的研究领域和侧重点不同。

"Public Resources"更强调资源的社会属性,该词语大多在行政学中谈及,是指属于社会公有、社会成员公用的自然资源及社会财富,是社会及社会成员公有公用的生产或生活资料,一般包括公共自然资源、公共设施、公共信

---

① 颜运秋、陈海嵩、余彦:《环境资源法》,中南大学出版社 2016 年版,第 295 页。

② 郑昭佩:《自然资源学基础》,中国海洋大学出版社 2013 年版,第 22 页。

息等,具有共用性、稀缺性、公共性、整体性等特点。① 最原始的航班时刻是由政府行政分配开始的,航班时刻是社会公有的一种资源,具有经济价值,绝大多数情况下航班时刻是由国家或政府开发并分配给航空公司使用的,任何对航班时刻的独占或垄断都会引起其他利益相关主体的强烈反对,公众(包括航空公司)是航班时刻资源使用的主要受益者,也只有对航班时刻进行有效的分配,才能达到航空机制整体的有效运行。航班时刻的稀缺性不再赘述(详细见上文航班时刻的特点)。因此,航班时刻具有"Public Resources"的性质。

"Common Resources"是经济学上的公共资源,分为"纯公共资源"和"准公共资源"("Pure common Resources"和"Quasi-common Resources")。依据萨缪尔森《公共支出的纯粹理论》一书中的观点,"纯公共资源"具有非排他性和非竞争性的特点,②这两个特点决定了公共物品的消费不可分割性,导致无法运用市场手段来分配资源。而航班时刻在实践中的应用充分证明,相比较实行单纯的行政手段进行分配,引入市场配置资源的手段更能避免航班时刻的滥用,发挥航班时刻的最大价值,因此在航班时刻的分配机制中,市场配置手段决定了航班时刻是具有竞争性的资源,其不具备"纯公共资源"的特征。

"准公共资源"是指介于私人物品和纯公共资源之间的一种准公共资源,是"人们共同使用整个资源系统但分别享用资源单位的资源",③其具备非排他性、竞争性和外部性的特点,如公共渔场、地下水资源等。

"准公共资源"的非排他性强调没有完全的私有产权,是任何个人或组织都可以获得的资源。按照目前全球绝大多数国家的法律和政策,航班时刻

---

① 参见雷晓明、赵成、王永杰:《中国公共资源问题:理论与政策研究》,西南交通大学出版社 2011 年版,第 5 页。

② 参见中国民航局政策法规司、中国民航大学编:《民航航班时刻管理的理论与实践——一种稀缺资源的应用研究》,中国民航出版社 2009 年版,第 33 页。

③ 雷晓明、赵成、王永杰:《中国公共资源问题:理论与政策研究》,西南交通大学出版社 2011 年版,第 3 页。

资源不属于任何航空公司或机场等私人主体所有,它是国家或政府通过无偿或有偿的方式分配给航空公司使用的资源,因此从航班时刻分配法律制度上来讲,航班时刻具有非排他性。再者,根据航班时刻分配法律规则,航班时刻有可能在下个航季会被重新分配给其他航空公司使用,这样的"轮流使用"机制也体现了航班时刻资源具有排他性。

"准公共资源"的竞争性是指个体对某一公共资源的使用会减损其他主体对该资源的使用。一旦某一航空公司获得某一航班时刻且未交付给其他航空公司使用时,那么其他航空公司即失去了获取和使用同一机场同一航线对应的同一航班时刻的权利,这对于未获得该航班时刻的航空公司来讲的确是一种利益减损,因此航班时刻也具备竞争性。

"准公共资源"具有负外部性,通俗来讲是指资源被过度使用、无效消耗的外部影响。实践操作中,由于航班时刻分配的独立性,航空公司只有在同时获得航线运营权、机场设施使用权利和航班时刻使用权时才能完成一次成功的执飞。如在不考虑航空公司再次交易的情形下,当航空公司在同一航季只申请到航班时刻的使用权时,将导致航班时刻的"搁置"问题,同时,各航空公司竞相获得航班时刻以便增加其在商业战场上的筹码,因此也出现了航班时刻被"囤积"的滥用现象。

现代意义上的"航班时刻"概念,既融入了行政色彩,又有市场支配的身影,航班时刻既有其社会属性,又具备"准公共资源"的性质,因此,航班时刻属于公共资源。

(3)航班时刻是否属于无形财产

财产包含财产和财产性权利,是具有金钱价值的权利所构成的集合体。财产区别于资产,资产对应的是企业的权利,①鉴于航班时刻的权属性质可知(详见下文"航班时刻的权利归属"),此处不宜用"资产"界定。同时,需要指出的是"无形财产"区别于"虚拟财产",虚拟财产是不具有实物形态,而以

① 参见杨汝梅:《无形资产论》,立信会计出版社2009年版,第7页。

特定形式存在的并为持有者带来相应利益的财产,[①]其具有非物质性,显然航班时刻并不属于虚拟财产。那么,航班时刻是无形财产吗?

"无形财产"的概念起源于古罗马法,盖尤斯在其著作《法学阶梯》一书中,首次将物划分为"有形物"和"无形物"。在第二编"物法"编第12条和第13条说,"有形物是有形的,是那些可以触摸的物品,例如:土地、人、衣服、金子、银子以及其他无数物品"。[②] 在第12条和第14条说,"无形物是无形的,是那些不能触摸的物品,它们体现为某种权利,比如:遗产继承、用益权、以任何形式缔结的债……实际上,继承权、用益权和债权本身都是无形的……"[③] 我国学者赞同罗马法对无形财产的定义,认为"无形物或无形财产为有形物所有权以外的权利体系,是一种将具体权利进行'物的主观拟制'的结果,无形财产本质上是一种权利,其存在是传统'物化思维'的产物"。[④]

综上定义得出,现代意义上的无形财产是指不具备一定形状,但占有一定空间或能为人们所支配并产生经济价值的物。时刻本是自然界的一种客观存在的物质形态,其不具有一定形状但是存在于空间之中,航空运输业的蓬勃发展使人类赋予时刻使用价值,以更好地平衡航空业发展存在的矛盾。航班时刻的运用给航空公司带来丰厚的经济利益,其不是"有体物",但是具有经济价值,因此航班时刻属于无形财产。

2. 航班时刻的法律属性

财产是一个法律概念,是指一个主体拥有且可以处分的有价值的物或权利。财产与权利是密切联系在一起的,财产总是意味着归属于某个人,某个人可以支配某个客体。物是人类社会最基本的财产形态,物权就是人类社会最基本的财产权。[⑤] 在英美法体系下,没有与大陆法系相对应的物权法典和

---

① 参见于玉林:《无形资产辞典》,上海辞书出版社2009年版,第3页。

② [古罗马]盖尤斯:《法学阶梯》,黄风译,中国政法大学出版社1996年版,第82页。

③ 同上。

④ 马俊驹、梅夏英:《无形财产的理论和立法问题》,载《中国法学》2001年第2期。

⑤ 参见高富平:《物权法》,清华大学出版社2007年版,第8页。

术语,与之对应的是其财产法体系,[①]航班时刻作为一种具有使用价值的自然资源,是可以直接归入其财产权体系下的。英美法体系下的财产法法典或法律汇编中,大多均涉及财产的权利或无体财产,但这些权利或无体财产本身的内容并不在这些法典或汇编中进行规定,而是通过各相应的法律或判例规则来规定各财产种类的内容。在适用英美法系的一些国家的财产法中,如美国《加利福尼亚州民法典》之财产法编就规定,"财产并不限于有体物,还包括无体的权利",[②]即其在事实上包括了有体物之外所有的财产性权利。在英美法体系下,航班时刻作为无形财产,自然具有财产法属性。

与之不同的是,在传统的大陆法系民法理论中,无形财产被归入物权和债权领域,航班时刻的非排他性说明其不属于债权。而在其物权法体系中物分为有体物和无体物,但大陆法系物权法所规范之物的客体仅限于有体物,[③]只有在法律有明文规定的情况下"权利"才可作为其物权客体。航班时刻作为一种"无形"财产,其不具备"有形物"的特点,因此其不属于严格意义上的传统大陆法系下物权的客体。

"准物权"是指大陆法系国家对民法物权之外某些对世财产权的统称,其多是一些特许物权,一般是民法和行政法共同作用的复合产物,特许物权是指基于基本事实或经过行政特别许可而生的权利。[④] "准物权系一集合概念,包含着一组差异颇大的特殊物权,其客体具有不确定性,且众多难以整齐划一,如渔业权、矿业权、水权等。"[⑤]"准物权"除具有复合性外,还具有公法性、非排他性等特点。

那么,航班时刻是否属于"准物权"呢?举一例以明之,渔业权就是一种准物权,权利人为获得水生动植物等利益,首先需获得实现支配特定水域的

---

① 参见[美]约翰·H.威格摩尔:《世界法系概览》,何勤华等译,上海人民出版社2004年版,第836页。

② 吴一鸣:《英美物权法——一个体系的发现》,上海人民出版社2011年版,第35页。

③ 参见陈华彬:《物权法原理》,国家行政学院出版社1998年版,第49页。

④ 参见崔建远:《准物权研究》,法律出版社2003年版,第26~27页。

⑤ 崔建远:《准物权研究》,法律出版社2003年版,第33页。

许可权;从渔业权作用的对象来看,既有特定的水域又有作用于该水域的水生动植物。① 同理,就航班时刻而言,航空公司为获得航班时刻权利必须首先取得国家或航班时刻所有权人的时刻运营许可权,其本质是一种行政许可权利。其次,航班时刻不仅包括飞机的起降时刻使用权,还包括因执行起降活动而使用机场基础设施的权利,航班时刻是一种复合权利,既要事先获得行政许可权又要与机场达成民事上的合作协议,其具备现有"准物权"的所有特征,因此航班时刻是一种"准物权"。

"准物权"的特性因与物权的性质十分相似,因此"准物权"在没有特别法规制的情况下,一般参照适用物权法律规则。物权作为财产,有两种表现形态:一是物之所有权;二是对他人之物的权利,表现为用益物权和担保物权。

航班时刻是一种自然资源,还是一种公共资源。目前,就全球大多数国家而言,政府都在航班时刻资源分配上起着重要的决定性作用,航班时刻也多是由政府进行分配,这也说明了各国政府对航班时刻资源主张的所有权性质,且这种主张具有强制性。

用益物权源于罗马法,是大陆法系国家物权制度特有的概念,是一个类概念,用益物权在大多数情况下是由所有权人设定的,允许他人在一定期限内使用特定物的一种法律安排,其属于他物权的范畴,是指因所有权人意志或法律规定的某种原因而形成的对他人之物在一定期间占有、使用和收益的权利。相对于担保物权,用益物权在于它是对他人之物占有、使用或享有利益,而不是对物价值的支配。而担保物权是对物的价值形态的支配,在担保物权实现之前,不涉及对物本身的直接支配。因航空公司获得航班时刻的使用权后,就会实际占有、使用并享受航班时刻带来的收益,所以对航空公司来说,航班时刻更偏向具有用益物权的性质。

综上可知,在英美法体系下,航班时刻在一般情况下是具有财产法属性

① 崔建远:《准物权研究》,法律出版社2003年版,第39页。

的，但其具体的法律属性还要回归到各国法律之中予以确定。而在大陆法体系下，航班时刻具备“准物权”的特点，其可以被归入“准物权”范围，同时，航班时刻针对不同的主体会具有所有权和用益物权的法律属性。

3. 航班时刻的权利归属

由前面对航班时刻法律性质的论证分析，可进一步明确航班时刻的所有权归属，是归属于国家、机场还是航空公司呢？关于航班时刻的权利归属问题，国家、机场、航空公司三方作为航班时刻的关键利益相关主体，无论从对航班时刻的直接分配、协调管理、容量提供还是实际使用等方面都主张各自对航班时刻的所有权，争论也从未停止。

而在各国法律和政策上，对航班时刻的权利归属是如何规定的呢？在美国联邦法规（Code of Federal Regulations，C. F. R.）第 14 卷第Ⅰ章第 F 子章第 93 部分第 S 子部分多处规定，在 C. F. R. 中关于航班时刻的分配问题上，多次提及了美国联邦航空管理局（Federal Aviation Administration，FAA）是航班时刻分配的“最终决定者”，[①]享有对航班时刻运营特许权的“绝对控制分配权”。FAA 是美国国会授权排他性管辖航班时刻的政府机构，这也说明了在美国航班时刻权属于国家。欧盟（不含英国）在航班时刻分配法律制度上，采用的是完全的行政分配模式，是由时刻协调人负责时刻的分配，时刻协调人是代表国家将时刻分配给航空承运人，这也说明了在欧盟航班时刻权属于国家。

同样地，我国《宪法》第 9 条明文规定了自然资源属于国家，集体所有的除外。航班时刻作为一种需要规制的自然资源，从我国宪法角度讲应该权属于我国政府。同时，在我国 2018 年颁布的《办法》第 4 条规定，“中国民用航空局、民航地区管理局对航班时刻实施管理，航空承运人享有平等的航班时刻使用权”，中国民用航空局、民航地区管理局是我国民用航空主管部门，其代表国家行使权力。再从我国近几年在航班时刻进行市场化分配改革的实

① Code of Federal Regulations，§ 93.223 Slot withdrawal，14 C. F. R. § 93.223.

践结果看,拍卖航班时刻所得的收入都上缴国库,这也说明了在我国航班时刻权属于国家。

在各国的法律和政策框架下,从法律规定的言语逻辑和实践中出现的航班时刻使用费归属等角度可以侧面反映出:目前,在全球绝大多数国家航班时刻的所有权实际上是权属于国家的。基于分配效率和缓解矛盾等原因的考虑,很多学者提出了一些航班时刻的所有权假想以简化并消除对时刻商业地位的管制,如外国学者欧文·冯·登·施泰纳(Erwin von den Steinen)在其"航班时刻的正式所有权和租赁规则"(Formal Ownership and Leasing Rules for Slots)一文中就提出"由机场占有时刻,航空公司租用(包括分租)时刻"的一种全新的时刻所有权模式。

关于机场,在最开始大多数国家的机场所有权其实是属于国家,国家出资建造机场,机场作为非营利性机构,由机场管理人进行管理,比如,在我国,机场大多数是政府出资建造的,其所有权是属于国家的。但"一般而言,不同机场提供服务的体制结构不同,这会使机场运营逐渐脱离政府部门的干预控制,比如在英国对一些机场实行私有化,在加拿大对机场进行'非营利性机构'的'公司化'改革"。① 不同国家的不同机场,其所有权可能不同。如果机场本身是由政府所有并控制的,那么即便机场拥有了航班时刻的所有权,但实质上航班时刻的所有权仍归属于出资建造它的国家。如果机场属于私人所有,无论其作为营利性机构还是非营利性机构,机场出于安全和效率等其他可能的考虑因素,认为机场作为航班时刻所需容量的提供平台,在航班时刻管理中掌握一定主导权,且航班时刻是产生于机场登机门、滑行道、跑道等起降设施基础上的,航班时刻将不能在其执飞活动如离开机场基建设施和人员服务方面发挥作用,因而主张对航班时刻的所有权。这种主张存在的问题是,其忽略了空域资源对航班时刻的钳制作用,时刻、航线和空域是三类紧紧结合相互依存的核心资源,"空中基础设施一般是由国家投资建设的,航班时

① [德]阿基姆·泽尼等编:《航班时刻——改革的国际经验与借鉴》,王利亚译,中国民航出版社2011年版,第343页。

刻本质上是空域资源,没有空中交通系统,航班是飞不起来的",[①]从这个角度讲航班时刻权属国家,而私人化的机场不应具有航班时刻的所有权,但是其可以获得机场经营收益、地方政府的政策红利等权益。

关于航空公司,航空公司认为其实际持有、使用航班时刻,没有航空公司的使用,航班时刻没有任何价值,因此其主张对航班时刻的所有权,或者是收益权(如果存在交易市场的话)。从法理角度分析,航班时刻作为自然资源,并不能由私人主体享有其所有权。另外,在法律规定和实践运用中,正如前文陈述的一样,美国在 C. F. R. 中将航班时刻作为一种行政运营许可权,而不是一项财产权利,FAA 无偿将航班时刻分配给航空公司使用,航空公司是航班时刻的"持有人",享有航班时刻的使用权和收益权。欧盟(不含英国)现阶段也未允许航班时刻的市场化交易,因此也未赋予航空公司对航班时刻的收益权。显然,正如前文所述,在我国航班时刻的经营收益是需要上缴国库的,航空公司也并未拥有航班时刻的收益权,但是其拥有航班时刻的使用权。因航空公司在时刻初次分配时已经支付了相应的对价,因此在航班时刻的二级交易市场中,其享有时刻交易产生的收益。综上所述,大多数国家都承认,虽然航空公司不应具有航班时刻的所有权,有些国家也不赋予其初次分配的收益权,但是航空公司享有使用航班时刻的权利,以及在二级市场交易的收益权。

(三)航班时刻分配制度的现有模式

综观全球,为适应航空运输业的高速发展,各国都在逐步探索新的模式以解决航空运输面临的最为严重的航班迟延、机场拥堵等问题。目前,航班时刻分配制度的现有模式主要有以下几种,分别是行政分配模式、市场分配模式和混合管理模式,其中混合管理模式也即行政分配和市场配置相结合的模式,而在实践中并不存在完全由市场配置的分配模式。

---

① 中国民航局政策法规司、中国民航大学编:《民航航班时刻管理的理论与实践——一种稀缺资源的应用研究》,中国民航出版社 2009 年版,第 62 页。

1. 行政性分配模式

国际民用航空运输协会发布的《世界航班时刻准则》作为航班时刻国际惯例,采用航班时刻行政性分配模式,目前欧盟也采用该种时刻分配模式,就是航班时刻以行政分配为主。该种分配模式的特点是具有明确的优先规则,航班时刻主要通过时刻协调人进行分配,不允许航班时刻进行市场交易配置。

在行政分配模式下,大多数国家适用"祖父权利"规则,历史航班时刻持有者在时刻分配中占据绝对性优势地位。享有"祖父权利"的航班时刻持有者仍要坚持"不用即失"规则,也就是要求执行航班时刻的使用率达到一定标准否则即会被主管部门撤回。"五五法则"适用于对新进入航空公司的时刻分配,这是在"祖父权利"占支配地位情况下,为建立公平竞争的分配秩序,维护中小航空公司的利益而作出的努力。在行政分配模式下,航班时刻分配规则虽然不允许进行交易,但是允许在航空公司之间以"一个换一个"的方式进行等量交换,这在一定程度上有利于航班时刻的灵活分配。

航班时刻的行政性分配,不是依据航空公司的申请意愿,而是依照"祖父权利"规则进行时刻的分配。虽然该模式下设立了维护新进入航空公司时刻分配权益的"五五法则",但是在"祖父权利"占绝对支配地位的情况下,中小航空公司在时刻分配中处于弱势地位,限制了航空运输业的良性竞争。航班时刻的行政性分配模式虽然能够维持航班运行的稳定性,但是具有天然效率低下的弊端,且不利于建立有序、竞争、高效的航班时刻分配秩序。

2. 行政性分配和市场化配置相结合模式

采用航班时刻行政性分配和市场化配置相结合模式的典型代表是美国。航班时刻的行政性分配和市场化配置相结合模式又称为混合管理模式。混合管理模式是在保留行政分配规则的基础上弱化了行政手段,通过引入市场交易机制来盘活航班时刻分配的制度。在实行航班时刻二级市场交易的国家,允许时刻的持有者在二级市场以买卖、转让、出租等形式进行市场交易。

美国历史上经历了三次重大的时刻分配制改革,由最初实行完全的行政分配模式开始，到引入二级市场交易，再到2000年至今进行的一级市场交易探索。美国曾积极探索在时刻初次分配中进行时刻拍卖，并提出拥挤时刻收费制度，但之后都没有在实践中进行下去。可以肯定的是，美国制定的二级转让"盲人市场"规则、"抽签分配机制"、"提高时刻豁免的最高限额"、"设立祖父权利有效期"等规则制度在实践中取得较好的效果。

航班时刻的分配机制中引入"市场交易"机制，在很大程度上能够增加时刻的流动性，避免时刻虚占，为新进入航空公司获得黄金航班时刻提供了很多机会。但是市场化配置机制也有其自身的弊端，如容易引起航班时刻交易价格过高、时刻交易市场出现不正当竞争行为等。

3. 小结

无论是航班时刻的行政分配模式，还是市场化配置模式，都存在各自的弊端。航班时刻行政分配更容易引发机场拥堵、航班迟延问题，且行政审批程序繁杂，分配程序透明度较低等。市场化配置航班时刻容易引发交易价格畸高、交易垄断和不正当竞争等现象。

现行的时刻分配制度面临的最主要的困难是，要在拥挤机场的现任航空公司和新进入航空公司之间寻求一种利益平衡。航班时刻的有效分配能确保机场基础设施得到最高效地利用，为机场使用者实现利益最大化。因此现有的航班时刻分配规则通过对以往历史惯例的不断突破和对新型分配规则的探索发展，试图创设一种平衡式规则，但实践总是在不断变化，各方主体的利益诉求也逐渐增多，建立一种公平高效的分配机制将是一个漫长的路程。

三、航班时刻分配制度比较分析

从全世界的范围来讲，我国的现代航空运输业发展算是后起之秀，欧美作为世界上最领先的国家，其航空制造业和运输业一直走在世界前列，①也

① 参见顾诵芬、史超礼：《世界航空发展史》，河南科学技术出版社1998年版，第185页。

是开展航班时刻分配和管理较早的国家。航班时刻分配制度由“先到先得”规则、“祖父权利”规则、“不用即失”规则、“五五法则”等规则构成,这些分配规则决定了不同航空公司之间获得的航班时刻数量与质量,这也就直接决定了各航空公司将会获得的经济效益。通过对不同国家航班时刻法律制度中的分配规则进行比较研究,找出更加能平衡各相关主体利益的制度,对构建和完善中国航班时刻分配制度具有重大意义,对建设中国特色社会主义航空强国具有重大推动作用。

(一)国际民用航空运输协会航班时刻分配规则

IATA 时刻分配规则即《世界航班时刻准则》代表了全球公认的政府和机场监管机构的最佳实践,是目前国际上的一种组织非常良好的时刻分配制度规则。IATA 航班时刻准则确保使用一致的政策、原则和流程将世界各地容量受限的机场的航班时刻分配给航空公司,对于管理全世界范围内时刻协调机场的需求来说非常有效。但是在 IATA 航班时刻准则下,并非所有的机场都是时刻协调机场,IATA 将全世界的机场分为三类,分别是一级机场、二级机场和三级机场。“一级机场,也称非协调机场(Non-Coordinated Airport),是指机场基础设施容量基本始终能满足机场使用者需求的机场;二级机场,也称时刻协导机场(Schedule Facilitated Airports),是指在一天、一周或某一航季中的某些时段可能出现拥塞,而进行航空公司和协助人共同协定的航班时刻表调整能够解决的机场”,[①]在一级机场和二级机场不进行航班时刻分配,因此也不适用历史优先权和航班时刻系列的规则。航班时刻主要在三级机场进行协调分配,“三级机场,又称完全协调机场(Full-Coordinated Airport),是指经过全面的需求和容量分析,确定因容量提供商尚未建设足够

① 国际民航运输协会编:《世界航班时刻准则》(简体中文第 8 版),资料来源:https://www.iata.org/policy/slots/Pages/slot-guidelines.aspx,最后访问日期:2019 年 8 月 25 日,第 12 页。

的基础设施,或政府对机场施加条件限制,从而无法满足需求的机场”。[①] 时刻协调人在进行航班时刻分配时会参照不同的标准,如祖父条款、“不用即失”条款、“先到先得”规则、“五五法则”“一个换一个”原则等。

1. 历史优先权规则

历史优先权是航班时刻分配制度的核心,也是航班时刻初始分配中的首要规则和先锋标准。历史优先权,可以理解为“历史时刻优先权利”,它是对“祖父条款”和“不用即失条款”等规则的直接运用,其只适用于相应的同航季[②]而非连续的航季,且局限于相应的运营期、运营日。根据 IATA,航班时刻是否具有历史优先权资格,应在遵循以下规则的基础上进行判断。

“祖父条款”,又称“祖父权利”(Grandfather’s Rights),是指航空公司对于历史上占有的时刻享有优先分配的权利,或者说是指“上一年持有和使用一个起降时刻的航空公司在下一年的同一季节有权利再一次持有和使用”。[③] 历史时刻调整具有优先性,这是“祖父权利”规则支配下的一种表现。与此同时,对历史时刻因运营或其他方面的原因而做的调整应优先于对总的可用容量内同一时刻的首次申请,这也是历史时刻享有航班时刻分配最高优先级的表现,在可用容量范围内航班时刻冲突的情况下,历史航班时刻调整优先于新提交的航班时刻申请。“祖父权利”支配下的时刻分配规则,历史惯例在事先直接决定了航班时刻的使用权归属,在下一航季的航班时刻分配中只要经符合条件的历史航班时刻持有人再次申请,航班时刻的持有人仍为原航空公司,时刻分配结果几乎不会发生变化。这种分配方式一方面很难保护想去获得时刻的新进入者和其他潜在航空运营人的权利,另一方面不利于缓解各机场的交通压力,尤其是在拥挤机场和替代机场。

---

① 国际民航运输协会编:《世界航班时刻准则》(简体中文第 8 版),资料来源:https://www.iata.org/policy/slots/Pages/slot-guidelines.aspx,最后访问日期:2019 年 8 月 25 日,第 12~13 页。

② 国际民航运输协会《世界航班时刻准则》第 10 条规定:“同航季是指相邻的夏秋航季(两个夏秋航季)或相邻的冬春航季(两个冬春航季),这与两个连续的航季(一个夏秋和一个冬春航季)相反。”

③ 余英:《网络型产业的政府管制:机场管制研究》,广东经济出版社 2008 年版,第 66 页。

"不用即失"(Use It or Lose It)条款,又称为"二八法则",是指"只有当航空公司能够向协调人证明其航班时刻系列在上年同航季分配的时间段内使用率至少达到了80%时,才能获取历史优先权",①否则将会丧失资格。历史航班时刻确定的基础为历史航班时刻基准日期②之前保留的航班时刻系列。③ 对于在历史航班时刻基准日期之后新分配的航班时刻系列,初始分配当日该系列中的航班时刻数量是计算80%使用率的基础,其时间范围是整个业务运营时间段。在历史航班时刻基准日期之前取消的时间段达连续5周或以上,会导致具备历史优先权资格的时段不连贯,而如果不连贯的时段被认作相同航班业务的一部分,则80%的使用率仍将按照整个运营时段中的运营总数来计算,这将会减少历史优先权的获取资格。而在历史航班时刻基准日期之后取消的时间段,在计算使用率时都被视为未使用的航班时刻系列,除非由于超出航班公司控制能力的不可预见且无法避免的自然原因或社会原因,如机场或空域关闭、恶劣天气、劳工运动等,导致航空业务中断或无法按计划飞行。对航班时刻系列作出的与时间无关的临时变更(如飞机型号、航班号、航线或业务类型)不会影响历史优先权资格。IATA引入"不用即失"条款的目的是减少航班时刻的无效率使用,避免航空公司囤积航班时刻以形成市场垄断,该规则与"祖父权利"规则密切相连,是在"祖父权利"基础上对航空公司更高的准入标准要求。

临时分配的航班时刻因具有临时性,④不具有历史优先权资格。所谓临

---

① 国际民航运输协会编:《世界航班时刻准则》(简体中文第8版),资料来源:https://www.iata.org/policy/slots/Pages/slot-guidelines.aspx,最后访问日期:2019年8月25日,第35页。

② 国际民航运输协会《世界航班时刻准则》第10条规定:"历史航班时刻基准日期即UTC时间1月31日23时59分(夏秋航季)和UTC时间8月31日23时59分(冬春航季)。UTC是国际协调时间,也可用Z或GMT表示。"

③ 国际民航运输协会《世界航班时刻准则》第10条规定:"航班时刻系列是指至少5个航班时刻申请在同航季内均匀分布,占用各周内同一天的相同时间,且分配结果与申请一致;若无可能,则分配在大致相同的时间。"

④ 国际民航运输协会《世界航班时刻准则》第8条规定:"在整个航季完成之前、于航班时刻大会会议截至日期前送交航空承运人的信息被认为是临时性的。"

时分配的航班时刻是指当某一航班时刻系列出于非历史性因素变为空闲时，协调人可将这些航班时刻临时重新分配给另一家航空公司，获得临时时刻的航空公司不能通过使用此类航班时刻系列主张相应的历史优先权资格。但是如果最初临时分配的航班时刻之后被当作航班时刻系列由航空公司进行申请，并在航季结束时构成了航班时刻系列，则其可能成为航空公司申请历史优先权的基础。

滥用航班时刻将丧失获得历史优先权的资格。如果航空公司“不在已分配的航班时段内运营或者不以事先协调的方式来使用航班时刻的”，①则构成航班时刻的滥用。除此之外，航班时刻滥用的情形包括但不限于以下行为：保留无意用于运营、转让、互换或共同运营的航班时刻；保留航班时刻的目的并非用于计划运营，而是阻止其他飞机运营商使用机场容量；申请无意运营的航班时刻；申请航班时刻的目的并非用于所述运营，而是意图提高优先级。禁止航班时刻滥用是保证构建公平竞争环境的重要手段和措施，对保证航班时刻的有效分配也至关重要。

2. 新进入者权利规则

在 IATA 时刻分配规则下，新进入者享有获得航班时刻分配的第二优先等级。IATA 对“新进入者”身份的定义为，如在任意日内对航班时刻系列发起的申请被接受，且在该日所持有的航班时刻数小于 5 的航空承运人，同时 IATA 规定新进入者仅限于航空公司。IATA 对新进入者权利的保护体现于“五五法则”之中，所谓的“五五法则”是指“在初始航班时刻分配时，航班时刻池内 50% 的航班时刻必须分配给新进入者，除非新进入者提出的申请少于 50%，协调人将按照全天的协调参数公平对待新进入者和其他航空公司的申请”。②

在该分配规则下，新进入者有权申请航班时刻，如果新进入者已分配到

① 国际民航运输协会编：《世界航班时刻准则》（简体中文第 8 版），资料来源：https://www.iata.org/policy/slots/Pages/slot-guidelines.aspx，最后访问日期：2019 年 8 月 25 日，第 36 页。

② 同上书，第 33 页。

的航班时刻与其申请的时间相差在1小时内,但在航班时刻大会结束前新进入者仍未接受该已分配时刻的,则该航季内时刻协调委员会将不会保留其新进入者的身份。航空公司在提交航班时刻申请时应向协调员说明该时刻申请是否享有新进入者身份,如果新进入者不满意协调人对其航班时刻申请的答复,可以要求召开协调委员会会议寻求解决方案。

“五五法则”在一定程度上是对传统“祖父权利”原则的新突破,其赋予新进入者优先获得航班时刻的权利,但是阻碍了其他非新进入航空公司、非历史时刻使用者等有能力运营航班时刻的中小型航空公司公平获取航班时刻的权利,同时又难以对抗基于“祖父权利”形成的固化分配规则,显然其作用并不是很大。

3. 交易规则

IATA 时刻分配规则鼓励航空公司之间互换航班时刻。在三级机场,任意数量的航空公司之间可以自由等量互换分配的航班时刻。在互换涉及新分配的航班时刻情况下(除了历史航班时刻或调整后的历史航班时刻以外的航班时刻),如果协调人认为这种互换不会改进该航空公司的运营状况,则可以拒绝这种互换。参与航班时刻互换的航空公司必须向协调人告知每一次互换信息情况,如果互换涉及补偿或报酬,应按照要求向相关方披露互换细节,披露的细节包括涉及互换的航空公司名称、互换的时刻以及互换的时段等信息,并在协调人网站上予以公布,以体现时刻分配的透明性。

IATA 时刻分配规则下也允许航空公司之间转让航班时刻。无论是否以补偿或报酬为目的,只要国家相关法律不予禁止,航空公司之间可以进行航班时刻转让,但只能转让给正在或计划在相同机场运营的另一家航空公司。与航班时刻互换一样,航班时刻转让也必须向协调人履行通知义务,如果转让涉及补偿或报酬,应按照要求向相关方披露转让细节,披露的细节包括涉及转让的航空公司名称、转让的时刻以及转让的时段等信息,并在协调人网站上予以公布。但是转让航班时刻存在禁止的情形,即新分配的航班时刻在运营满两个同航季之前不允许转让,这是为了防止航空公司利用新进入者身份提高时刻分配的优先级,而仅以转让给其他航空公司为目的获取航班时刻的现象发生。

虽然 IATA 没有引进完全的市场分配机制,但是在其航班时刻分配政策的某些规则下,其使用了“互换”“转让”等含有交易性质的词语来灵活分配航班时刻,这也说明 IATA 允许航空公司之间可以通过“一个换一个”(one for one)的方式交换各自的航班时刻。有目共睹的是,一个机场的航班时刻一旦被确定,变化也不会太大,故航空公司分配政策仍然依据“祖父权利”规则。

综上所述,IATA 航班时刻分配规则是航班时刻的行政分配的典型模式。其对航班时刻分配遵循的历史优先权规则做了比较详细具体的规定,历史优先权规则主要是“祖父权利”的运用。那些试图进入拥挤机场的航空公司认为“祖父权利”是反竞争的,但 IATA 认为目前尚找不到可被各方接受的替代分配制度,且目前的分配体系是有效率的。

(二)欧盟航班时刻分配法律规则

欧盟最早于 1993 年通过立法颁布了第(EEC)95/93 号规章《通勤机场时刻分配一般规定》,这比美国晚了 8 年之久。第 95/93 号规章经历了两次重大修订,最后一次是在 2004 年 4 月 30 日修订形成了第 793/2004 号规章,修订主要局限于对一些专业术语的解释,在时刻分配方面并无较大变化。欧盟第 95/93 号规章和第 793/2004 号规章最大的区别就是对航班时刻和新进入者的解释不同,其关于时刻的解释已在第一部分阐释过,此处不再赘述;关于对新进入者解释将在下文予以详细说明。欧盟完全依靠行政手段分配航班时刻,并排斥在时刻分配中引入市场机制。但值得注意的是,当时的英国已经在其航班时刻分配制度中允许时刻交易,且早在英国还没有相关允许交易的法律和政策之前,其国内就存在了一种补偿性质的“灰色市场”,在“灰色市场”航空公司之间可以“交换”为幌子进行时刻的货币性交易,当时的英国政府对此也是睁一只眼闭一只眼,英国政府的这种态度间接加强了民间的私下交易,因为这样做显然有助于提高航班时刻的有效配置和经济效益。①

1.历史优先权规则

欧盟第95/93号规章第8条规定,“航空承运人已经运营过且被协调员收回的航班时刻,在下一个同等的航班时刻期间内,该航空承运人有权要求同样的航班时刻”。② 该条规定说明了欧盟适用“祖父权利”规则,即允许在位航空公司永久持有他们以前在拥挤机场获得的航班时刻,这是历史优先权的体现。同时,在欧盟新修订的第793/2004号规章中的“鉴于”部分着重提及了“祖父权利”对维持航空运营不可或缺的稳定性和必要性。但有变化的是,第793/2004号规章第8条是对“祖父权利”有保留地接受,其允许对基于“祖父权利”而持有的航班时刻进行时间上的调整,这也意味着会把一定比例的祖父时刻放回到时刻池中进行重新分配,以避免“祖父权利”妨碍竞争的问题。这一规定与美国对“祖父权利”设置时效期的操作和效果一致,使新进入者有机会获得更多的新的航班时刻,保证航班时刻的流动性,确保时刻的充分竞争。

“祖父权利”被解读为国际惯例,涵盖了“不用即失”规则。欧盟第793/2004号规章继续沿用了“不用即失”规则,且在以往的基础上提高了航班时刻的利用率门槛。其规定“除特殊情况外,如果航空承运人无法向时刻协调人充分证明在该航季至少80%的利用率,则会取消其下一航季该时刻的使用权”。对于所有的航空承运人,无论其运营定期航班还是不定期航班都必须严格遵守满足时刻80%的利用率要求。“祖父权利”和“不用即失”二规则仍然在欧盟机场航班时刻分配中发挥着至关重要的作用,欧盟委员会确信沿用航班时刻历史惯例有利于乘客和航空公司双方各自利益。

2.新进入者权利规则

欧盟关于“新进入者”定义有一个先后变化。欧盟第95/93号规章规定

① See James D. Reitzes etc., “Competitive Effects of Exchanges or Sales of Airport Landing Slots”, *Rev Ind Organ* 46, 2015, pp. 95 – 125.

② 中国民用航空局运输司、中国民航大学编:《航空运输市场管理政策与法规:欧盟、澳、日、新部分》,中国民航出版社2009年版,第146页。

的新进入者一般是指“申请机场某一天的航班时刻,且其在该机场该日所拥有的或者所分配到的航班时刻少于4个的航空承运人”,且其规定“在相关日在某特定机场拥有总的航班时刻3%以上的航空承运人,或者该日在机场系统拥有总的航班时刻2%以上的航空承运人,不得视为该机场的新进入者”。而新修订的第793/2004号规章认为“新进入者可以理解为增强地区性航空运输服务的充分供给,并且在共同体内部航线上增加潜在的竞争”,其重新定义新进入者是“在任一机场、任何一天申请一个航班时刻或者连续航班时刻的航空承运人,假如它的申请被接受,这一天它在该机场所拥有的航班时刻仍然少于5个的航空承运人”,且“某一日在一个特定机场拥有的航班时刻超过时刻总量5%的航空承运人,或者某一日在机场系统拥有的航班时刻超过时刻总量4%的航空承运人,不得视为该机场的新进入者”。

欧盟与IATA在新进入航空公司方面适用的分配规则都是“五五法则”,其具体规定是“时刻池中50%的时刻要首先分配给新进入的航空公司,除非新进入的航空公司需求少于50%的时刻数量”;同时其规定,如果分配给新进入航空公司的航班时刻,是其申请前或后一个小时之内的时刻,但航空公司未接受该时刻的,则其新进入者身份将会被取消。第793/2004号规章还对新进入者转让或交换航班时刻进行了限制,新进入者在两个对等航季的时期内,不得转让或交换航班时刻。从对新进入者的规定可知,欧盟对于新进入者范围在第793/2004号规章中得以扩大,能够更好地保护新进入者的权利,且只有真正的新进入者才能优先分配到时刻。

3. 交易规则

欧盟时刻分配遵循的最基本原则是确保能最大限度地利用机场稀缺的容量。因此通过经济手段调节供需矛盾逐渐引起欧盟的重视,新修订的第793/2004号规章对“时刻流动性”、时刻转让和时刻交换进行了规定。欧盟第793/2004号规章第8a条允许进行航班时刻的转让和交换,在母公司与子公司之间,和同一母公司的不同子公司之间可以进行航班时刻的转让;两个航空承运人之间可以“一个换一个”的方式进行交换;转让和交换都应当通知协调人并经协调人批准。同时第 8a 条还规定,“时刻不允许在承运人之间,或承运人与独立实体之间以货币补偿的形式进行转让”,这也说明欧盟禁止航班时刻的有偿转让。

在欧共体委员会内部,就航班时刻的市场化交易机制进行了多次提议与探讨,除英国、卢森堡和荷兰外,其他成员国都表示在没有对引入市场准入机制的冲击进行深入分析之前,不能将航班时刻市场交易合法化。欧盟目前没有引入时刻的市场分配机制,仅允许在次级交易进行时刻的交换和转让。而在英国的灰色市场上已经存在航班时刻的市场交易行为。航班时刻的交易在确保新进入者市场准入方面存在一定缺陷,对新进入者来说,在拥挤机场能够获得的时刻数量将会越来越少。因此,欧盟第 793/2004 号规章与 IATA 适用的航班时刻分配机制一致,二者都不实行航班时刻的市场化配置,但允许时刻的转让和交易。

欧盟在 2004 年颁布的第 793/2004 号规章是对第 95/93 号规章的修订案,且共同规制着欧盟共同体机场航班时刻的分配。欧盟最新的航班时刻分配的法律规则基本沿用了 IATA 的时刻分配规则,无论是从“祖父权利”“二八法则”以及保证新进入者权利的“五五法则”等时刻分配规则,还是为分配时刻设立的协调人、协调委员会等管理制度方面的内容,[①]欧盟与 IATA 规定得十分相似。由于单一行政分配模式下产生的低效率等弊端,欧盟一直在探讨是否需要引进像美国一样的时刻交易机制以提高航班时刻资源管理的灵活性。

(三)美国航班时刻分配法律规则

美国作为当今世界上航空运输最发达的国家,其民用航空事业在 20 世纪 20 年代末就超过了欧洲。美国最早在航空运输领域关于航班时刻的立法于 1969 年就有了《高密度规则》,而在 1966 年其国内航空运输实践中就早已

---

① 参见[德]阿基姆·泽尼等编:《航班时刻——改革的国际经验与借鉴》,王利亚译,中国民航出版社 2011 年版,第 381 ~382 页。

有了航班时刻的雏形。从1968年开始至今,美国经历了三次航班时刻分配制度改革,其不断探求航班时刻有效分配的制度,也是目前世界上航班时刻分配制度最领先的国家之一。与IATA和欧盟不同的是,经过多年的实践发展,当今的美国采用混合管理的航班时刻分配制度,其运用行政手段和市场手段来共同管理航班时刻的分配,以求航班时刻分配制度能更加灵活、透明、有效率。

1.历史优先权利规则

美国1969年颁布的《高密度规则》(High Density Rule,HDR)是对机场实施准入管制的最早法律规定,这也是美国航班时刻分配第一阶段(1968~1985年)的开端。在这一阶段美国采用航班时刻完全行政分配模式,其本质是实行基于“祖父权利”原则的历史优先权分配规则,航班时刻的分配和使用都是无偿的。HDR规定了5家机场属于高密度机场,在高密度机场实行航班时刻数量限制,使用航班时刻需要提交申请并经审批才可。

因完全行政分配模式的弊端,美国在航班时刻改革的第二阶段,也即引入市场交易手段分配航班时刻阶段,在该阶段“祖父权利”支配下的时刻分配仍然发生在美国一小部分拥堵机场中。在C.F.R.中第14卷第Ⅰ章第F子章第93部分第S子部分第93.215节载明,“航空公司可以在未来的相应航季内永久性持有其历史上在肯尼迪国际机场使用的航班时刻,但应在规定的时间内以书面形式向美国联邦航空局履行了通知义务”。[①] 此条款说明了美国在航班时刻初始分配中仍然保留适用“历史航班时刻优先”的规则,这是对“祖父权利”的直接应用。对于历史航班时刻的申请,只要由航班时刻管理办公室确认并经FAA首席决策顾问最终决定通过后既可由原航空公司继续持有相同航班时刻。这也说明了在航班时刻的初始分配中,规定了“永久性历史航班时刻”优先的规则,且其历史时刻仍然沿用“祖父权利”原则。与IATA类似的是,美国航班时刻分配也遵循“不用即失”规则,在C.F.R.中

① Code of Federal Regulations, § 93.215 Initial allocation of slots. ,14 C.F.R. § 93.215.

第 14 卷第Ⅰ章第 F 子章第 93 部分第 S 子部分第 93.227 节第 a 项规定了任何在 2 个月内使用率低于 80% 的航班时刻将被 FAA 召回,这就意味着申请的航班时刻未在规定时间内达到 80% 的使用率,则就会丧失历史优先权资格。

在美国航班时刻改革的第三阶段,也即探索建立航班时刻一级市场阶段,美国想尝试废除“祖父权利”条款,进行航班时刻初级市场拍卖,对美国来讲这种尝试无疑是一项巨大的挑战。沿袭多年的“祖父条款”一直是航班时刻初始分配领域的核心规则,虽然有其先天的弊端但是其一直维持着航班时刻分配的稳定秩序,能不能废除“祖父权利”条款,废除其之后会引起什么问题且产生什么不可逆转的后果等等这些问题都是必须要考虑的焦点问题。初级市场“时刻拍卖”在美国并未进行下去,“祖父权利”未被废除,但美国在第三阶段对“祖父权利”规定了“有效期”,这为新进入的航空公司来讲无疑是一个十分利好的制度,该制度兼备了航班时刻分配运营的稳定性和公平性。

2. 新进入者权利规则

在美国采取混合管理的航班时刻分配制度期间,赋予了新进入者航班时刻市场准入的权利。美国对新进入者的身份界定条款体现在 C. F. R. 中第 14 卷第Ⅰ章第 F 子章第 93 部分第 S 子部分第 93.213 节中,从该定义中我们可知,美国对新进入者的定义是在 1985 年 12 月 16 日之后,从未在特定机场出售或放弃过航班时刻,且没有持有该机场任何航班时刻的通勤营运人或航空公司。[①] 美国采用了和 IATA 完全不同的界定标准,一方面美国对新进入者的身份界定不仅限于航空公司,还包括通勤营运人,而 IATA 规定新进入者只限于航空公司;另一方面,美国没有像 IATA 一样对新进入者身份设置较宽的限制条件,其仅规定从未持有、出售或放弃过航班时刻的运营人或公司为新进入者,而 IATA 规定的是在某特定日持有时刻数量小于 5 的航空公司为新进入者,这说明从时刻持有数量上看 IATA 规定的新进入者范围更广。

---

① Code of Federal Regulations, § 93.213 Definitions and general provisions, 14 C. F. R. § 93.213.

在 C. F. R. 中第 14 卷第Ⅰ章第 F 子章第 93 部分第 S 子部分第 93. 225 节第 h 项下载明了航班时刻分配中新进入者的优先权利，①在美国第二阶段的时刻分配改革中采取抽签方式进行时刻分配。所谓抽签，不是抽取航班时刻，而是通过随机抽签方式确定航班时刻选择的顺序，每一航空公司应在 5 分钟内作出决定，否则将失去该轮选择的机会。在首轮抽签循环中，新进入者优先于在位航空承运人获得分配的时刻，对新进入者会预留可分配航班时刻的 25% 且不少于 2 个的可用航班时刻容量供其优先选择，但总持有航班时刻的数量不得超过 12 个。同时，在航班时刻分配给新进入者的 90 天内，即使新进入者对航班时刻的使用率未达到 80%，也不会丧失优先权。如果在 90 天中的任意 2 个月时间中其航班时刻的使用率不低于 65% 的，航空公司可以提前出租其航班时刻，否则通过抽签获得航班时刻的航空公司不得在 90 天内出租其航班时刻。而 IATA 规定的是优先给予新进入航空公司可分配航班时刻的 50%，显然 IATA 规定对新进入者而言更加有利。

3. 交易规则

在美国采用混合管理的航班时刻分配模式期间，也即是美国实行航班时刻行政性抽签分配和二级市场交易相结合的阶段。美国航班时刻初次分配中没有引入市场交易手段，根据 C. F. R. 第 14 卷第Ⅰ章第 F 子章第 93 部分第 S 子部分第 93. 221 节的规定，②我们可知航班时刻在初次分配后，可在同一机场或者其他高密度交通机场在任何时间内以任何对价采取组合时刻或单一时刻方式进行买卖、租赁交易。美国对新进入者买卖、租赁其获得航班时刻设置了时间限制条款，根据该条款的其他规定，通过抽签分配获得航班时刻的新进入者和限定性在位承运人，必须使用其获得的航班时刻达到 60 天后才可以向其他新进入者或者限定性在位承运人进行买卖、租赁或其他交易。不同的是，根据 C. F. R. 第 14 卷第Ⅰ章第 F 子章第 93 部分第 S 子部分第 93. 219 节中相关规定可知，对于国际航班时刻和基本需求航班时刻不允

---

① Code of Federal Regulations, § 93. 225 Lottery of available slots. ,14 C. F. R. § 93. 225.

② Code of Federal Regulations, § 93. 221 Transfer of slots. ,14 C. F. R. § 93. 221.

许进行买卖、租赁或其他交易,但是这些时刻可以在同一机场以“一个换一个”的方式进行交换,且交换不应有对价存在。[①] 由此规定可知,在美国对涉及国防、外交等方面的国际航班和基本需求航班是不允许进行市场化交易的,只允许国内航班时刻进行市场化交易。除了对航班时刻交易的实质内容进行规定外,美国还对航班时刻交易涉及的程序进行了缜密细致的规定。根据 C. F. R. 第 14 卷第Ⅰ章第 F 子章第 93 部分第 S 子部分的内容,转让航班时刻需要向 FAA 部门履行一系列的程序义务,如提交书面转让证据、申请转让批准和确认等。

美国开创了航班时刻交易制度的先河,其国内最先在高密度机场开设了允许航班时刻市场交易的规定。[②] 市场交易机制的引进克服了单纯由行政分配航班时刻带来的弊端,使航班时刻资源在市场上更加灵活地分配给更需要的航空承运人,避免时刻虚占等问题。与此同时,二级市场交易制度也产生了交易收入归属等争议,为促进美国航班秩序朝着更加公平和效率的方向发展,美国自 2000 年开始再次进行航班时刻分配改革,此次改革是在以前分配制度的基础上进行航班时刻一级市场交易的实验,同时采取二级“盲人市场”的转让制度。

美国在第三次航班时刻改革中,在一级市场引入“拥挤航班时刻收费”“航班时刻拍卖”等制度。所谓的拥挤航班时刻收费“是指对于空域使用需要超过机场容量需要的航班时刻进行收费”,[③]以便改善机场地面容量。拍卖航班时刻是基于航班时刻资源的稀缺性和机场拥挤的现状提出,但由于上述两制度的实施会在实践操作中面临较多需要解决的问题,因此目前还没有进行推广应用。为规避航班时刻私下交易的混乱和通谋等不良现象,出现了

---

① Code of Federal Regulations, § 93. 219 Allocation of slots for essential air service operations and applicable limitations, 14 C. F. R. § 93. 219.

② See Benjamin Berlin, Graham Keithly, "Asserting Broad Authority or Circumventing Deregulation: FAA's Proposed Regulation of New York Airport Slot Transactions", *The Air & Space Lawyer* 28, 2015, p. 20.

③ 中国民航局政策法规司、中国民航大学编:《民航航班时刻管理的理论与实践——一种稀缺资源的应用研究》,中国民航出版社 2009 年版,第 135 页。

二级转让“盲人市场”制度,所谓的“盲人市场”指的是,对预计要进行买卖、租赁等交易的航班时刻及其交易双方的信息采取保密的措施,也即采用“保密投标”的方法进行交易。这种交易方式中由 FAA 做中间人,其作用类似于“招投标代理人”,航空公司将欲进行交易的航班时刻告知 FAA,由 FAA 进行公布该航班时刻交易中除出售人信息之外的所有信息进行招标,FAA 将出价最高的合格投标发给出售人由出售人决定是否成交,若交易达成,则在交易达成后公布双方交易当事人的身份信息。航班时刻二级转让“盲人市场”制度是在以前二级市场交易制度基础上改革发展而来的,其在实践中取得了一定的成效,促进了航班时刻二级转让市场公平竞争秩序的建立。

(四)拉丁美洲部分国家航班时刻分配法律规则

在拉丁美洲,民用航空业正经历着前所未有的增长,在位于哥伦比亚波哥大的埃尔多拉多国际机场(以下简称波哥大机场)、位于墨西哥的墨西哥城—贝尼托·胡亚雷斯机场(以下简称墨西哥机场)和位于巴西圣保罗的瓜鲁柳斯国际机场(以下简称圣保罗机场)都有航班时刻的规定,而在这些机场中实行的航班时刻规则都与 IATA 航班时刻国际标准规则不同,与其他航班时刻运营大国的规定也不相类似,且其各自内部规定也各有不同。①

1. 历史优先权规则

墨西哥机场在航班时刻分配制度上遵循着“祖父权利”规则,历史航班时刻使用者仍然具有时刻分配的首要优先地位。首先,根据墨西哥的规定,当两个以上航空公司申请同一个航班时刻时,航班时刻会优先分配给历史航班时刻使用者。其次,航班服务的准点率会作为第二优先分配的考量因素。“不用即失”原则在墨西哥机场表现为航班业务的准点率要求。与 IATA 国际标准规定不同的是,墨西哥机场要求航空公司提供至少 85% 的使用率,该

---

① See Jose Ignacio Garcia-Arboleda, “Airport Slot Regulation in Latin America: Between Building the Fortress and Protecting the Newcomers”, *Issues in Aviation Law and Policy* 12, 2013, p. 574.

使用率标准高于 IATA 规定的 80% 国际标准。同时,其亦规定,如果非因不可归责的原因导致航班迟延、取消等其他未按规定计划执飞的情形,这些时刻将会被墨西哥民用航空主管部门撤回,而这一规定与 IATA 的规定是一致的。最后墨西哥还规定,在同航季长期提供有效运营业务的航空公司享有时刻分配的第三优先权。墨西哥机场的航班时刻优先权获取资格大体规则上与 IATA 规定的较为相似,但是其规定了比 IATA 更高的使用率,这种高标准能够更有效地利用稀缺的机场基础设施容量,同时也能为时刻竞争者提供更广阔的公平竞争环境,增加获取航班时刻的机会。

值得注意的是,哥伦比亚的波哥大机场同样适用"祖父权利"规则,但是其突破了"祖父权利"规则适用的首要优先地位。根据波哥大机场航班时刻的相关规定,可用航班时刻的 80% 应分配给从事定期航运业务的航空公司,这说明了在波哥大机场定期航班享有航班时刻分配的最高优先权,而不考虑各航空公司在过往使用特定航班时刻的历史记录,这也就意味着航班时刻并不优先分配给享有历史权利的航空公司,历史时刻持有者并不享有时刻分配的首要优先地位,这是与 IATA 规定的明显不同之处。另外,当两个以上的航空公司同时申请一个航班时刻时,航班时刻会优先分配给在过去三个月内提供"最准时服务"的航空公司,只有在这种情形下如果申请一方为历史航班时刻使用者,则其优先于其他航空公司获得航班时刻。同时,在波哥大机场会以一种非常特殊的方式强制执行历史优先权,根据其规定,"对于同一航班时刻的申请,拥有更充足时间去运营的航空公司享有优先权"。这一规定也很快引起了理论界中的混乱,因为各方对"同一时刻"的理解不同也就导致歧义。有些航空公司为获取时刻,将规定中的"同一时刻"解释为"航空公司可以向另一航空公司要求提供已分配的并正在运营中的航班时刻",而这一解释会导致竞争对手故意滥用规则的问题,显然不符合哥伦比亚法律规定的公平性和合理性。除此之外,航班时刻运营所服务的市场大小和航空公司计划使用多大载客容量的航空飞机也是波哥大机场分配航班时刻优先考虑的因素,而很多国家航班时刻分配制度中未将该条所涉因素考虑进去。

在巴西圣保罗机场,航班时刻分配规则没有"祖父权利"条款以及类似规定等的历史优先权规则。在巴西,航班时刻分配采用"圆桌轮流规则"和"抽签分配规则",即先由航空公司通过抽签方式决定进行航班时刻分配的顺序,第一位航空公司首先分配得到航班时刻组合,然后第一位航空公司将转变为第二轮时刻分配的最后一位,依次循环进行轮流分配。其中,可用航班时刻的80%将会分配给在位的航空公司,但是并不实行历史优先权规则,每个航空公司都可以在公平竞争的分配环境中获得一组航班时刻,剩余20%的航班时刻将分配给新进入者。巴西机场通过这种"圆桌轮流规则"保证了每位航空公司都享有同等的机会公平获得航班时刻。显然,美国在其第三次航班时刻分配改革中探索的废除"祖父权利"规则下的运营模式在巴西得到了实践。

2. 新进入者权利规则

墨西哥机场和波哥大机场都没有对新进入航空公司设立具体的规定,这也是与 IATA 航班时刻规则规定的最大不同。在墨西哥机场容量饱和状态下,新进入者需要花费更多的金钱才能获得机场的航班时刻,通常情况下,新进入者很难申请到可用的航班时刻。波哥大机场对新进入者的界定较为宽泛模糊,任何从未在机场运营过的航空公司都被视为新进入航空公司,且不区分国际航空还是国内航空公司。

与此形成对比的是,在巴西圣保罗机场,对新进入者适用的航班时刻分配规则进行了专门具体的规定。在圣保罗机场,新进入者指"从未在任何机场进行过运营但有意运营的航空公司,或者虽在机场运营过,但在一天内持有少于3组航班时刻或在一周内持有少于21组航班时刻的航空公司"。根据巴西圣保罗机场的"圆桌轮流规则",新进入者有权利在圆桌会议上占据一个时刻分配的位置,且每向在位航空承运人分配4组航班时刻,就必须向新进入者分配1组航班时刻。巴西"圆桌轮流规则"目标是为新进入者和在位航空承运人提供一个中立公平的时刻分配规则,但在实践中的运行效果并不理想,其不但使新进入者更难获取航班时刻,反而将对在位航空承运人的航班时刻计划配置额固化为“祖父权利”,直接导致各航空承运人之间的不平等待遇问题。

3. 交易规则

《墨西哥城国际机场一般运营规则》规定了墨西哥城航班时刻分配规则,根据其中的规定,航空公司或航空承运人之间可以自由的以交换、转让等无偿或有偿的交易方式分配其已经使用一年以上的航班时刻,且时刻交易应通知墨西哥航空主管部门,否则墨西哥航空主管部门有权要求撤回该航班时刻。除此之外,在墨西哥没有关于航班时刻交易的其他规则。由于墨西哥航空主管部门没有义务去审查交易中可能存在的反竞争行为,这也导致了一些问题。例如,在实践中一些在位航空公司或者较大规模的航空公司出于排挤竞争对手的考虑,通过高竞价获得航班时刻。而对于该种交易,任何参与交易的各方主体都没有义务去披露交易信息,这就导致在实践操作中很难去认定该种交易涉嫌反竞争行为,因此难以构建一个公平竞争的环境。

《哥伦比亚民用航空规则》规范着波哥大机场航班时刻的运营,与 IATA 规定得一样,经哥伦比亚民航局批准,航班时刻的交易只允许在航空公司之间进行,且被交易的航班时刻使用率要求达到 80% 以上,但是该规则的弊端是没有就航班时刻 80% 的使用率要求规定时间限制,同样在实践中会存在反公平竞争的行为。

巴西《航班时刻管理一般规则》①是巴西国家民航局于 2006 年 7 月 3 日通过的第 2 号法案。根据该法案中有关航班时刻分配制度的规定,只有基于优化航班时刻运营或改进经济、技术性能的需要,航空公司之间才允许以“一个换一个”的方式交换航班时刻,且该种交换需要经过巴西国家民航局的事先批准。该法案并没有规定该种交换是否会支付适当的补偿或报酬,但是可以明确的是,在巴西禁止将航班时刻的交换进行“商业化”,否则国家民航局将会撤回该航班时刻。从此规定可知,与 IATA 一样,巴西并没有引入航班

① Brazil-Agência Nacional de Aviação Civil, Ato Resolução No. 2 de 3 de Julho de 2006.

时刻市场化分配机制,而是通过“一个换一个”的方式灵活分配航班时刻以避免航班时刻的虚占浪费等问题。

(五)小结

在论文的第二大部分对现今航班时刻的主要分配规则进行了比较研究,首先介绍了国际公认时刻分配标准——IATA 制定的航班时刻准则,其次对欧盟、美国、墨西哥、哥伦比亚、巴西等国家在航班时刻分配制度上彰显的特色或者收效显著的规则进行论述。通过以上比较分析可得出以下几点结论:

“祖父权利”规则作为目前航班时刻分配机制的核心规则,是保障机场容量利用效率的一个非常重要的规则,且在大多数国家的航班时刻分配制度中都有其发挥作用的身影。该权利在民用航空业的航班时刻分配制度中运行了将近半个世纪的时间,其确保了新的航班时刻表是基于历史惯例,在过去可行的时刻表基础上进行修订而成的,因而在很大程度上保证了航班运行的连续性、一致性和稳定性。“祖父权利”规则可以发挥两大优势:一是它使旅客习惯于某一航空公司的航班时刻,从而减少旅客查找和交易成本;二是它为机场和空中交通管制部门提供了高度确定性,如果在每航季航班时刻表都全部重新制定或时刻都全部重新分配的话,那么这种确定性是不会存在的。

“不用即失”规则最早于 1985 年引入,目的是鼓励航空公司有效率地使用航班时刻,避免航班时刻持有者虚占囤积时刻。现如今,IATA 国际标准和美国等大多数国家将航班时刻的使用率门槛设置为 80%,并且规定了 3 个月的使用率时间限制,而在拉丁美洲的部分国家还有将航班时刻的使用率规定为 85% 的情形,对所有未达到规定使用率的航空公司已分配的航班时刻进行撤回并重新再分配。一定程度上该规则为新进入航空公司或其他航空公司获得航班时刻提供了更多机会。

新进入航空公司作为承担航空运输的一分子,在航班时刻分配国际标准和大多数发达国家分配制度中都为其留有一定比例的分配席位,以保证其可以优先获得航班时刻。但是“祖父权利”规则的设置很大程度上限制新进入航空公司公平获得航班时刻的权利。而在拉丁美洲的有些国家并不设立"新进入者相关制度",其认为专门为保障新进入者权利的"新进入者制度"本身就是不公平的制度,其区别了新进入者和其他航空公司在获取航班时刻方面的地位与权利,这样的不公平制度产生的分配结果本身也是不公平的。

航班时刻市场交易机制的引入,盘活了原由"祖父权利"规则支配的固化的航班时刻分配制度,为航班时刻的真正需求者提供获取航班时刻的机会,为航班时刻的有效运营提供了制度保障。从目前各国的实践来看,美国在航班时刻市场分配机制探索方面走在全球最前列,且诞生了很多有价值的制度,如二级转让"盲人市场"制度等。美国率先引入航班时刻的二级市场交易机制,之后为平衡各相关方的利益又试图引入"一级市场交易机制",如探索航班时刻一级市场拍卖制度等。①

不可否认的是,除上述分配规则之外,在航班时刻的分配制度中还存在很多有价值的规则或标准正在规范着整个航空运输业的有效发展,如"全年无休制""宵禁制度""本地准则""业务和市场类型"等规则制度。

综上所述可得知,解决机场拥挤和时刻延误问题,既需要通过引入市场手段灵活的配置时刻资源,同时又需要"国家之手"这支有形的行政力量来进行调节规范。行政规范既包括对事前的航班时刻规则进行设置,又包括因市场弊端引起的反公平竞争行为的事后救济等措施,这也为构建和完善中国航班时刻分配制度提供了很好的借鉴。

四、中国航班时刻分配制度及其法治进路

(一)中国航班时刻分配制度

1. 中国的航班时刻分配制度现状

我国最早在2005年由中国民用航空局首次出台了关于规范航班时刻的

---

① See Daniel R. Polsby, "Airport Pricing of Aircraft Takeoff and Landing Slots: An Economic Critique of Federal Regulatory Policy", *California Law Review* 89, 2001, p. 805.

试行办法,之后陆续下发了暂行办法、实施细则、通知等相关法律文件对航班时刻分配制度进行改革。在此期间,我国航班时刻长期采用行政分配的主模式,适用“行政分配”“祖父权利”“无偿使用”等分配规则,实质上还是在更多的维护大型航空公司、在位航空公司的利益,而新进入航空公司很难获得航班时刻。另外,在此阶段虽然允许在极强的行政力量控制下进行时刻的交换和调整,但是并不允许航班时刻进行交易,这严重限制了航班时刻配置的灵活性与效率性,无法构建一个公平竞争的航班时刻分配秩序。

在航空承运人要求改革的呼声逐渐高涨的情况下,我国从 2015 年开始探索航班时刻市场改革道路,首次启动了在繁忙机场航班时刻资源市场改革试点项目。根据改革试点方案,本次试点项目采取初级市场和次级市场共同推进的方式,通过市场配置获得的航班时刻资源具有 3 年的使用权,不需要换季时刻协调,不具有所有权;在初级市场获得的航班时刻可以在次级市场进行交换、转让、出租、出借、出售等方式的交易,交易完成后需进行报备;以行政分配方式获得的航班时刻,在次级市场可基于“一对一”原则进行交换;交易和交换可基于无偿和有偿;如有滥用情形,航班时刻资源将会被召回。

上述改革试点具体应用到实践操作中时,先是对广州白云机场的 9 组航班时刻进行了“拍卖”,该次“时刻拍卖”对所有航空公司一视同仁,不区分所有制性质,不区分规模大小,各航空公司平等参与竞拍,竞价最高者以第二高价位作为成交价。白云机场的“时刻拍卖”,有利于发挥时刻的最大经济价值,且赋予了市场上最需要该特定航班时刻的航空公司公平获得时刻的分配机会,尤其是新进入航空公司,但也产生了一些消极影响:其一,时刻拍卖所得的收益归于国家引起了理论界及实际交易中各相关利益主体的激烈争论;其二,通过高价拍到时刻的航空公司会将拍卖成本转嫁给消费者,加重了消费者的负担;其三,高昂的竞拍价格也阻止了众多中小型航空公司的脚步,很大程度上限制了其发展。这次“拍卖”不仅对探索中国航班时刻分配制度意义非凡,对全世界来说也是一次先进的尝试。

紧接着在上海浦东机场进行了“时刻抽签 + 使用费”分配模式试点,其操作规则为:分别对新进入航空公司、主基地航空公司和其他在位航空公司分类组建“时刻池”进行两轮次抽签,第一轮按照一个时刻系列组合对应一次抽签的原则,随机排定三类抽签池的抽签顺序;第二轮在第一轮排定的抽签池中随机抽签,中签航空公司在时刻池中选择一个时刻系列组合。从浦东机场的时刻抽签分配模式中,可以看出试点方案赋予了每家航空公司获取航班时刻的公平分配机会,打破了以往由行政分配模式主导下的不公平准入现象,但这种分配模式的随机性也会导致航空公司在初次分配中错过其心仪的目标时刻,而幸运的是其可以在次级市场再进行交易。

我国航班时刻市场配置试点改革取得了一定成效,这直接体现于2018年颁布的《民航航班时刻管理办法》(以下简称《办法》)。《办法》结合我国实践发展,力求与IATA国际标准相一致,采用初级市场行政化配置和次级市场市场化配置相结合的分配模式,初级分配依然遵循“历史优先权”“不用即失”“新进入者优先分配”等相关分配规则,以历史航班时刻为最优先分配级,对新进入者分配时刻池中20% ~50%的时刻,最后剩余的时刻分配给在位航空公司;在次级市场以申请为前提,允许历史航班时刻在满足规定运行时间的条件下进行交换、转让、共同经营,交换按照同一机场“一个换一个”的原则进行,转让只能对正在或计划在同一机场运营的航空承运人。中国民用航空局和各地区管理局负责对在各机场的航班时刻运营进行监督。

随着北京大兴国际机场的投产运营,2019年北京进入“一市两场”时代,大兴国际机场和首都机场成为北京双枢纽机场。根据2019年年初发布的《北京大兴国际机场转场投运及“一市两场”航班时刻资源配置方案》(以下简称《方案》)等相关文件的指示规定,在北京两个国际机场新增的航班时刻均遵循主基地航空公司优先分配原则,仅东航集团和南航集团分别占有大兴国际机场新增航班时刻比例为40%,合计为80%。根据该规定,同等条件下,新进入航空公司优先于在位航空公司获得时刻,相对于已经分配给东航和南航的时刻而言,新进入航空公司不会获得更多更好时段的航班时刻。从《方案》附件1《各公司冬春和夏秋航季历史时刻数量》表来看,南航、东航和国航三大航空公司占据了几乎全部的历史航班时刻。

2. 中国航班时刻分配制度存在的问题

现阶段,我国航班时刻分配制度采用行政分配和市场分配相结合的模式,市场化路程还处于刚起步阶段。《办法》确立了"祖父权利"、"不用即失"规则、"五五法则"、"市场交易"等逐渐在与国际航班时刻标准接轨的规则,将在很大程度上促使我国民营和小型航空公司获得更有利的高速发展,总体来看在最新的分配政策下,我国各航空公司都将会受益于行业发展。但应引起注意的是,我国的航班时刻分配制度依然存在一些问题。

(1)缺乏航班时刻法律定性

目前,在我国的法律体系中没有对航班时刻进行明确的法律定性。从我国政府出台的各相关文件可以看出航班时刻分配被界定为一种行政许可权,但是在我国民法体系尤其是物权法体系中没有对航班时刻的法律属性、权利归属进行明确的规定。航班时刻作为一种能产生经济价值的稀缺资源,各相关利益主体都竞相争取其权益,而不明确的法律规定导致在实践操作中经常出现各种问题:航班时刻是否应由政府进行行政管制?航班时刻是否都能进行市场交易?时刻交易的收益应归属于谁?

同时值得注意的是,我国试点改革中的"时刻拍卖"也在理论界挑起了有关航班时刻资源的法律归属的"千层浪"。在2019年颁布的《办法》中并没有将"拍卖"这一交易方式纳入市场配置体系之中。拍卖是具有一套明确规则的市场交易制度,该制度以市场交易参与者投标竞价为基础,决定资源的分配和价格。① 我国是世界上第二个开展"时刻拍卖"探索的国家,第一个是在2009年的美国,在理论界"时刻拍卖"本是最佳的分配时刻的模式,其让时刻资源回归市场,发挥市场的作用来调解稀缺的时刻资源,而在实践中,时刻的拍卖虽然使各方都获得了巨大的经济利益,但也引起了各利益相关方的争夺战,在国家法律和政策规定中航班时刻权属的不确定性问题也将这场争

① 参见中国拍卖行业协会编:《拍卖通论》,中国财政经济出版社2006年版,第2页。

夺战的战火烧向了理论界,对时刻拍卖的收入归属也是各有各说。

(2)未确立公平合理的竞争规则

我国2019年颁布的《办法》并没有从实质上确立一个公平合理的竞争规则。虽然我国目前施行的航班时刻规则给予了新进入航空公司获得航班时刻一定比例的优先分配权利,但是其仍然彰显的是历史航班时刻持有者的绝对优势地位。在我国中国国际航空股份有限公司(以下简称国航)、中国南方航空股份有限公司(以下简称南航)、中国东方航空公司股份有限公司(以下简称东航)三大航空公司的支配控制下,基地航空公司在枢纽机场中的地位难以撼动,中小航空公司在初次分配中仍然难以获得其梦寐以求的航班时刻,即便是在航班时刻的次级市场上中小航空公司由于其财力有限也很难获得其想要的航班时刻。

据统计,我国三大航空公司在民航运输总周转量中占比超过7成,在航线占比中仍占绝对优势,①在航班时刻的分配中占据主要地位,民营航空公司和小型航空公司获得黄金时刻的机会仍然占相对较小的比例。换句话说,民营和中小航空公司仍然没有被公平对待。市场分配机制如何具体有效地应用到实践中,如何平衡现阶段的各方矛盾,如何构建稳健运行的时刻分配秩序以保障航空安全仍是亟待解决的问题。必须引起重视的是,在航班时刻的分配实践中,目前我国航空业已经形成了以三大航空公司为主导,多家航空公司并存的局面。因此建立公平公正、高效有序的航班时刻分配秩序仍是现阶段我国时刻分配制度亟须努力的方向。

(3)缺乏航班时刻有效监督管理

我国关于航班时刻监督管理所涉及的相关组织机构的设置从形式上看似乎什么机构都有,但是却难以保障其发挥应有的实质性作用。航班时刻监督管理制度涉及很多内容,如确保航班时刻协调委员会的中立地位、对航空公司进行分类管理、保障航班时刻信息的公开透明等。《办法》对以上几个

① 参见《以中国国航、东方航空、南方航空三大航空公司为例,看航空业的投资前景》,载投资界网:https://news.pedaily.cn/201804/430459.shtml,最后访问日期:2019年4月1日。

主要部分都进行了规定,有些规定还有待在实践中进行观察并加以完善,如航班时刻信息公开制度等;有些规定得过于模糊,如对航班时刻协调委员会的规定。

IATA设立的航班时刻协调人是由民航主管机构、机场管理机构、使用该机场的航空公司及其代表组织协商后委任的具有航班时刻表安排方面的知识及协调经验的人员;且时刻协调人在职能和财务方面都必须保持独立,并以中立、透明及不带歧视的方式行事;时刻协调委员会对时刻协调人提出有关容量、航班时刻分配等事项的建议,并监控机场航班时刻使用,其是由经常使用机场的所有航空公司及其代表组织、机场管理机构、机场交通管制机构和通用/商务航空代表等相关主体组成,时刻协调人以观察员身份出席。IATA规定了全面具体的航班时刻管理机制,且各机构能够发挥其实质的作用,以保证航班时刻分配的透明性和公平性。

《办法》在有关术语含义部分对航班时刻协调人进行了解释,认为其"是指具体负责航班时刻协调配置工作的人员",显然该规定过于含糊,其没有说明协调人是由谁委任的,也没有说明协调人具体的协调配置工作地点。同样我国法律上还规定,"航班时刻协调委员会是由民航地区管理局、机场管理机构、空中交通管理机构、航空承运人代表和其他利益相关方组成,航班时刻管理部门、协调人列席",此规定一样是过于宽泛模糊化的,其没有就航班时刻协调委员会的成立组织程序进行规定,也没有像IATA一样说明是在该机场运营的"所有"航空承运人均可加入时刻协调委员会,尤其是新进入航空公司、中小型航空公司的代表。

另外,我国航班时刻管理委员会设置流于形式,①不能引起各方重视。法律虽然规定"航班时刻管理部门和协调人应当坚持中立、透明、非歧视的原则行事",但航班时刻管理部门作为我国民用航空局的代表机构,其不能独立于民航局而存在,且其同时要依据民航局的规定做事,从国家航空布局战略

① 参见中国民航局政策法规司、中国民航大学编:《民航航班时刻管理的理论与实践——一种稀缺资源的应用研究》,中国民航出版社2009年版,第191页。

出发其是否能对所有的航空公司保持中立、非歧视态度?谁来对时刻管理部门进行监督?这些问题在法律中都没有进行明确的规定。

(二)中国航班时刻分配制度的法治进路

我国航班时刻市场化分配机制还处于起步阶段,而欧美航班时刻分配制度经历了将近半个世纪的发展,已经形成了一种较为稳定的分配模式。无论是行政分配模式还是混合管理模式,都在时刻的分配中发挥了更多积极的作用:两种分配模式的运行效率和规范程度都比较高,是各相关利益主体共同认可并接受的公平合理的分配制度;两种分配模式都建立了公开、透明的分配程序和管理制度,为各航空公司营造一个公平竞争的环境;两种分配模式都建立了航班时刻分配的监督管理制度,组建航班时刻协调委员会等机构保障航班时刻分配的公正严肃性;在市场化配置方面,两种分配模式都对一级市场交易、完全市场配置机制抱持谨慎态度。可以说,无论是在航班时刻分配的上层建筑还是具体实践中,国外都有可供我国借鉴的经验和教训。航空运输具有世界性,航班时刻的分配是全球各个国家民航政府主管部门的重要职能,是民航业共同聚焦的关键问题,科学合理的分配机制才能保证稀缺的航班时刻资源得到充分有效的利用。

1. 澄清航班时刻法律属性

我国航空事业发展较晚,航班时刻更是基于航空实践的发展需要而产生的一种有使用价值的资源。在我国目前的法律规定之中,没有对航班时刻进行明确的定性,难以确定航班时刻的权利属性,这就直接导致通过拍卖航班时刻所得的收益归属不明确问题,各利益相关主体竞相主张对航班时刻的权利。理论界更偏向认为航班时刻类似于用益物权性质,认为航班时刻的持有人享有时刻的占有、使用、收益的权利。从世界各国的法律规定来看,无论是大陆法系国家还是英美法系国家,虽然没有从民法领域对航班时刻进行明确的规定,但在行政法领域几乎都将航班时刻作为一种行政许可权看待,我国也不例外。我国民用航空局在其颁布的部门规章中将航班时刻作为一种行政许可权，我国在试点实践中进行的“时刻拍卖”收益最终都收归国库，这也表明了我国国家对航班时刻这一资源归属的态度，认为其应该属于国家所有，但这一试点之后再无实行，这就又为航班时刻的归属问题再次打了个问号。

比较好的做法是，一国政府或其代表机构在航班时刻的初次分配中通过无偿或较低的价格分配航班时刻给航空公司，由此而获得初次分配或初级市场交易的所得用于机场基础设施等容量的投资建设，这样既能扩充机场容量减轻机场建造的巨大压力，又能有利于航空公司更为便利便宜地使用机场基础设施，同时避免机场和航空公司对航班时刻的争夺。这样的做法实质上是将航班时刻这一公共资源所产生的价值再惠及各使用航班时刻的主体之中，使各主体产生一种心理认同：通过其各自努力创造的时刻属于公共资源，是各方共同行为产生的有价值的资源。为使这一有使用价值的公共资源得到有序高效的利用，国家有必要通过其行政手段加以干涉，以求能够达到一种利益平衡。从现今的发展情况来看，我国应将航班时刻尽快纳入“物权法”体系，明确其国家所有的公共资源法律属性，以便更好实施航班时刻分配制度。

2. 坚持行政分配模式

当今世界并不存在完全由市场配置的航班时刻分配模式，原因是在资源有限论下市场调节存在弊端。市场调节资源配置是通过供求和价格的波动来实现的，具有明显的自发性、盲目性和滞后性弊端，单纯的市场配置并不能达到理想的效果，反而容易造成资源的浪费。[①] 航班时刻如果单纯通过市场手段进行配置，首先由于航班时刻权属不清容易引发争抢混乱；其次即便在忽略时刻权属这一先决条件因素情况下，假设航班时刻能在市场上进行有序的分配，由于市场自身的弊端，容易出现哄抬时刻价格的现象，更容易引起时刻的市场垄断问题。

中国特色的社会主义经济制度充分证明了资源的高效利用需要发挥“有

---

① 参见郑红亮主编：《论市场在资源配置中的决定性作用》，广东经济出版社2015 年版，第2 页。

形之手”和“无形之手”的共同作用。各国尤其是美国的时刻改革经验和教训也再次强调了引入市场调节机制的同时更离不开政府的行政调节手段。航班时刻的行政分配模式,逐渐形成了一种自上而下的稳定有序安排,其通过“先到先得原则”在航班时刻的最原始分配之初,便给与了各航空公司最公平的准入门槛。当最初的新进入航空公司逐渐拥有历史优先权资格,成为享有“祖父权利”的历史航班时刻持有者时,这时已经形成了初具规模的半固定式时刻分配模式。由“祖父权利”支配下的时刻分配模式虽然对后来的新进入航空公司来说不太利好,但从航空事业的全局观出发,行政分配是国家理智决策的结果,很大程度上能够维持一种稳定有效的分配模式。因此,坚持行政分配是对航班时刻高效、有序、稳定分配的重要保障。

3. 设立“祖父权利”时效期

当今全球大多数国家在其航班时刻分配制度中仍然沿用“祖父权利”规则,这在一定程度上说明了“祖父权利”的稳定性和有效性。但“祖父权利”规则的运用对新进入航空公司来说无疑是巨大的“绊脚石”,正如前文中多次提到的“祖父权利”是新进入航空公司公平获得时刻的不可移除的障碍。从我国现阶段的航空业发展情况来看,“祖父权利”仍是我国航班时刻分配的重要规则,只要航空公司一直符合获得航班时刻历史优先权的要求就不会丧失其“祖父权利”这一“特权”,既然“祖父权利”在我国不能像在巴西一样完全不采用,那么针对“祖父权利”引起的弊端我们就要寻求新的解决途径。

《办法》中没有对“祖父权利”设置时效期,这里的时效期也可以称为有效期。只要历史航空公司不触犯禁止性规定其就可以一直享受“历史时刻”带给其的权利和利益,而在实践中,历史航空公司所拥有的历史时刻多是价值更高的黄金时刻,如果黄金时刻没有进行轮流使用的和分配,新进入航空公司就永远难以获得该黄金时刻。美国 2006 年在拉瓜迪亚机场对依据“祖父权利”条款初始分配的航班时刻设置有限了 3 ~ 13 年的时效期。该规则在生效后第 4 年开始,每年有 10% 的航班时刻将会到期并被重新赋予 10 年的有效期进行再次分配,这种操作有利于新进入航空公司相对公平的获得航班时刻,每年按比例到期也确保了时刻分配的流动性和稳定性。我国现有的规定中没有相关制度,应设立“祖父权利”的时效期限以保障航班时刻在现阶段更加相对公平的分配。

4. 引入二级转让“盲人市场”制度

二级转让“盲人市场”是美国在航班时刻分配制度最新改革中的一种规则,其是指对拟进行交易的航班时刻采用“保密投标”的方法,航空承运人向FAA发出欲进行出售、出租的航班时刻信息,同时向FAA提供一个最低的投标价,FAA将航班时刻的信息对外公布寻求投标人,FAA将最高价格的合格投标信息发送给招标航空公司,招标航空公司在规定时限内决定拒绝或接受,在此期间招标航空公司和投标航空公司的身份信息予以保密直至交易达成时公开。二级转让“盲人市场”通过对交易双方基本信息进行保密,避免了交易双方私下的不正当合谋,规避了航班时刻二级市场交易存在的无人管理的混乱现象,有利于完善时刻分配二级市场的契约安排。

我国航班时刻法律制度允许在二级市场进行时刻的交换、转让和共同经营,且规定航班时刻转让需要向协调人提出申请并经航班时刻管理部门同意后确认,但这并不能从根源上避免时刻二级市场存在的合谋等排挤竞争对手的交易。在航班时刻分配的二级市场中,大型航空公司为了能够继续在下个航季享有历史优先权资格,往往将其多余的航班时刻以无偿或有偿的方式出租给其他航空公司,要求其他航空公司在一定时段内达到一定的执飞率或使用率,以保证时刻不会被撤回而继续持有。这样的操作将会使好的航班时刻一直保持在持有历史时刻的航空公司手中,中小型航空公司如果不能满足其要求,将会失去在二级市场公平交易的机会。同时,这样的操作不利于航班时刻的流动分配,难以保证交易的正当和公平,而引入二级转让“盲人市场”恰好可以规避这样的风险。

5. 引入“圆桌规则”轮流分配机制

放眼全世界,巴西在其航班时刻分配中没有采用“祖父权利”规则,而是采用其特有的“圆桌规则”。“圆桌规则”相当于完全废除了“祖父权利”,其规则是不区分航空公司的性质、规模等要素,所有航空公司以“一司一票”的原则通过抽签决定分配时刻的顺序,以“轮流”的方式进行时刻的有序分配。虽然巴西也规定80%的航班时刻分配给在位航空公司,20%的航班时刻分配给新进入航空公司。但引人注目的是,其“圆桌规则”从理论上似乎可以确保各航空公司获得时刻的公平性,但却在这种“公平”性前附加了很大的随机性。因此从某种意义上讲,使用这一规则能保证各航空公司获得时刻分配的形式公平,但并不能确保时刻分配的实质公平。

“圆桌规则”有点类似于我国在2015年试点改革中的“抽签制”,在公平性前都附加了随机性,但由于实践的复杂性和航空公司众多各异的利益追求,这一规则可以算作目前为止可以采取的平衡措施中较为被普遍认同和接受的一种方式了。我国航班时刻分配制度属于稳中求进型,可以预见的是“祖父权利”规则在很长时间内是不会被废除的,是否适用“圆桌规则”也要结合我国的实际情况进行抉择,无疑这将是一次大胆的选择。但可以肯定的是,“圆桌规则”的这种公平轮流模式在复杂的时刻分配机制中更能为各航空公司所认同和接受。

6. 强化航班时刻的监督管理制度

良好的航班时刻监督管理制度是分配制度有效发挥作用的保障。针对我国航班时刻监督管理不力的问题,笔者提出以下建议。

第一,完善航班时刻协调人及协调委员会制度。航班时刻协调人应在职能和财政上的独立,在协调机场由航班时刻协调人协调需求矛盾,出现争议时最终的决定由航班时刻协调人和航班时刻管理委员会通过投票的形式作出;补充并完善航班时刻协调委员会产生的程序、具体的组成、决策与议事机制,保证航班时刻协调委员会是各相关利益方主动共同作用的组织,保持其中立性地位。

第二,健全航班时刻二级市场交易的程序。规定航空公司定期向监管机构报告其航班时刻交易和持有情况;对航班时刻的交易履行通知、披露等义务;监管机构有权定期或不定期地对各航空公司执行航班时刻的情况进行检查及调查。

第三,加强行政处罚力度。针对那些浪费时刻的行为建立处罚机制,对于不按照规定执行航班时刻、未在规定期限内执行航班时刻的航空公司以及不及时归还空闲航班时刻等行为,应加强对其进行警告和行政罚款的力度;对于存在囤积、垄断航班时刻等不正当竞争行为的相关主体,设立处罚机制。在航班时刻分配制度中适用处罚措施,可以平衡时刻供需矛盾,提高容量的利用效率。

第四,建立争议解决申诉和投诉机制。规定正常的申诉和投诉渠道和受理机制,比如,申诉需提交给协调委员会,委员会在收到申诉后 1 个月内进行处理,航空公司也可以向协调人提出解决建议。

五、结　　语

航班时刻是一个实践先于理论发展的事物,最早在 1966 年的美国华盛顿机场产生,之后在美国 1969 年《高密度规则》中作为对机场实施准入管制的规定。随着航空运输业的高速发展,航班时刻分配在美国历经了 3 次改革,到如今美国采用行政性分配和市场化配置相结合的制度来解决机场拥堵和航班迟延问题。

早期世界上大多数国家采用行政性分配模式,在此模式下基于"先到先得""祖父权利""有效使用""不用即失""五五法则"等规则,持有历史航班时刻的航空公司在航班时刻分配中占据了绝大优势,也为其带来巨额的经济收益,与之牺牲的是新进入航空公司和其他在位航空公司获得的航班时刻。为了盘活航班时刻分配机制,解决日益严重的机场拥堵和延误问题,美国在全世界率先引入了航班时刻市场交易分配制度,通过"买卖""租赁"等交易方式平衡航班时刻供需矛盾,增强航班时刻在不同航空公司之间的流通性,为健全平等、有序、高效的航班时刻分配制度提供参选方案。美国在市场分配制度中的很多规则都很有借鉴意义,如为了减低在"祖父权利"支配下的航空公司的绝对优势地位,同时又不丧失由“祖父权利”规则构建的分配稳定性和高效性,美国通过对“祖父权利”设立时效性来平衡航班时刻初次分配的矛盾;为规避大型航空公司通过垄断航班时刻而继续享有历史优先权的红利,美国在航班时刻二级转让市场采用“盲人机制”,通过匿名交易的方式在航空公司之间建立公平竞争的交易环境。

在《芝加哥公约》没有对航班时刻进行规定的情形下,IATA 制定了世界航班时刻分配准则这一国际标准。IATA 世界航班时刻分配机制采用行政性分配模式,设立了明确的优先规则,如“祖父权利”“有效使用”“不用即失”“五五法则”等这些规则都是 IATA 最显著的特征规则,其中最基本的规则就是基于航空公司对机场的历史使用而进行时刻分配。同时,在 IATA 分配机制下设立的航班时刻协调人,必须遵循透明、中立和非歧视的原则来在各航空公司之间进行航班时刻的分配。目前,世界上大多数国家沿用 IATA 航班时刻分配规则,欧盟就是其“效忠者”。无疑,行政化的航班时刻分配制度虽不是最理想的,但却是最稳定有效的分配模式,其保证航班时刻资源不会被过度利用的同时兼顾了长期稳定、安全的有效使用。

与世界主流航班时刻分配制度不同的是,在拉丁美洲的巴西、哥伦比亚以及墨西哥等国家,实行着完全不同的分配制度。巴西航班时刻分配制度中压根没有规定“祖父权利”这一被大多数国家奉为圭臬的核心规则,哥伦比亚降低了“祖父权利”在航班时刻分配中的首要优先地位,墨西哥在沿用“祖父权利”规则的基础上提高了时刻使用率的标准;在这之中更加值得注意的国家是巴西,巴西采用“圆桌规则”来分配航班时刻,不区分各航空公司的地位和规模因素。虽然“圆桌规则”在巴西实践中并不理想,但是这种规则很能照顾到处于弱势地位的航空公司利益,且从理论上看其更加能彰显时刻分配的公平性。同时,以上 3 个国家都允许航班时刻进行市场化交易,以促进航班时刻在航空公司之间的流转和有效使用。

现今,一些大型机场面临严重的容量不足问题,航班时刻分配变得越来越市场化,航空公司之间的竞争也越来越激烈。经验表明,机场拥堵和时刻紧张的问题总是难以避免，建立完善的航班时刻分配制度能够引导航空公司正确有效地使用航班时刻，能够平衡航班时刻的供需矛盾。

航空运输具有世界性的特点，航空运输业是国家的重要基础性产业，是综合运输体系的有机组成部分，其发达程度是一国国家综合实力和现代化水平的重要标志。毋庸置疑，航空法的产生、发展自始至终都是围绕着航空运输业活动的。可以说，航空法所调整的最主要的对象就是航空运输关系，航班时刻分配问题无疑是由航空运输活动衍生而来的。构建和完善航班时刻分配制度，有利于正确调整民用航空法律关系，合理有效地配置航班时刻资源，协调各利益相关方的利益，保护民用航空活动当事人各方合法权益，推动我国航空大国和世界航空强国的建设。

资　　讯

悼念著名国际航空法学家迈克尔·米尔德教授(1931~2018年)

郑　派[*]

加拿大麦吉尔大学(McGill University)航空法与空间法国际研究所(International Institute of Air and Space Law, IIASL)荣誉主任、国际民航组织(International Civil Aviation Organization,ICAO)法律事务与对外关系局前任局长及首席法律官员、世界著名权威国际航空法学家迈克尔·米尔德(Michael Milde)教授,于2018年5月6日在加拿大安大略省伦敦逝世,享年87岁。

米尔德教授生于捷克古城布拉格,精通英语、捷克语、德语、俄语和法语等5国语言。其后的职业生涯中,他的学术履历包含至少3项法学博士学位与为数众多的其他法律资质。他1955年毕业于布拉格查理大学(Univerzita Karlova)并留校任教,自1966年

* 法学博士,华东政法大学讲师,荷兰莱顿大学(Universiteit Leiden)航空法与空间法国际研究所(IIASL)访问学者,俄罗斯"促进航空"航空法与空间法研究所(Aerohelp)专家组成员。

起连续25年供职于国际民航组织的诸多法律岗位,1983年起连续8年担任国际民航组织法律事务与对外关系局(以下简称法律局)局长和首席法律官员。其间,米尔德教授主管一系列航空安全与安保国际公约及议定书的谈判和议定事宜,这些工作对国际航空法的发展与完善具有重要意义,至今依然影响深远。为表彰其杰出贡献,国际民航组织秘书长和理事会主席于1991年授予米尔德教授国际民航组织"功勋金章"(Gold Badge of Merit)。

鉴于米尔德教授在国际航空公法与国际航空私法领域享有的杰出的专业造诣和公认的世界级威望,他于1989年起受邀担任加拿大麦吉尔大学航空法与空间法研究所法学教授,并连续9年担任该研究所主任,连续17年为来自世界各国的学生们讲授航空法知识。在其引导和努力下,麦吉尔大学航空法与空间法研究所在教学与科研方面均取得了长足发展,成为业界公认的从事航空法研学的世界一流平台,并于1996年获得国际民航组织嘉奖的最高殊荣——爱德华·沃纳奖(Edward Warner Award)。正如麦吉尔大学航空法与空间法研究所现任主任布莱恩·F.哈弗尔(Brian F. Havel)教授所言:"米尔德教授是一位鼓舞和启迪人心的教育家;学生心中富于洞见、充满活力和尽心尽责的国际航空公法与国际航空私法教师。他乐此不疲地与学生、青年学者和事业起步期的专业人才开展交流对话,并乐于为那些未来可能在他如此钟爱的航空法领域开展职业生涯的人们提供咨询与建议。"若干年后,为表彰和答谢米尔德教授在教育和学术两方面为提升航空法与空间法研学水平所做的贡献,麦吉尔大学校董事会授予其航空法与空间法研究所"荣誉主任"(Director Emeritus)身份。

米尔德教授撰写了不胜枚举的书籍和论文,其代表作《国际航空法与国际民航组织》(*International Air Law and ICAO*)在学界内外享有盛誉。荷兰莱顿大学(Universiteit Leiden)航空法与空间法国际研究所主任帕布罗·门德斯·德·莱昂(Pablo Mendes de Leon)教授将米尔德教授敬称为"国际航空法业界的标杆人物"。米尔德教授游历世界多国,不仅是众多国际航空法会议、学术论坛和大学课堂的座上宾,也是许多知名国际法学刊的编委会成员。自1989年起,他曾连续13年担任麦吉尔大学航空法与空间法研究所的"旗舰出版物"、知名国际学刊《航空法与空间法年刊》(*Annals of Air and Space Law*)主编,持续推进国际航空法与外层空间法的研究和发展。此外,自1991年起,米尔德教授一直以独立法律顾问的身份,为不同国家的政府机构和航空产业提供法律意见,并持续关注着《芝加哥公约》和国际民航组织的新近发展与实践。甚至在2006年正式退休以后,他依旧笔耕不辍,继续投身于他一生热爱的国际航空法事业。

迈克尔·米尔德教授享年87岁。作为一名功勋卓著的学者、教师和友人,他将被熟识他的亲人们、同事们和学生们深深缅怀。麦吉尔大学航空法与空间法研究所于2018年秋季举办了米尔德教授的特别追悼会,缅怀他的人生、颂扬他的功绩。

资讯来源

1. Brian F. Havel, "In Memory of Professor Michael Milde (1931 – 2018)", *Air & Space Law* 43, 2018, pp. 367 – 370.

2. Michael Milde, *International Air Law and ICAO* (Second Edition), Eleven International Publishing, 2012, pp. ix – xiii.

3. McGill University Institute of Air & Space Law, "In Memoriam: Professor Dr. Michael Milde (1931 – 2018)", Accessed May 9, 2018. https://mcgill.ca/law/channels/news/memoriam-professor-dr-michael-milde-1931-2018-287112.

4. McGill University Institute of Air & Space Law, "Remembering Professor Michael Milde (1931 – 2018)", Accessed May 17, 2018. https://mcgill.ca/iasl/press/2018/michaelmilde.

5. Montreal Gazette, "Michael Milde Obituary", Accessed May 19, 2018. http://www.legacy.com/obituaries/montrealgazette/obituary.aspx?pid=189050310.

中国国际法学会2019年学术年会国际航空法边会简报*

2019年5月18日晚，由西北政法大学郑斌航空与空间法研究所、航空法治现代化协同创新中心、国际法学院主办的中国国际法学会2019年学术年会国际航空法边会，在西北政法大学北校区五号教学楼309智慧教室举行。本次航空法边会的主题为国际航空法的新发展与热点问题，会议于晚7时正式开始，北京理工大学法学院院长、教授李寿平老师担任会议主持人，会议共分为4个议题，通过主讲与与谈的方式进行。

第一个议题是埃塞空难涉及的法律问题，由中国海事仲裁委航空争议解决、调解中心主任聂颖老师作为主讲人，聂颖老师首先提到埃航空难是航空业近期最为热点的问题，其影响是世界性的，所以波音公司需要针对此次空难的危机化解准备一整套的应对方法，舆论的控制则是其中非常重要的方面，波

* 本简报由西北政法大学国际法学院2016级硕士研究生王思炜和西北政法大学国际法学院2018级硕士研究生刘静根据参会嘉宾发言整理。

音公司的新闻发言人也深知在美国这样奉行极端索赔制度的国家,其所发布的每一项声明都有可能被作为呈堂证供。其次,聂颖老师还特别提到了危机管理的作用,如何在事故发生后进行解决、防止类似事件再次发生才是航空公司需要特别关注的问题,最大程度上避免出现釜山空难时期各个部门相互推诿的现象。此外,航空保险中的类型划分、理赔方案的专业性、个人信息的收集也在一项空难事故的解决过程中产生重要的影响。最后,针对上述几个方面的问题,聂颖老师认为中国的律师只有在充分了解美国不同部门之间的法律规定的基础上,充分进行风险的评估,对管辖权的界定与责任的承担范围进行清楚的认知后,才能切实地维护我国的利益。随后,西北政法大学航空法治现代化协同创新中心副主任周亚光老师作为与谈人针对该问题发表了自己的看法。周老师提到波音公司的飞机在运行前都需要通过试航检测,那么在本次埃航空难中,波音公司是否可以将此作为一项免责事由进行提出?在进行严格的检验程序后,产品责任的划分与界定标准的认定又是一个值得探讨的问题。李寿平老师认为,除了上述几个方面外,在涉及多国取证的情形下,一个国家的瑕疵是否可以作为其他国家的免责事由也将是未来不可避免的重要问题。

第二个议题是空天一体化的国际新发展,担任此议题的主讲人是李寿平教授,其认为现阶段人类仅能对 20 千米以内的空气空间以及 100 千米以上的外层空间部分进行充分利用,而对于 20 ~ 100 千米的临近空间部分却由于空气稀薄无法满足飞机运行的空气反推而并未得到真正的运用。但在这部分领域内实际上兼具其他两个部分的优势,即飞机监测的清晰性与航空器运行的持久性,所以部分国家已经开始进行相关的试验并取得了不错的成绩,所以空天一体化实际上已经存在,只是暂时未进行公开。正是由于临近空间所处的特殊位置与在该区域内所运行飞行器的多样性特点,不能再使用传统方式进行限制,具体适用什么样的规则进行规制则是我们未来需要面对的问题。所以,在未来的一段时间内,法律规则一定会以碎片化的形式呈现,不同的空间范围甚至会存在不同的管辖要求。

随后西北政法大学郑斌航空与空间法研究所副教授师怡老师表示通过聆听李寿平老师的分享收获很多,其认为未来临近空间领域内将会面临国际法与国内法两个层面的问题:在国际法层面,由于临近空间范围内并不能简单的适用《芝加哥公约》等相关国际公约,未来不可避免的需要重新通过跨境合作等双边或多边的方式建立新的规则;而在国内法层面上,对于临近空间的开发主体资格,也需要各国国内行政法依据本国主体与外国主体进行具体规制。张丝路老师则从国家主权范围界定、临近空间的法律地位明确、军事机密的保护与军事化的利用与自卫权的适用等几个方面提出了自己的看法和理解。

第三个议题是航空产品事故中的政府赔偿责任,由华东政法大学国际法学院副教授于丹老师作为主讲人。于丹教授认为,在飞机上市前都需要进行严格的适航许可程序,其中又包括型号合格证和生产合格证等多个方面,且往往认证周期都非常的长,那么当出现产品问题时,除了飞机制造商外,进行认证的政府部门又是否需要承担责任。因为在实践中有观点认为,为了缩短与波音之间的差距,美国联邦航空管理局(Federal Aviation Administration,FAA)故意缩短了认证时间,但实际上除了FAA承担飞机的检验工作外,空客的工程师也会被聘请作为空客的检验员,即为飞机的适航委任制。那么,当出现飞机产品事故时,受害方到底是否可以将适航认证机构作为被告方,虽然在实践中已经存在先例,但是第三方与认证机构之间实际上并不存在直接的联系。美国针对此种情况规定有自由裁量权例外,联邦法院也适用了这项例外,认为适航认证应属于FAA的自由裁量范围,如何进行适航检测属于FAA的自由,其不应为此承担责任。根据美国的适航认证规则和判例,于丹教授认为,我国的飞机企业也即将上市,也可能会出现上述的问题,但根据我国《民用航空器适航管理条例》,在我国对政府提起诉讼是存在可能的,但政府在适航认证是仅发挥监管者的角色而并非安全责任人,况且依据产品责任起诉的赔偿范围和赔偿标准也更高,对于消费者而言更有利。

西飞民机公司法律审计室主任于涛表示,是否能够通过适航认证将责任划归至政府,实际上仍需要通过调查报告认定,但政府在调查报告中往往并不是责任承担主体。与谈人周亚光老师表示美国联邦侵权赔偿法与航空法之间并非对立关系,政府的身份并非为保险人而仅是抽检人。在实践中,也存在判决FAA承担责任的情形,若是将政府需要承担责任的判定标准界定为:应履行而未履行,既未改变原有法律要求还能促进法律的实际发展。西北政法大学郑斌航空与空间法研究所副所长张超汉副教授也发表了自己的观点,张老师认为中国也逐步向航空大国发展,中国应积极借鉴、参考美国的自由裁量权与委任代表制度,作为解决我国日后政府是否需要承担责任问题时的参考。

第四个议题是欧盟机场投资援助机制分析,担任该议题的主讲人是西北政法大学郑斌航空与空间法研究所博士研究生时杜鹃,其提到机场属于航空价值链的核心地位,欧盟对机场设施的补贴问题有较为统一的立法规定,是在区域一体化层面进行的尝试,其经验可能给中国未来的发展提供范本和对多边谈判提供参考标准。欧盟对机场的投资援助经历了相当漫长的时期,主要包括三个阶段:第一,1957~2000年,欧盟将补贴作为一般经济政策措施,未对其进行统一的立法。另外,欧盟于1957年制定了《欧洲经济共同体条约》,由理事会决定如何将其适用于海运或空运,并排除竞争规则对运输部门的适用;法院也认为援助手段应适用于航空运输领域。第二,2000~2010年,机场基础设施被纳入国家援助计划,机场数量得以空前增长,但如果继续对机场提供援助,那么很有可能导致机场容量过剩,从而对欧盟造成不必要的损失,该阶段的投资援助机制虽较大程度地支持了机场的发展,但仍存有亟须完善的部分。第三,2010年至今,机场投资援助规则现代化,从20世纪70年代起,欧盟就开始致力于改革援助制度,并在20世纪80年代得到了空前的增长,20世纪90年代达到了援助的顶峰,如2011年颁布了《通往单一运输区路线图》;2012年通过国家援助现代化实现机场一体化、自由化和可持续发展以及2014年航空指南对航空进行分类和细化了规则,进一步凸显援助制度对机场发展的效果。时杜鹃还提到,根据《欧盟运行条约》第107条的规定,欧盟可对“一般性”机场基础设施进行界定,评估援助措施对机场造成的竞争优势或对内部市场秩序造成的扭曲程度。中国在发展航空业的过程中,可充分借鉴欧盟的投资援助机制,不断地修订立法;区分一般与非一般基础设施;设定豁免机制。

南开大学法学院教授左海聪老师表示,对于埃航空难,应从国际统一法的角度考虑;目前,国际社会缺乏对“临近空间”的法律规制,给国际条约和国内行政法留下了规制的空间;政府在空难事故中承担监督责任,而非承担赔偿责任;欧盟的援助制度相当复杂,尤其是对农产品的补贴机制最具影响力。中国可借鉴欧盟对一般与非一般基础设施的分类和对应的豁免制度。

随后,西北政法大学国际法学院副教授杨蔚林补充道:补贴问题实际上属于宏观经济学的范畴,任何问题都是多个学科的综合。欧盟是人类法律的实验室,但由于中国飞机产业具有自身发展的特点,如其尚处于初级发展阶段,因此中国应对欧盟的制度进行有取舍的借鉴。

西北政法大学国际法学院副教授刘学文老师提到机场建设从本质上讲是投资问题,各国可基于 WTO 对补贴的规定分析欧盟的补贴机制,如补贴专向性问题与反补贴措施等;国内机场之间的交流可能会出现竞争性行为,而涉及国际服务的机场可能产生不正当竞争。

最后,本次国际航空法边会主持人李寿平老师作了总结。李寿平老师认为,作为首次在 2019 年中国国际法年会中出现的边会会议非常成功,通过今晚的报告大家都收获颇丰,不仅是理论学习,甚至对未来航空产业的发展都非常有意义。在此,应积极响应西北政法大学王瀚教授的号召,组建团队进行专题研究,为中国航空未来的发展提出更多建议。最后,希望在座的各位通过能够通过本次边会了解航空法、航天法的魅力,能够让同学们对航空航天产生兴趣,将是此次边会最大的收获。

西北政法大学郑斌航空与空间法研究所2018年学术活动大事记

1. 王瀚教授应邀出席西咸新区“探索西安建设自由贸易港”咨政研讨会

2018年1月7日西咸新区“探索建设自由贸易港”研讨会在空港新城召开，是在党的十九大报告提出赋予自由贸易试验区更大改革自主权，探索建设自由贸易港的国家战略部署以来，陕西省召开的首个研究西安建设自由贸易港的咨政研讨会，会议特别邀请来自国家部委、省市相关主管部门以及陕西省高校知名专家学者为西咸新区大胆创新、探索建设自由贸易港“把脉支着”。

西咸新区党工委副书记、管委会主任康军主持研讨会。陕西省商务厅厅长、陕西省自贸办主任赵润民，陕西省发改委副主任徐强，陕西省口岸办专职副主任陶绍卿，陕西省自贸办专职副主任翟北秦，西安市委政研室副主任李传顺，西安市发改委副主任赵寅科，国际港务区管委会副主任苏国锋西咸新区党工委委员、空港新城党委书记、管委会主任贺键，商务部国际贸易经济合作研究院副院长李光辉，中国民航大学临空经济研究中心主任曹允春,原中国社科院经济研究所所长裴长洪,商务部国际贸易经济合作研究院产业国际化战略研究所所长崔卫杰,西安交通大学“一带一路”自贸研究院服贸中心主任冯宗宪等著名专家出席会议,我校三秦学者特聘岗教授、郑斌航空与空间法研究所所长王瀚教授应邀出席会议。

王瀚教授就陕西省自由贸易区试验区建设的法治驱动与引领、西安建设自由贸易港探索陆海内外联动、东西双向互济的全面开放新模式、西安自贸港建设的涉外法治建设、国际化法律服务等问题作了专题发言,《陕西日报》、陕西省自由贸易实验区官网、“一带一路”官网、央讯网、《三秦都市报》等多家媒体作了相关报道。

2. 西安国际物流港管委会黄瑜晖副主任一行来我校国际法研究中心调研

2018 年 1 月 18 日西安国际物流港管委会副主任黄瑜晖、崔华,西安国际物港管委会招商局局长吕志,管委会干部宣霏一行 4 人来我校国际法研究中心调研。我校国际法研究中心主任王瀚教授,商学院副院长李晓宁教授,科研处副处长程启悃副处长,丝绸之路区域合作与发展法律研究院副院长吕江副教授,郑斌航空与空间法研究所副所长张超汉博士,跨境电商研究所副所长张夏恒博士参加了调研座谈会。

王瀚教授对黄瑜晖副主任一行来我校国际法研究中心调研表示欢迎。黄瑜晖副主任说明了此次调研的目的和意义,介绍了西安国际物流港在国际商贸物流、电商发展、融资租赁、文化旅游等方面的基本情况,并指出临空经济是西安国际物流港发展的核心,“一带一路”建设为西安国际大物流体系建设带来了极大的发展机遇。崔华副主任和吕志局长介绍了目前国家陆港建设的布局情况、西安国际物流港的定位,以及关于成立淘宝大学、京东大学及其课程设置的计划,并提出了目前西安国际物流港发展面临的法律问题,期待借助西北政法大学的师资和专家智库优势,与我校寻找更多的合作领域。调研座谈会上,王瀚教授指出党的十九大报告已明确加强铁路、公路、水运、航空、管道、信息、物流等基础设施网络的建设,我国将以“一带一路”建设为契机,构建全球物流和供应链服务体系,全面提升全球连接、全球服务、全球解决方案的能力。针对西安国际物流港的发展现状和存在的问题,王瀚教授作了整体“会诊”与“把脉”,谈了自己的观点,期待双方未来在港口建设与多式联式、智库建设、科学研究、信息采集、人员培训、课程设置、行政执法等领域有更多合作空间。座谈会上,李晓宁教授、程启悃副处长也结合自己的分管领域作了发言和交流。

座谈结束后,黄瑜晖副主任一行参观了我校郑斌航空法与郑天锡国际法图书馆。此次调研座谈进一步拓宽了我校与实务部门的合作渠道,彼此加深了解,为我校发挥智库平台优势作了基础和铺垫。

3. 张超汉博士参加科技创新与航空法的变革学术会议

2018 年 2 月 4 日,科技创新与航空法的变革学术会议在中国民航管理干部学院教学楼第二会议厅隆重召开。全国政协文史和学习委员会副主任委员李家祥(原中国民用航空局局长)、全国人大法工委民法室原副主任扈纪华、北京市法学会专职副会长杜石平、清华大学法学院党委书记黎宏教授、北京市知识产权法研究会会长宿迟、奥凯航空有限公司副总裁娄春华、中国民航管理干部学院党委书记沙洪江等来自政府、民航理论与实务界的专家学者160 余人出席了此次会议。我校郑斌航空与空间法研究所副所长张超汉博士应邀参加了会议,并当选为北京市航空法学会理事。

会议开幕式由北京市航空法学研究会会长董念清教授主持。此次会议主要围绕民航法治建设、新时代中国民航的国际化与法律风险防控、航空承运人责任与航空产品责任、航空争议的仲裁与调解、航权谈判与航班时刻拍卖等五个议题展开深入讨论。张超汉博士在下午航空承运人责任与航空产品责任这一议题环节作了题为“从美国法院判例实践看航空产品责任管辖权的确定”的主旨讲演。张超汉博士认为航空产品责任案件具有显著的国际性特征,由此决定了案件国际裁判管辖的确定和分配问题。管辖权的确定直接影响案件程序规则的启动和法律选择的结果,并最终影响当事人权益的维护。张超汉博士结合美国法院确定四类航空产品责任案件管辖权的实践,分析了美国法院在每一类案件中行使对人管辖权的原则、标准和方法,并结合中国大飞机制造的实情,为维护中国航空器制造商的权益和防范航空产品责任风险,结合美国实践,提出了四点启示和意见。张超汉博士的发言受到与会专家学者的认同和关注。

另外,在主旨发言环节,张超汉博士还与代理"MH370 案件"的中方律师张起淮和美方律师弗洛伊德·A. 威斯纳(Floyd A. Wisner)就该案件在美国华盛顿州提起航空产品责任诉讼的管辖权问题以及美国法院行使不方便法院的情况做了交流。

4. 王瀚教授等受邀参加"一带一路"航空法研讨会

2018 年 4 月 28 ~ 29 日,原西北政法大学副校长、郑斌航空与空间法研究所所长王瀚教授,郑斌航空与空间法研究所副所长张超汉博士,2017 级博士研究生时杜娟受邀参加了"一带一路"航空法研讨会。此次会议由武汉大学主办,国家高端智库武汉大学国际法研究所承办,中国民用航空局国际合作服务中心协办。来自国家民航局政策法规司、国际航空运输协会、新加坡及我国香港、澳门特别行政区政府民航法律官员和来自自由贸易试验区、中国国际航空公司、东方航空公司、南方航空公司等实务部门和 20 多所高等院校的专家学者 150 多人参加了会议。4 月 28 日上午,研讨会开幕式在武汉洪山宾馆举行,武汉大学常务副校长冯友梅、国际民航组织秘书长柳芳、中国民用航空局副局长王志清发表致辞。国际民航组织对外关系与法律局局长黄解放博士主持论坛开幕式和主题研讨。

研讨会下设五个议题,参会代表围绕"一带一路"与民航立法新发展、航空公司与"一带一路"法律事务、"一带一路"与航空器融资租赁、航空法研究热点问题、"一带一路"与航空争议解决机制进行了主题发言。深入分析了中国内地、中国香港、澳门特别行政区和新加坡民航立法的新发展,航空企业境外活动的风险防范,航空器融资租赁的国际国内立法与司法实践,当前航空法所面临的人权保护、无人机监管、航空器登记改革,航空商事仲裁等专业问题。

王瀚教授就“当前国际航空发展的若干新趋势”进行了主题发言，指出国际航空法当前应该加强研究的三大问题：一是国际航空运输安全与合作。该问题主要涉及如何规制武力攻击民用航空器入刑入罪，而当前的国际航空刑法对该问题的规定较为模糊和原则化，应该进一步明确实施武力攻击民用航空器的责任主体。在发生地区武装冲突时，国际民航组织、各个国家、航空公司应当加强信息沟通。此外，在航空事故调查、搜寻、救援的问题上，需要进一步研究可否突破调查报告用途的限制，能否作为民事责任、行政责任、刑事责任的证据，以及如何建立科学的搜寻与救援费用分摊机制。二是国际航空运输所面临的环境保护挑战。欧美国家近年来实施了一系列的航空碳排放的减排政策，特别是欧盟单边采取的ETS减排措施，对中国大飞机将来进入欧盟航空市场形成了巨大的阻碍。王瀚教授指出，应该深入研究中国大飞机的适航认证、欧美国家航空运输的反补贴政策和立法以及大飞机的减排问题。三是国际航空立法一体化问题。王瀚教授指出，应重视对国际航空公约文本的研究，提高该领域的研究水平。此外，国际航空运输领域的问题除了统一国际公约能够解决的外，还存在大量的需要冲突法解决的问题，比如，在航空器上缔约、结婚、立遗嘱等行为，航空器光机保险，航空器融资，航空器物权等，因此要加强航空冲突法的研究。王瀚教授的发言受到了与会人员的高度关注和积极讨论。

会议期间王瀚教授分别拜会了国际民航组织秘书长柳芳博士、国际民航组织法律事务与对外关系局局长黄解放博士和新加坡民航局法律司司长陈秀花，就我校开展航空法研究、人才培养和学术交流情况和今后合作研究等事宜交换了意见。

本次研讨会上，王瀚教授提交的参会论文《美国航空产品责任诉讼中的惩罚性损害赔偿问题研究》、张超汉博士的《欧美通用航空产品责任诉讼中的抗辩事由》、周亚光的《航空公司实质所有权与有效控制的国际立法与实践》、博士研究生时杜娟的《欧盟机场投资援助制度解析》四篇论文获得“武大国际法”优秀论文奖。

5. 王瀚教授接受西安晚报、西安电视台专访:临空经济示范区的设立,将改写西安对外开放的格局

“临空经济示范区的设立是西安发展的重大机遇,将改写西安对外开放的格局。”在谈到近日批复设立的西安临空经济示范区时,西北政法大学副校长、航空法治现代化协同创新中心主任王瀚这样说道,示范区的设立突破了西安作为内陆型城市对外开放中不通达的限制,对于发展外向型经济起到了决定性作用。

说起国家级经济新区,“临空经济”这一概念在大家的印象里并不熟悉,王瀚解释道,临空经济示范区其实是我国在新时代形成的全面对外开放新格局的一种新型经济开发区。

“这一开放型经济的特殊功能试验区,主要利用城市作为航空运输枢纽这一优势,实现航空运输与现代装备制造业、航空服务业等产业高度融合的经济开发区,属于国家经济开发区的新类型。”王瀚表示,临空经济示范区就是基于快捷的运输方式将本地生产要素与全球的生产链、价格链、市场链有效对接,打通国内与国际市场以及国内区域间的合作,用航空生产要素的高度融合引领和驱动区域经济发展。

“其实现在许多城市都在争取临空经济示范区,而西安最终获批设立,离不开城市的独特优势。”王瀚表示,国家选择西安,其实是基于对外开放的新经济形势,以及推进“一带一路”倡议的选择。

作为新一批获批示范区的城市,西安首先拥有得天独厚的地理区位优势,亚洲腹地,中国中心,让西安在“一带一路”向西开放中处于引领西部各省的地位,西安市经济发展快速势必能够带动其他中西部城市向欧洲市场、西亚、中亚开放,成为对外开放的重要节点和支撑城市。王瀚解说道,城市的开放度其实就是需要借助临空经济的发展,西安作为节点城市,能够将中西部各省份航空生产要素和国际航空市场的生产分工有效对接,从而带动当地经济发展。

此外，王瀚告诉记者，西安的产业基础雄厚。作为国家重要的航空航天产业、电子信息和装备制造业基地，先后引进了三星、美光、华为、中兴等一批航空指向性较强的领军企业。同时，西安也是国际一流旅游目的地，具有发展文化旅游产业的先天优势，2017年，西安市接待国内外游客1.8亿人次，旅游客流对临空经济支撑作用巨大。

“临空经济的专业性较强，而西安丰富的人才资源正为发展临空经济提供着充足的人力资源。”据了解，西安目前拥有各类科研开发机构3000多个，省部级以上重点实验室、工程技术研究中心231家，两院院士67位，各类专业技术人员80万人，密度居全国之首，是丝绸之路经济带上科创资源汇聚富集的高地。

优势的航空制造业、丰富的科教资源、军工产业的密集，对推动现代临空经济产业体系的构建起到了关键作用，这也是西安从多个城市中突出重围的原因。

王瀚提出，临空经济的发达对有效利用国际资源、推动当地经济发展、扩大当地发展空间十分必要。临空经济发达城市可以利用交通运输的便捷性吸引优质国际企业前来投资，引入现代化企业生产体系，同时吸引国际组织设立分支机构，甚至举办国际性文化节、体育赛事。

“临空经济的发展，其实是给西安对外开放插上了一对翅膀，示范区设立后我们需要做的工作还很多。”王瀚认为，接下来要着力统筹陕西综合交通运输体系，公路、铁路全方位地与国际航线实行对接，增强航空运输的网络体系建设，同时增强陆港联运，为陕西外向经济发展提供便利。

同时，王瀚表示，要积极引进外资以及支撑临空经济发展的产业，加速现代化航空经济产业体系的构建。加快航空关联产业、偏好产业的建设，比如，飞机发动机研制、维修、飞行员培训、航空物流产业等，要为临空示范区发展提供有特色的产业体系支撑。

王瀚认为，临空经济示范区的设立其实也是对政府的一次考验。“给贸易自由化、便利化带来了新的要求，也对政府管理贸易投资提出了新的要求。”王瀚说,相关部门要努力落实“负面清单管理模式”,对正面清单领域的投资要降低企业入驻条件,扩大企业自由创业空间,为临空经济发展提供高效快速的管理模式。对贸易自由流动方面,要尽快引入“单一窗口”的现代化运营模式,运用信息化手段,实现企业一次性提交、一次性受理、一次性审核、一次性办结、多项手续共用一个平台,大幅度提高效率,减少成本,为经济发展创造更好环境。

“示范区的设立为西安带来了机遇,但也带来了关于开放环境和国际化经营方面的新课题,值得我们研讨,在临空经济领域不断进步。”王瀚说。

6. 张超汉博士成果获陕西省第十三次哲学社会科学优秀成果奖

2018 年 7 月 17 日,陕西省社科联第五次代表大会开幕式在陕西宾馆陕西大会堂隆重开幕。省委书记胡和平出席开幕式并作重要讲话,省委常委、省政府常务副省长梁桂宣读了《陕西省人民政府关于表彰第十三次哲学社会科学优秀成果的通报》(陕政函〔2018〕90 号),省委常委、省委宣传部部长庄长兴主持开幕式。

会议表彰了陕西省第十三次哲学社会科学优秀成果。郑斌航空与空间法研究所副所长张超汉博士独立完成的《国际航空运输事故承运人先行付款制度研究》一文获论文类三等奖(青年成果)。

陕西省哲学社会科学优秀成果奖是我省哲学社会科学研究领域的最高奖项,每二年评选一次,旨在鼓励陕西省广大哲学社会科学工作者积极进行科学研究,繁荣发展哲学社会科学事业,更好地为中国特色社会主义建设和陕西经济社会发展服务。

7. 张超汉博士著作获 2017 年“中国国际法学优秀科研成果奖”并被实务部门关注采纳

近日,中国国际法学会公布了 2017 年度“中国国际法学优秀科研成果奖”获奖名单。我校郑斌航空与空间法研究所副所长、陕西省“三秦学者”创新团队成员张超汉博士参评的成果《国际航空产品责任研究》获得本年度著作类优秀成果奖(著作类唯一获奖成果)。

该著作于2017年由法律出版社出版,受中国博士后科学基金特别资助项目"中国大飞机发展战略法律保障机制研究"和陕西省"三秦学者"创新团队科研经费资助,是张超汉博士近10年集中研究国际航空产品责任法律问题的一个归纳、梳理和总结。该书是国内首部围绕国家大飞机发展战略,从实体和程序两个层面全面、系统研究大飞机在设计、制造、适航、交易、运营、维修等过程出现的产品责任问题以及争议解决的国际航空法专题著作,拓展了中国国际私法研究的新领域,填补了国内在该领域的研究空白,对于维护我国大飞机制造商及相关企业的权益提供了充分的法律依据。

该著作出版后引起中国商用飞机有限责任公司(以下简称中国商飞公司)、中国航空工业集团有限公司等实务部门的极大关注、肯定和好评。该书被中国商飞公司采纳应用,并致函我校感谢,作为该公司全体法务人员必备的参考用书,对中国大飞机主制造商及相关产业方防范航空产品责任风险和应对航空产品责任诉讼提供了有益的法律建议和智力支持。

"中国国际法学优秀科研成果奖"是中国国际法学会(外交部主管)于2009年设立的奖项。该奖分为优秀著作奖和优秀论文奖,每年评选一次,原则上每年评选出优秀著作2部,优秀论文5篇,奖励对象侧重中青年学者,尤其是青年学者。本次与张超汉博士同时获奖的其他五位作者分别是清华大学博士研究生导师陈卫佐教授,山东大学法学院院长、博士研究生导师沈伟教授,武汉大学博士生导师黄志雄教授,华东政法大学助理研究员包毅楠和刘雪红。

8. 国际民航组织法律事务与对外关系局局长黄解放博士访问我校

2018年7月4日,我校"三秦学者"特聘岗教授、郑斌航空与空间法研究所所长王瀚教授在雁塔校区丝绸之路区域合作与发展法律研究院会见了国际民航组织对外关系与法律局局长黄解放博士、武汉大学国际法所副所长邓朝晖女士一行,西北政法大学国际法学院院长刘亚军陪同会见。黄解放博士自1988年起参加国际民航组织活动,后担任民航组织法律顾问,在国际民航组织工作时间长达20多年。2018年3月16日国际民用航空组织第213届理事会任命黄解放为法律事务与对外关系局局长,是自国际民航组织成立后70多年的首位担任该职务的中国籍专家。

黄解放局长参观考察了我校郑天锡国际法与郑斌航空法图书馆及航空法研究所的学术研究情况。郑天锡国际法与郑斌航空法图书馆藏书由著名航空法学家郑斌先生捐赠,主要包括郑斌先生及其父亲郑天锡收藏的经典国际法和外空法著作、著名国际法院判例、重要国际条约谈判资料和知名国际法学术刊物等3000余册。王瀚教授向黄解放局长介绍了图书的保管情况,及航空法人才培养与科研情况,并强调郑天锡国际法与郑斌航空法图书馆资料的重要价值,感谢黄解放局长对图书资料获赠的大力支持。

随后,我校航空法治协同创新中心举行了"航空强国与航空法治建设"座谈会,与会嘉宾有西北政法大学航空法治协同创新中心主任王瀚教授,武汉大学国际法所副所长邓朝晖,西北民航管理局法规处处长朱勇民,西部机场集团副总秦占欣,民航西北地区管理局党委办公室主任方瑞丰,《中国社会科学报》西北记者站主任陆航,西安交通大学法学院苏金远教授,西北政法大学国际法学院院长刘亚军教授、副院长潘俊武教授、副院长张光教授、刘萍教授以及航空法治现代化协同创新中心成员师怡副教授、张望平副教授、张超汉副教授、周亚光博士、华雨婷博士、张丝路博士、时杜娟博士研究生等,黄解放局长参会并作重要讲话。座谈中,与会嘉宾就航空法治的最新动态进行讨论,并梳理了新时代背景下航空法研究的重点议题。

黄解放局长指出中国航空法治建设任重道远,以航空环境法的新问题为例,民航组织理事会最近通过的碳排放制度试图以市场机制将碳排放市场化,在36个理事国当中,南非和坦桑尼亚缺席,4个国家反对,30票赞成(包括美国和西欧),中国对此提出保留(弃权),碳排放市场化对于发展中国家和最不发达国家来说将是一个严峻的挑战。

王瀚教授指出当前航空法的研究要紧跟大数据、人工智能等新时代热点问题,深入研究欧盟《通用数据保护条例》与适航标准认定、航空企业海外兼并之间的关系。从陕西服务"一带一路"建设的需求来讲,亟待开放第五航权，完善国际航线网络布局与发展规划，优化西安临空经济示范区国际化、便利化和法治化营商环境，助跑西安国际化大都市建设、西安咸阳国际航空枢纽功能升级与陕西临空经济示范区的发展。从人才培养的现状来看，需要筹划中国航空法教育基金，与国际民航组织形成常态实习对接关系，培养理论与实务并重的航空法治人才队伍。

邓朝晖副所长向与会嘉宾介绍了“德恒访问学者项目”，提出西北政法大学航空法研究团队实力雄厚，希望能够进一步接洽，与武汉大学国际法所进行深入合作，联合培养航空法治人才，实现共建共赢。

朱勇民处长介绍了民航监管的最新动向：一是解决民航监管力量不足的问题和实现监管现代化。建立监管事项库，明确监管的边界；统一全国的监管平台；鼓励企业自查。二是推行民航信用制度。旅客信用实行全网联通，信用等级信息共享；企业信用实行国内国外统一入网。三是为了解决通用航空过度监管的问题，朱勇民处长建议将散见于民航规章中的立法，统一于民航法中，并将无人机纳入通用航空中统一立法。

座谈中，周亚光博士就防空识别区、经济专属区上空法律地位等问题与苏金远教授进行了交流和讨论。方瑞丰主任等就航空法的地位与未来发展与参会人员进行了交流。

黄解放局长对我校航空法治现代化协同创新中心取得的成就给出了高度的赞赏，表示将积极支持西北政法大学航空法学科建设，支持我校打造具有国际影响力的航空法研究重镇，并就2018年10月国际民航组织法律局与国家民航总局合作，由西北政法大学郑斌航空与空间法研究所承办“2010年北京国际航空保安公约研讨会”一事与王瀚教授交换了意见。黄解放局长希望航空法治协同创新中心能够稳步发展，协同纳新，构建“空天丝路”与“地面丝路”的对接，服务于国家“一带一路”建设。王瀚教授向黄解放博士对西北政法大学航空法人才的培养和学科建设的支持表示感谢！

9. 王瀚教授陪同国际民航组织法律事务与对外关系局黄解放局长调研考察我省临空经济发展情况

我校国际法研究中心学术顾问、联合国国际民航组织法律事务与对外关系局局长黄解放博士应中华人民共和国外交部邀请来京出席“一带一路”国际法治合作论坛,并于2018年7月4~6日专程来陕调研临空经济、机场管理、航空产业发展等方面的问题。陕西省“三秦学者”特聘教授、我校郑斌航空与空间法研究所所长王瀚教授,我校国际法学院副院长张光教授,国家高端智库武汉大学国际法研究所副所长邓朝晖博士,我校郑斌航空与空间法研究所副所长张超汉博士陪同调研。

7月4日黄解放局长一行5人来陕西空港新城管理委员会就临空经济和国际航空运输竞争力等问题展开考察。空港新城党委书记、管委会主任贺键会见了黄局长,党委委员、管委会副主任韩娜主持座谈会。韩娜介绍了空港新城基本区位情况、“保税+自贸+临空”的叠加优势、航空物流、高端人才引进政策。贺键主任结合空港新城四大片区规划和产业布局,从交通优势、高标准规划先行优势、体制机制优势和人才创新优势等方面介绍了空港新城发展情况。黄解放局长对空港新城临空经济和航空运输的快速发展予以肯定,希望空港新城充分发挥政策红利、区位禀赋和人才优势,着眼更高的开放标准,借鉴成都和郑州等地的先进经验,开拓国际视野,建设更具国际竞争力的临空经济产业体系。

7月6日黄解放局长一行5人赴西部机场集团有限公司调研,西部机场集团公司党委书记,董事长王海鹏会见了黄局长,对黄局长一行来集团考察、指导表示欢迎。随后举行座谈会,机场集团副总经理秦占欣博士汇报了机场建设、航线管理、西安咸阳国际机场航空客、货运现状及目前存在的问题。座谈后,双方还就西安国际门户枢纽机场建设与陕西对外开放等问题做了探讨。

7月6日黄解放局长调研考察了西安阎良国家民用航空高技术产业基地管理委员会,参观了西飞公司,并与基地管委会纪委书记张炎就中国大飞机制造、通用航空产业发展、航空业军民融合、中国航空法治问题举行座谈。

黄解放局长来陕调研期间，还访问考察了西北政法大学航空法治现代化协同创新中心、参观了郑斌航空法、郑天锡国际法图书馆，并与西北政法大学国际法学院领导，航空法研究团队进行座谈，就航空法人才培养、科学研究、对外交流、学术平台建设等问题提出了建议。黄局长表示将极力支持我校航空法特色研究方向发展和国家航空航天法高端智库建设。

10. 张超汉博士赴爱尔兰参加第 11 届全球航空法大会

受加拿大麦吉尔大学航空与空间法研究所名誉所长保罗·史蒂芬·邓普西（Paul Stephen Dempsey）教授和英国泛欧人身伤害律师组织首席执行官沃尔夫冈·雷拖（Wolfgang Resch）博士的邀请，我校郑斌航空与空间法研究所副所长张超汉博士作为中国唯一学者代表于 2018 年 10 月 18～21 日赴爱尔兰参加了第 11 届全球航空法大会。来自美国、中国、英国、德国、法国、俄罗斯、加拿大、西班牙、澳大利亚等全球 41 个国家的近 200 位航空理论与实务界的专家、学者参加了此次会议。

本次会议主要围绕航空承运人责任的新发展、航空器及其零部件制造商的责任、航空事故及恐怖主义的政府责任、机场及维修商的责任、航空事故诉讼争议解决及保险、航空器融资租赁、美国和爱尔兰的航空立法及司法实践等七大主题展开研讨。19 日上午，张超汉博士在会议第二单元以“航空产品责任诉讼中三大理论与实践难题”为题，就航空产品责任诉讼对国际统一运输责任体系的影响与破坏、欧美航空产品责任期间的差异对航空器国际贸易的影响与乘客对航空器国籍的选择、航空产品责任诉讼中的双重赔偿等三个问题作了主旨演讲，阐述了自己的观点。另外，在 20 日上午的“美国航空产品责任司法实践”主题研讨环节，张超汉博士还作为评论人，对美国律师斯图尔特·弗朗克尔（Stuart Fraenkel）博士和杰弗里·埃利斯夫（Jeffrey Ellisf）博士关于美国航空产品责任诉讼中的非方便法院原则、法律冲突问题的发言作了评议与交流。张超汉博士的发言和评议紧扣大会主题，思路清晰、观点明确，受到与会学者的极大肯定与赞赏。

主旨演讲前，张超汉博士还宣介了我校以王瀚教授为主任和首席专家的郑斌航空与空间法研究所在师资团队、科学研究、社会服务与对外合作交流等方面的基本情况,使西方学者对我校郑斌航空与空间法研究所及航空法特色研究方向有了一个全面、深入的了解。

11. 国浩律师事务所(北京)高级合伙人高峰律师作“航空公司之民事赔偿责任”专题讲座

2018 年 10 月 23 日晚上 7 时 30 分,国浩律师事务所(北京)高级合伙人高峰律师在西北政法大学雁塔校区研究生综合楼三楼国际法学术报告厅以“航空公司之民事赔偿责任”为题作学术讲座。讲座由国际法学院副院长张光教授主持,张望平副教授担任评议人,张超汉博士、周亚光博士、刘冰博士研究生、国际法专业硕士研究生及我校部分本科生参加了本次讲座。

高峰律师首先深入解读了其在专业实践中总结出的航空运输赔偿案件处理规律,以此为基点,深入剖析了民用航空运输中的法律规制及各类民事赔偿案件具体的解决思路。高律师梳理了我国民航法体系的五大渊源,接着详细解析了我国《民用航空法》的主要内容,明确了航空事故的界定、航空公司侵权与违约责任竞合时的选择以及诈弹风波中航空公司的责任承担问题,比较了新旧《消费者权益保护法》在航空运输责任案件中的适用,并重点分析了民用航空运输中超售和代码共享的概念及处理规则。随后,高律师详细介绍了我国各级民航主管机关,厘清了民航行政诉讼中的职责权限,解释了民用航空运输中争议较大的相关事项,如特价机票中退改签的效力问题、航空旅客运输中民事责任的归责问题等,重点解析了航空公司的过错、责任期间、免责以及损害赔偿事项等问题,并就这些问题提出了建设性的解决思路。最后,高峰律师结合民用航空运输中航空公司赔偿案件的复杂性,重申了从法律角度寻求解决思路的必要性,并激励与会学坚守法律信仰,共同推进我国航空法制的发展。

在互动环节,与会师生踊跃提问,提问涉及代码共享中的欺诈问题、相关服务产品的市场界定、民航运输中优先通道、民航运输中无因管理以及航空公司的免责等问题,高峰律师的耐心解答进一步引发了更加广泛的讨论。张望平副教授在总结中感谢高峰律师带来的精彩讲座，并鼓励在座的研究生和本科生用开拓的眼光去看待航空法领域的问题，结合自身的学习兴趣探寻研究热点。

12. 王瀚教授应邀参加西咸新区空港新城第五航权研讨会

2018年11月23日国务院印发《关于支持自由贸易试验区深化改革创新若干措施的通知》，明确提出在对外航权谈判中支持西安机场利用第五航权，在平等互利的基础上允许外国航空公司承载经西安至第三国的客货业务，积极向国外航空公司推荐并引导申请进入中国市场的国外航空公司执飞西安机场。为落实好国家政策，解决实际利用第五航权的过程中存在的问题，12月5日西安空港管委会召开西咸新区空港新城第五航权研讨会。这是国务院有关通知出台后，西安地区就如何更好地利用第五航权而召开的第一次研讨会。

我校“三秦学者”特聘岗教授、国际法研究中心主任、丝绸之路区域合作与发展法律研究院院长王瀚教授，应西安空港管委会邀请参加会议，并就西安机场如何利用第五航权建言献策。王瀚教授认为，充分利用航权，优化航线，进而实现航线网络的重新布局，对于通过民航驱动西安地区进一步对外开放，产业转型升级，打造内陆型改革开放新高地，具有十分重要的意义。王瀚教授指出，航权事关航空公司对于机场、空域的使用，应针对货运第五航权以及客运第五航权，分别调研航空公司的实际需求。同时，为吸引航空公司在西安建设运输基地，王瀚教授认为，应在国内外广泛宣传西安机场的位置优势。为此，王瀚教授提出应当以中欧航空运输枢纽为西安机场的全球定位，并建议设立第五航权领导小组负责西安利用第五航权的顶层设计并与国家民航局的政策沟通，同时负责对外宣传西安机场。

13. 纪念改革开放40周年学术讲座——中国民航强国法治建设三人谈

2018年12月8日为纪念改革开放40周年，利用“制止与国际民用航空有关非法行为的公约(《北京公约》)”法律论坛召开间隙，西北政法大学国际法学院邀请陕西省“三秦学者”特聘教授王瀚，中国海事仲裁委员会航空争议仲裁中心主任聂颖和上海璞燕信息科技信息有限公司总经理、上海社会科学院研究生院兼职教授吴建端,在西北政法大学雁塔校区研综楼国际法报告厅做了题为《中国民航强国法治建设》的学术讲座。讲座由西北政法大学国际法学院院长刘亚军教授主持,国际法学院50余名师生参加了论坛。

刘亚军首先对《北京公约》法律论坛作了介绍并致词。随后,西北国际法研究中心主任王瀚教授为聂颖、吴建端颁发了兼职研究员聘书,并合影留念。

吴建端总经理首先介绍了成为一流企业的经营理念,指出法科学生要进行跨专业的学习,所谓跨专业并不是指跨出法学这一专业单独学习其他专业知识,而是指要学习好与法学专业相关的知识,特别指出要打好民商法学的基础。航空产业是“现代工业之花”,到2035年航空产业更加关注“社会发展”“经济”“政治”“新技术”这些问题,尤其是新技术的问题。作为一名研究者,要学会沟通,沟通是研究者的基本技能。聂颖主任侧重于实务方面的讲授:建议先学好有关航空法的专业知识,企业要将危机处理、管理纳入风险管理。王瀚教授指出:其一,全球航空已进入关键的三个时段,即安全、协调、绿色,并提出武力攻击民用客机是否能成为国际罪行的疑问;其二,航空发展对于全球的发展越来越重要,对GDP的贡献与日俱增,要把航空发展作为战略性驱动;其三,作为航空业的两大载体——空间与机场,毫无疑问是航空领域不可忽略且十分重要的课题。

西北政法大学郑斌航空与空间研究所副所长张超汉博士认为,民航强国有四个构成要件,即航空公司强、机场强、制造强、空管强,并提出了空管的责任究竟是归于私人还是归于国家的问题。此次讲座的成功举行,使同学们清晰认识到中国航空发展的现状,并对于航空法有了进一步的学习和体会。

14. 慕亚平教授在我院做学术讲座

2018年12月8日下午2时30分,西北政法大学国际法学院邀请中山大学慕亚平教授在雁塔校区研究生综合大楼国际法报告厅举办“民用航空争议解决”专题讲座。讲座由国际法学院副院长张光教授主持,西北政法大学王瀚教授、张望平副教授、张超汉博士、周亚光博士担任与谈人,国际法学院50

余名硕士研究生参加。

慕亚平教授首先讲述了其代理的全国首例国际航空器留置权案件——“广州白云机场诉美国通用航空公司案”。他介绍了案件发生的缘由、设计案件中遇到的问题、案件起诉以及争议的焦点、案件的解决及体会与收获。慕亚平教授指出,此次案件妥善解决了如何处理国有资产保护和国际法的关系问题,是商业留置概念首次适用于航空器上,取得了良好的示范作用。王瀚教授与慕亚平教授对本案有关国际私法法理问题进行了商榷,指出我国在航空物权制度方面的缺失,即没有关于航空器留置权的规定。各位与谈人积极发言,在场多名学生也提出了自己对本案的理解和问题,并和各位老师进行积极探讨。

慕亚平教授介绍的这起经典案件涉及法学理论及其在实践中具体灵活应用问题,引起了广泛的争鸣,给学生以重要启发。最后,张光教授代表国际法学院对慕亚平教授的到访和精彩讲座表示衷心的感谢。讲座在热烈掌声中圆满结束!

15. 国际民航组织运输局副局长西尔万·莱弗耶(Sylvain Lefoyer)先生访问我校国际法研究中心及郑斌航空与空间法研究所

2018年12月9日国际民航组织运输局副局长西尔万·莱弗耶先生应邀访问我校国际法研究中心及郑斌航空与空间法研究所并与相关人员座谈。我校国际法研究中心主任、郑斌航空与空间法研究所所长王瀚教授,国际交流与合作处李立处长,国际法学院长刘亚军教授以及航空法研究团队的师怡副教授、张望平副教授、张丝路博士参加了会见和座谈。

西尔万·莱弗耶副局长首先参观了国际法研究中心的郑斌航空法图书馆与郑天锡国际法图书馆,对丰富的馆藏图书表示非常赞叹,认为图书馆的藏书量已经达到世界级水准,足以吸引更多的专家学者来西北政法大学讲学与研究。

随后的座谈会由李立处长主持,李处长首先欢迎西尔万·莱弗耶副局长的到访,希望我校和国际民航组织运输局今后在业务交流方面加强联系。

王瀚教授在发言中指出,很荣幸和西尔万·莱弗耶副局长在西安相见,尤其是在12月7日这一国际民航日那天和西尔万·莱弗耶先生一起开会探讨,印象深刻,希望今后和国际民航组织加强联系,在多领域进行更加深入的交流与合作。王瀚教授最后表示欢迎西尔万·莱弗耶副局长以后再来西安,再来西北政法大学访问。

西尔万·莱弗耶副局长表示,非常高兴在他第一次来中国的时候就能访问西北政法大学,更令他高兴的是学校在航空法领域做出的贡献非常突出。西尔万·莱弗耶先生认为西北政法大学航空法学科的整体水平居于世界领先地位,希望未来能在航行飞行安全、航空网络安全等领域加强与学校的合作。

最后,王瀚教授向西尔万·莱弗耶副局长赠送了航空法专著和礼品,座谈会在热烈的气氛中结束。

16.《制止与国际民用航空有关的非法行为的公约》航空法律论坛在西安隆重召开

2018年12月7日适逢国际民航日,由中国民用航空局与西北政法大学主办,西北政法大学国际法研究中心、陕西省国际法学科三秦学者创新团队、中国民航局国际合作服务中心、国家高端智库武汉大学国际法研究所承办的,题为"迈向安全、协调、绿色的国际民航新时代——《制止与国际民用航空有关的非法行为的公约》(《北京公约》)航空法律论坛"在西安隆重召开。

《北京公约》是航空法领域第一部以中国首都名称命名的国际条约,已于2018年7月1日正式生效。《北京公约》吸收了联合国反恐公约近些年取得的新原则、新成果,反映了国际反恐公约的发展趋势,增加了新罪名,弥补了原航空安保公约体系的空白和不足,为打击威胁民航安全的国际恐怖主义行为提供了有效手段和有力的法律保障,引起国际社会强烈反响。在国际民航组织的积极倡导下,目前已有26个国家确定了加入公约。《北京公约》将在今后为打击危害民航的恐怖主义活动和其他犯罪行为,保障旅客的生命财产安全,提供强有力的法律保障。

中国民用航空局副局长吕尔学、陕西省副省长陈国强、司法部立法四局副局长董超洁、国际民航组织法律事务与对外关系局局长黄解放、西北政法大学校长杨宗科教授、国际民航组织运输局副局长拉弗耶先生、亚洲国际航空暨太空法研究会董事会主席程家瑞教授、民航西北地区管理局局长王长益、西部机场集团董事长王海鹏、中国民航局国际合作服务中心孟庆芬、北京理工大学法学院院长李寿平、广东外语外贸大学法学院院长袁泉教授、西北政法大学国际法学院院长刘亚军、西北政法大学航空法研究团队及国际法学院部分师生等航空法理论界与实务界代表150余人参会,《中国民航报》《中国社会科学报》、中国社会科学网等媒体全程报道。在中国民用航空局安全监察专员魏亚军主持下,中国民用航空局副局长吕尔学、陕西省副省长陈国强、司法部立法四局副局长董超洁和西北政法大学校长杨宗科先后致辞,国际民航组织法律与对外关系局局长黄解放博士、运输局副局长拉弗耶做大会主旨演讲,主旨演讲由陕西省"三秦学者"特聘教授王瀚主持。

中国民航局吕尔学副局长在致辞中回顾了《北京公约》在北京签订时的情景,强调了《北京公约》在国际航空安保法律发展中的重要地位,对中国批准、加入国际民用航空多边公约的情况以及深度参与国际民航公约的制定与修订情况作了介绍。

陕西省副省长陈国强在致辞中介绍了陕西民航近年来的发展情况。陕西省近年来不断加密国内干线航班,持续开通新的洲际航线,客货运输总量近年来保持了10%以上的增速。陈国强副省长希望民航界能助力陕西打造门户机场枢纽,构建"空中丝绸之路"新起点,为陕西谱写追赶超越的新篇章作出新的更大贡献。

司法部立法四局副局长董超洁在致辞中强调了《北京公约》的重要意义,认为《北京公约》是过往法律实践与未来法律预防的综合性成果。董超洁副局长对司法部目前推进《民用航空法》的修订工作作了介绍,强调了《民用航空法》修订与《北京公约》之间的"国际法—国内法"重要互动关系。

杨宗科校长在致辞中介绍了西北政法大学80多年传承红色基因办学

史、70余年法学教育史,以及西北政法大学在国家法治人才培养的重要地位。杨校长指出,西北政法大学国际法学科有着深厚的学术积淀,国际法研究中心与郑斌航空与空间法研究所在学术成就、智库成果、国际合作、协同创新机制建设等方面获得了具有国际与国内影响力的重要成果。

在西北政法大学国际法研究中心主任、陕西省"三秦学者"特聘教授王瀚主持下,国际民航组织法律事务与对外关系局局长黄解放博士、运输局副局长拉弗耶先后作大会主旨演讲。国际民航组织法律与对外关系局局长黄解放博士作"航空安保工作的新发展"的主旨报告,作为《北京公约》主要推动者,黄解放博士对《北京公约》的起草与缔结过程作了精彩介绍。国际民航组织运输局副局长拉弗耶作了"国际航空安保形势及政策"的主旨报告,并与参会学者就热点问题深入探讨互动。

当日下午,王瀚教授在论坛的主题研讨环节致辞。王瀚教授强调,《北京公约》是我国深度参与国际航空法律秩序全球治理的重大成果,在国际航空法的立法史上具有里程碑意义。本次会议是公约生效后,国内航空实务界与法律界首次系统讨论公约实施的会议,也是我国首次由中国民航局与地方高校联合举办的学术会议,对我国航空法律的修订以及公约在我国的实施具有重要的推动意义。

著名航空法专家、亚洲国际航空暨太空法研究会董事会主席程家瑞先生作了"国际航空法新维度——国际航空安保法"(New Dimensions of International Air Law-International Air Law of Security)的主旨演讲。其他与会的航空法理论界与实务界代表分别围绕"《北京公约》核心条款的适用及与我国相关法律的衔接""不循规旅客非法干扰行为的法律规制""航空安保国际合作与冲突地区民航飞行风险的法律应对""无人机安全监管及国际航空安保法的新发展"四个议题的相关法律问题展开深入研讨。

17. 王瀚教授等就国际航空安全治理问题接受中国社会科学报专访

2018年12月7日"《制止与国际民用航空有关的非法行为的公约》航空法律论坛"在西安召开。来自国内外从事航空法研究的学者以及航空管理机构和从业者代表,聚焦航空法律问题,围绕"不循规旅客非法干扰行为的法律规则""航空安保国际合作与冲突地区民航飞行风险的法律应对""无人机安全监管及国际航空安保法的新发展"等议题,进行了深入探讨。

自"一带一路"倡议提出以来,民航为"一带一路"沿线国家互联互通提供航空整体解决方案,极大地丰富了"一带一路"倡议的内涵,在浩瀚的天空中构架起了合作的桥梁。2018年7月《北京公约》正式生效。作为国际航空安保公约缔结的重要成果,《北京公约》为民航安全提供了强有力的国际法依据和保障。

"民用航空在加强世界各国互联互通、促进政治文化交流和经贸合作中发挥了重要的作用。树立构建人类命运共同体意识,加强民航领域航空安保国际合作,倡导学术界参与国际组织立法,可以促进国内法治理论探究,为进一步完善国际法律体系提供中国方案、中国智慧,保护全球民航体系。"国际民航组织法律事务与对外关系局局长黄解放告诉记者,《北京公约》中文文本为正式法律文本,是国际航空领域航空安保统一立法的重要成果,为国际社会协调立场,统一行动,加强航空安全合作,实施国际航空安全治理提供了全新的国际法律依据,将为国际社会防范民航领域的恐怖主义活动、打击民用航空非法行为,维护航空安全发挥国际法法治保障作用。

黄解放表示,从第一部关于航空违法犯罪的《东京公约》通过至《北京公约》正式生效,国际航空安保公约体系发生了重大的更新。《北京公约》在国际航空法的发展史上具有里程碑意义,为当代全球航空安全提供了全新国际法律规则体系。加深对《北京公约》与我国现行国内立法衔接关键问题的深入研究,可以进一步推动中国政府参与国际民航法律制定,迈向安全、协调、绿色的国际民航新时代。

西北政法大学教授王瀚介绍,20世纪六七十年代,随着航空运输业的蓬勃发展,在国际民航组织与各缔约国的不懈努力下,诞生了得到国际社会广泛认可的三大公约,即《东京公约》《海牙公约》《蒙特利尔公约》,确立了关于民航安保的国际公约体系基本框架。然而,随着航空运输业的飞速发展,与民航相关的新型违法犯罪活动也层出不穷,例如,将航空器作为武器,或实施生物、化学和核武器攻击等。在这一背景下,2010 年国际民航组织在北京举行了航空安保外交会议,目的是更新《海牙公约》《蒙特利尔公约》及其议定书,共有 76 个国家的代表和 4 个国际组织的观察员与会。大会通过了《北京公约》和《制止非法劫持航空器公约的补充议定书》(以下简称《北京议定书》)。

实施"一带一路"倡议,实现互联互通是关键,交通运输是基础。航空运输具有国际化程度高、速度快、适应性强,适合长距离的人员往来、货物流动等特点,在互联互通中具有独特优势。近年来,航空公司积极开辟"一带一路"沿线国家的国际航班,取得了重要进展。围绕"互联互通""反恐安全"两大主题,中国已与 100 余个国家和地区签署了双边政府间航空运输协定,其中与"一带一路"沿线的 60 余个国家签署了双边政府间航空运输协定,与东盟签订了首个区域性航空运输协定。

司法部立法四局副局长董超洁表示,航空运输具有速度快、覆盖面大、影响范围广等特点。我国现行《民用航空法》《民用航空安全保卫条例》和相关部门规章建立了包括安全检查、机场控制区通行证、驻停航空器专人警卫、承运行李货物专人监管等内容的民用航空安全保卫基本制度,为我国民用航空事业的安全、稳健发展提供了重要的法律保障。学术界的相关研究将为推进我国《民用航空法》在修订过程中落实《北京公约》精神,进一步完善民用航空安全保卫制度,确保民用航空安全运行,稳步迈向安全、协调的国际民航新时代发挥重要作用。

长期以来,中国积极参与国际航空安保合作,遵守国际公约,以负责任的态度,深入开展相关研究,为航空运输产业的健康发展,构建安全便捷的交通体系,保障人民生命财产安全作出了不懈努力。中国民用航空局副局长吕尔学表示,中国民航积极主动融入民航国际合作领域,已经批准、加入 26 项重要的国际民用航空多边公约。同时,中国民航一直致力于国际民航法律的跟踪、学习和研究,近 30 年来,深度参与了多部民航公约的制定修订。《北京公约》和《北京议定书》体现了国际社会对中国民航实力与地位的高度认可，体现了中国民航的高度国际化和领先的航空安保理论研究水平，希望中国民航法律建设的实践，能为国际民航立法贡献中国智慧，提供中国经验。《北京公约》《北京议定书》与另外三大公约一起，将为打击民航领域的恐怖主义活动和其他犯罪行为发挥至关重要的作用。

吕尔学提出，步入新时代，国际民航和中国民航面临着许多新的问题、新的挑战，我们应当与其他缔约国一起，加强《北京公约》与《北京议定书》的研究和推广，在构建人类命运共同体理念下，使更多国家能够积极加入，通过《北京公约》和《北京议定书》搭建起一个各国通力合作的平台，共同维护国际民用航空的安全。

会议由中国民用航空局与西北政法大学主办，西北政法大学国际法研究中心、中国民航局国际合作服务中心、武汉大学国际法研究所承办。

18. 王瀚教授等参加北京航空法学会 2018 年年会暨 2018 航空法治论坛

2018 年 12 月 16 日西北政法大学国际法研究中心主任、郑斌航空与空间法研究所所长王瀚教授，研究所特邀研究人员、华东政法大学国际法学院于丹副教授，研究所研究人员、国际法学院张望平副教授参了加北京航空法学会 2018 年年会暨 2018 航空法治论坛。本次论坛由北京航空法学会主办，主题是改革开放与航空法治建设，来自国内的 60 余位专家学者及实务工作者参加了本次论坛。

12 月 16 日上午论坛开幕式在中国民航管理干部学院国际会议中心举行，开幕式由北京航空法学会会长、中国民航管理干部学院航空法研究中心主任董念清教授主持，时任中国国际法学会会长、时任中国政法大学校长黄进出席开幕式并致辞。黄进教授指出，改革开放 40 年来，我国航空业发生了巨大变化，航空业已成为全面维护国家安全的战略基石，是推动科学进步、服务经济社会发展的重要力量。研究航空法是国家战略的需要，是国防建设的需要，是航空业自身发展的需要。黄进教授建议积极推动航空法理论研究和创新，大力加强航空法人才的培养。加强立法和规划，建立比较完备的民航法规和标准体系,需要航空法理论的支持和支撑,需要建立起中国的航空法理论体系,为全球航空业发展以及国际航空法提供中国方案和中国理论。

在专业讨论环节,与会专家学者围绕“中国民航的法治建设”“航空法人才培养”“无人机的应用与监管”“航空法实务”等问题展开了深入研讨,王瀚教授就航空法理论研究和人才培养进行了主题发言,指出我国航空法的研究工作在民国时期就已经起步,但至今并未形成体系化和规模化,这一现象亟待解决。王瀚教授建议国内的高校和研究机构在航空法的理论研究以及人才培养方面应当构建战略联盟,形成优势互补,合力打造在世界范围内具有影响力的航空法研究和人才培养体系。于丹副教授和张望平副教授分别就国外航空法人才培养对我国的启示以及无人机的立法监管进行了发言,并和与会的其他学者进行了充分的交流。

本次论坛还颁发了北京航空法学会首批“航空法治建设杰出成就奖”,王瀚教授与国际民用航空组织法律事务与对外关系局局长黄解放、中国海事仲裁委员会航空争议仲裁中心主任聂颖、北京蓝鹏律师事务所创始合伙人张起淮获此殊荣。

《中国航空法评论》稿约

《中国航空法评论》是由陕西省哲学社会科学重点研究基地——西北政法大学国际法研究中心和西北政法大学郑斌航空与空间法研究所主办，由法律出版社出版的文集。

本文集秉承弘扬学术，探究法理，注重国际国内立法与司法实践的特色，力求收录海内外与航空法律、航空政策相关的一切研究成果。本文集涉及航空法热点问题评析、航空公约述评、国际国内航空法立法动态、航空案例研究、资料信息、译文摘录、学位论文等内容。

本文集面向国内外征集稿件，热忱欢迎国内外专家、学者、学界同人及同学不吝赐稿。稿件要求如下：

一、本文集欢迎选题新颖、有独到见解和学术价值的航空法中英文论文或资料信息。

二、来稿形式不限，学术专论、评论、判解研究、译作等均可，篇幅长短不拘。

三、来稿须同一语言下未曾在任何纸质和电子媒介上发表，请勿一稿多投。

四、来稿应附有作者简介(姓名、学位、工作单位、工作单位及职务、职称、研究领域和通信方式及 E-mail 地址等)。基金资助的论文应对基金项目名称、项目编号予以注明。

五、译作请附寄原文,并附作者或出版者的翻译书面授权许可。译者需保证该译本未侵犯作者或出版者的任何权利,并在可能的损害产生时自行承担损害赔偿责任。本文集主编及编委会不承担由此产生的任何责任。

六、本文集注释使用脚注,每页重新编号,不使用尾注注释规范。具体注释规范请参考文集样刊格式。

七、本文集实行文责自负原则。

八、本文集欢迎对收录的文章、案例和相关资料信息予以转载、摘登、翻译和结集出版,但应尊重原作者依照《著作权法》所享有的权利,在实施转载时请注明“转自《中国航空法评论》20 × ×年第 × 卷”,以及原作者、译校者署名,同时书面通知执行主编。

九、凡向本文集投稿,即视为接受本稿约。

执行主编:张超汉

投稿邮箱:aviationlawreview@ 126. com

图书在版编目(CIP)数据

中国航空法评论. 第四卷 / 王瀚主编. -- 北京 : 法律出版社, 2019
ISBN 978 -7 -5197 -4071 -9

Ⅰ. ①中… Ⅱ. ①王… Ⅲ. ①航空法-研究-中国 Ⅳ. ①D922.296.4

中国版本图书馆 CIP 数据核字(2019)第 256398 号

中国航空法评论(第四卷)
ZHONGGUO HANGKONGFA PINGLUN (DI-SI JUAN)

王　瀚 主编

策划编辑 沈小英
责任编辑 沈小英
　　　　 张泽华
装帧设计 李　瞻

出版 法律出版社
总发行 中国法律图书有限公司
经销 新华书店
印刷 北京虎彩文化传播有限公司
责任校对 马　丽
责任印制 吕亚莉
编辑统筹 法治与经济出版分社
开本 710 毫米 ×1000 毫米　1/16
印张 27.25
字数 417 千
版本 2019 年 12 月第 1 版
印次 2019 年 12 月第 1 次印刷

法律出版社/北京市丰台区莲花池西里 7 号(100073)
网址/www. lawpress. com. cn
投稿邮箱/info@ lawpress. com. cn
举报维权邮箱/jbwq@ lawpress. com. cn
销售热线/400 -660 -8393
咨询电话/010 -63939796

中国法律图书有限公司/北京市丰台区莲花池西里 7 号(100073)
全国各地中法图分、子公司销售电话:
统一销售客服/400 -660 -8393/6393
第一法律书店/010 -83938432/8433　西安分公司/029 -85330678　重庆分公司/023 -67453036
上海分公司/021 -62071639/1636　深圳分公司/0755 -83072995

书号:ISBN 978 -7 -5197 -4071 -9　**定价:**188.00 元
(如有缺页或倒装,中国法律图书有限公司负责退换)